交通与运输类系列教材

智能交通系统

Intelligent Transportation Systems

王晓原　孙　锋　郭永青　编著

西南交通大学出版社
·成都·

内容简介

本书采用中英文对照的方式，通过简洁明了的内容体系框架、插图、表格等新颖形式，从什么是智能交通系统（ITS）、ITS 是如何工作的、ITS 的体系框架和标准、ITS 的效益是什么、如何进行 ITS 的规划和投资、如何启动 ITS、转型及发展中国家的 ITS、从长远看 ITS 是什么样的等方面进行了深入的分析和论述。本书打破了传统书籍固有的形式，更能吸引读者的注意力。

本书可作为高等院校交通运输与交通工程专业及其他相关专业的研究生和本科生教材或讲义，也可作为各类专业人员的自学参考书。

图书在版编目（CIP）数据

智能交通系统 = Intelligent Transportation Systems：汉英对照 / 王晓原，孙锋，郭永青编著. — 成都：西南交通大学出版社，2018.3（2023.8 重印）

交通与运输类系列教材

ISBN 978-7-5643-6026-9

Ⅰ.①智… Ⅱ.①王… ②孙… ③郭… Ⅲ.①交通运输管理 – 智能系统 – 高等学校 – 教材 – 汉、英 Ⅳ.①U495

中国版本图书馆 CIP 数据核字（2018）第 013000 号

交通与运输类系列教材

智能交通系统
Intelligent Transportation Systems

王晓原　孙锋　郭永青　编著

责任编辑	周　杨
封面设计	何东琳设计工作室
出版发行	西南交通大学出版社 （四川省成都市二环路北一段 111 号 西南交通大学创新大厦 21 楼）
邮政编码	610031
发行部电话	028-87600564
官网	http://www.xnjdcbs.com
印刷	成都中永印务有限责任公司
成品尺寸	185 mm × 260 mm
印张	20.75
字数	670 千
版次	2018 年 3 月第 1 版
印次	2023 年 8 月第 2 次
定价	58.00 元
书号	ISBN 978-7-5643-6026-9

课件咨询电话：028-87600533

图书如有印装质量问题　本社负责退换

版权所有　盗版必究　举报电话：028-87600562

前言 _ PREFACE

　　智能交通系统（Intelligent Transportation Systems，ITS）是将先进的信息技术、通信技术、传感技术、控制技术以及计算机技术等有效地集成运用于整个交通运输管理体系，而建立起的一种在大范围内、全方位发挥作用的，实时、准确、高效的综合运输和管理系统。它通过人、车、路的和谐、密切配合提高交通运输效率，缓解交通阻塞，提高路网通行能力，减少交通事故，降低能源消耗，减轻环境污染。

　　"智能交通系统"课程是交通工程和交通运输专业的基础必修课，通过学习该课程学生可掌握ITS的基本知识和ITS各子系统的工作原理，了解ITS的体系框架、标准和效益，熟悉ITS在交通领域的应用，领会ITS对提高交通运输效率的意义，并能从长远展望ITS发展的未来，为分析和解决交通运输系统中的实际问题打好基础。

　　本书是在收集近年来国内外ITS最新研究成果的基础上，结合作者在这一领域的科研和教学实践编写而成的。全书采用中英文对照的形式，内容新颖，共分为八章：第一章介绍什么是ITS，第二章介绍ITS是如何工作的，第三章介绍ITS体系框架和标准，第四章介绍ITS的效益，第五章介绍如何进行ITS的规划和投资，第六章介绍如何启动ITS，第七章介绍转型及发展中国家的ITS，第八章介绍ITS的发展趋势。本书可作为开设"智能交通系统"课程的教材或讲义，也可为从事智能交通系统设计、开发和运营等工作的相关工作人员提供理论、方法和应用案例。

　　本书由王晓原、孙锋、郭永青编著，其他参与编写的人员包括：刘亚奇（第一、二章），汪海波（第三、四章）、田伟（第五、六章）、刘振雪（第七、八章），王云云、刘丽萍、刘菲菲在此基础上进行了全书的统筹编校，于翠翠、王方、孔栋、陈晨、阚馨童、孙懿飞、赵新越、冯凯、张露露、孙一帆也参与了大量工作。

　　本书的结构框架和内容参考了美国学者John C. Miles编著的 *ITS Handbook* 以及由陈干、王笑京等编译的该书中译本，此外，还引用了《智能交通系统工程导论》（电子工业出版社）、《智能交通技术及其应用》（机械工业出版社）、《智能运输系统概论》（人民交通出版社）等教材，本书的部分图片来源于国内外ITS相关的研究成果和应用实例，在此对上述资料的作者和提供者们表示最衷心的感谢！

　　由于编者水平有限，书中难免存在一些不妥之处，欢迎广大读者及同行专家批评指正。

编者

2017年6月

目录 _ CONTENTS

Chapter 1 What are Intelligent Transport Systems

第一章 什么是智能交通系统 ………………………………………………………… 1

1.1　Definition of ITS　ITS 的定义 ………………………………………………… 1
1.2　Background of ITS　ITS 的背景 ……………………………………………… 2
1.3　ITS Application Areas and Users　ITS 的应用领域和用户 ………………… 6
1.4　Basic Concepts　基本概念 …………………………………………………… 11
1.5　Advanced Traffic Management Systems　先进的交通管理系统 ………… 24
1.6　Advanced Traveler Information Systems (ATIS)　先进的出行者信息服务系统 ……… 31
1.7　Advanced Vehicle Control Systems (AVCS)　先进的车辆控制系统 …………………… 38
1.8　Commercial Vehicle Operation Systems　商用车辆运营系统 …………… 43
1.9　Advanced Public Transport Systems (APTS)　先进的公共交通系统（APTS）……… 46
1.10　Electronic Payment Systems (EPS)　电子支付系统 ……………………… 52
1.11　Security and Emergency Response Systems　安全和紧急事件应急系统 ……… 57
1.12　Conclusions　结论 …………………………………………………………… 62

Chapter 2 How do Intelligent Transport Systems Work

第二章 ITS 是如何工作的 ………………………………………………………… 64

2.1　ITS Technologies　ITS 技术 ………………………………………………… 64
2.2　Data Acquisition　数据获取 ………………………………………………… 68
2.3　Gaining Intelligence: Data Processing　获取智能：数据处理 …………… 77
2.4　Communications and Data Exchange　通信和数据交换 ………………… 83
2.5　Information Utilization　信息利用 …………………………………………… 90
2.6　Electronic Payment　电子付费 ……………………………………………… 95
2.7　Human Factors　人为因素 ………………………………………………… 103
2.8　Conclusions　结论 …………………………………………………………… 109

Chapter 3　What about ITS Architecture and Standards

第三章　ITS 体系框架和标准 ································· 111

3.1　ITS Architecture　ITS 体系框架 ································· 111

3.2　ITS Standards　ITS 标准 ································· 125

3.3　Conclusions　结论 ································· 128

Chapter 4　What are the Benefits of ITS

第四章　ITS 的效益是什么 ································· 129

4.1　Who Benefits from ITS　谁能从 ITS 中获益 ································· 129

4.2　What are Specific Benefits　ITS 的效益是什么 ································· 132

4.3　Benefits to Roads Network Operations　对道路网络运营的效益 ································· 142

4.4　How are Benefits Evaluated　如何进行 ITS 效益评价 ································· 151

4.5　Advice on ITS Evaluation　关于 ITS 评价的建议 ································· 160

4.6　Conclusions　结论 ································· 165

Chapter 5　How do I Plan and Finance ITS

第五章　如何进行 ITS 的规划和投资 ································· 166

5.1　Context for ITS Deployment　ITS 实施背景 ································· 166

5.2　The ITS Framework Plan　ITS 框架规划 ································· 173

5.3　Strategies Implementation　战略执行 ································· 180

5.4　Financing and Contracts　投融资与合同 ································· 189

5.5　Public-Private Partnerships　公共-私营合作 ································· 193

5.6　Conclusions　结论 ································· 200

Chapter 6　How do I Launch ITS

第六章　如何启动 ITS ································· 201

6.1　Launching ITS at the Program Level　在规划层面开展 ITS ································· 201

6.2　Launching ITS at the Project Level　项目层面启动 ITS ································· 206

6.3　Regional ITS Deployment　区域 ITS 部署 ································· 225

  6.4 Conclusions 结论 ·········· 232

Chapter 7 What about ITS in Transitional Developing Countries

第七章 转型及发展中国家的ITS ·········· 234

  7.1 Special Considerations 特殊的考虑 ·········· 234
  7.2 ITS Status and Plans in Transitional and Developing Countries 转型及
     发展中国家 ITS 的现状和发展规划 ·········· 238
  7.3 Myths and Realities 误解和现实 ·········· 249
  7.4 Advice to Transitional and Developing Countries 对转型及发展中国家的建议 ····· 252
  7.5 Questions For Decision-Makers 决策者面临的问题 ·········· 264
  7.6 Advice to Major Industrialized Countries 对主要工业发达国家的建议 ·········· 269
  7.7 Conclusions 结论 ·········· 271

Chapter 8 What about ITS in the Long-Term

第八章 ITS 的发展趋势 ·········· 272

  8.1 Future Scenarios 未来的情景 ·········· 272
  8.2 Forward-thinking ITS Programs and Projects 前瞻性的 ITS 系统计划和方案 ·········· 277
  8.3 Delivering the Future of ITS 描述 ITS 的未来 ·········· 306
  8.4 Conclusions 结论 ·········· 308

附录 1 运输评价方法在 ITS 中的应用 ·········· 309

附录 2 ITS 单元成本 ·········· 314

参考文献 ·········· 323

Chapter 1　What are Intelligent Transport Systems
第一章　什么是智能交通系统

1.1　Definition of ITS　ITS 的定义

ITS（Intelligent Transport Systems）is a generic term for the integrated application of communications, control and information processing technologies to the transportation system. The resultant benefits save lives, time, money, energy and the environment. The term "ITS" is flexible and capable of being interpreted in a broad or narrow way. "Transport telematics" is a term used in Europe for the group of technologies that support ITS.

ITS（智能交通系统）是对通信、控制和信息处理技术在运输系统中集成应用的通称。这种集成应用产生的综合效益主要体现在挽救生命，节省时间和金钱，降低能耗以及改善环境等方面。ITS 是灵活的，可以用广义和狭义的方式进行解释，在欧洲支撑 ITS 的技术群被定义为"运输的远程信息处理"。

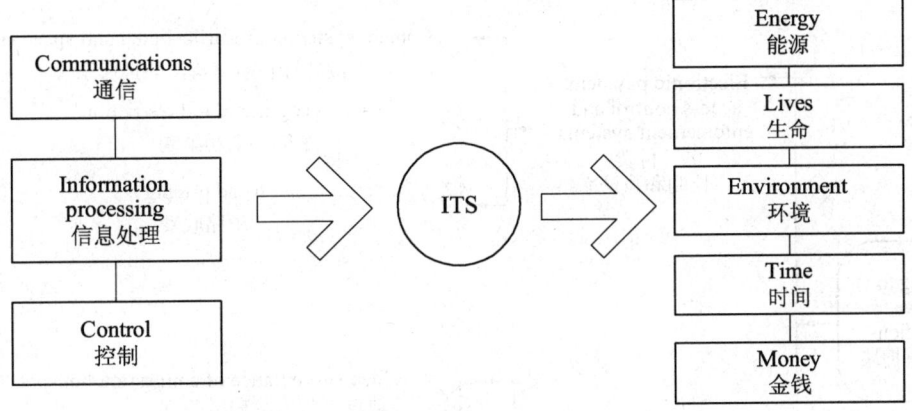

Figure 1.1　Comprehensive benefit diagram
图 1.1　综合效益框图

ITS covers all modes of transport and considers all elements of the transportation system: the vehicle, the infrastructure, and the driver or user, interacting together dynamically. The overall function of ITS is to improve decision making, often in real time, by transport network controllers and other users, thereby improving the operation of the entire transport system. The definition encompasses a broad array of techniques and approaches that may be achieved through stand-alone technological applications or as enhancements to other transportation strategies.

ITS 覆盖了所有的运输方式，并考虑运输系统中动态、相互作用的所有要素——汽车、基础设施、驾驶员或用户。ITS 的总体功能是通过改进（通常是实时地）交通网络的管理者和其他用户的决策，改善整个运输系统的运行。ITS 的这一定义包含一个技术和方法组成的宽阔阵列，这些可以通过独立的技术应用获得，也可以作为其他运输策略的增强因素来达到预期目的。

1.2　Background of ITS　ITS 的背景

1.2.1　Origins 起源

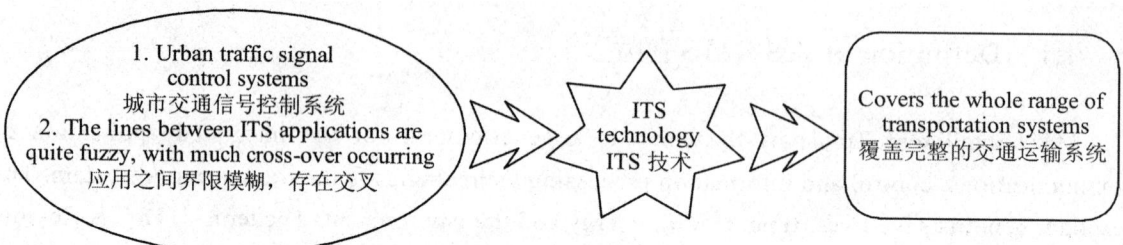

Figure 1.2　Origins of ITS

图 1.2　ITS 的起源

1.2.2　Motivation for ITS　ITS 的目的

1. Helping to relieve congestion　帮助缓解拥堵

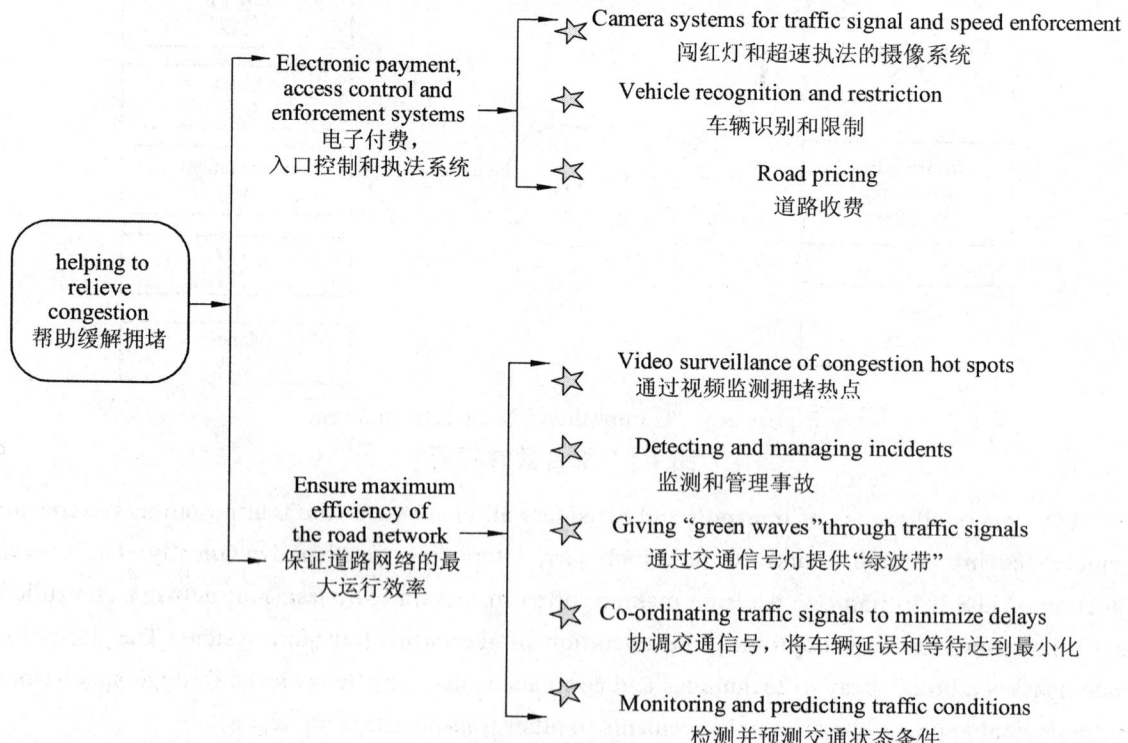

Figure 1.3　Framework of ITS helping to relieve congestion

图 1.3　ITS 帮助缓解拥堵的框架图

2. Safety and environmental benefits 安全和环境效益

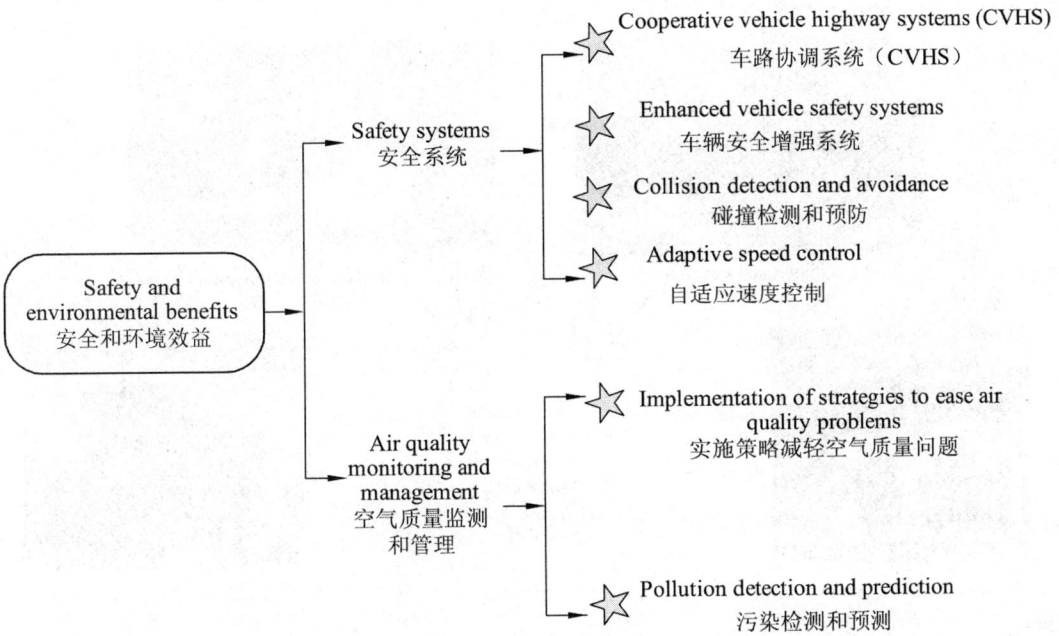

Figure 1.4 Framework of safety and environmental benefits

图 1.4 安全和环境效益框架图

3. Making public transport more attractive 让公共交通更具吸引力

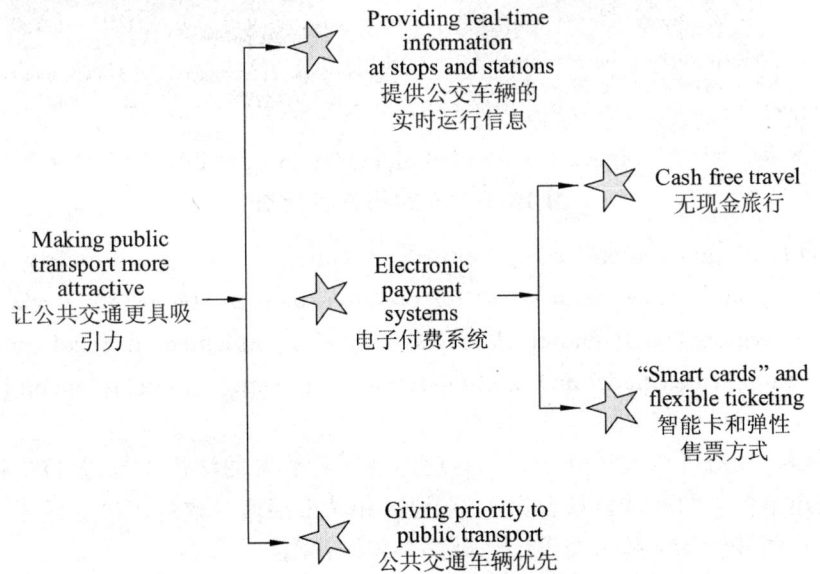

Figure 1.5 Application of ITS in public transport

图 1.5 ITS 在公共交通中的应用

1.2.3　ITS Deployment　ITS 的部署

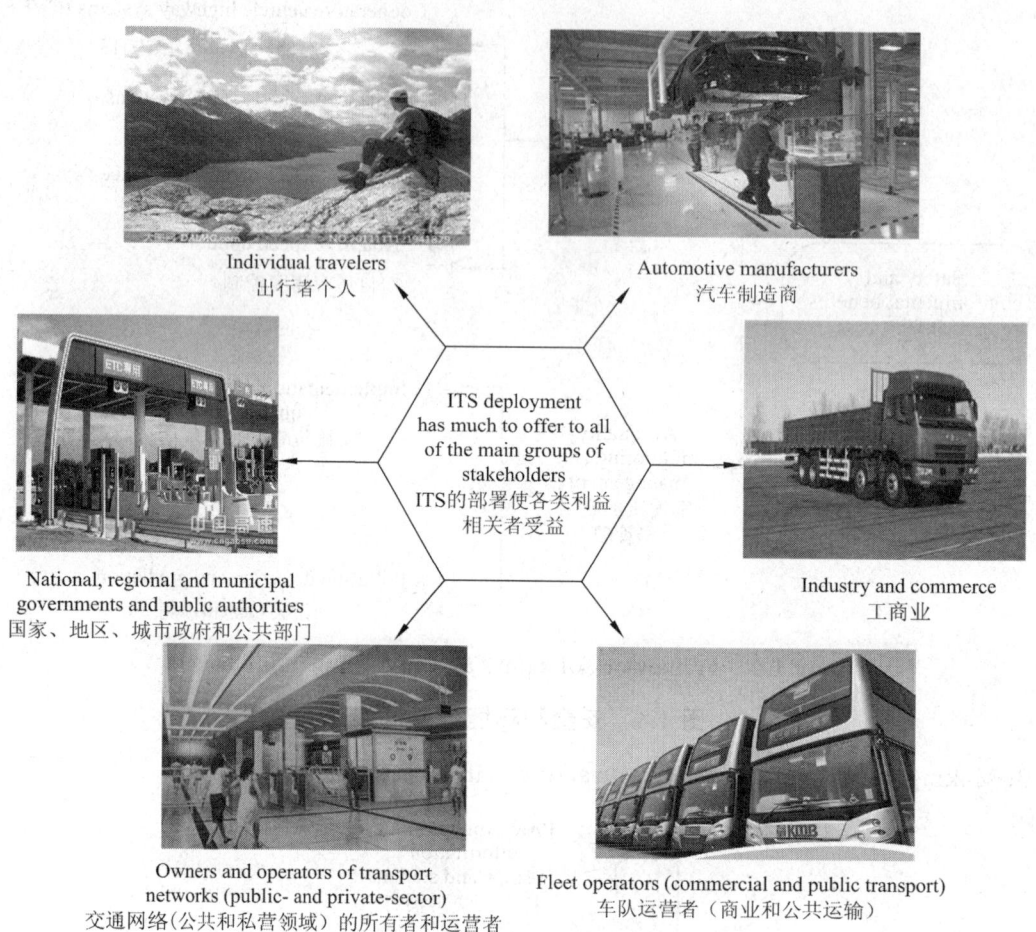

Figure 1.6　Stakeholders benefit of ITS
图 1.6　ITS 的相关者受益

At national level, governments can pave the way with enabling legislation (e.g. regulations for road user charging) and create frameworks for private-sector involvement(e.g. via public-private partnerships). At regional and municipal levels, they can implement demand management and integrated information (intermodal and multimodal) and payment systems, to encourage intermodal travel.

在国家层面，政府可以通过立法（如对道路使用者收费的法规）推进 ITS 部署，也可以为私营企业搭建平台（如通过公私合作）。在地区和城市层面，政府可以通过需求管理、信息集成（交互模式和多模式）和付费系统，鼓励多模式出行。

Operators of road, rail, tram and waterway networks and the associated transport interchanges (from road to rail and transit, and the airports, ports and ferry terminals) can manage their operations with better information and can provide users with safer or more reliable travel conditions.

公路、铁路、有轨电车、水路网络以及相关交通交汇处（从公路到铁路和公共交通系统、机场、码头、渡轮及换乘点）运营者可以利用更充分的信息来管理自己的业务，并能为用户提供更安全或更可靠的出行条件。

From the market perspective, public authorities are major customers for applications such as traffic management and control, and road user charging. They also collect significant quantities of traffic data, which can be made directly available to road users, or to private-sector service providers for incorporating into commercial value-added services for the travelling public. Beyond these, the market will naturally tend to focus on developing products and services for key groups such as road and public transport operators; automotive manufacturers (as purchasers of original equipment manufacturer (OEM) equipment); fleet operators and the motoring public (as sources of demand for OEM equipment and purchasers of retrofits).

从市场的观点来看，公共部门是应用的主要客户，这些应用包括交通管理和控制以及向公路使用者收费。公共部门也收集大量的交通信息，这些信息可以直接提供给道路使用者，或提供给私营的服务供应商，从而将此信息合并到为公共出行提供的商业增值服务中。此外，市场也会自然地趋向于为重要群体开发产品和提供服务，诸如道路和公路交通运营者、汽车制造商（原始设备制造商（OEM）设备购买者）、运输公司运营者和驾车族（OEM设备需求人及改装部件购买者）。

Automotive manufacturers can achieve significant product differentiation and customer loyalty by developing appropriate in-vehicle telematics products. Vehicle fleet owners can run more cost-effective services and save on energy costs. Businesses can move goods and services more efficiently.

汽车制造商通过发展适合的车载资讯通产品能够实现更明显的产品差异化和提高用户忠诚度。运输公司所有者能够提供更经济、节能的运营服务。企业能够更加便捷地运输货物并提供更有效的服务。

Individuals can plan journeys better, enjoy safer travel, avoid delays, and make informed choices between modes. All transport providers and users can enjoy greater security.

个人旅行者可以更好地计划行程，享受更安全的旅行，避免延误和方便地在不同交通模式中进行选择。所有交通运输服务的提供者和用户都能够享受到更多的安全保障。

Figure 1.7　On-board satellite TV
图 1.7　车载卫星电视

Ultimately, many ITS benefits are likely to be invisible to the end user: ITS will simply improve safety, security, efficiency and comfort of the transport system and the environment without the general public being aware that ITS is at work. Therefore there is an important role for public awareness programs to show transport users how they can enjoy increased safety and security, better information, greater convenience and reduced journey time; and how populations as a whole can enjoy the healthier environments produced by sustainable mobility.

最后，ITS 的许多好处对最终用户而言似乎是不可见的——ITS 改善了交通运输系统的安全、保障、效率、舒适性和环境，公众却并没有意识到这是 ITS 作用的结果。因此，对公众的宣传尤为重要，它使交通用户了解如何才得以享受不断提高的安全和保障、更好的信息服务、更便捷的出行和出行时间的节省以及全体人民如何得以享受由可持续的机动性所创造的更健康的环境。

1.3　ITS Application Areas and Users　ITS 的应用领域和用户

1.3.1　Improving Safety and Security　改善安全和可靠性

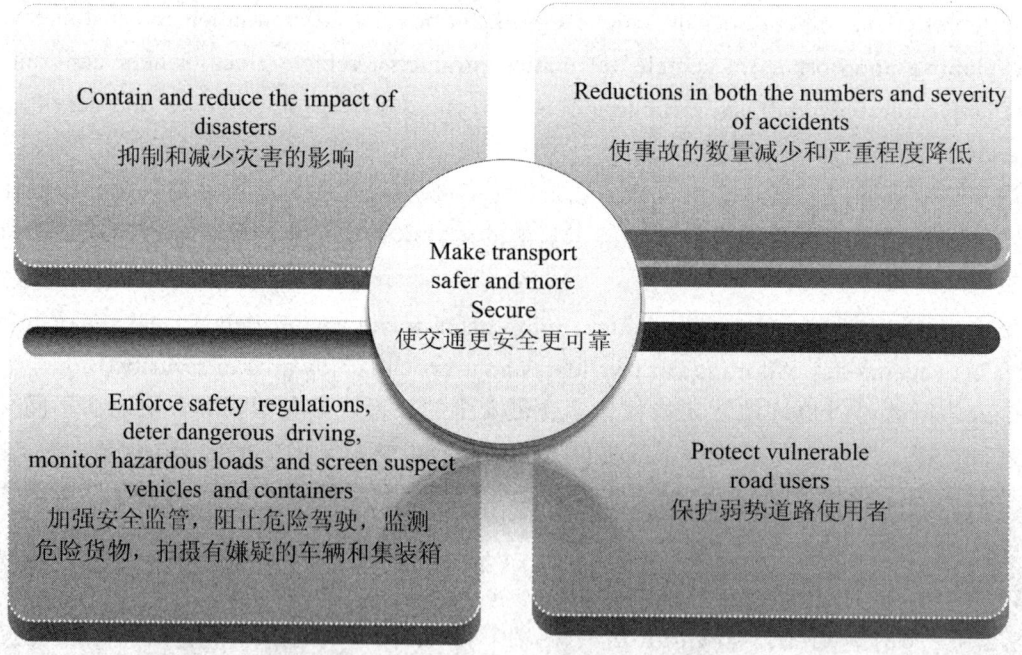

Figure 1.8　Improving safety and security

图 1.8　改善安全和可靠性

ITS services can make transport safer and more secure. They can maximize its capability to contain and reduce the impact of disasters, natural and man-made.

ITS 服务能够使交通更安全更可靠，它们能最大限度地抑制和减少自然和人为灾害的影响。

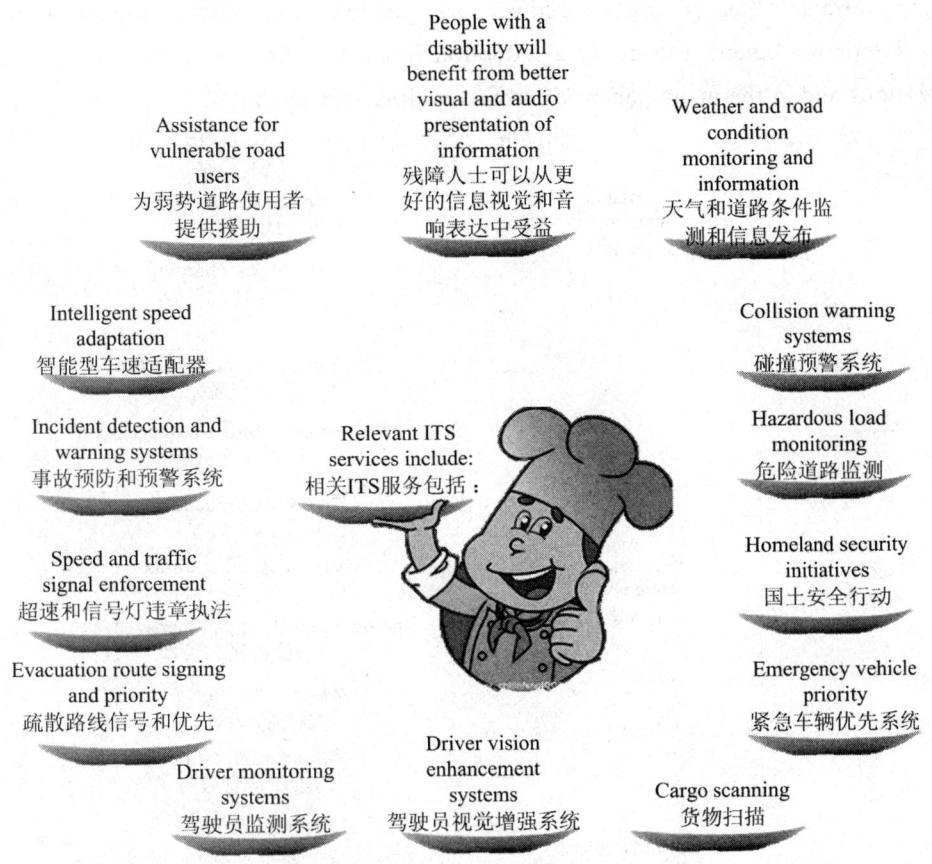

Figure 1.9　Relevant ITS services

图 1.9　相关 ITS 服务

1.3.2　Helping to Relieve Congestion　帮助缓解拥堵

Congestion is a major problem for all transport networks, and increasing the efficiency of existing transport systems is a major goal of ITS programs around the world. Congestion can be reduced by instrumenting networks to improve their real-time operation; introducing control systems; managing demand; and encouraging off-peak travel or the use of alternative modes.

对所有交通网络来说，拥堵都是一个主要问题，提高现有交通系统的有效性是世界范围内 ITS 计划的主要目标。通过网络手段改善路况的实时管理、引进控制系统、管理需求、鼓励非高峰期旅行或出行方式的改变可以减少拥堵。

1.3.3　Environmental Monitoring and Protection　环境监测和防护

Public concerns about the environmental impact of our transport systems have intensified in recent years. Worldwide, the use of motor vehicles still shows no sign of decreasing and road traffic continues to rise. As a result, the environmental impacts from emissions and noise have become increasingly serious. Clearly urgent actions are needed from the transport sector toward environmental improvement, especially a reduction in carbon dioxide (CO_2) and nitrogen oxides (NO_x) emissions and in the management of urban and inter-urban traffic.

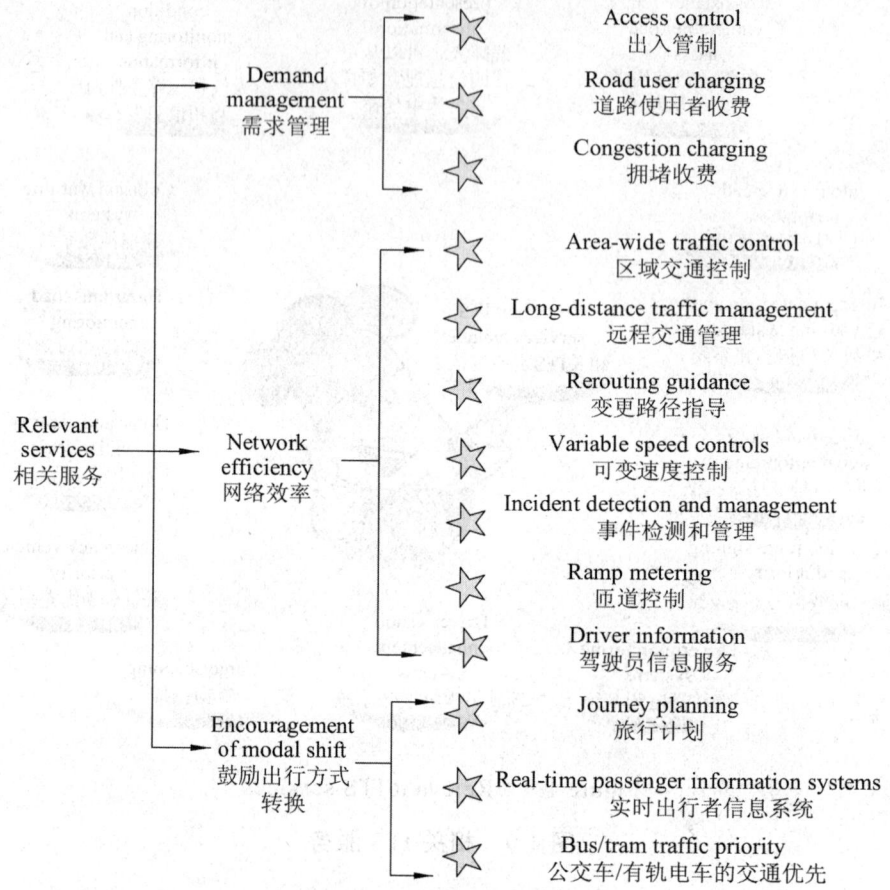

Figure 1.10　Relevant services

图 1.10　相关服务

近年来，公众越发关注交通系统对环境的影响，世界范围内仍然未见机动车辆使用下降的迹象而且道路交通量持续增长，由此产生的排放物和噪声对环境的影响日益严峻。为了改善环境，政府部门迫切需要采取行动，特别是减少二氧化碳（CO_2）和氮氧化物（NO_x）的排放以及城市和城间交通的管理。

Making transport systems run more efficiently can also bring corresponding benefits for the environment. ITS have much to offer here. For example, reducing traffic congestion or encouraging more people to travel by public transport directly reduces vehicle emissions and consequently air pollution. Environmental monitoring and evaluation of various environmental parameters is becoming especially important, in order to quantify the effects of policies and programs.

在使交通系统运行更有效，为环境带来相应的益处方面，ITS 能够做得更多。例如：缓解交通拥堵或鼓励更多人使用公共交通出行能够直接减少机动车尾气的排放，减少空气污染。为了量化政策和方案的效果，环境监测和评价的各种参数尤为重要。

Figure 1.11　Vehicle emission exhaust
图 1.11　汽车尾气排放

Figure 1.12　Traffic congestion brings trouble to the residents
图 1.12　交通拥堵给居民带来困扰

1.3.4　Productivity and Operational Efficiency　生产率和运营效率

ITS can make transport operations more efficient. Fleet management systems can reduce administrative and operational costs and deliver substantial improvements in productivity. Wider benefits include more rational use of the highway infrastructure, reduced congestion and pollution, and less risk of accidents due to monitoring vehicle and driver condition.

ITS 能够使运输运营更有效率。车队管理系统可以减少管理和运营成本，并且使生产率大为提高。更广泛的好处，包括更合理地使用高速公路基础设施，减少拥堵和污染，通过监测车辆和驾驶员状况而减少事故风险。

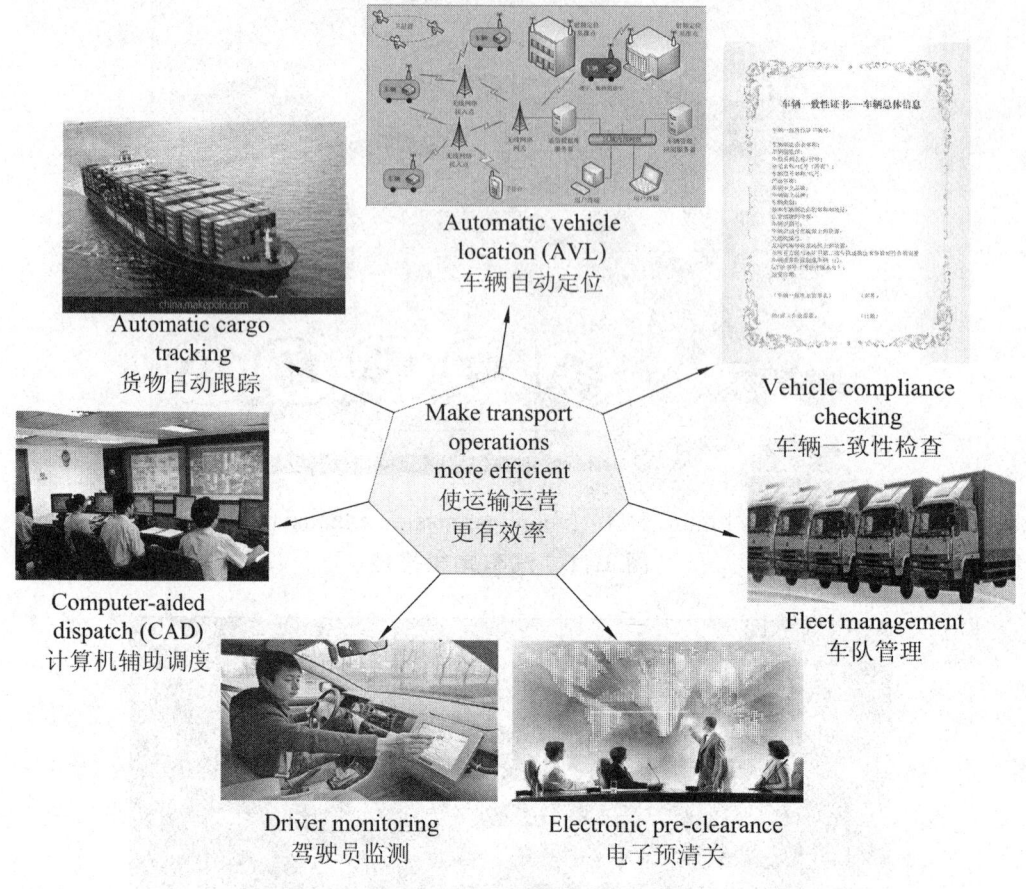

Figure 1.13　Related service of ITS
图 1.13　相关 ITS 服务

1.3.5 Comfort Factors　舒适因素

Users of any transportation system need to feel comfortable, confident and secure. Route confirmation, journey time estimates and clear advice on approaching interchanges and connections all play their part. Speed controls, ramp metering, advance incident and congestion warnings, and alternative route guidance can make road journeys easier and less stressful. Facilities such as multimedia systems that provide both entertainment and navigation can do this too. Public transport users also expect high standards of comfort, convenience and service. ITS can provide the real-time passenger information, automated scheduling and priority systems needed to improve public transport.

任何交通系统使用者都需要感到舒适、可靠和安全。路线确认、旅行时间预测以及有关换乘和连接的清晰建议都非常重要。速度控制、匝道控制、事故和拥堵预警以及可选路经指导均能够使道路旅行更容易，并能减少旅行者的压力。多媒体系统等设施可以提供娱乐和导航功能。公共交通工具使用者也期望高标准的舒适、便利和服务。ITS 可以提供实时乘客信息、自动化的时刻表安排和改进公共交通系统所需的优先系统。

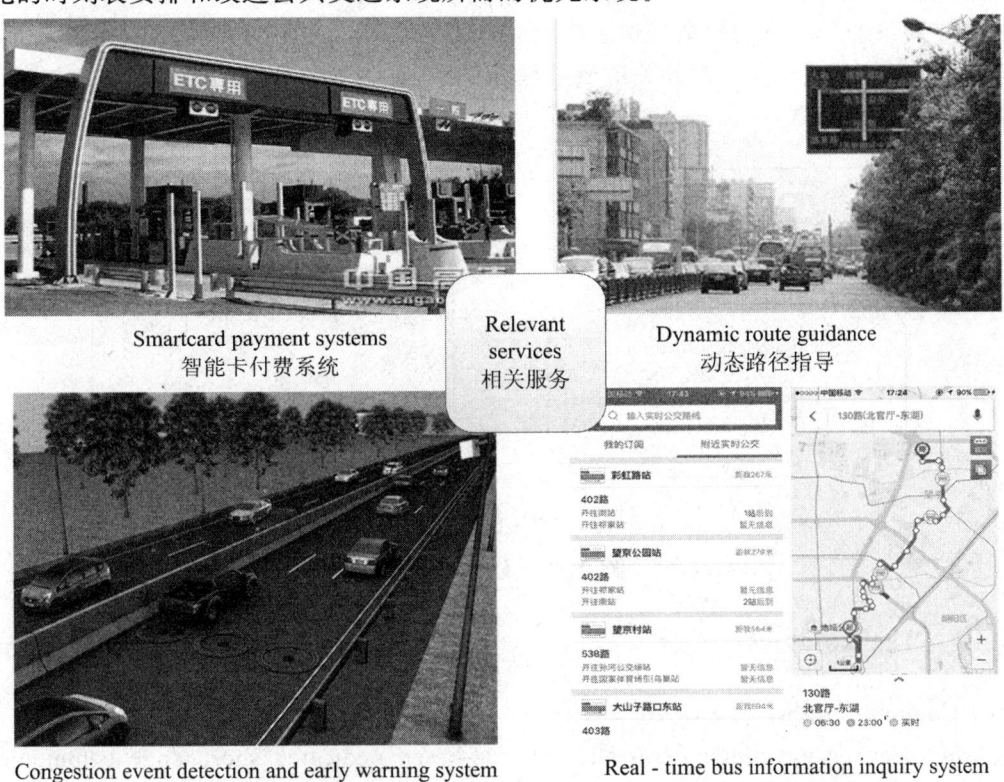

Figure 1.14　Relevant services
图 1.14　相关服务

例　美洲虎高级音响系统 "Jaguar Alpine Premium Sound System"

　　In 2003, Jaguar introduced an optional multimedia system allowing drivers and passengers to enjoy individual access to satellite Navigation or information/ entertainment via radio, CD/DVD players and TV. Those in front seats have touch-screen monitors that double as control panels for multimedia and in-vehicle functions such as climate control. Those in rear seats have video screens mounted in the back of front-seat headrests, with control panel set in armrests. Fibre-optic cables carry data around the vehicle.
　　2003年，美洲虎公司引入了可选配的多媒体系统，该系统能给驾驶员和乘客提供个人卫星导航服务和通过无线电台、CD/DVD播放机和电视机提供信息或者娱乐。前座安装的系统有触摸屏监视器，作为多媒体和车内功能的控制台，如温度控制。后座安装的设备有在前座的头枕后边装有视频屏幕，在扶手装有控制面板，在整个车辆上通过光纤来传输数据。

1.4　Basic Concepts　基本概念

　　ITS offers immense scope for integration, and some argue that it is only through integration of ITS components that ITS will achieve its full impact. Key ingredients are thorough planning, good communications and effective coordination of partners and stakeholder interests.

智能交通系统（ITS）为集成提供了极大的空间，有些人认为只要通过对 ITS 组件的集成，ITS 就能发挥其完整的效果。但是关键要素是需要完整的计划、良好的交流和对参与者和利益主体的利益的有效协调。

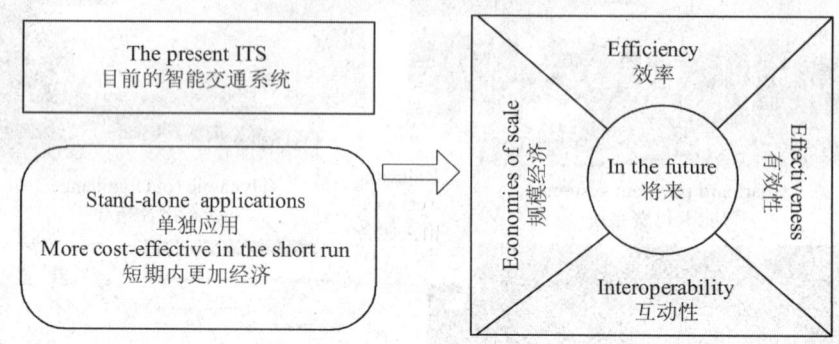

Figure 1.15 Change of ITS
图 1.15 ITS 的变化

1.4.1 Technologies 技术

（1）Communications 通信

① Microwave, short-range radio and infrared-based dedicated short-range communications (DSRC): used for EFC; commercial vehicle operations (CVO) pre-clearance.

微波、短程无线通讯和基于红外的专用短程通信（DSRC）——用于电子收费系统和商业车辆营运的预清关。

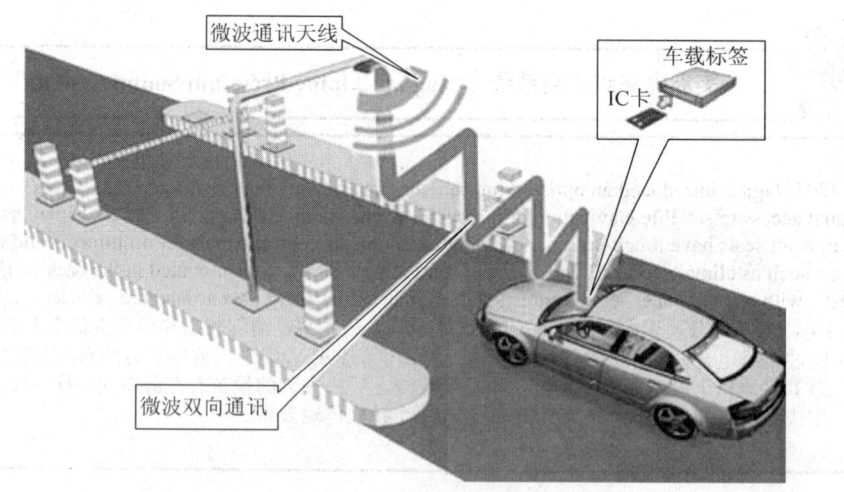

Figure 1.16 Application of microwave communication in EFC system
图 1.16 微波通讯在电子收费系统中的应用

② Mobile communications: used for real-time travel information; fleet management; emergency response.

移动通信——用于实时出行信息、车队管理、紧急反应。

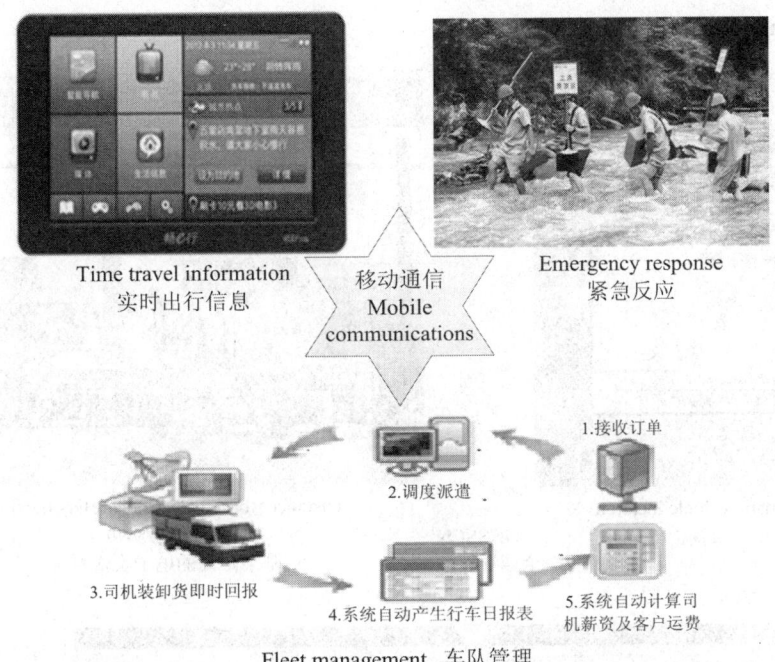

Figure 1.17　Application of mobile communication

图 1.17　移动通信的应用

③ The Internet: used for real-time travel information; trip planning; traffic images; payment.
因特网——用于实时出行信息、旅行规划、交通图像和付费。

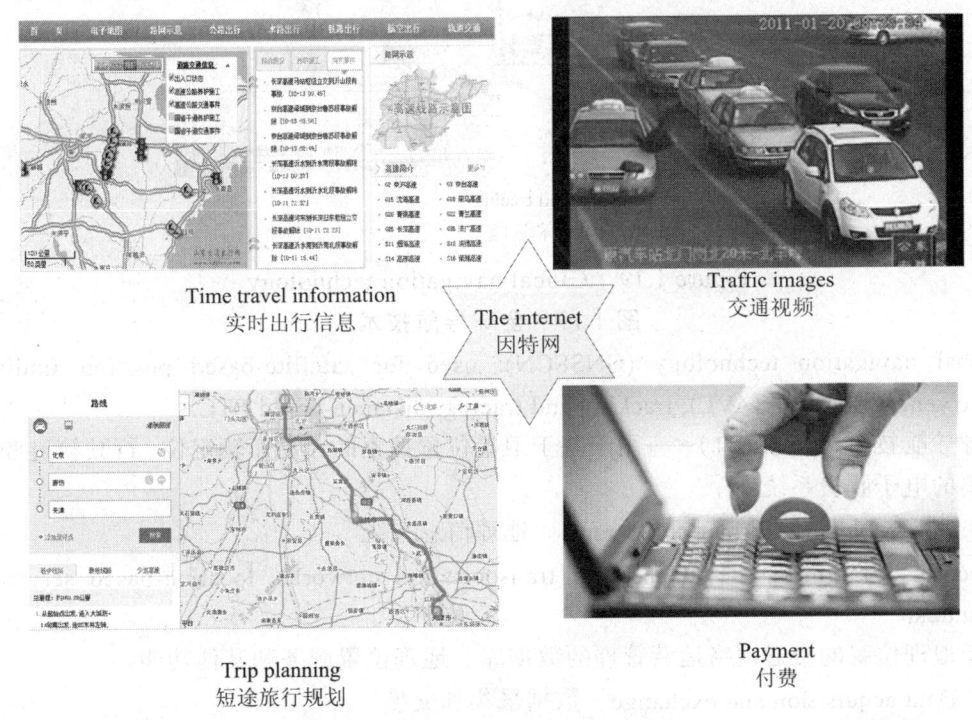

Figure 1.18　Application of internet

图 1.18　因特网的应用

（2）Geographical location 地理定位

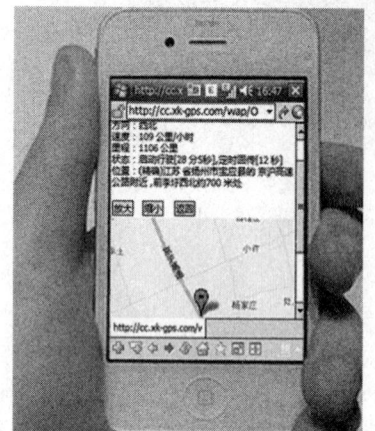
Automatic vehicle location
自动车辆定位

Distance - based electronic toll collection (ETC) system
基于距离的电子收费系统

GNSSCN
全球导航技术

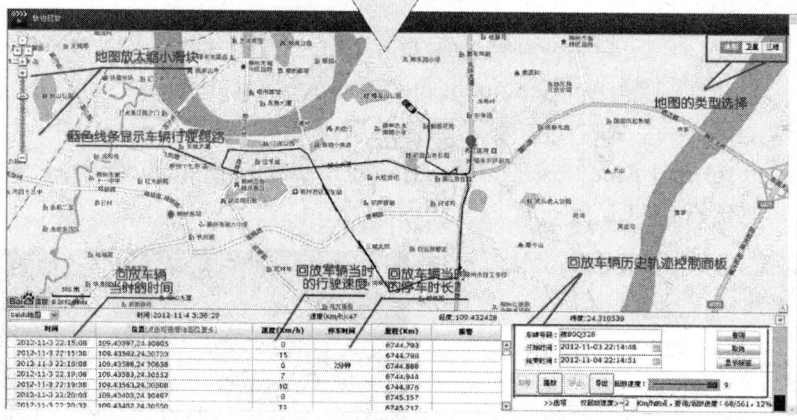
Tracking and tracing
行驶轨迹和追踪

Figure 1.19 Global navigation technology

图 1.19 全球导航技术

Global navigation technology (GNSSCN): used for satellite-based position finding for automatic vehicle location (AVL); tracking and tracing; distance-based ETC.

全球导航技术（GNSSCN）——用于基于卫星位置搜索的自动车辆定位、行驶轨迹和追踪、基于距离的电子收费系统。

（3）Geographical Information Systems 地理信息系统

Used for location-based databases of transportation networks, location-based services and other features.

基于地理位置的交通网络运营管理的数据库、地理位置服务和其他功能。

（4）Data acquisition and exchange 数据采集和交换

Used for real-time traffic management and information.

用于实时交通管理和信息。

Figure 1.20 Location-based platform of transportation network
图 1.20 基于地理位置的交通路网运营管理平台

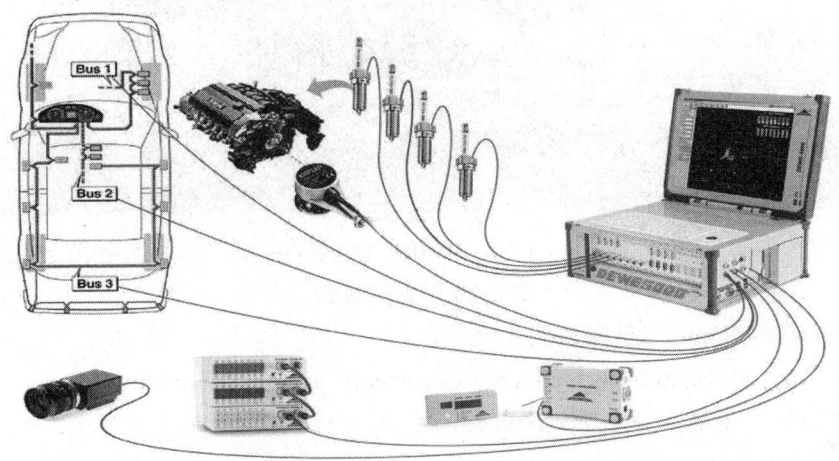

Figure 1.21 Data acquisition
图 1.21 数据采集

（5）Camera systems and artificial vision 摄像系统和人工视觉
Used for enforcement and security
用于执法和保安。

Figure 1.22 Road monitoring
图 1.22 道路监控

（6）Detection and classification　检测和分类

Used for traffic management, incident management, compliance, safety, security.

用于交通管理、事件管理、执行、安全、保安。

Figure 1.23　Traffic management

图 1.23　交通管理

（7）In-vehicle systems　车内系统

Used for travel information, vehicle control systems, accident avoidance.

用于出行信息、车辆控制系统、事故预防。

Figure 1.24　In-vehicle systems of Volvo XC90

图 1.24　沃尔沃 XC90 车内系统

（8）Digital mapping 数字地图

Figure 1.25　Three-dimensional digital map
图 1.25　三维数字地图

These are databases of road and transportation networks stored on digital media (e.g. CD-ROM) using agreed data dictionaries and standardized location referencing. Digital maps are a key building block for ITS. Used for traffic management, traffic information, route guidance, car park management and routing, lorry route monitoring; recreational facilities direction.

在数字媒体（如 CD-ROM）上都储存有道路和交通网络的数据库。这些数据库均使用了行业内的数据词典和标准化的区位描述。对于 ITS，数字地图是一个关键的构件模块。用于交通管理、交通信息、路线指导、停车管理和停车路线规划、货车路线监控、娱乐设施方位指示。

1.4.2　Key Actors　关键因素

For a city or region, ITS is just part of an overall transport plan or package of measures. No single ITS service can be a complete solution in itself. Table 1.1 illustrates the wide range of ITS methods that are available. A deployment framework is therefore needed, mapping out the desired result and key stages and obstacles along the way.

对于一个城市或者地区来说，ITS 只是整个运输规划或者整套措施的一部分，没有一个单独的 ITS 服务自身是一个完整的解决方案。表 1.1 列举了能够利用的多种 ITS 方法。因此，需要一个部署框架，制定出该框架的期望结果、关键阶段和障碍。

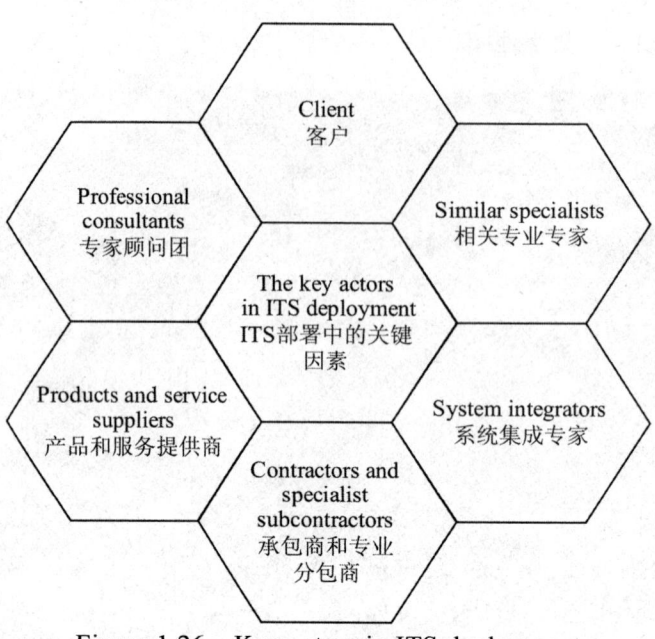

Figure 1.26　Key actors in ITS deployment
图 1.26　ITS 部署中的关键因素

Table 1.1　ITS methods and applications included in the "ITS City Pioneers" Toolbox
表 1.1　包含在"ITS City Pioneers"工具箱中的 ITS 方法和应用

Theme 主题	ITS Methods and Applications ITS 方法和应用	
Traffic Management 交通管理	Urban Traffic Control 城市交通控制 Intersection Control 交叉口控制 Highway Management 公路控制 Ramp Metering 匝道控制 Dynamic Speed Adaptation 动态速度调适 Access Control 出入口控制	Parking Management 停车场管理 Incident Management 事故管理 Vulnerable Road User Facilities Supervisory Management 弱势道路使用者设施监督管理 Traffic Regulations Enforcement 交通法规实施 Traffic Environmental Management 环境交通管理
Integrated Payment Systems 集成收费系统	Public Transport Payment 公共交通收费 Parking Payment 停车场收费	Urban Tolling 城市通行费 Urban Road Pricing 城市道路分级收费
Collective Transport Management 综合交通运输管理	Fleet and Resource Management 车队和资源管理 Public Transport Priority 公共交通优先权	Car Pooling/Sharing Management 小汽车合伙/共乘管理 Taxi Management / Demand 出租车管理 Responsive Transport 应招运输

Theme 主题	ITS Methods and Applications ITS 方法和应用	
Traffic and Travel Information 交通和出行信息	Public Transport Information 公共交通信息 Traffic Information 交通信息	Pre-trip Journey Planning 出行前行程规划 Route Guidance and Navigation 路线引导和导航
Freight Transport Management 货物运输管理	Hazardous Goods Management 危险品管理 Fleet management 车队管理	Freight Management 货物运输管理 Co-ordinated City Logistics 城市协同物流管理
Security and Emergency Management 安全和应急管理	Rescue Services Incident Management 紧急事件营救服务管理 Breakdown and Emergency Services 紧急事件服务	Public Transport Security 公共交通安全

1.4.3　System Approach　系统方法

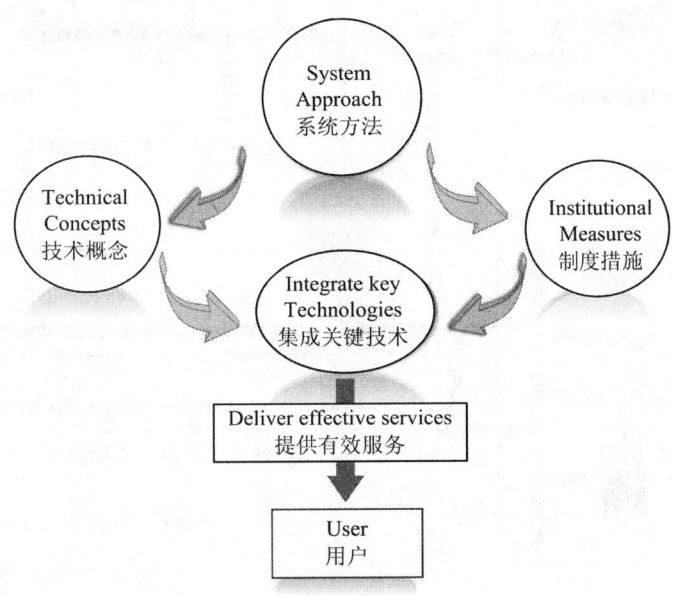

Figure 1.27　Frame of system approach
图 1.27　**系统方法框架图**

The application of information and control technologies to transport systems is at the core of ITS. The amalgamation of technologies to perform ITS functions is based on the principles of systems engineering. Many transportation problems arise from the lack of timely, accurate and easily usable information, or from the lack of appropriate coordination among decisions makers. Dealing with a life-threatening incident on an expressway, for example, needs close coordination of traffic management, driver information and emergency management systems. As the capabilities of high-tech solutions continue to increase, and costs decrease, so will the capabilities and costs of ITS functions. At the same time, these technologies will build on top of each other to produce synergy. For example, information gained from Electronic Fee Collection (EFC) may also provide probe vehicle data for traffic management. However, an agency does not need to invest in all the latest high-tech electronics in order to start applying ITS to its most urgent problems.

信息技术和控制技术在交通系统中的应用是 ITS 的核心。系统工程原理是综合各种技术形成 ITS 各种功能的基础。很多交通问题的产生在于缺乏实时、准确和易于使用的交通信息，或在于决策者间缺乏适当的协调。例如，在处理高速公路上发生的威胁生命安全的事件时，需要交通管理系统、驾驶员信息系统以及紧急事件管理系统的密切配合。随着"高技术"解决方案能力的持续增强和成本的降低，ITS 的能力和成本也遵循着同样的趋势。同时，这些技术互为基础，从而产生协同效应，例如由电子收费（EFC）系统获得的信息也可以为交通管理提供浮动车数据。但是，任何一个管理机构都没有必要在开始用 ITS 解决其最迫切的问题时，就投资于所有最新的高科技电子技术和设备。

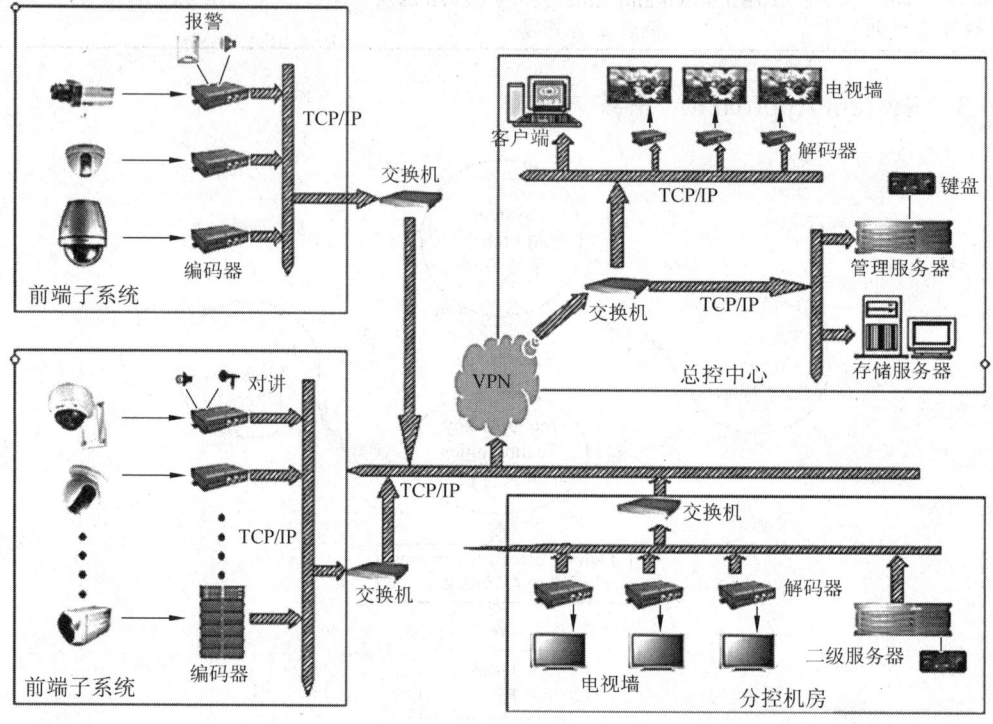

Figure 1.28　Network monitoring system
图 1.28　联网监控系统

1.4.4　Coordination　协调

ITS deployment typically involves coordinating a number of agencies with common interests in improving mobility and safety: transport providers and transport network operators in an intermodal transfer (passenger or freight); traffic police and rescue services in an emergency management plan; or traffic control and information centers for real-time traffic information. Therefore a priority with ITS is to consult the widest possible range of interests and build local partnerships for combined action and joint problem-solving. These may well include new actors, e.g.

financial institutions, retailers, broadcasters, telecommunications operators and commercial service providers. There is often a role for an ITS champion in taking initiatives, driving forward consultation and keeping all partners and actors on track.

ITS 部署通常要协调许多在改善机动性和安全性方面具有共同利益的机构，如：在联运转移（客运或货运）中的运输服务提供商和路网运营管理运营商，应急管理计划中的交通警察和救援服务部门，还有提供实时交通信息的交通控制和各类信息中心等。因此，对 ITS 而言，最重要的是征求尽可能广泛的利益相关方的意见，在本地形成能够联合行动和共同解决问题的伙伴关系。这些伙伴可能还包括一些"新角色"，如：金融机构、零售商、广播电台、通信运营商以及商业服务提供商等。ITS 支持者通常承担的工作是倡导立项、推动沟通和确保所有伙伴和参与者各尽其职。

1.4.5　ITS Architecture　ITS 体系框架

The term "architecture" describes a structured framework within which the components of ITS systems are brought together.

"体系框架"这个术语描述了一个结构化的架构，在此架构内，ITS 的各个组成部分被联系在一起。

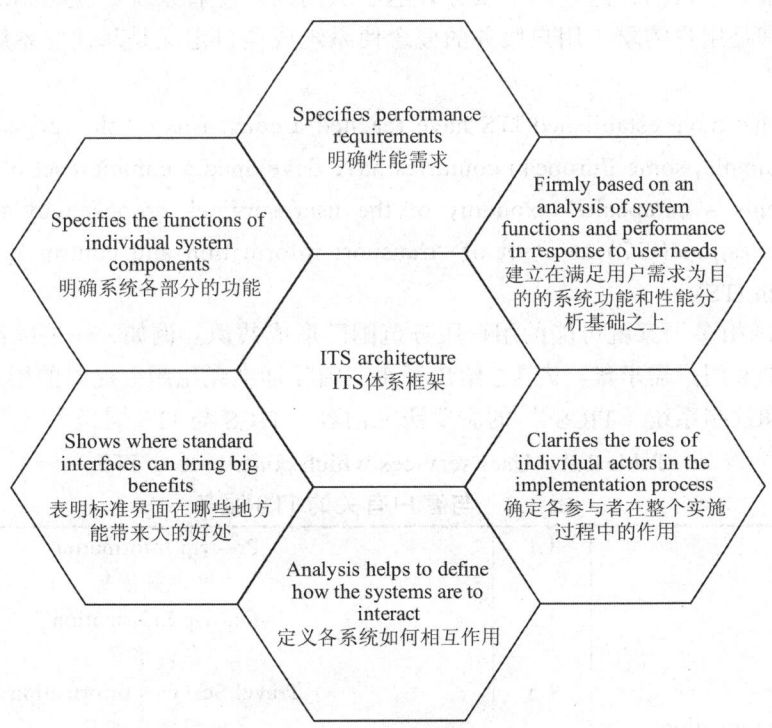

Figure 1.29　ITS architecture
图 1.29　ITS 体系框架

ITS architecture does not assume the use of specific ITS applications, technologies or components. It should be generic to allow freedom for system developers to design what they see as optimum solutions, while meeting appropriate standards and accommodating the interfaces needed for interoperability and future extensions. If the design provides for interchangeability of components it will encourage competition and allow scope for future improvements in cost, design, functionality and safety.

ITS 体系框架并没有设定确切的 ITS 应用、技术和组件。它容许系统开发者可以灵活地选择他们认为最优的解决方案，同时满足合适的标准以及具备交互性和未来系统扩展所需要的各类接口。如果设计提供了部件的可互换性，那么就会鼓励竞争和允许在成本、设计、功能和安全等方面的持续改善。

1.4.6　User Services　用户服务

ITS covers many development fields, and is or will be implemented in various schemes. But the fields of ITS can be identified by user services which represent what the systems will achieve from the users' perspective. The concept of user services allows system or project definition to begin by establishing the high level services that will be provided, to address identified problems and user needs.

ITS 覆盖了很多发展领域，并且现在是，将来也会以各种不同方式实施。但是，ITS 应用领域是由用户服务确认的，这些用户服务表达了从用户角度看系统所应达到的功能。为解决现存问题并且满足用户需求，用户服务的概念使系统或项目定义是从建立系统将要提供的高层服务开始。

Countries that have established ITS have reached a consensus on the range of possible user services. For example, some European countries have developed a common set of ITS user needs. Table 1.2 presents a composite taxonomy of the user services proposed by the International Standards Organization (ISO) as a set of "transport information and control systems" (TICS—synonymous with ITS).

建立 ITS 的很多国家就可能的用户服务范围已形成共识。例如，一些欧洲国家已经发展了一套通用的 ITS 用户需求集。表 1.2 给出了由"国际标准化组织"提出的用户服务分类，作为"交通信息和控制系统（TICS）"的主要研究内容（TICS 与 ITS 同义）。

Table 1.2　User services which contribute to ITS

表 1.2　与客户有关的 ITS 服务

Traveler Information 出行者信息	1.1	Pre-trip Information 出行前信息
	1.2	On-trip Information 在途信息
	1.3	Travel Services Information 出行服务信息
	1.4	Route Guidance and Navigation-pre-trip 路线引导和导航——出行前
	1.5	Route Guidance and Navigation-on-trip 路线引导和导航——在途
	1.6	Trip Planning Support 出行计划支持

续表

	2.1	Traffic Management and Control 交通管理和控制
Traffic Management and Operations 交通管理和运营	2.2	Transport Related Incident Management 与交通相关的事故管理
	2.3	Demand Management 需求管理
Traffic Management and Operations 交通管理和运营	2.4	Transport Infrastructure Maintenance Management 交通基础设施维护管理
	2.5	Policing and Enforcement 政策与执法
	3.1	Vision Enhancement 视觉增强
	3.2	Automated Vehicle Operation 自动车辆运行
Vehicle Services: Driver Assistance and Vehicle Control 车辆服务——驾驶员辅助和车辆控制	3.3	Collision Avoidance 避撞
	3.4	Safety Readiness 安全提醒
	3.5	Pre-crash Restraint 碰撞前限制
	4.1	Commercial Vehicle Pre-clearance 商用车辆预清关
	4.2	Commercial Vehicle Administrative Processes 商用车辆管理进程
	4.3	Automated Roadside Safety Inspection 自动路侧安全检查
Freight Transport and Commercial Vehicle Operations 货物运输和商用车辆运营	4.4	Commercial Vehicle On-board Safety Monitoring 商用车辆车载安全监控
	4.5	Freight Transport Fleet Management 货物运输车队管理
	4.6	Intermodal Information Management 联运信息管理
	4.7	Management and Control of Intermodal Centers 联运中心管理和控制
	4.8	Management of Dangerous Freight 危险品运输管理
Public Transport Operations 公共交通运营	5.1	Public Transport Management 公交运输交通管理
	5.2	Demand Responsive and Shared Transport 需求响应和共享运输

续表

Emergency Services 紧急事件服务	6.1	Transport Related Emergency Notification and Personal Security 交通相关紧急事件发布和人身保障
	6.2	After Theft Vehicle Recovery 被盗车辆寻找
Emergency Services 紧急事件服务	6.3	Emergency Vehicle Management 应急车辆管理
	6.4	Hazardous Materials and Incident Notification 危险品和事故发布
Electronic Payment 电子收费	7.1	Transport-related Electronic Financial Transactions 交通相关的电子金融业务处理
	7.2	Integrated Payment System 综合收费系统
Personal Safety 个人安全	8.1	Public Travel Security 公众出行保障
	8.2	Safety Enhancements for Vulnerable Road Users 弱势道路使用者道路使用安全措施
	8.3	Safety Enhancements for Disabled Road Users 残疾人道路使用安全措施
	8.4	Safety Provisions for Pedestrians using Intelligent Junctions and Links 行人安全预防措施
Weather and Environmental Conditions Monitoring 气候和环境状况监测	9.1	Weather Monitoring 气候监测
	9.2	Environmental Conditions Monitoring 环境状况监测
Disaster Response Management and Coordination 灾害响应管理和协调	10.1	Disaster Data Management 灾害数据管理
	10.2	Disaster Response Management 灾害响应管理
	10.3	Coordination with Emergency Agencies 各类应急机构协调
National Security 国家安全	11.1	Monitoring and Control of Suspicious Vehicles 可疑车辆的监测和控制
	11.2	Utility, Structures and Pipeline Monitoring 公共设施、结构物和管线监控

1.5 Advanced Traffic Management Systems 先进的交通管理系统

ATMS is designed to ensure optimal, safe and efficient use of the capacity of urban and inter-urban road networks.

设计先进的交通管理系统（ATMS）是为了保证城市内和城际间的道路网络通行能力得到

合理、安全、高效的使用。

Figure 1.30 Traffic Management Systems
图 1.30 交通管理系统

Relevant applications include:
相关的功能包括：
(1) Incident detection and response;
事件检测和应急反应；
(2) Traffic management for special events;
特殊事件的交通管理；
(3) Urban traffic control;
城市交通控制；
(4) Coordination of traffic signals to minimize delays and control traffic queues;
协调交通信号以降低交通延误和控制交通排队；
(5) Vehicle flow and demand management;
车流和需求管理；
(6) Re-routing guidance;
变更路径导航；
(7) Traffic management on long-distance (including cross-border) corridors;
长途交通走廊的管理（包括跨界运输）；
(8) Weather warning systems;
天气预警系统；
(9) Enforcement.
执法。

To deliver these systems, national, regional and urban authorities invest in modern, computerized traffic management centers (TMCs) and traffic control centers (TCCs). These centers generate important sources of data that can be processed to inform and advise motorists via traffic information centers (TICs) and value added services as demonstrated by Berlin's Transport Management Centre.

为了传送这些系统的管理信息，国家、地区和城市当局投资设立了现代化的、计算机化的交通管理中心（TMC）和交通控制中心（TCC）。这些中心是数据的重要来源，处理后的数据通过交通信息中心（TIC）通知乘车的人们，或给他们提出建议；这些中心同时提供类似于柏林运输管理中心的增值服务。

> **例** **Berlin's transport Management Center 柏林交通运输管理中心**
>
> Since the start of 2003 a fully operational, public-private transport management center (VMZ Berlin) has been monitoring, processing and disseminating information on Berlin's traffic and transport system to the general public and businesses. It provides basic mobility services for no charge and value-added services for a fee. Apart from some minor subsidy, VMZ's private operator will have to cover operating costs by developing commercial information services. VMZ is intended to influence travel demand through provision of appropriate information services. VMZ was set up as a public-private partnership with the investment costs for hardware and software borne by the Berlin government. Thus the system is owned by the state and operated on its behalf by the private consortium comprising DaimlerChrysler Services AG and Siemens AG.
>
> 从2003年年初开始,政府和私营企业合作的运输管理中心（柏林VMZ）,监控和处理柏林交通运输信息,并对公众和企业发布实时信息服务。该中心提供免费基础移动服务和有偿延伸服务。除了较少补助外,VMZ私营企业必须通过开发商业信息服务,筹集运行所需的费用。VMZ通过适当的信息服务来调整出行需求。柏林政府成立了政府和私营企业合作的VMZ并承担了软硬件的投资费。该系统的所有权属于国家,由DaimlerChrysler Services AG和Siemens AG运行该系统并从中获利。

1.5.1　Urban Traffic Control (UTC)　城市交通控制

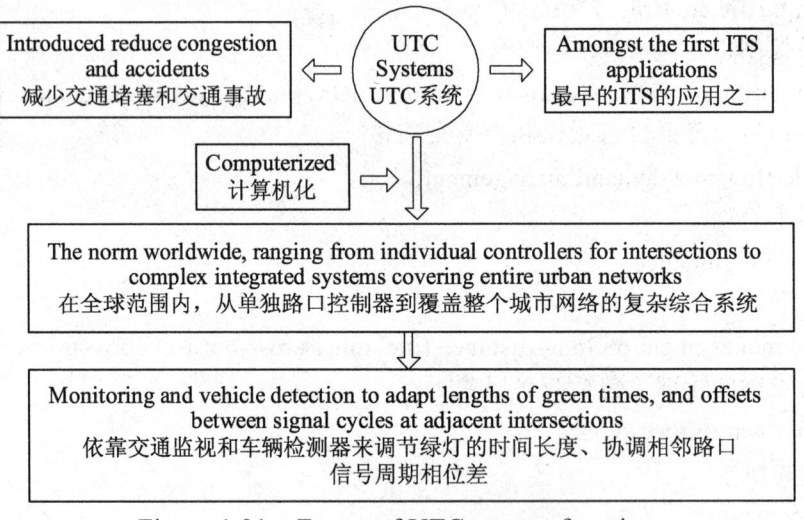

Figure 1.31　Frame of UTC system function

图1.31　UTC系统功能框架图

UTC systems have four basic functions: UTC系统有四种基本功能:

(1) Automatic collection of data on traffic volumes and speeds, using devices including in-road sensors, CCTV, automatic number plate recognition (ANPR) and floating vehicle data (FVD);

利用道路中的传感器、CCTV、自动牌照识别（ANPR）、浮动车数据（FVD）等设备自动收集交通量和速度等数据;

(2) Control of traffic signals based on this data;

根据以上数据控制交通信号;

(3) Provision of data for travel information services;

为出行信息服务提供数据；

(4) Automatic incident alerts to relevant organizations.

自动事故报警，并通知有关部门。

例 The 2000 Sydney Olympics 2000年悉尼奥林匹克运动会

The Roads and Traffic Authority (RTA) of the Australian State of New South Wales deployed an advanced version of SCATS. SCATS 6, based on a distributed PC architecture, analyzed real-time traffic data from vehicle detectors and produced signal timings suitable for prevailing traffic conditions. RTA personnel controlled traffic using a suite of color graphics windows on their PCs, corresponding to four levels of the traffic system:

The whole-area, indicating regional boundaries and conditions at the six most heavily trafficked subsystems.

Selected regional areas, with traffic flows coded from light to heavily congested.

Selected subsystems, showing traffic flows and densities as monitored by strategically located detectors.

Intersection displays showing layouts and phasing designs.

澳大利亚新南威尔士州的道路交通管理局（RTA），采用了SCATS系统的高级版本。基于分布式的PC结构，SCATS6分析车辆检测器的实时交通数据，产生适合主要交通状况的控制信号。RTA人员通过PC机上的一套彩色图形窗口来控制交通，对应交通系统的四个水平：

全部区域，显示6个商业聚集区的子系统的地区边界和交通状况；

被选择的区域，根据交通流量的不同堵塞状态从轻到重进行编码显示；

被选择的子系统，显示按战略布设的检测器监控的交通流及其密度；

交叉口区域，显示交叉口的平面布局和相位设计。

例 Re-routing in CENTRICO 欧洲运输通信合作项目中的路径变更引导

The European Commission (EC) has set up CENTRICO to improve traffic management and information on the 75,000 km Trans-European Road Network (TERN). The CENTRICO area (Belgium, Northern France, Western Germany, Luxembourg, The Netherlands and South-East England, UK) experiences very high traffic volumes. To help users avoid congestion and incidents, cross-border rerouting corridors operate between Koln (Germany) and Eindhoven (The Netherlands) and between Antwerp (Flanders) and Rotterdam (The Netherlands). Variable message signs (VMS) at decision points display a special rotatable routing arrow.

为改善交通管理和提供信息，欧盟委员会在7500km的泛欧道路网上建设了CENTRICO。CENTRICO（管理）的区域（比利时、法国北部、德国西部、卢森堡、荷兰和英国的东南部）交通量大，为了帮助道路使用者避开交通堵塞和交通事故，在德国科隆到荷兰埃因霍温，佛兰德斯的安特卫普到荷兰鹿特丹的交界地段采用绕行路线，在做出换道决策地点的可变信息板上显示特殊的可交替变化的路线引导箭头。

1.5.2 Freeway corridor and expressway management 高速公路协调与管理

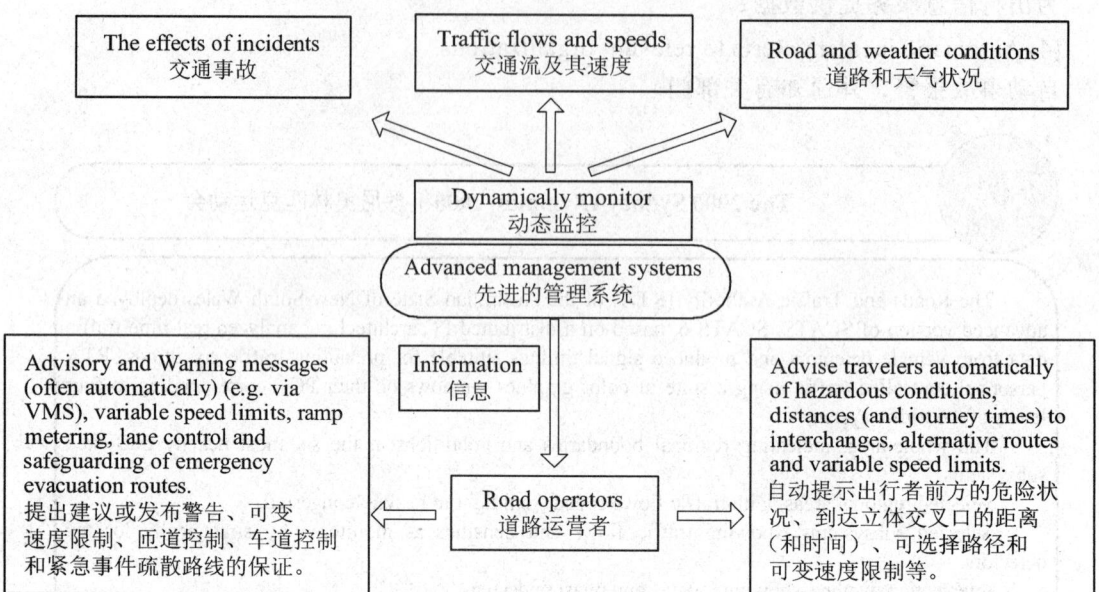

Figure 1.32 Management system of freeway
图 1.32 高速公路管理系统

例 **Effects of Japanese UTC Deployment 日本UTC的使用效果**

Reducing congestion: The Japanese UTC system substantially reduces traffic congestion by linking accurate signal controller operation to prevailing traffic conditions and giving drivers traffic information via traffic message and travel time displays.

Reducing pollution: Because it reduces the number of stops vehicles need to make in congestion, it also cuts fumes and noise and so reduces environmental pollution.

Reducing accidents: It reduces accidents caused by frustrated drivers by smoothing vehicle flows and giving reliable information on traffic conditions and travel times to specified destinations, e.g. via variable message signs.

Saving energy: It saves energy by smoothing traffic flows and reducing travel time to destinations, so reducing fuel consumption.

减少堵塞：通过将精确的交通信号控制器与占主导地位的交通状况相关联，以及通过交通信息发布和出行时间显示为驾驶者提供交通信息，日本的UTC系统大大地减少了交通堵塞；

减少污染：通过减少堵塞引起的停车次数，减少燃油消耗和噪声，从而减轻了环境污染；

减少事故：通过可变信息情报板疏导车流，提供可靠的路况信息和到特定目的地的出行时间，减少了由于疲劳驾驶造成的交通事故。

节约能源：通过疏导车流和缩短到达目的地的出行时间，减少燃料消耗，节约能源。

1.5.3 Demand Management 需求管理

One way of reducing congestion is by managing traffic demand. This can involve relatively straightforward access control techniques or categorizing vehicles (e.g. by their number plates) to restrict flows entering given areas (e.g. historic city centers).

减少交通堵塞的方法之一是交通需求管理，包括使用相对直接的进入控制技术或车辆分类（依据车牌）来约束进入特定区域（例如历史名城的市中心）的车流量。

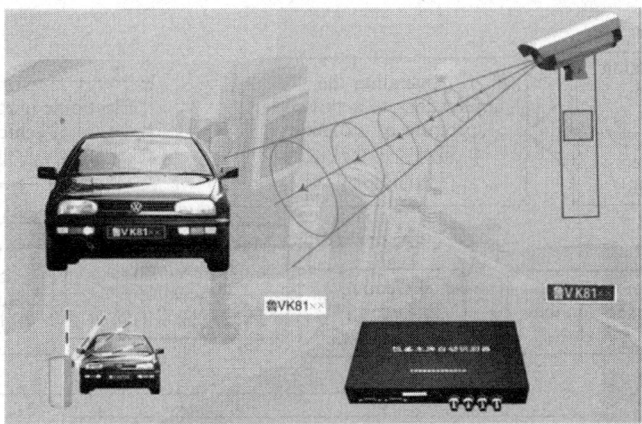

Figure 1.33　Automatic license plate recognition
图 1.33　车牌自动识别

More intensive measures include charging for use of the road during congested periods, or the introduction of special high-occupancy vehicle (HOV) lanes.

更有效的交通需求管理措施包括在交通堵塞期间向道路使用者收费，或是设立特殊的高载客车辆（HOV）专用车道。

Figure 1.34　Electronic Road Pricing (ERP) for congestion in Singapore
图 1.34　新加坡公路拥堵电子收费系统（ERP）

例　**Access control in Barcelona, Spain**　西班牙巴塞罗纳准入控制

Barcelona has implemented various demand management strategies in order to reduce traffic levels in environmentally sensitive areas within the city center. The access zones are controlled by a network of control gates, physically enforced by retractable bollards, to limit access to authorized vehicles only, which are equipped with smartcard or in-vehicle transponders. At the same time the system gives priority to important road users including residents, pedestrians and delivery vehicles. The initial La Ribera zone was introduced in 1995 and has now been extended to 4 other areas. Surveys conducted in La Ribera demonstrate that traffic entering the zone has been reduced by 78%, with travel times across it being reduced by 18%. The level of residents' acceptance of the scheme has been high (in excess of 70%) and impacts on the local economy are generally positive. However, the evidence does show a change in business type within the zones to those less dependent on car-based custom.

为了减少城市中心环境敏感区域的交通水平，巴塞罗那已经实施了多种需求管理策略。准入地区实行路网入口控制，由可伸缩的柱子在物理上控制，只让有授权的配备智能卡或者车载应答器的车辆通过。同时，系统优先放行重要的道路使用者，包括居民、行人和运送货物的车辆。LaRibera 地区最初在1995年建立了该系统，现在已经被扩展到其他4个区域。调查结果表明，这项措施使进入 LaRibera 地区的交通量减少了78%，从而使穿越此地带的出行时间减少18%，当地居民的满意度超过70%，同时也对当地的经济产生了积极的影响。然而证据也表明，该地带之内的商务正在向对车辆依赖较少的类型转变。

1.5.4 Enforcement 执法

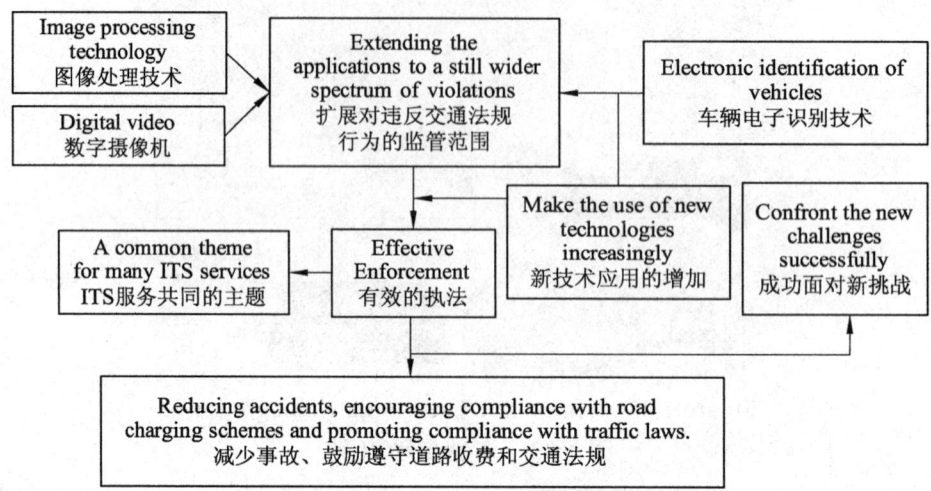

Figure 1.35　Effective enforcement
图 1.35　有效执法

Figure 1.36　Road monitoring
图 1.36　道路监控

Automatic enforcement technologies are being applied to new types of violations, e.g. following distance, lane keeping, congestion charging and toll payment.

自动执法技术正被应用于处理新的违法行为上，例如跟车间距、电子收费、车道保持、拥堵收费。

Figure 1.37　Electronic toll collection system
图 1.37　电子不停车收费系统

1.6 Advanced Traveler Information Systems (ATIS) 先进的出行者信息服务系统

Traveler information systems (TIS) are designed to give accurate information on traffic conditions so that travelers and fleet managers can adjust times, routes and modes of travel and delivery. Drivers can be warned to change their planned route to avoid incidents, congestion or severe weather conditions (based on historical as well as real-time current data). TIS may also give yellow pages type information.

出行者信息系统（TIS）给出行者和车队管理者提供关于交通状况的精确信息，以使他们能够调整时间、路线以及出行和送货的方式，提醒驾驶者改变预定的行驶路径，以避免事故、交通堵塞和恶劣的天气（依据历史和当前的实时数据）。TIS 还可以给出黄页式的信息。

Figure 1.38 Air parking lot
图 1.38 空中停车场

Figure 1.39 ATIS action frames
图 1.39 ATIS 作用框架图

ATIS applications have two main requirements:
ATIS 的应用有两个主要要求：
(1) Detailed system operations information, often generated by ATMS.
由 ATMS 产生详尽的系统运行信息。

(2) Means of communicating this information to travelers.

将这些信息传输给出行者的方式。

While ATMS is generally a public-sector responsibility, ATIS is often developed in partnerships between the public and private sectors. ATIS data is, in fact, the doorway to a whole new generation of commercially-viable, value-added traveler services made available through private sector service providers.

一般来讲，ATMS 服务由公共部门负责，而 ATIS 则通常由公共部门和私营部门合作开发。实际上，ATIS 数据是通向商务新时代的通道，而私营服务商的出现使得为出行者提供增值服务成为可能。

1.6.1　In-vehicle ATIS　车载 ATIS

The simplest forms of ATIS involve in-vehicle radio traffic reports, from general broadcasters, on queues and incidents; and highway advisory radio (HAR) "local casts" on conditions in known congested locations.

ATIS 的最简单形式包括：车载无线电交通广播提供的关于车辆排队和交通事故的信息；公路路况广播（HAR）播送的已知堵塞路段的状况。

Recent developments include the RDS/TMC system in Europe, incorporating a traffic message channel (TMC) within a radio data system (RDS) and now available on FM radio side-band transmissions. As a further refinement, European companies including iTIS and Trafficmaster (UK) and Mediamobile (France) have developed congestion monitoring and journey time information services that relay information to in-vehicle units. One of the most highly-developed systems is Japan's Vehicle Information and Communication System, VICS. Many countries are now investing in traffic control centers and traffic information centers which are at the hub of ITS (evidence of the way in which ATMS and ATIS are logically converging).

Figure 1.40　Involve in-vehicle radio traffic reports

图 1.40　车载无线电交通广播

最近的发展包括欧洲的 RCVS/TMC 系统，将交通信息频道（TMC）嵌入一个无线数据广播系统（RDS），而且现在可以在调频广播边带上传输。作为进一步的改进，欧洲的一些公司，包括 iTIS, Trafficmaster（英国）和 Mediamobile（法国）开发了交通堵塞监测和旅行时间信息服务，能将相关信息传输给车载单元。发展最快的系统之一是日本的道路交通信息通信系统（VICS）。一些国家正在投资建设作为 ITS 核心的交通控制中心和交通信息中心（ATMS 和 ATIS 功能有效的融合）。

> **例** VICS (Vehicle Information and Communication System)
> VICS（道路交通信息通信系统）
>
> Japan's VICS system for in-vehicle traffic information has operated since 1996. Data from police headquarters and road operators feeds into the Japanese Road Traffic Information Centre, which is connected by dedicated high-speed digital lines to the VICS Centre. This transmits processed information to media centres and FM broadcasting stations, which provide it in turn to in-vehicle units (IVUs) via radio (quasi-microwave) beacons, largely for expressways; infrared beacons, largely for trunk roads; and FM multiplex broadcasts from local stations, for wide-area coverage. Information is free to drivers, who can receive it in text display, simple graphic display, or map display.
>
> 1996年日本实施了提供交通信息的VICS系统。警察厅和道路运营者将数据提供给日本道路交通信息中心，该中心与VICS中心由高速专用数字线路连接。VICS中心将处理后的信息传递给媒体中心和调频广播台转发至车载接收单元（IVU），在高速公路上主要是无线电（微波）信标，城市干路上主要通过红外信标，而本地电台的调频多路广播则主要用于广域覆盖。此类交通信息对驾驶者是免费的，可以以文本、简单图形或者地图的形式提供给驾驶者。

1.6.2 Infrastructure-based ATIS 基于基础设施的 ATIS

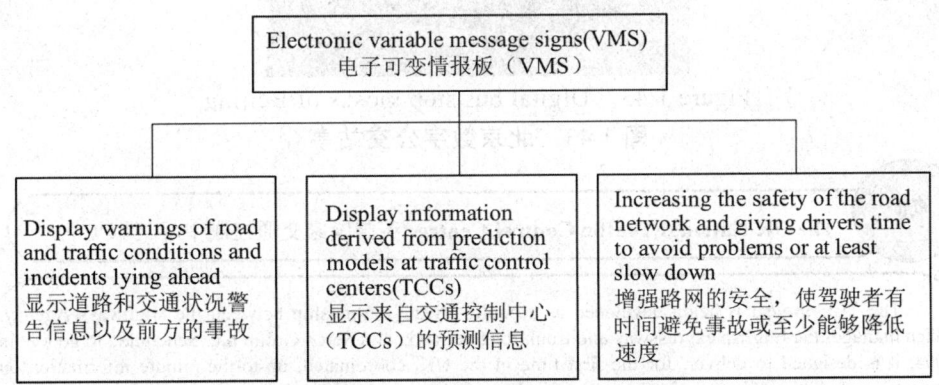

Figure 1.41　Effect of electronic variable message signs (VMS)
图 1.41　电子可变情报板的作用

Automatic detection of incidents and queuing traffic, coupled with automatic setting of VMS, has brought noticeable reductions in secondary accidents on instrumented expressways. VMS can also display information derived from prediction models at traffic control centers (TCCs). Other infrastructural media include electronic information kiosks located at service areas or interchanges.

事故和车辆排队的自动检测加上 VMS 的自动设置，使安装这种设施的公路显著减少了二次交通事故。VMS 还可以显示来自交通控制中心（TCC）预测模型的信息。其他的设施还包括设置在服务区或者交叉路口的电子信息亭等。

Figure 1.42　Electronic variable message signs (VMS)
图 1.42　电子可变情报板（VMS）

Figure 1.43　Digital bus stop kiosks of Beijing
图 1.43　北京数字公交站亭

例　The UK National Traffic Control Centre　英国国家交通控制中心（TCC）

　　The TCC project is being developed as a public-private partnership between the Highways Agency, which manages the English expressway and trunk road network, and Serco Group plc. Scheduled to go live in 2004, it is designed to deliver, for the first time in the UK, coordinated, up-to-the-minute information on strategic roads (ultimately to be integrated with other transport modes). The information will feed an Internet-based Travel Information Highway (TIH), which will allow open exchange of, and provide a market for, transport data. Value-added service providers (VASPs) will process this, to make it more accessible to users, and add enhanced services e.g. route planning via channels including the Internet, cell phones and digital audio broadcasting (DAB).

　　TCC项目以政府和私营合作的模式发展，即由掌管着英国高速公路、公路网主干线的公路局以及信嘉集团联合开发。项目计划在2004年推出，在英国首次实现实时道路交通协调策略的信息发送（最终将与其他的交通信息发布方式相融合）。信息将被提供给基于因特网的高速公路出行信息平台（TIH），这将为交通信息的提供、交换、发送提供一个市场。增值服务提供商（VASP）将提供支撑服务，使服务更加顺畅地到达用户，并且还会提供增强服务，例如通过因特网、移动电话和数字音频广播（DAB）的方式为客户制定路径。

1.6.3　Location-independent ATIS　独立于位置的 ATIS

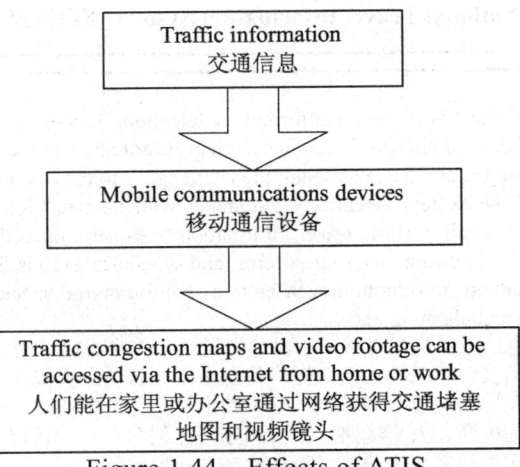

Figure 1.44　Effects of ATIS
图 1.44　ATIS 的作用

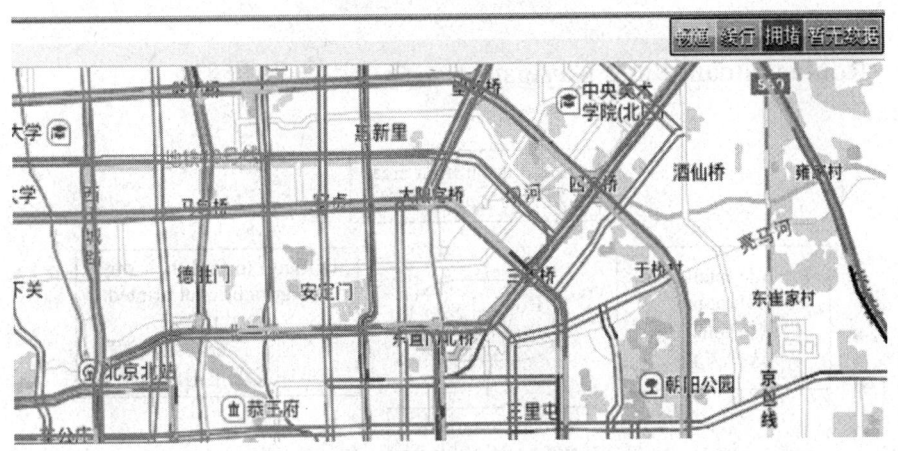

Figure 1.45　Beijing traffic live diagram
图 1.45　北京交通实况图

Figure 1.46　Touch-screen Web phone
图 1.46　具有 Web 功能的触摸屏电话

> **例** 511 National Travel Information System 511国家出行信息系统
>
> The concept behind the "511" travel information telephone service is to have a secure exclusive national three-digit telephone number to disseminate travel information to the traveling public throughout the United States. Although the service is national, the challenge is to provide information which is relevant and timely to travelers. The system is entirely automatic with no need for human intervention unless specifically requested by the caller. Basic travel information (weather and road conditions, traffic updates, public transportation service interruptions, routes, fares, and schedules, etc.) is free. Some 511 services may charge for additional, premium information such as tourist information, special events, parking locations and lot status, trip routing and planning, etc.
>
> "511"出行信息电话服务是全美唯一为出行者发布全美交通信息的3位数电话号码。虽然服务范围覆盖全美,但是如何及时有效地为公众提供信息是本项目的最大挑战。如果呼叫用户没有特殊需求的话,本系统将由电脑自动接听和应答。基本的出行信息是免费的,包括天气和路况信息、交通最新资料、公交服务的中断、公交线路、票价和排班计划等。511中的有些服务是收费的,包括旅游信息、大型活动、停车指导和剩余泊位、出行路径和计划编制等。

1.6.4　Route Guidance and Navigation　路径引导和导航

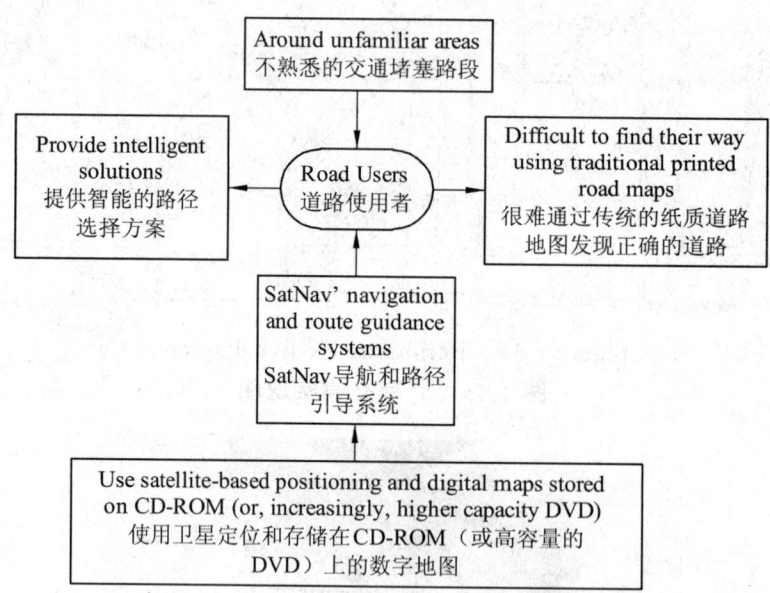

Figure 1.47　Structure of road users route choice system

图1.47　道路使用者路径选择系统结构图

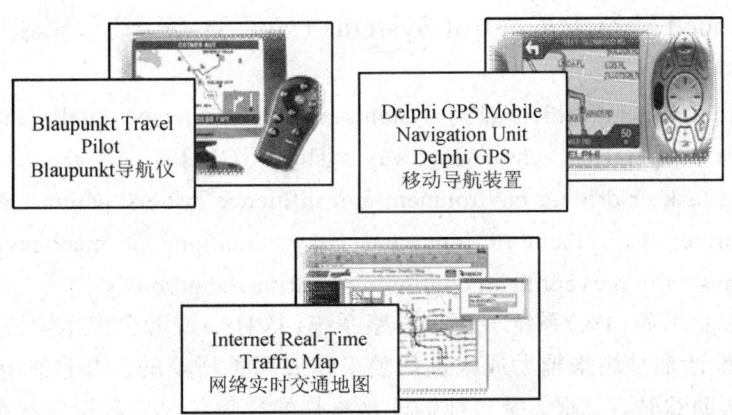

Figure 1.48 Devices for displaying travel and traffic information
图 1.48 用于显示旅行和交通信息的设备

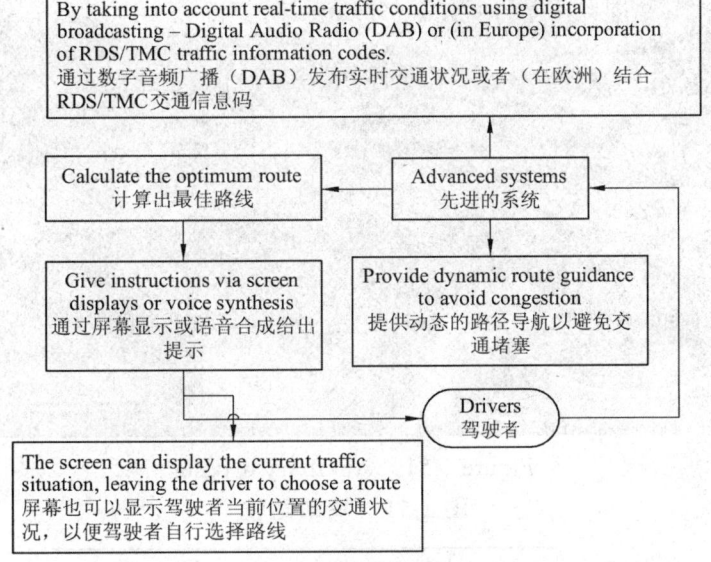

Figure 1.49 Structure of route guidance systems
图 1.49 路径引导系统结构图

Figure 1.50 Car monitor
图 1.50 车载显示器

1.7 Advanced Vehicle Control Systems (AVCS) 先进的车辆控制系统

AVCS cover intelligent vehicle (IV) systems and the projected intelligent vehicle-highway systems (IVHS) or cooperative vehicle highway systems (CVHS). All are designed to assist or modify the driving task or driving environment and influence drivers' actions. AVCS can actively help drivers to drive; warn them of imminent risky situations or manoeuvres (conscious or inadvertent); or physically prevent them continuing to drive dangerously.

AVCS 包括智能车辆（IV）系统、智能车-路系统（IVHS）或者合作车辆公路系统（CVHS）。所有智能系统的设计都是用来辅助或改进驾驶工作或驾驶环境的，并且影响驾驶者的行为。AVCS 能主动地协助驾驶者驾驶，警告他们即将来临的危险状况或者操作状态（有意识的或无意识的）或在物理上防止他们继续危险驾驶。

Figure 1.51　Auxiliary driving
图 1.51　辅助驾驶

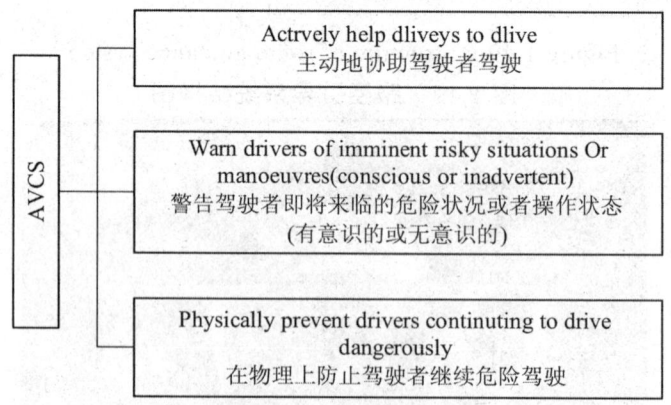

Figure 1.52　Function of AVCS
图 1.52　AVCS 的功能

Other AVCS technologies under development include:
AVCS 技术的发展由以下因素驱动：

Technologies already available include: traction control, the antilock braking system (ABS), which has paved the way for the electronic stability program (ESP) for skid recovery; and adaptive cruise control(ACC), which has recently appeared in top end vehicles. ACC's use of radar sensors to maintain safe headways points towards future AVCS aimed at keeping vehicles safely positioned on the road.

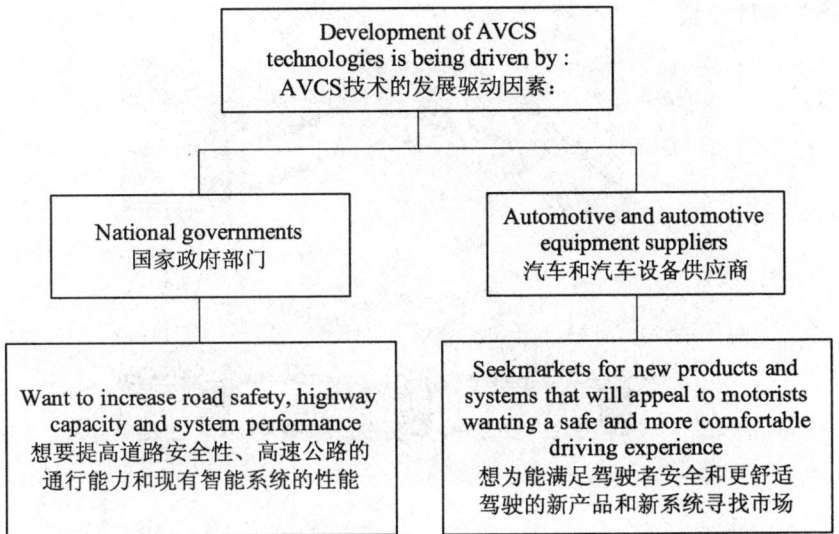

Figure 1.53　AVCS technology development driver factors
图 1.53　AVCS 技术的发展驱动因素

现已投入使用的 AVCS 技术包括：牵引控制，防抱死制动系统（ABS）（为用于制动恢复的电子稳定装置（ESP）的研制铺平了道路）以及配置在高级车辆上的自适应巡航控制（ACC）技术。ACC 使用雷达传感器保持与前车的车距，未来的 AVCS 技术的目的是为保证车辆的安全而确定其在道路上的位置。

Figure 1.54　ACC of Audi
图 1.54　奥迪的自适应巡航系统

These will warn of, and help avoid, unplanned lane changes and the risk of lateral as well as longitudinal collisions with obstructions including other vehicles and pedestrians, and automatically deploy crash restraints such as air bags, so reducing seriousness of any impact. At the same time, they will trigger automatic emergency alerts.

车载智能系统将在以下情况下辅助驾驶：无计划的车道变换，躲避横向和纵向的障碍物（包括其他车辆和行人），并自动启动碰撞保护装置（如气囊），减轻事故的伤害。同时，还可以自动触发紧急事件警报。

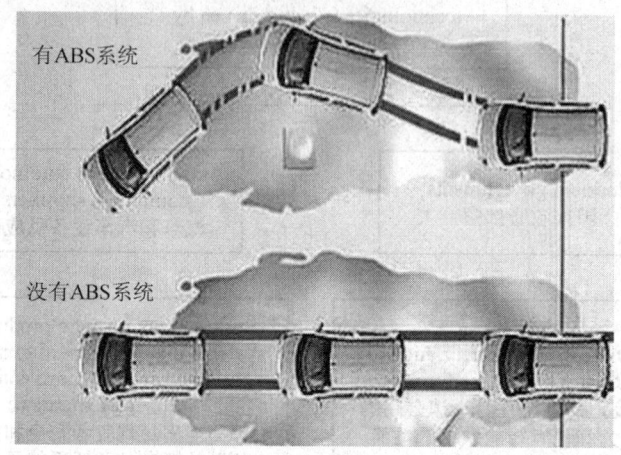

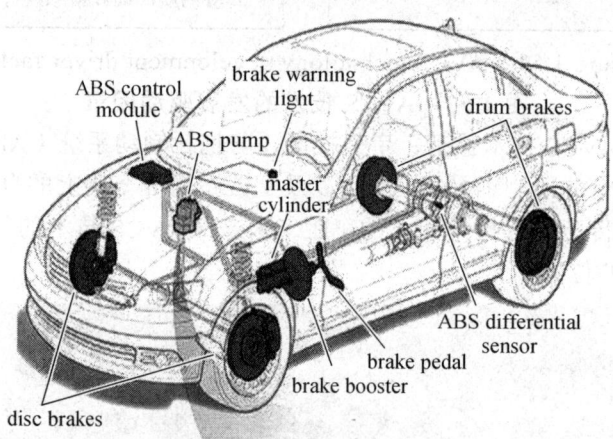

Figure 1.55　Antilock braking system
图 1.55　防抱死系统

Figure 1.56　Air bags
图 1.56　安全气囊

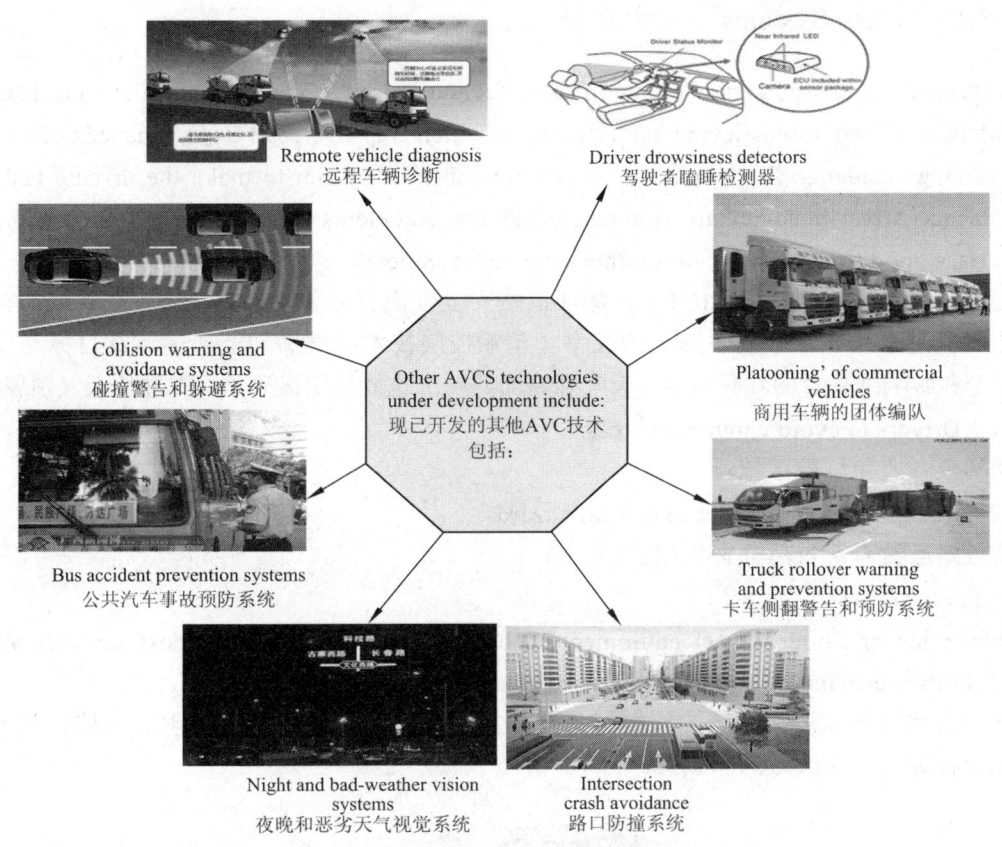

Figure 1.57　Other AVCS technologies under development
图 1.57　现已开发的其他 AVC 技术

例　Platooning with CHAUFFEUR　利用CHAUFFEUR的车辆编队

The volume of goods moving on European roads is expected to double between 1995 and 2010. Without remedial action, the effects will be longer journeys (for private as well as commercial vehicles), higher costs and aggravated environmental pollution. The CHAUFFEUR project, led by German automotive DaimlerChrysler AG, has addressed the problem by developing a 'platooning' system that can increase the density of freight traffic without prejudicing safety. It involves linking two or more trucks by 'electronic towbars' that let them travel in close convoy, so occupying less road space with only the leading one driven. Prototype trucks have been trialled on the Brenner highway in Austria.

预计到2010年，欧洲道路的货运将比1995年翻一番。没有相应的补救措施，将会有更长时间的行程（无论是私人车辆还是商用车辆），增加车辆行驶成本，加剧环境恶化。CHAUFFEUR项目由德国戴姆勒克莱斯勒牵头，开发"团体编队"系统，在不破坏运输安全的前提下提高货物运输车辆行驶的密度。它包括只用一个引导车，用"电子拖杆"将两辆或更多辆卡车接连组成车队，使车辆近距离行驶，以节省道路空间。原型样车已经在奥地利Brenner公路上做过测试。

1.7.1　Safety Systems　安全系统

Advanced Information and Communication Technologies (ICT) can contribute significantly to road safety, enabling sophisticated safety systems which improve road users' chances of avoiding and surviving accidents. Developments in vehicle control that aim to make the driving task safer and influence driver behavior are summarized above. Accidents can also arise from weather and road-surface conditions. Advanced weather warnings enable:

先进的信息和通信技术（ICT）在保证道路安全方面有显著贡献，复杂安全系统能提高道路使用者躲避事故和从事故中逃生的几率。车辆控制技术的发展如上所述，其目标是使驾驶更加安全和影响驾驶者的驾驶行为。天气和路面的状况也能够引发事故，先进的天气预警可以：

（1）Drivers to avoid dangerous areas.

使驾驶者避免危险区域；

（2）Road operators to react to natural hazards.

使道路运营者对自然危害做出反应。

Such as: 例如：

Winter ice or floods, direct equipment such as snow ploughs to the most severely-affected areas; Prioritize evacuation and emergency vehicle access routes.

冬天结冰区域和洪水区域，直接配备诸如扫雪车等设备给受灾最严重的区域；优先疏散和紧急营救进入受灾区域的车辆。

Figure 1.58　Snow ploughs

图 1.58　扫雪车

Figure 1.59　Disaster relief vehicles

图 1.59　救灾车辆

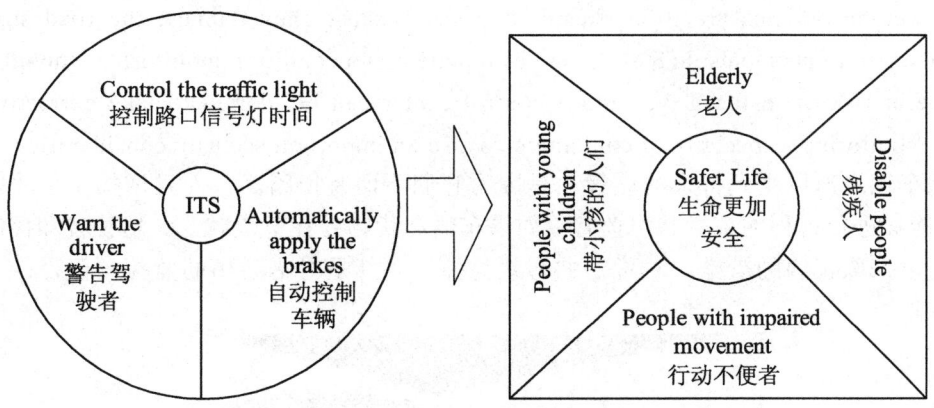

Figure 1.60 Cyclists and pedestrians can also benefit from ITS
图 1.60 ITS 对行人和骑行者的益处

Accidents can also arise from weather and road-surface conditions. But the advanced weather warnings could make the road operators to react to natural hazards and drivers to avoid dangerous areas.

糟糕的天气和路面的状况能够引发事故，但是先进的天气预警使道路运营者对自然危害做出反应，使驾驶者避开危险区域。

1.8 Commercial Vehicle Operation Systems 商用车辆运营系统

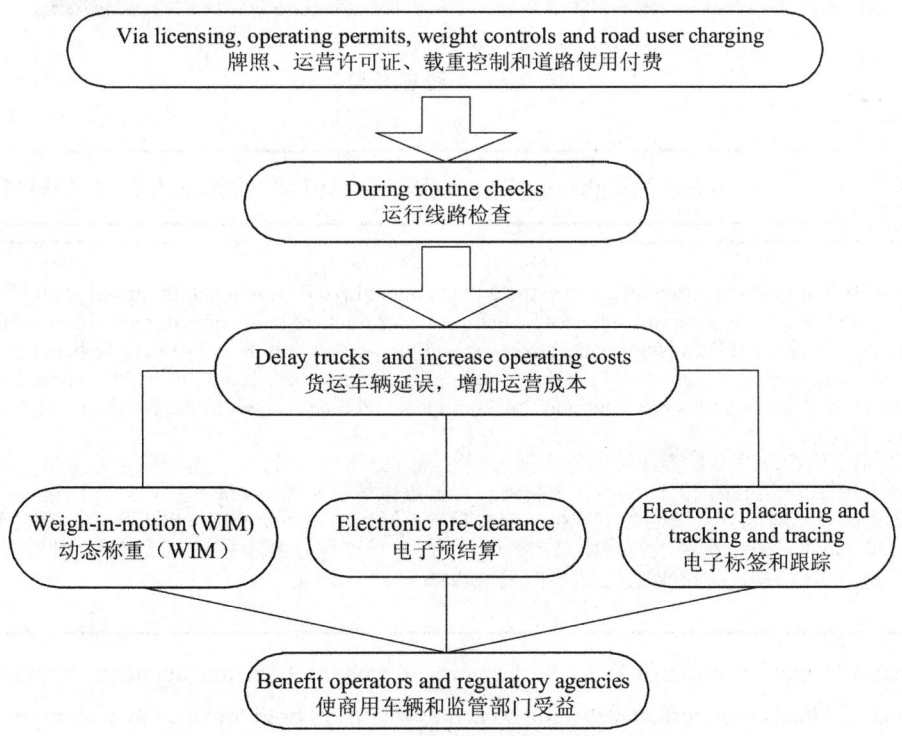

Figure 1.61 Commercial Vehicle Operation Systems
图 1.61 商用车辆运营系统

43

Overweight vehicles are of particular concern because they damage the road surface and increase the risk of accidents. ITS also enables remote cargo condition monitoring; should a vehicle or load be at risk, both the driver and a control center can be alerted to take corrective action. Effective monitoring, especially of containers, is also an important security consideration.

超重车辆之所以受到特别的监管，是因为它们不但有损路面，而且增加了事故发生的风险。ITS 能够进行远程的载货状况监督，如果车辆和货物处在危险状态，驾驶者和控制中心都会被警告以采取正确的措施。对货物的有效监控，尤其是对集装箱的监控，仍是一个重要的安全性因素。

Figure 1.62 Overweight vehicles

图 1.62 超重车辆

例 **A virtual Weigh-In-Motion (WIM) station 虚拟动态称重（WIM）站**

Overweight vehicles attempting to avoid a conventional fixed weight station installed on US Interstate Highway 75 (I75) in the state of Kentucky by using a lesser road are being caught by a virtual weigh station. It consists of a piezo WIM system, lane controller and high-resolution digital camera. When a truck passes, the system captures its image, weight and (by measuring the time between axles passing) speed, length and classification. Resulting files are date- and time-stamped, and then relayed to the physical weight station for action if necessary.

超重车辆尝试避开设置在美国肯塔基州州际高速公路75（I75）的传统固定称重站，通常会选择一条人迹罕至的公路，但这样的行为目前已经被虚拟称重站粉碎。WIM包括了一个压力动态称重系统，车道控制器和高分辨率的数字相机。当载货汽车通过时，系统捕捉车辆的图像，获得车辆的重量、速度（通过计算卡车经过特定距离的时间得到）、长度和分类的数据。具有日期和时间的结果文件被传递给实际的称重站，以便在需要时采取措施。

Automatic Vehicle Location (AVL) is the core of modern fleet management. It helps operators manage fleets and loads more effectively, and so achieve gains in both logistics and economics.

自动车辆定位（AVL）技术是现代车队管理的核心。它能更加有效地帮助运营商管理车队和货物，在物流管理和经济上都获得收益。

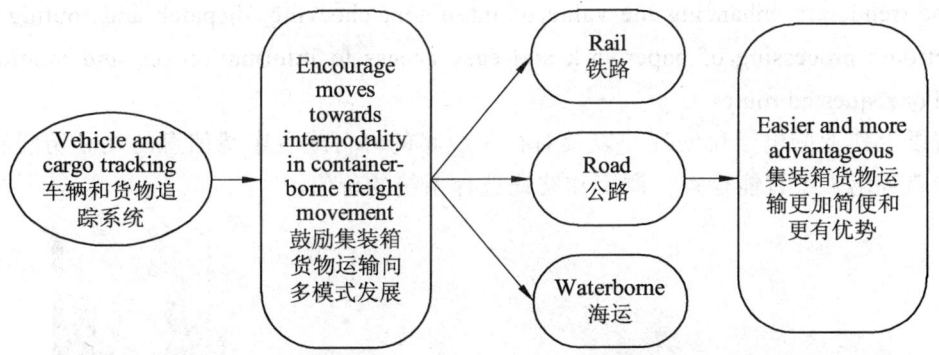

Figure 1.63　Vehicle and cargo tracking
图 1.63　车辆和货物追踪系统

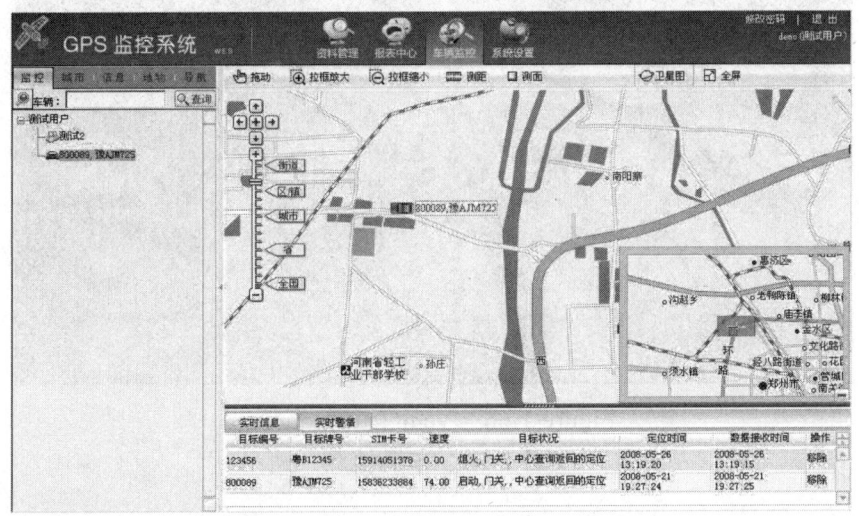

Figure 1.64　GPS-logistics on track
图 1.64　GPS 定位-物流在途追踪

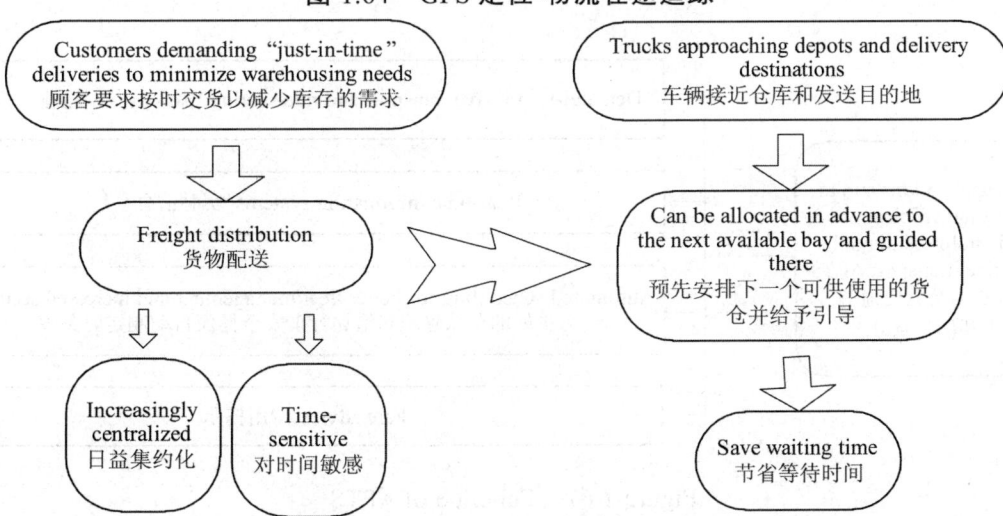

Figure 1.65　Frame of logistics distribution
图 1.65　物流配送框架图

These trends are enhancing the value of intelligent checking, dispatch and routing systems, with electronic processing of paperwork and easy access to information on, and monitoring of, permitted or requested routes.

随着纸上作业的电子化处理，以及对行车线路的许可或者申请信息的便利访问和监控，这些发展趋势增强了智能检查，调度和路线选择系统的价值。

Figure 1.66　Vehicle detection

图 1.66　车辆检测

1.9　Advanced Public Transport Systems (APTS)　先进的公共交通系统（APTS）

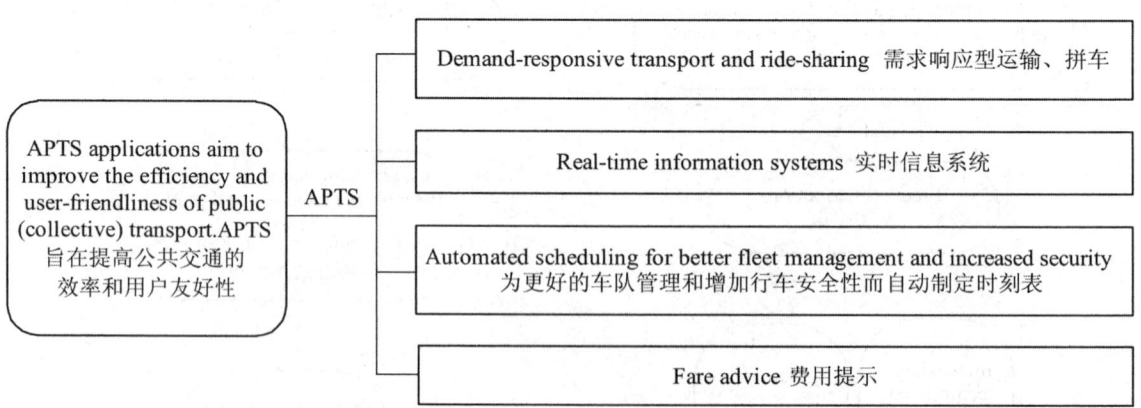

Figure 1.67　Function of APTS

图 1.67　APTS 的功能

All help to position public transport within integrated, multimodal systems that will encourage people to rely less on cars, and so help reduce traffic congestion and environmental pollution.

以上所有措施，将有助于将公共交通融入集成的多模式系统，鼓励人们减少依赖私人小汽车出行，以减少交通堵塞和环境污染。

1.9.1　Public Transport Information　公共交通信息

One way of promoting greater use of public transport is by providing reliable and easily-accessible real-time passenger information (RTPI). Automatic vehicle location (AVL) can drive real-time information systems giving service running and connection times and route advice in-vehicle, at-stop, at home or work, on the street or using other transport modes.

推进人们更多地利用公共交通的一个方法就是提供可靠的、可方便访问的实时乘客信息（RTPI）。自动车辆定位（AVL）使得实时信息系统能够为在车内、车站、家里、工作地点、街道上以及使用其他交通模式的人们提供运行和换乘时刻和路线建议等信息。

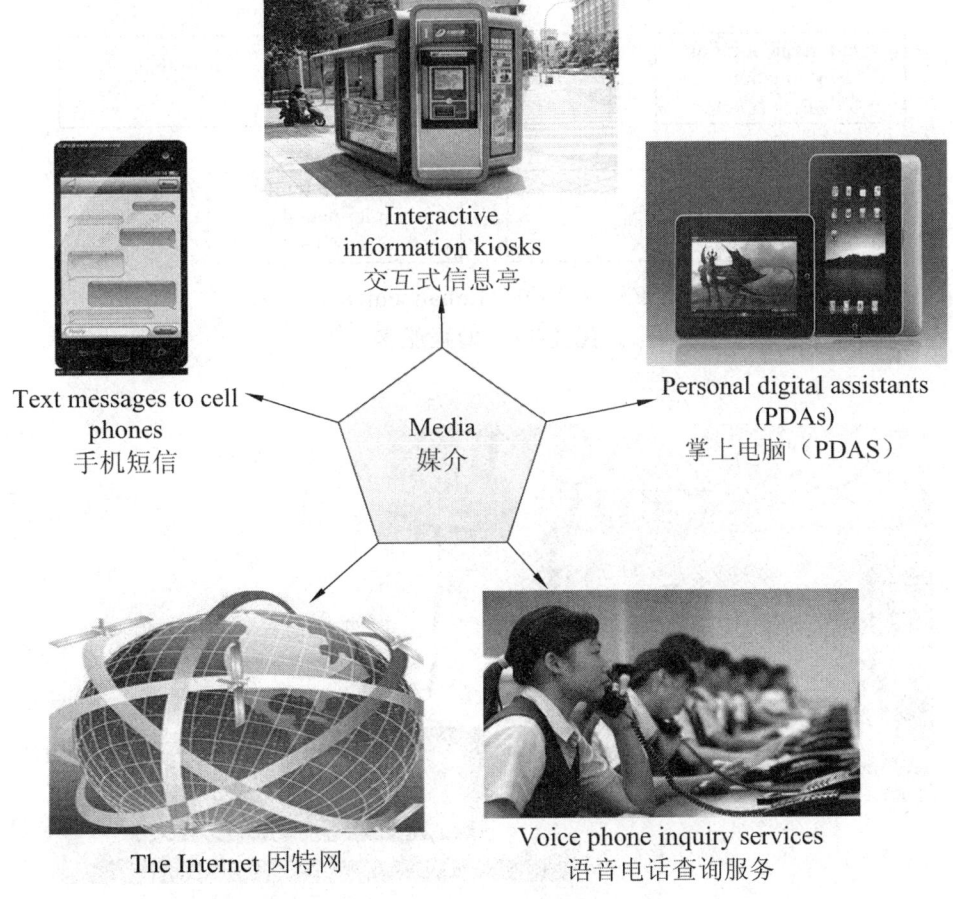

Figure 1.68　Public transportation information media
图 1.68　**公共交通信息媒介**

> **例** **Commercial Vehicle Border Crossing between Canada and the US**
> **加拿大和美国之间的商用车辆过关通道**
>
> Cross-border mobility between Canada and the US has been impacted twice in recent years. First, the North America Free Trade Agreement (NAFTA) encouraged heavier commercial flows, resulting in delays of up to an hour for laden trucks. Second, the September 11th 2001 terrorist actions increased the risk of security breaches at the world's longest undefended frontier. Both countries have collaborated in the Free and Secure Transport (FAST) programme, which dedicates special lanes to trucks equipped with radio frequency identification (RFID) transponders. These send control agents electronic data for checks against preclearance information.
>
> 近年来，加拿大和美国间通关机动性已经两次受到影响。第一，北美自由贸易协定（NAFTA）鼓励载重更大的商用车队，致使满载车辆通关延迟增加到1个小时。第二，2001年9月11日的恐怖袭击，增加了这个世界上最长的未布防的边境线上保安缺口的风险。这两个国家已经就自由而安全的运输（FAST）计划展开合作，为安装射频识别（RFID）装置的车辆设置专用车道。射频识别装置给管理部门发送电子数据，以核查车辆的预结关信息。

| "On-arrival" location information 到达的位置信息 | Journey planning 行程设计 | Fare options 付费提示 |

| Booking services 预订服务 | On-arrival' tourist information 旅行者信息 |

Figure 1.69　Enhancements
图 1.69　增强服务

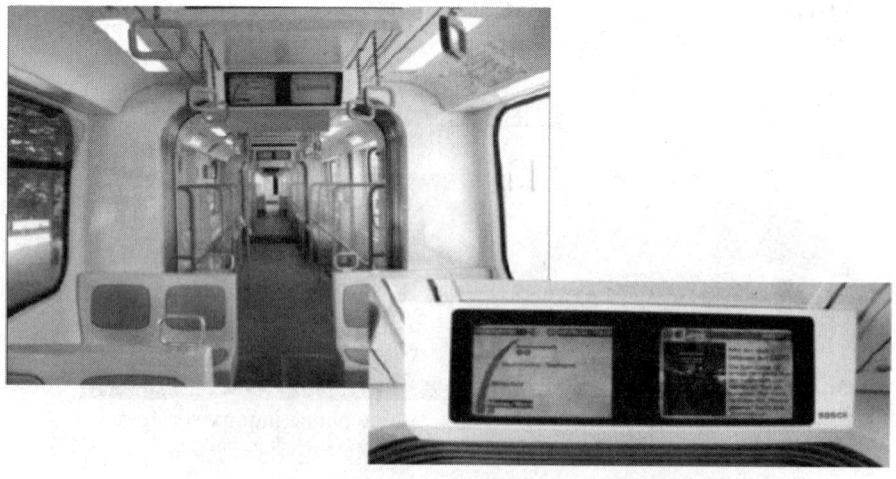

Figure 1.70　In-train passenger information display
图 1.70　列车车厢内旅客信息显示图

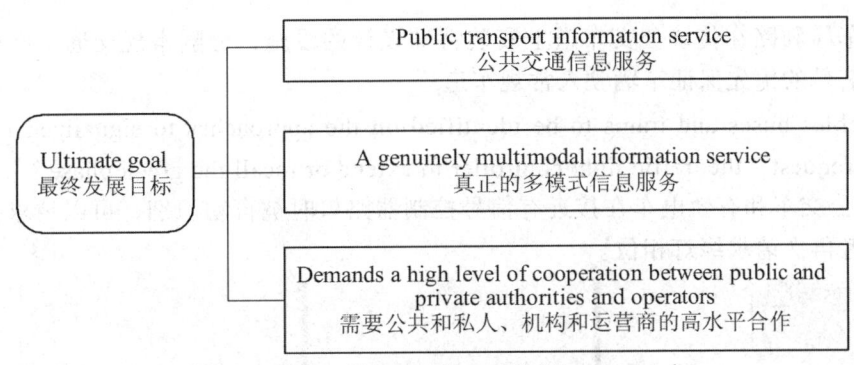

Figure 1.71　Frame chart of ultimate goal

图 1.71　最终发展目标框架图

例　**Heavy Vehicle Electronic Licence Plate (HELP)**　重型车辆电子牌（HELP）

PrePass is a US electronic pre-clearance scheme. It is run by the non-profit Heavy Vehicle Electronic Licence Plate (HELP) partnership between US freight operators and government agencies. Pre-qualified trucks equipped with transponders can comply at highway speeds. HELP has joined forces with the US East Coast E-Zpass tolling consortium to use the same transponders for both preclearance and toll payment, with scope for extension to border crossings.

PrePass是美国的一项电子预结关计划。它是美国货运运营商和政府机构合作的非盈利的重车电子许可牌照联合组织。预检合格的卡车装配有应答器，它能够在公路行驶速度下实现应答。HELP联合了美国东海岸电子收费财团的E-Zpass收费联盟的力量，在预清关和电子收费中都使用相同的收发机，范围扩大到了通关边境。

1.9.2　Public Transport Priority　公共交通优先

Public transport vehicles can be given priority by urban traffic control (UTC) systems.

公共交通车辆通过城市交通控制（UTC）系统获得优先权。

The guided bus way supplements conventional bus lanes with specially-designed track sections that deter general traffic. At the end of a bus way section, traffic signal priority gives access to general lanes.

Figure 1.72　Bus lanes

图 1.72　公交专用道

公共汽车导驶路在传统公交车道上安装特殊设计的设施，分隔常规交通。在公交车道的末端，交通信号的优先保证车辆驶入常规车道。

AVL enables buses and trams to be identified on the approaches to signalized intersections, where they "request" the traffic light controller to extend or recall the green phase.

AVL 使公交车和有轨电车在接近有信号控制器路口时被自动识别，可以请求交通信号控制器延长或者再次请求绿灯相位。

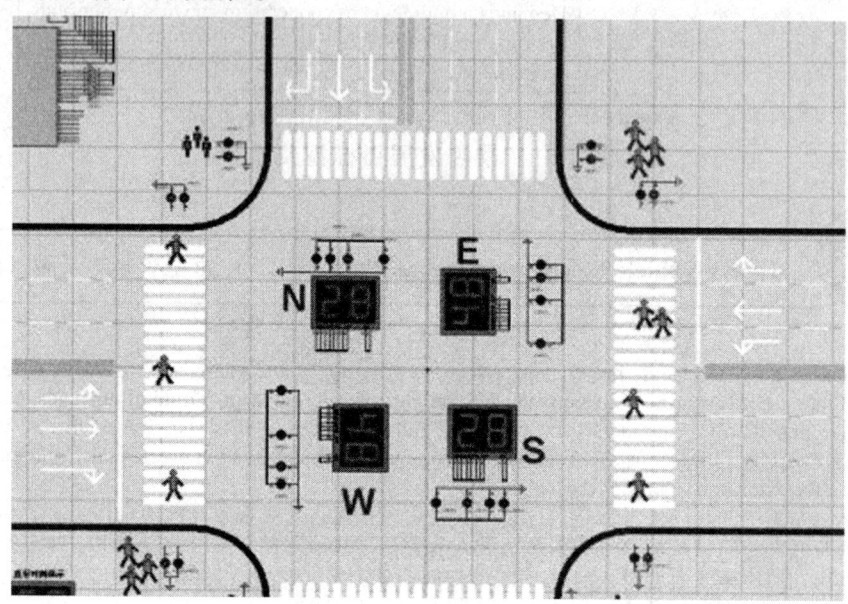

Figure 1.73　Signal control
图 1.73　信号控制

例　Lane Transit District (Oregon, USA)　车道变换区域（美国俄勒冈）

Lane County, in the US state of Oregon, centers on the twin communities of Eugene and Springfield. Population growth has indicated the need for new public transport investment, and the county is opting for a bus rapid transit (BRT) system with traffic signal priority, satellite positioning-based AVL and automated stop announcements and (eventually) real-time passenger information. Block signaling will control bi-directional single-lane sections, built to save land and costs. The County sees the protection of rights of way for the BRT as securing the possibility of a future higher-technology light rail.

美国俄勒冈州的县级公路，位于尤金和斯普林菲尔德两个社区的中心。人口的增长表明了对新公共交通的投资需求，县政府倾向于采用具有交通信号优先权的快速公交（BRT）系统，基于卫星定位的AVL，自动停车报站及（最终）实时乘客信息。区域信号控制双向的单车道，节省土地和成本。县政府将对快速公交系统（BRT）路权的保护看成是对未来可能兴建的高科技轻轨的路权的保护。

Detection can be via inductive loops under the road surface, roadside beacons, or satellite-based positioning systems.

对公共交通车辆的检测，可以通过埋设在道路表面以下的环形线圈、路侧装置或者卫星定位系统实现。

1.9.3　Public Transport Fleet Management and Logistics　公共交通车队管理和物流服务

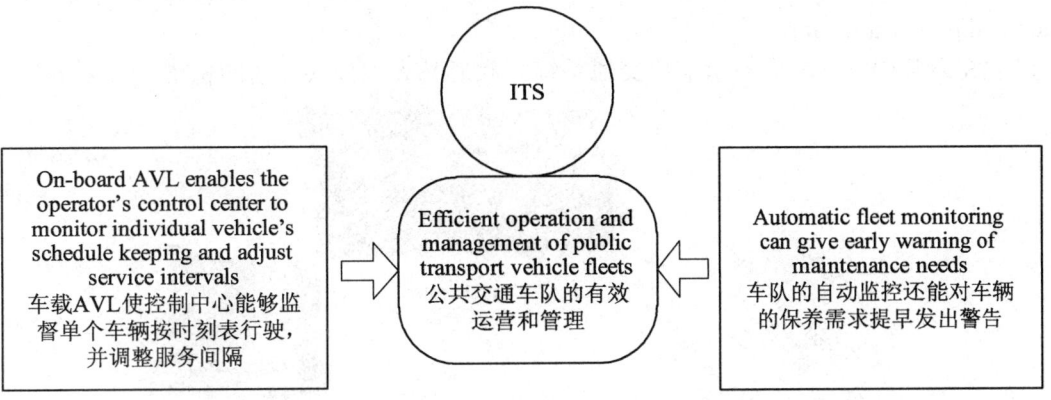

Figure 1.74　ITS support efficient operation and management of public transport vehicle fleets
图 1.74　ITS 支持对公共交通车队进行有效运营和管理

Door opening/closing detection systems and automated fare collection (AFC) provide operators with valuable passenger data.

车门开/关自动检测系统和自动售检票系统（AFC）向运营者提供有价值的乘客数据。

Figure 1.75　Valuable passenger data
图 1.75　有价值的乘客数据

Use to evaluate route usage and refine services to meet passenger demands and roster vehicles and drivers more effectively, and improve financial management.

用来评价路线使用情况，优化服务以满足乘客的需求，提高值班车辆和驾驶员的效率，以及改善财务管理。

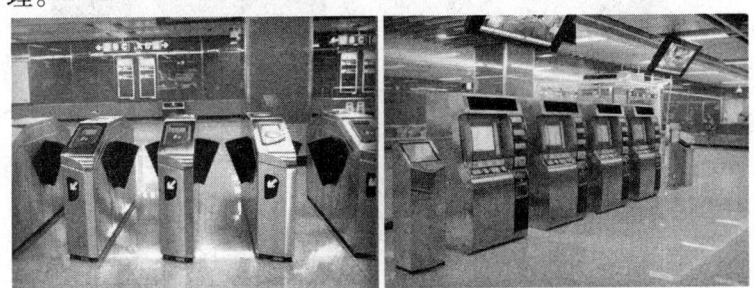

Figure 1.76　Automated fare collection system
图 1.76　自动售检票系统

1.9.4　Flexible Shared Transport Services　灵活共享的交通服务

ITS-based shared and demand responsive transport systems are bridging the gap between private and public transport.

以 ITS 为基础的共享和需求响应交通系统是联通私人和公共交通的桥梁。

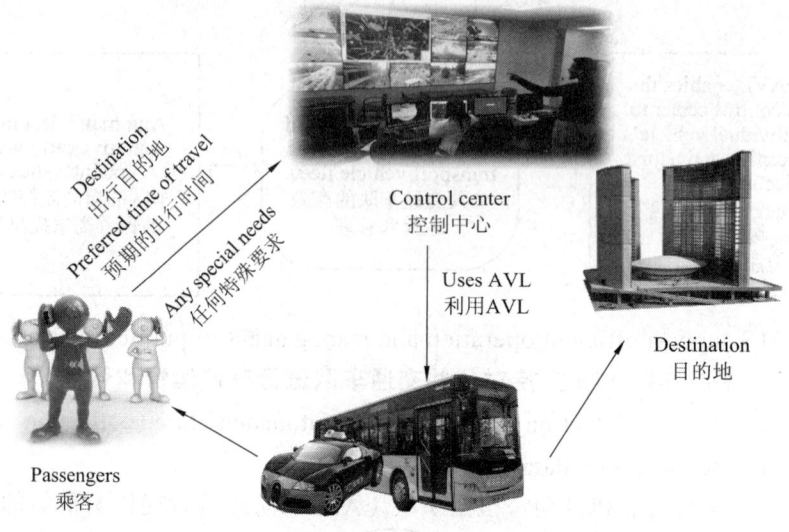

Figure 1.77　transport services

图 1.77　交通服务

1.10　Electronic Payment Systems (EPS)　电子支付系统

Modern EPS systems offer major advantages over cash payment for transport and highway operators, their passengers and customers.

现代 EPS 系统为运输、高速公路运营商、乘客和消费者提供了优于现金支付的付费方式。

Figure 1.78　Payment methods

图 1.78　付费方式

ETC (Electronic Toll Collection) / EFC (Electronic Fee Collection) is now well developed on expressways, bridges and tunnels across the world.

现在 ETC 与 EFC 系统已经在世界范围内的高速公路、桥梁和隧道上广泛应用。

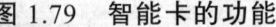

Figure 1.79　Function of smartcards

图 1.79　智能卡的功能

Figure 1.80　Smartcards

图 1.80　智能卡

EPS also offer prospects of interoperability within and across transport modes and systems, using a single, intelligent payment medium.

EPS 系统还提供了互操作性的前景，使得在跨越运输模式和系统之间使用单一的智能卡介质进行结算成为可能。

1.10.1　ETC/EFC Systems　ETC 与 EFC 系统

ETC/EFC enables drivers to pay tolls and other road-use fees (e.g. in urban congestion charging schemes) automatically without stopping at plazas.

ETC 与 EFC 系统能够实现自动支付通行费和其他道路使用费（如城市拥堵收费等）。

DSRC-based EFC systems need substantial infrastructural investment in gantries for mounting reading antennae over charging lanes.

建设以 DSRC 为基础的 EFC 系统，要在收费车道上架设安装天线的门架，因此需要充足的基础设施投资。

ETC/EFC
Infrared
红外
Dedicated Short Range Communications (DSRC) technology
专用短程无线通信技术
Microwave
微波
Read at an identifying in-vehicle electronic tag (transponder) automatically
自动读取车载可识别电子标签

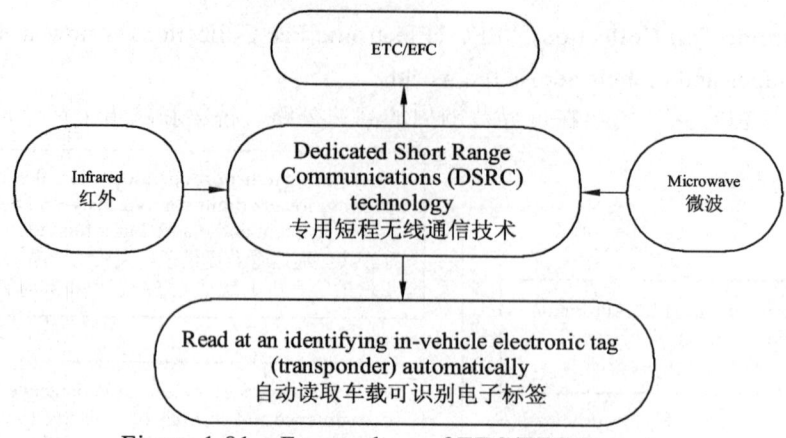

Figure 1.81 Frame chart of ETC/EFC Systems

图 1.81 ETC 与 EFC 系统框架图

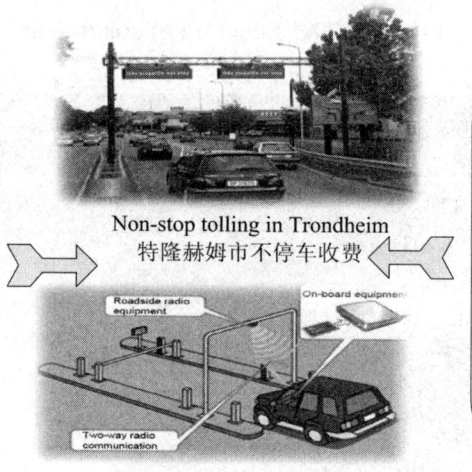

Payment can be by invoicing the registered transponder owner; or debiting a stored-value tag or smartcard inserted into an in-vehicle unit (IVU)
付款可以是对已注册的应答机所有者记账，也可以从插入车载单元（IVU）的储值标签或智能卡中扣除
Non-stop tolling in Trondheim
特隆赫姆市不停车收费
Roadside radio equipment
Two-way radio communication
Advanced systems that carry out transactions at expressway speeds are in operation on the all-electronic.For example Highway 407 in Toronto (Canada) and the Melbourne City Link in Australia
先进系统可以在高速公路行驶速度下实现交易。比如加拿大多伦多的407全电子高速公路和通往澳大利亚墨尔本的高速公路

Tolling technology(Japan)
日本收费技术

Figure 1.82 Example of Non-stop tolling

图 1.82 不停车收费案例

Use satellite technology
利用卫星技术来定位
Virtual positioning systems
虚拟定位系统（VPS）
Use satellite technology
利用卫星技术来定位
Vehicles equipped with special in-vehicle units (IVUs)
配备特殊车载单元（IVU）的车辆
Known as GNSS-CN, for global navigation satellite system – cellular networks
GNSS-CN，即全球卫星导航系统—蜂窝移动网络

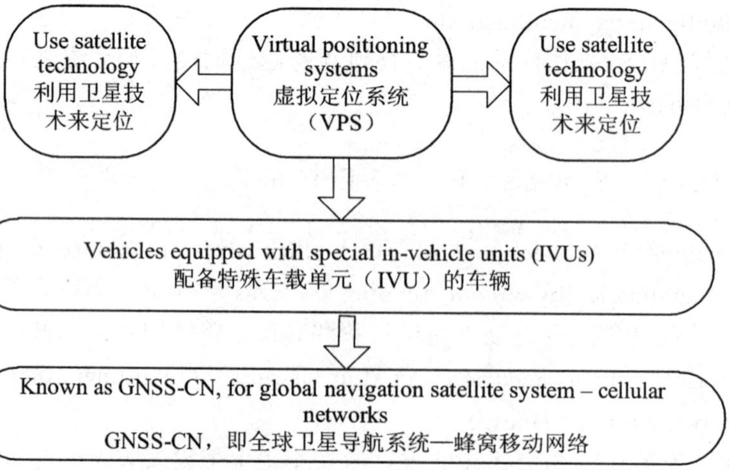

Figure 1.83 Frame chart of VPS

图 1.83 虚拟定位系统（VPS）框架图

Advantages of VPS
虚拟定位系统（VPS）的优势

- Within tolled networks or charging zones, VPS measure the distance they travel. VPS then either communicates charging data to a control center, using wireless CN links, or deducts the charge from a stored-value smartcard inserted into the IVU.
  在收费路网和收费点，虚拟定位系统（VPS）测量配备车载单元（IVU）车辆的行驶距离，然后通过无线蜂窝网将收费数据传送到控制中心，或是从车载单元的储值智能卡中扣除费用。

- VPS offer road operators wide flexibility in varying charging boundaries and "value pricing" (i.e. tailoring charges to traffic flows or times of day/week).
  为道路经营者在变换收费边界和付费价格等方面提供了广阔的灵活性（例如针对交通流和一天内或一周内的时段设定收费标准）。

- In charging for the exact distance travelled, it lets road users compare costs with those of alternative modes, so encouraging a multimodal outlook.
  对精确的行驶距离的收费，可以让道路使用者与其他可选择模式的收费费用相比较，促进多模式的前景。

Figure 1.84　Advantages of VPS
图 1.84　虚拟定位系统（VPS）的优势

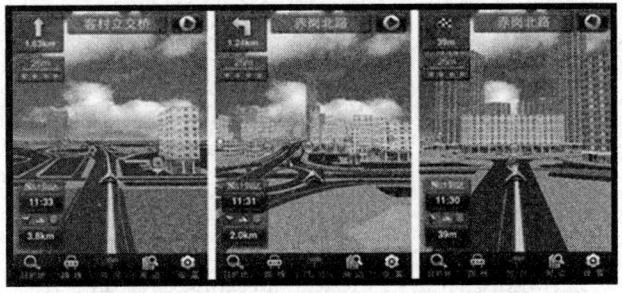

Figure 1.85　Application of VPS
图 1.85　虚拟定位系统（VPS）的应用

In charging for the exact distance travelled, it lets road users compare costs with those of alternative modes, so encouraging a multimodal outlook.

对精确的行驶距离的收费，可以让道路使用者与其他可选择模式的收费费用相比，促进多模式的前景。

例　　　　Melbourne City Link　　墨尔本的City Link

City Link is a privately-operated, fully-electronic, 22-km expressway linking Melbourne, Australia's second city, with its airport, port and industrial areas. It uses DSRC technology. Users pre-register by opening a toll account or buying a day pass (via the Internet, if they wish). Account-holders receive an e-TAG transponder. Gantry-mounted readers automatically debit accounts for each of the eight toll zones the vehicle passes through. Enforcement of evasion is by gantry-mounted cameras that photograph vehicle number plates.

连接澳大利亚第二大城市墨尔本与机场、海关和工业区的城际通道是私营的、全电子化的、22km长的高速公路。它采用DSRC技术收费。使用者可以预先开设费用账户，或者购买一天的通行权（如果使用者愿意，也可以使用因特网购买）。账户的持有者收到一个电子标签的收发机，配置天线的读卡器在车辆通过任何一个收费区域时都自动在账户上借记。对逃避的监管是通过门架上架设的相机抓拍车辆的车牌实现的。

Apart from reducing delays to road users, EFC cuts labor costs for toll road operators and improves security by reducing payment evasion. Enforcement is typically strengthened by automated number plate recognition. In addition, its two-way communications channels can be used for other transactions and services (e.g. parking payment and traffic information). ETC/EFC also has the potential to reduce queues at the toll gates, which is a major cause of congestion.

除了减少道路使用者的延误外，EFC 系统还降低了道路经营者的劳动力成本，并通过防止漏缴，提高了安全性。自动车牌识别技术巩固了收费管理。另外，其双向通信信道可以用于进行其他交易和服务（例如停车收费和交通信息）。ETC 与 EFC 系统还在解决收费站排队这个主要拥堵问题方面具有应用价值。

1.10.2　Public Transport Fares and Ticketing　公共运输费用和票务

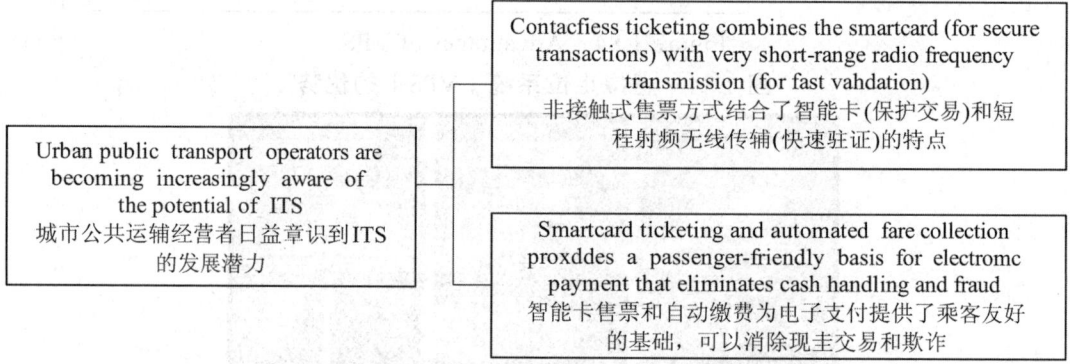

Figure 1.86　Potential advantages of ITS
图 1.86　ITS 潜在的优点

The memory and processing capabilities available on smartcard microchips allow development of flexible and innovative products for paying fares and other transport- related charges.

智能卡微芯片的记忆和处理能力允许为付费和与交通有关的付费开发灵活的和创新的产品。

The technology is also capable of being extended into an "electronic purse" for small cash payments at newspaper kiosks and convenience stores. The high volume of cash transactions in public transport makes it particularly suitable for realizing this concept.

这项技术能够扩展成为"电子钱包"，在报亭和便利店用于小额现金支付。公共交通中的大量现金交易使这项技术特别适合实现这个概念。

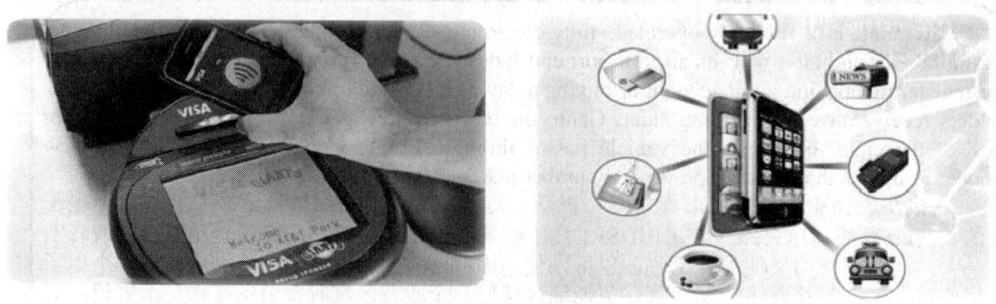

Figure 1.87　Electronic payment
图 1.87　电子付费

For operators, analysis of transactions offers a useful analytical tool for service planning and modification.

对于运营者来说，交易分析为服务的制定和修正提供了一个有价值的分析工具。

1.11 Security and Emergency Response Systems 安全和紧急事件应急系统

The terrorist attacks on the USA of 11 September 2001 highlighted the vulnerability of all freight and passenger modes and infrastructures to terrorist assault when transport was used as a weapon.

美国 2001 年 9 月 11 日遭遇的恐怖袭击，突出了货物、乘客和基础设施在把交通工具作为武器使用的恐怖袭击中的易受攻击性。

Figure 1.88　911 Event of United States

图 1.88　美国"9·11"事件

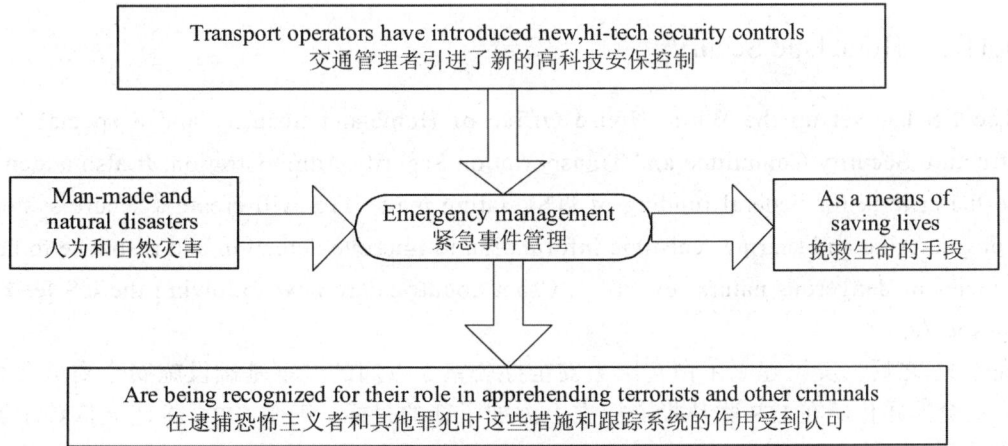

Figure 1.89　Emergency management system

图 1.89　紧急事件管理系统

Figure 1.90　Road transport emergency plan drills
图 1.90　道路运输突发事件应急预案演练

> **例**　**Go Transit (Toronto, Canada)　多伦多（加拿大）公共交通系统**
>
> Toronto (Canada) public transport operator GO Transit's smartcard AFC system is being progressively deployed on seven rail corridors and an extensive bus network, serving five million people in the Greater Toronto area. It uses dual interface contact/contactless smartcards, which were introduced after an intensive public education program. Passengers can buy and load their cards at ticket offices and external retail outlets, and check balances at special reader terminals, introduced for travellers' comfort.
>
> 多伦多（加拿大）公共交通运营商GO Transit的智能卡AFC系统，逐渐在7个轨道交通和广大公交网络中得到应用，为在多伦多广大地区的五百万人服务。智能卡有接触式的和非接触式的双重接口，通过一个集中的公共教育节目介绍之后，智能卡开始普及。为了方便乘客，乘客可以在售票口和零售店购买智能卡和为智能卡充值，并且还可以在专用读卡器上查询余额。

1.11.1　Homeland Security　国土安全

The US has set up the White House Office of Homeland Security and a special National Infrastructure Security Committee and Transportation Security Administration. It also added a new goal to the criteria for Federal funding of ITS, stating that; "ITS will create a secure system that relies on gathering and sharing real-time information to improve detection and response to national emergencies or dangerous natural events". Other countries are now following the US lead. Early priorities were:

在 9.11 之后，美国建立了白宫国土安全办公室、专门的国家基础设施安全委员会和运输安全委员会。并且还在 ITS 联邦投资标准上添加了新的目标，声明"ITS 将建立依赖于实时信息收集和共享的安保系统，用于改善对国家紧急事件和自然灾害的检测和响应"。其他国家也纷纷跟随美国的引导。早期的优先项是：

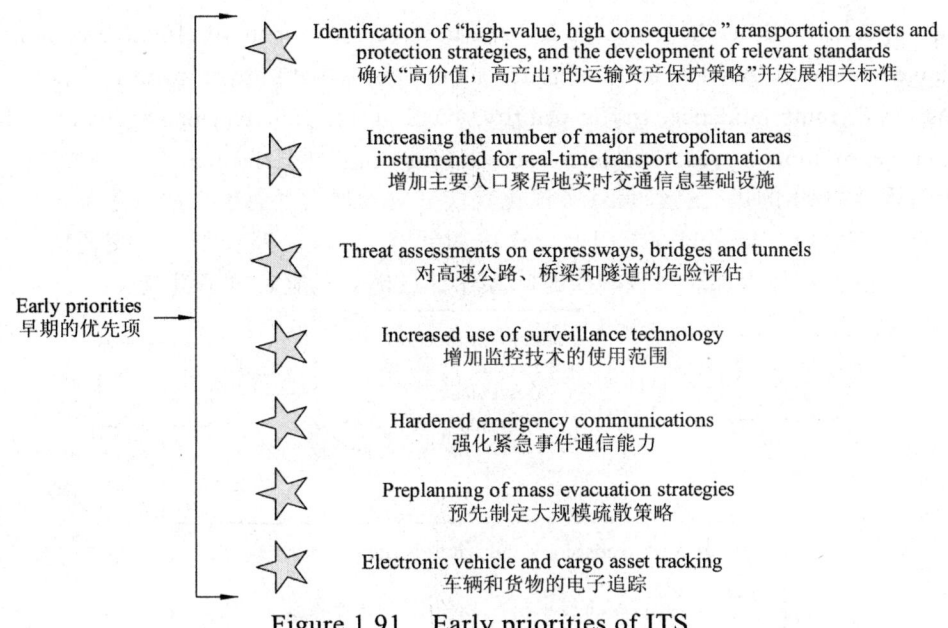

Figure 1.91　Early priorities of ITS

图 1.91　ITS 早期的优先项

1.11.2　Emergency Management Systems (EMS)　紧急事件管理系统（EMS）

EMS must respond to events ranging from a terrorist attack or natural disaster, through severe weather or exceptional road conditions, to an incident involving a single vehicle.

FMS 必须处理的事件范围从恐怖袭击、由恶劣气候条件或特殊道路状况造成的自然灾害到单一车辆的交通事故等。

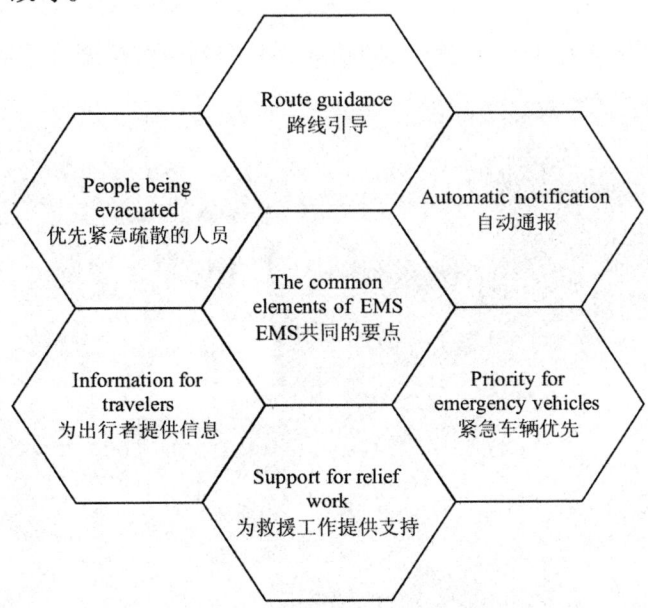

Figure 1.92　Common elements of EMS

图 1.92　EMS 共同的要点

ATMS operations throughout the world have been refined for more effective response to new risks of large-scale emergencies, and integrated more closely with government and police security operations. AVL, route guidance, traffic priority, VMS arrays and fleet management technologies all contribute to minimizing reaction times and ensuring optimal performance.

世界范围 ATMS 的运行已经得到了优化，能够对大规模紧急事件的新危险做出更加有效的响应，并且与政府和警卫安保部门的合作更加紧密。AVL、路线引导、交通优先、可变情报板陈列和车队管理技术都对减少响应时间和保证最优的性能做出了贡献。

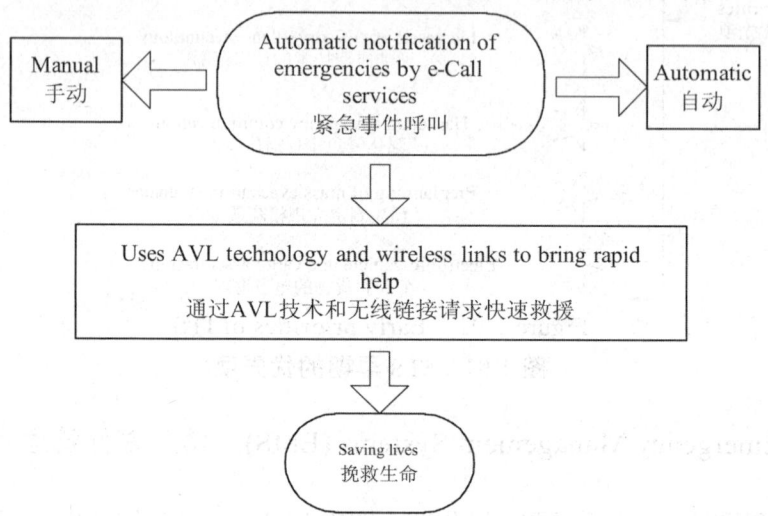

Figure 1.93　Automatic notification of emergencies by e-Call services
图 1.93　紧急事件呼叫系统

In remote areas, doctors can monitor patient condition and advice on first aid before hospital arrival.

在偏远地区，急救医生可以监控病人的状况，并在到达医院之前采取紧急措施。

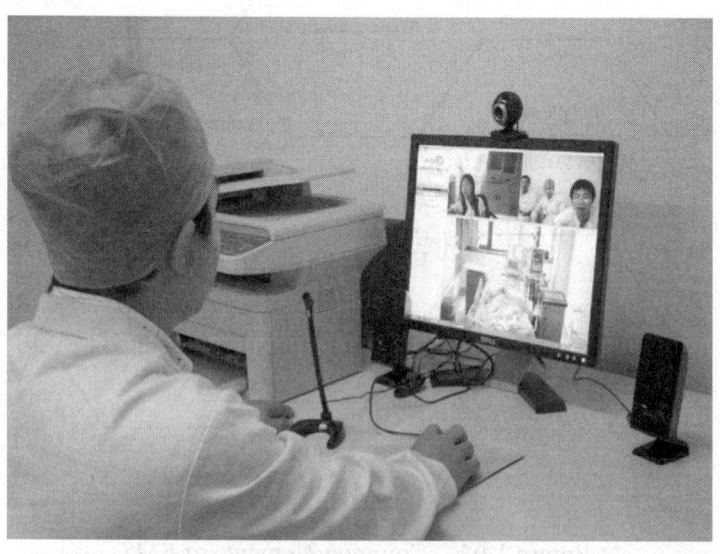

Figure 1.94　Doctors remote monitoring of the patients
图 1.94　医生远程监控病人

1.11.3　Security in Transport Operations　运输管理中的安保

Increased security and safety concerns have highlighted the security risks inherent in hazardous loads and vehicles or containers that could carry weapons.

对安保和安全关注的增加，突出了危险货物和车辆或可能装有武器的集装箱所固有的安全隐患。

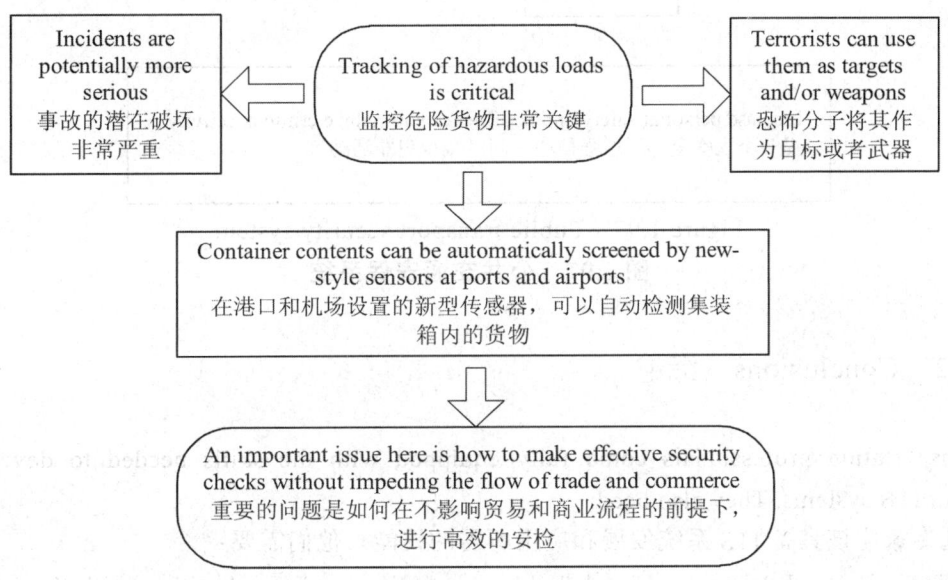

Figure 1.95　Loads tracking system diagram

图 1.95　货物监控系统图

Personal security for public transport users and staff is the highest priority. Large numbers of people are at risk in any incident, and they need to know that help is at hand when needed.

值得最优先考虑的是公共交通的用户和工作人员的人身安全。在任何事故中都有很多人面临危险，他们需要知道一旦发生危险，救援就在附近。

Figure 1.96　Public traffic accident

图 1.96　公共交通事故图

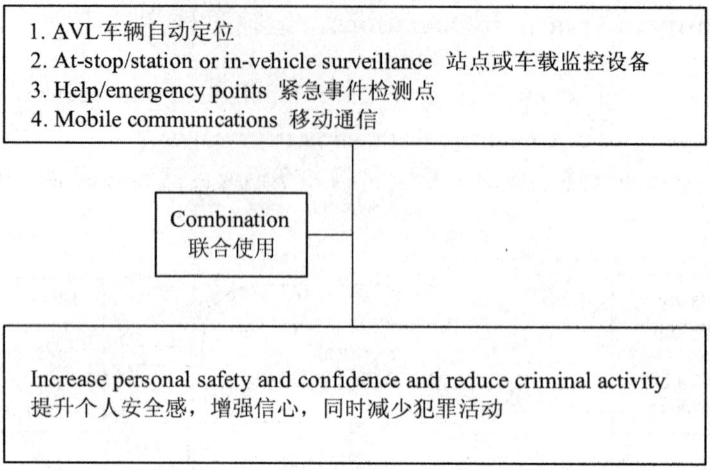

```
┌─────────────────────────────────────────────────────┐
│ 1. AVL 车辆自动定位                                  │
│ 2. At-stop/station or in-vehicle surveillance 站点或车载监控设备 │
│ 3. Help/emergency points 紧急事件检测点              │
│ 4. Mobile communications 移动通信                    │
└─────────────────────────────────────────────────────┘
                          │
                 ┌────────────────┐
                 │ Combination    │
                 │ 联合使用        │
                 └────────────────┘
                          │
┌─────────────────────────────────────────────────────┐
│ Increase personal safety and confidence and reduce criminal activity │
│ 提升个人安全感，增强信心，同时减少犯罪活动            │
└─────────────────────────────────────────────────────┘
```

Figure 1.97　Public transport security system

图 1.97　公共交通安保系统

1.12　Conclusions　结论

Transportation professionals come fully equipped with the skills needed to develop and implement ITS systems. They also need:

交通专家应该具备 ITS 系统发展和应用所需的技能。他们需要：

(1) To understand the needs of stakeholders including public authorities (with their electoral constraints), transport operators, commercial and financial partners, and road users (not least those who are vulnerable).

充分理解利益相关方的需要，包括：公共机构（受到选举制约）、交通运营商、商业和金融合作伙伴以及道路使用者（不仅是弱势道路使用者）。

(2) To appreciate the impact and limitations of new technology, as well as its operation and potential benefits.

正确评价新技术的影响和局限性以及其运营和潜在的利益。

(3) To be able to meet the challenge of building, and working with, wide-ranging stakeholder groups and partnerships.

能够应对与大范围的利益相关方和合作伙伴共同建设和工作的挑战。

(4) To accept the importance of a systems approach, within multi-agency frameworks.

能够认识到多构框架下系统方法的重要性。

(5) To assess available systems and services for relevance to specific applications, cultures and stages of economic development.

能够根据现有特定的技术应用水平、文化背景和经济发展阶段，实现可行的 ITS 系统和服务。

(6) To be realistic in drawing up timescales and implementation schedules and use a step by step approach.

能够切合实际地描绘阶段性的 ITS 蓝图，脚踏实地地逐步实现原定计划。

(7) To be able to work with financial institutions on funding ITS deployment.
能够与在 ITS 部署上投资的金融机构合作。

(8) To be able to communicate effectively with end users.
能够有效地与终端客户沟通。

Chapter 2　How do Intelligent Transport Systems Work
第二章　ITS 是如何工作的

This chapter introduces the main ITS enabling technologies and explains why transport professionals should involve human factor experts at an early stage of design of ITS equipment and facilities.

本章介绍 ITS 主要可使用的技术，并阐述为什么在 ITS 设备和设施设计的早期运输专业人员应该包括人因学专家。

2.1　ITS Technologies　ITS 技术

2.1.1　Functions of ITS Components　ITS 部件的功能

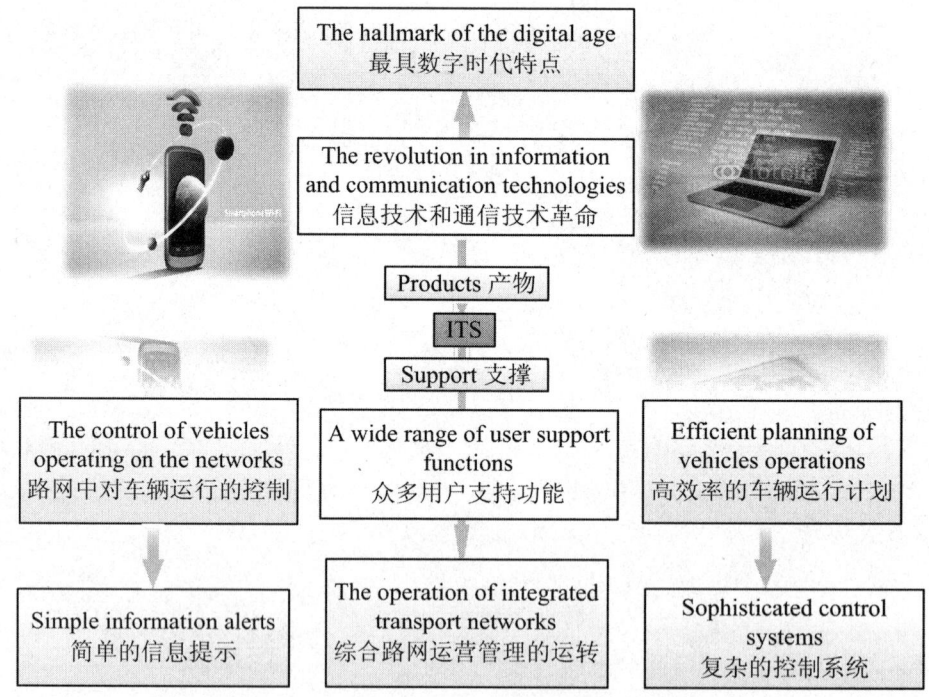

Figure 2.1　Frame chart of ITS technologies
图 2.1　ITS 技术框架图

Essentially, these ITS services can be thought of as an information chain.
从本质上说，这些 ITS 服务可视为一个信息链。

Relatively new technologies and system concepts in ITS
在 ITS 中，相对较新的技术概念和系统概念

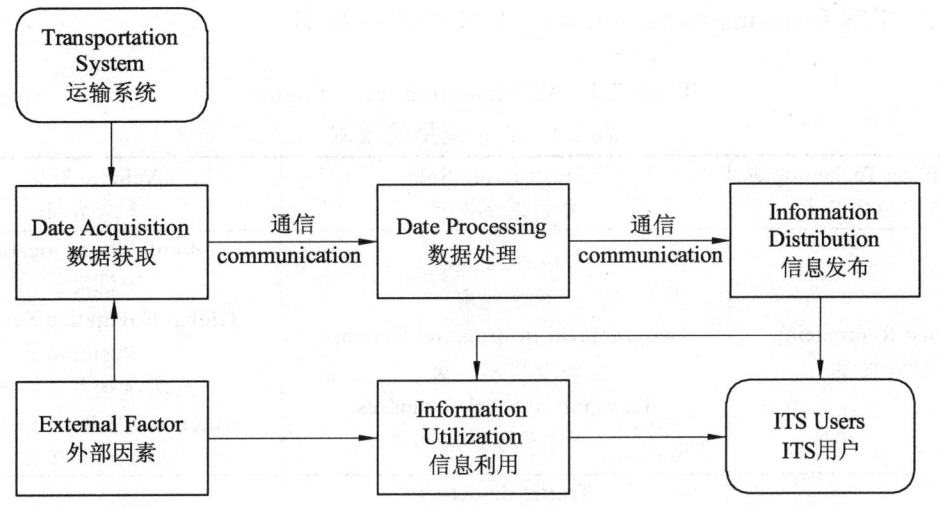

Figure 2.2　Information chains of ITS services
图 2.2　ITS 服务信息链

(1) Information exchange and decision coordination involving multiple centers;
多个中心间的信息交换与决策协调；

(2) Information acquisition and integration between the vehicle and the road infrastructure;
车与道路基础设施间的信息获取和集成；

(3) Information exchange with new private-sector organizations;
与新型的民营组织的信息交换；

(4) Information exchange with non-transport organizations.
与非运输组织的信息交换。

Figure 2.3　Dynamic route guidance
图 2.3　动态路径引导

2.1.2　ITS Enabling technologies　ITS 使用的技术

Table 2.1　ITS Enabling technologies
表 2.1　ITS 使用的技术

ITS Enabling Technologies ITS 使用的技术	Infrastructure Side 基础设施方面	Vehicle Side 车辆方面
Location Referencing 位置提供	Digital maps 数字地图 Geographical Information Systems 地理信息系统 Transport network databases 交通网络数据库	Mobile phone location 手机定位 Global Navigation Satellite Systems 全球导航卫星系统 Automatic Vehicle Location 自动车辆定位
Data Acquisition 数据获取	Traffic detectors 交通检测器 Weather monitoring 气象监测 Automatic Incident Detection 自动事件监测	Automatic Vehicle Identification 自动车辆识别 Vehicle probes 探测车
Data Processing 数据处理	Data dictionaries 数据词典 Data fusion 数据融合 Data exchange 数据交换	On-board computers 车载计算机 Digital map matching 数字地图匹配
Communications 通信	Fixed microwave links 固定的微波链路 Optical fiber networks 光纤网 Beacons (DSRC) 信标 Cell phone networks 蜂窝电话网	DAB receiver DBA 接收器 Cell phone receivers 蜂窝电话接收机 Highway Advisory Radio, RDSTMC 公路咨询广播，RDSTMC 接收器 Transponders 无线电应答器
Information Distribution 信息发布	Dynamic Message Signs 动态情报板 Internet 因特网 Kiosks 书报亭，音乐台，广告亭，问询处等	Handsets and Personal Digital Assistants 手机和个人数字辅助设备 In-vehicle units 车载单元
Information Utilization 信息使用	Incident detection 事件监测 Demand management 管理决策 Congestion monitoring 拥堵监测	Route guidance 路径引导 Advanced Driver Assistance Systems 先进的驾驶辅助系统

续表

Advanced Driver Assistance Systems 先进的驾驶辅助系统（ADAS）	Dynamic Message Sign 动态情报板（DMS）
Automatic Incident Detection 自动事件监测（AID）	Dedicated Short Range Communications 专用短程通信（DSRC）
Automatic Vehicle Identification 自动车辆识别（AVI）	Geographical Information System 地理信息系统（GIS）
Automatic Vehicle Location 自动车辆定位（AVL）	Global Navigation Satellite System 全球导航卫星系统（GNSS）
Digital Audio Broadcasting 数字音频广播（DAB）	Highway Advisory Radio 公路路况广播（HAR）
Data Exchange protocols 数据交换协议（DATEX）	Urban Traffic Control 城市交通控制（UTC）

Table 2.1 shows examples of enabling technologies for ITS and a way of categorizing them. Some of these technologies are already familiar to many transportation professionals.

表 2.1 列举了 ITS 使用的技术及一种分类方法。其中一些技术，对许多运输专业人士而言已经是很熟悉了。

Others may be relatively new, including those transferred from the defense industry in the past decade, such as GNSS and the Internet. However, all of these technologies are available off the shelf in the open market.

另一些技术在运输行业就相对较新，包括那些在过去十年里从国防工业转移过来的技术，比如 GNSS 和因特网，不过，这些技术实际已经可以从公开市场上直接获取。

Figure 2.4 Beidou global navigation satellite system planning model
图 2.4 北斗全球卫星导航系统规划模型

2.2 Data Acquisition 数据获取

2.2.1 Road-based data sources 基于道路的数据源

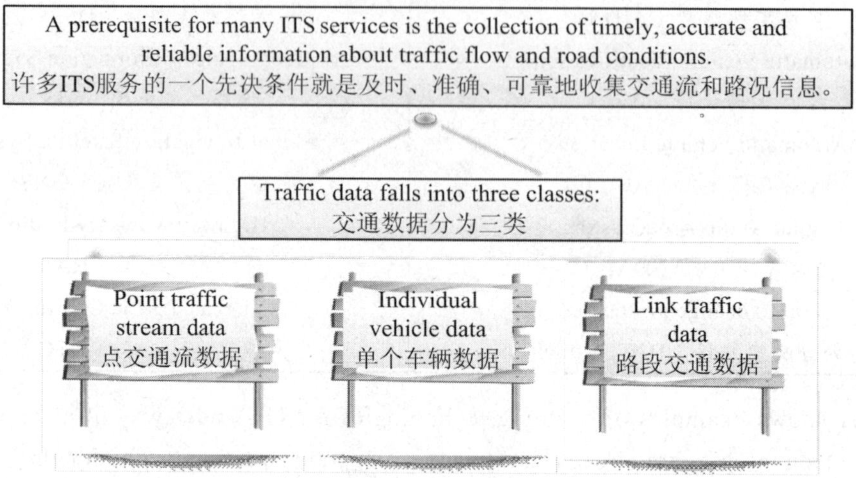

A prerequisite for many ITS services is the collection of timely, accurate and reliable information about traffic flow and road conditions.
许多ITS服务的一个先决条件就是及时、准确、可靠地收集交通流和路况信息。

Traffic data falls into three classes:
交通数据分为三类

- Point traffic stream data 点交通流数据
- Individual vehicle data 单个车辆数据
- Link traffic data 路段交通数据

Figure 2.5 Traffic data classes
图 2.5 交通数据种类

For many years, traffic surveillance has been achieved by inductive loop detectors, which can sense the presence of a vehicle. A single loop buried under the lane pavement can perform vehicle counting. Double loops in the same lane separated by a fixed distance can measure vehicle speed. As vehicle speed slows below a certain threshold, loop detectors can indicate traffic congestion.

长期以来，交通监视是由感应线圈检测器实现的，这种技术可以检测到车辆的存在。车道路面下埋设单个线圈可以完成车辆计数，同一条车道内按照固定距离布设双线圈可以测量车速，当车速低于一定阈值时，线圈检测器可以指示交通拥堵。

Figure 2.6 Ground sense coil
图 2.6 地感线圈

Figure 2.7　Other types of traffic sensors

图 2.7　其他交通传感器

Video image detectors (VID) through image processing are one of the more recent technologies to be applied to traffic detection.

基于图像处理的视频图像检测器（VID）是近年来应用于交通检测的许多技术之一。

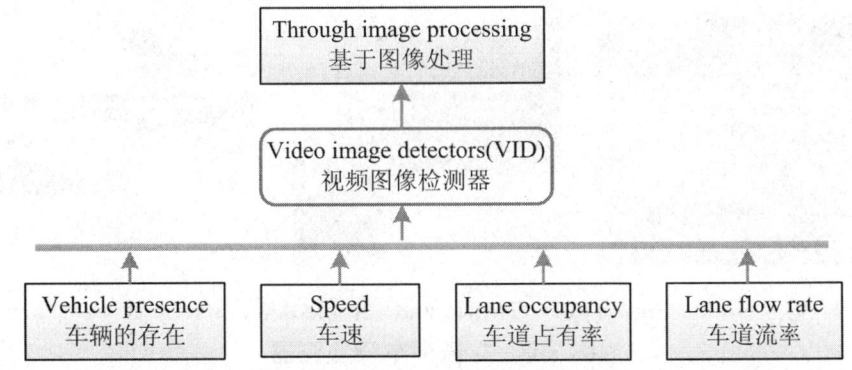

Figure 2.8　Available information after image processing

图 2.8　图像处理后可获得信息

There is nothing better than live video images to help the traffic center operator monitor complicated traffic situations and make appropriate decisions.

动态视频图像最能帮助交通管理中心操作人员监视复杂的交通状态并做出适当的决定。

Visual images from closed circuit television (CCTV) are therefore obtained by the traffic management center to complement the traffic detectors (in Figure 2.9).

交通管理中心将来自闭路电视（CCTV）的可视图像作为交通检测器的补充信息，如图 2.9 所示。

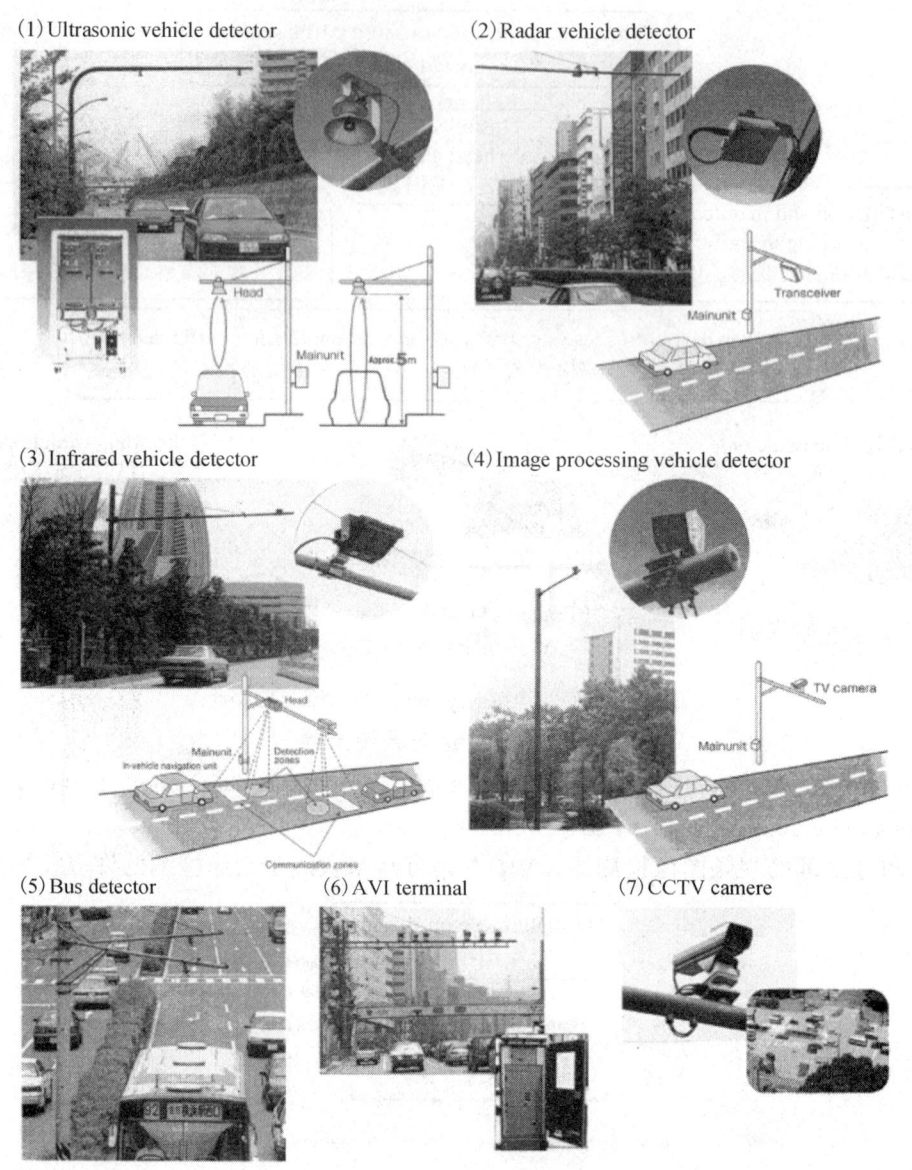

Figure 2.9 Traffic and vehicle detectors
图 2.9 交通和车辆检测器

Traffic management center apply departments of input information to traffic information and management.

交通管理中心将各部门的输入信息运用于交通信息与管理。

On the vehicle side, data regarding vehicle conditions such as speed, fuel level, oil pressure, engine temperature, etc. are familiar to all drivers. Acquisition of these data through in-vehicle sensors is important for vehicle operation and maintenance.

在车辆一侧，与车辆状况相关的数据，如车速、油位、油压、发动机温度等都是驾驶员熟悉的信息，但是通过车内传感器获取这些信息对于车辆运营和维护就很重要。

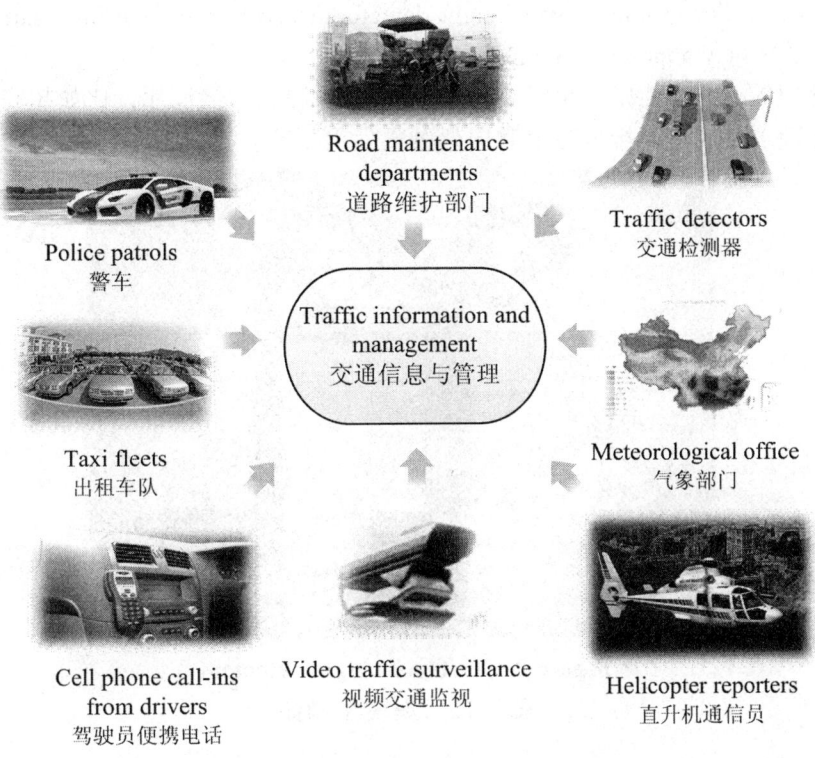

Figure 2.10 Traffic information and management

图 2.10 交通信息与管理

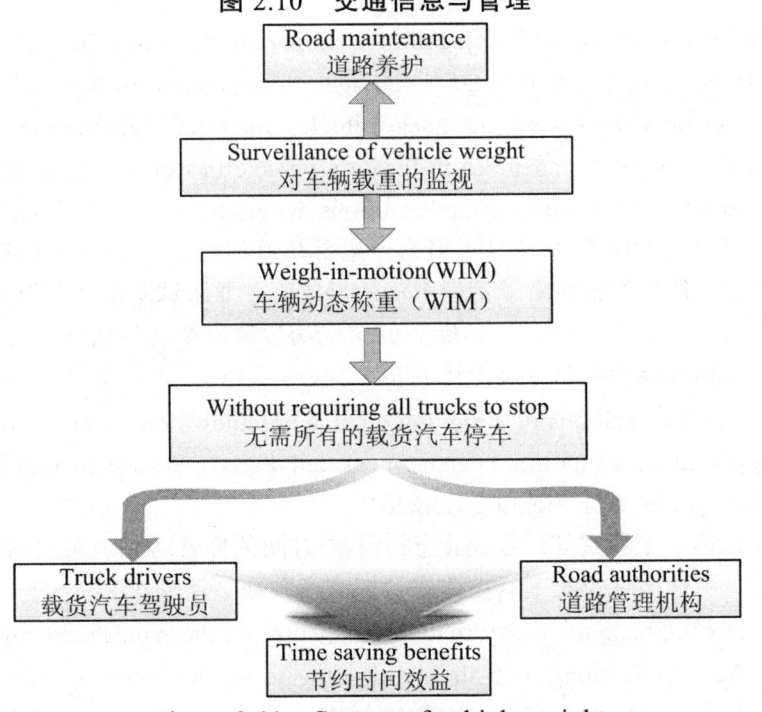

Figure 2.11 System of vehicle weight

图 2.11 车辆载重系统

Measurement of vehicle dimensions by ITS technologies is also needed for some functions in traffic management. For example, over-height detectors (based on the cutting beam principle) can warn the drivers as they approach a tunnel.

在交通管理的一些功能中，也需要运用 ITS 技术测量车辆尺寸，比如超高检测器（基于遮挡光束的原理）可在车辆接近隧道时向驾驶员发出预警。

Figure 2.12　Over-height detectors
图 2.12　超高检测器

2.2.2　Vehicle-based data sources　基于车辆的数据源

In ITS, information about vehicle location is important for both the individual driver who wants to know where he or she is in order to navigate or to obtain location-relevant information, and for the fleet operator who wants to track vehicles for fleet management purposes. Vehicle location is invaluable for public agencies to locate a vehicle in trouble for rescue purposes, or to find stolen vehicles or vehicles transporting hazardous materials.

在 ITS 中，有关车辆定位的信息不但出于想要知道其位置以便出行或获取定位相关信息的驾驶员很重要，而且对于那些出于管理车辆的目的而想要跟踪车队的车队运营商也很重要。车辆定位在帮助公共行政机构确定遇到麻烦的车辆的位置以便实施营救、寻找被盗车辆或寻找运输危险物品车辆方面的价值更是无可衡量。

Moreover, when the locations of a moving vehicle are known on a link at two different times, the travel time on the link (or link time) can be measured directly. A vehicle used for this purpose is known as a "probe vehicle" or a "floating vehicle".

而且，当获知移动车辆在某一线路上两个不同时间的位置时，就可直接测得车辆在该线路上的行驶时间。用作该目的的车辆被称作"探测车"或"浮动车"。

In addition, tyre slippage on an icy road and moisture on the windshield can also be detected and reported by the vehicle along with its location to the traffic center. In this case, the vehicle serves as a "probe" for both traffic and road/weather conditions (in Figure 2.13).

另外，轮胎在结冰的道路上打滑以及挡风玻璃的湿气，也可检测后随着车辆定位信息由车辆一同发往交通中心，如图 2.13 所示。

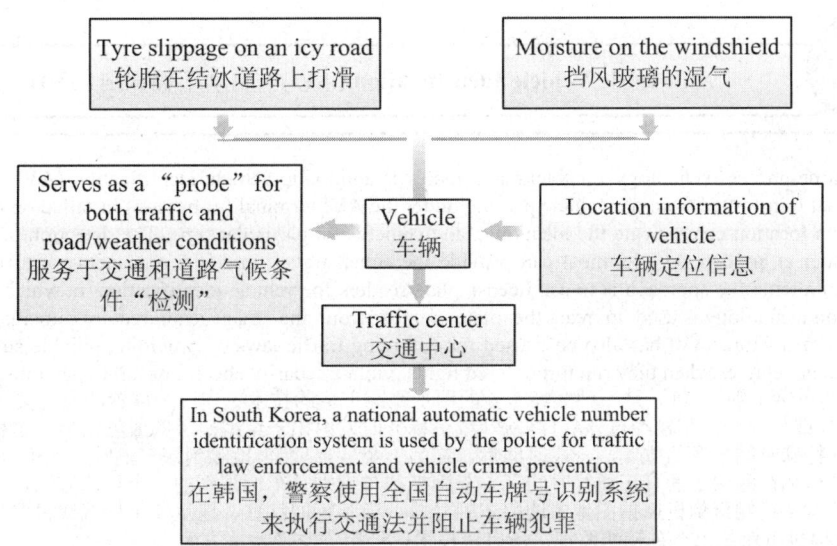

Figure 2.13　Collection and application of vehicle information
图 2.13　车辆信息的采集与应用

Automatic Vehicle Identification involves equipment installed on the infrastructure. Vehicle probes based on AVI requires installation of appropriate equipment on the infrastructure (either roadside beacons where passing vehicles are equipped with a tag or transponder that can be recognized or camera-based license plate readers which rely on image processing techniques).

AVI 包括安装在基础设施上的设备。基于 AVI 的车辆检测需要在基础设施上安装合适的设备（可以是路侧信标，识别装有电子标签或无线收发装置的过往车辆，也可以是以图像处理技术为基础的基于摄像机的牌照抓拍与识别）。

Figure 2.14　Red light captures
图 2.14　闯红灯抓拍

> **例** **Automatic Vehicle Identification (AVI)　自动车辆识别(AVI)**
>
> A time-proven technology for tracking vehicles is automatic vehicle identification (AVI). A coded radio signal transmitted from the vehicle passing under the AVI terminal (or beacon) installed on the gantry at a known location can indicate the location of the vehicle at a particular time. The detection of the same vehicle later at another AVI terminal can provide the actual travel time in a road network to the traffic center. An alternative approach is to use license plate readers for vehicle identification, in which character recognition technology is used to read the plate number from the image captured by cameras installed on the infrastructure. AVI has also been used for enforcing traffic laws by providing reliable surveillance of individual vehicles when they run through red lights, violate security checks, or fail to pay tolls.
>
> 自动车辆识别（AVI）是一种久经考验的用于跟踪车辆的技术。在已知位置的龙门架上安装AVI终端（或信标），车辆经过该AVI终端（或信标）时发射出一组编码了的射频信号，这样就能表明在某一特殊时间车辆的位置，一段时间后，在另一个AVI终端再检测到该车辆时，就可以向交通中心提供车辆在路网上的真正通行时间了。车牌抓拍与识别是车辆识别的一个可选方法，它运用字符识别技术从路侧摄像机抓拍图像中读取车牌号码。当车辆闯红灯、违反安全检查或付费失败时，AVI可以提供可信的单个车辆的监视，所以该技术已经用于交通执法方面。

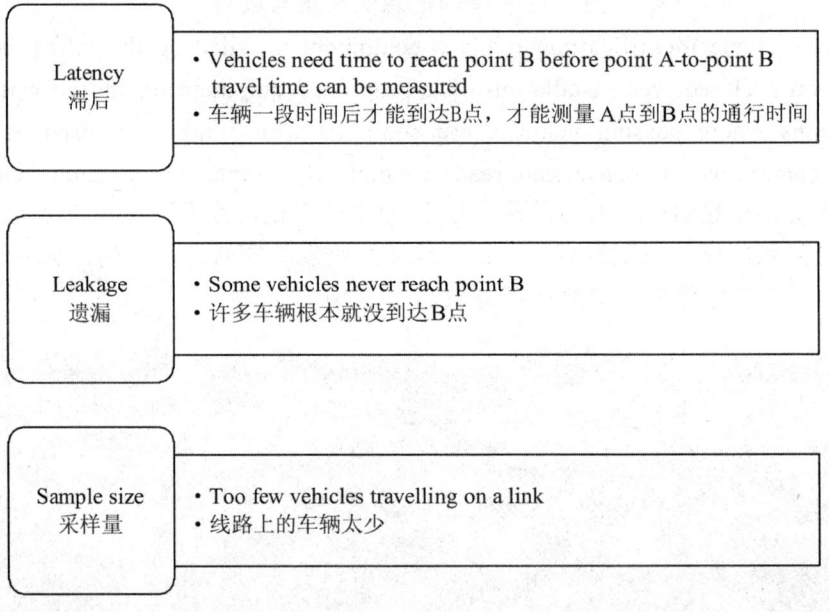

Figure 2.15　Three challenges to measure travel time using a probe vehicle

图 2.15　利用探测车辆来测量旅行时间面临的三个挑战

Thus, reliable measurement of travel time by probe vehicles depends on the sample size and successful matching. These issues are being solved, as more vehicle fleets are equipped with AVI and AVL.

因而，用探测车辆可靠地测量旅行时间依赖采样量和成功的匹配。随着更多的车队装备AVI 和 AVL，这些问题正在得以解决。

2.2.3　Transport Network data sources　运输网络数据源

In addition to the data from traffic and vehicles, a considerable investment is needed in data concerning the transport networks themselves. The basis for ITS in many cases are detailed and reliable databases of network links, inter-connections and other features, supported by a sound location referencing system.

除了来自交通和车辆的数据外，与运输网络本身相关的数据也需要相当大的投资。许多情况下，ITS 的基础是详细可靠的网络链接、互连和其他特征的数据库，这些是由一个完善的位置参照系统支持的。

With the advent of hand-held GNSS receivers and vehicles equipped with AVL, the business of accurately locating network has become much easier
随着手持GNSS接收机和装配AVL车辆的出现，准确定位网络变得非常容易

Network features need to be described in terms which the user will easily comprehend
网络特征需要使用易于用户理解的术语来描述

Similarly for road information, reliable coding of the network is needed for location based services
道路信息也是如此，基于位置的服务都需要对路网进行可靠的编码

Figure 2.16　Advantages of transport network
图 2.16　网络运营的优点

Capturing data on transport networks is very labor-intensive, involving detailed reference to maps and plans, aerial photographs, and on-site surveys. Videoing the network from a moving vehicle is often used to reduce the amount of time spent on the ground. Viewing these video images is an effective form of desk-based data capture. The images can be studied frame-by-frame if detail is required, whereas the fast forward control allows unimportant sections to be skipped.

在路网上捕获数据是一个劳动密集的工作，包括详细地查阅地图和平面图，航空摄影及定点测量。为了减少在现场的时间，经常在移动的车辆上对路网进行录像。观察这些视频图像是一种基于桌面的地图数据捕捉的有效形式。

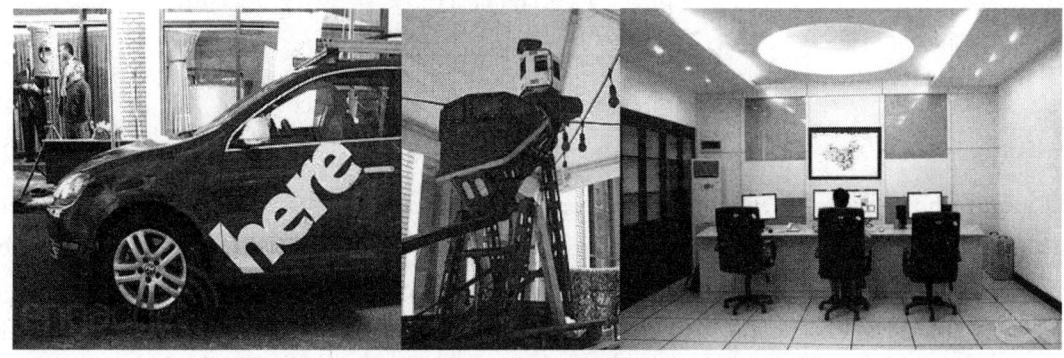

Figure 2.17　Video footage
图 2.17　视频录像

At the time of data capture, careful attention must be given to the way the database will be used, since at some future occasion someone will have to interpret the data.

由于在将来的某些情况下要解释这些数据，所以在数据捕捉的同时，必须关注数据库的使用方式。

Figure 2.18　Database

图 2.18　数据库

Opportunities exist for automating data capture and eliminating human error. However, the process remains very time consuming.

自动数据捕获和人为错误消除都是有可能的，但是其处理过程比较耗时。

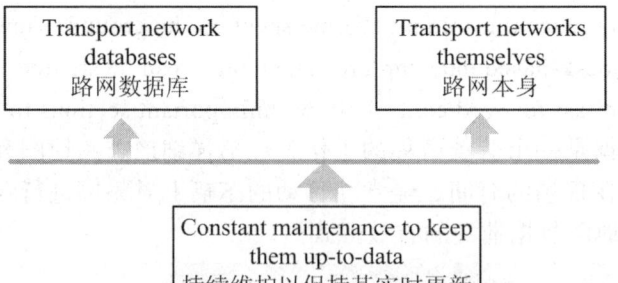

Figure 2.19　Data update and maintenance

图 2.19　数据更新维护

Careful checking is essential to avoid errors which can lead to features being incorrectly located, sometimes wildly misplaced. The long-established maxim of "RIRO" (rubbish in, rubbish out) applies to ITS as much as any other branch of Information Technology.

仔细检查是避免数据库错误的基础，数据库错误会导致路网位置特征不正确，有时还会出现大量的错误位置。长期以来建立 RIRO 的最大化原理应用于其他信息技术分科，也应用于 ITS。

2.3 Gaining Intelligence: Data Processing 获取智能：数据处理

2.3.1 Traffic and Travel Information 交通与旅行信息

1. Data fusion 数据融合

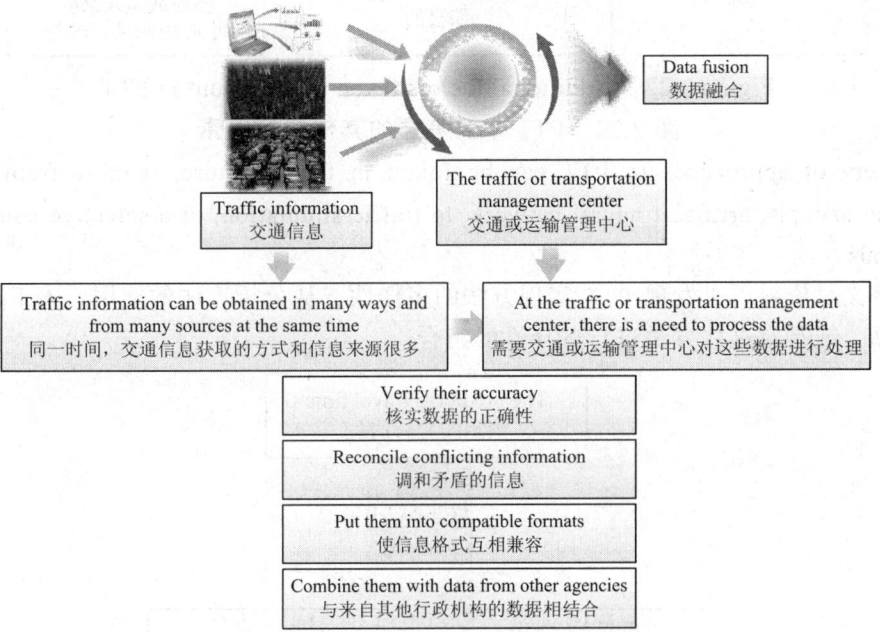

Figure 2.20 System of data fusion

图 2.20 数据融合系统图

2. Data processing 数据处理

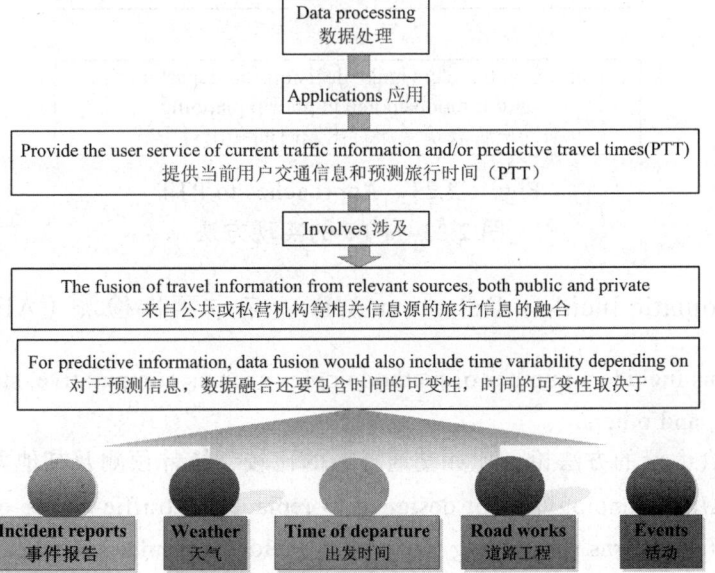

Figure 2.21 System of data processing

图 2.21 数据处理系统图

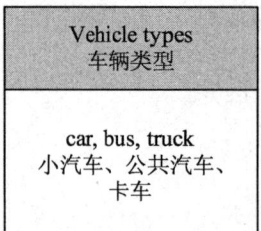
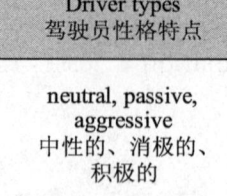

Figure 2.22 Additional factors taken into account in PTT
图 2.22 PTT 中要考虑的其他附加因素

A variety of approaches to PTT can be found in the literature, ranging from the use of analytical algorithms, artificial neural network, to traffic simulation, or a selective combination of these methods.

从很多文献资料可以发现 PTT 实现方法的多样性, 从分析算法的使用、人工神经元网络到交通仿真, 或是对这些方法进行选择性的组合。

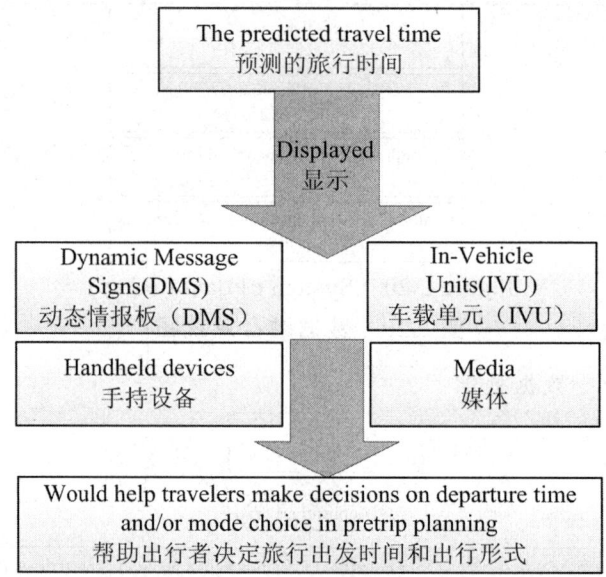

Figure 2.23 Approaches to PTT
图 2.23 PTT 的实现方法

2.3.2 Automatic Incident Detection(AID) 自动事件检测（AID）

The algorithms include a number of methodologies such as comparative, statistical forecasting of traffic behavior, and others.

验证算法包含大量的方法论, 比如交通行为的比较、统计预测及其他方法。

In general, AID technology is not designed to replace the traffic center operator but to alert him or her of traffic patterns resembling those in an incident. Human confirmation through CCTV or site visits is still needed.

一般而言, AID 技术的目的并非要替代交通中心操作人员, 但它可以提醒操作员注意那些与某交通事件相似的交通模式，实际还是需要通过 CCTV 或现场考察来人为证实。

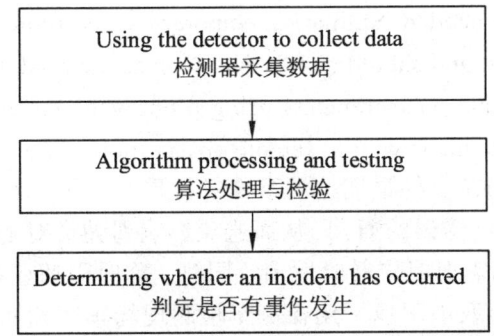

Figure 2.24　Flow chart of automatic incident detection
图 2.24　**自动事件检测流程图**

例　Automatic Incident Detection　自动事件检测

　　Automatic Incident Detection (AID) has proven helpful in reducing incident detection time, and in speeding up rescue operations and traffic diversion around incident sites. There are also other applications of AID. For example, AID has been used to estimate traffic conditions or degree of congestion (slow-moving, congested, free-flow). AID cameras have been used for travel time estimation, based on the idea that AID can determine the mean speed of each segment along the covered stretch. The method is also used to automatically display driver alerts on DMS and to trigger a mandatory speed limit upstream of the incident.

　　自动事件检测已被证实在减少事件检测时间、加速营救实施、事件地点交通分流方面都是有益的。AID还有其他应用，比如AID已被用于评估交通状况和交通拥堵程度（缓慢移动、拥堵、自由流）。由于沿摄像机拍摄区域所覆盖的路段上，AID可以测定每一小段路程上的平均车速，所以AID摄像机也已被用于通行时间评估。该方法也已用于在DMS上自动显示驾驶员警视信息并触发强制限速。

Figure 2.25　System of AID
图 2.25　**自动事件检测系统**

　　Positive confirmation of the end of an incident is as important as early detection. It is essential to identify reliably the beginning and the end of an incident so that drivers are not given wrong advice which destroys confidence in the ITS systems. DMS alerts need to be displayed quickly and cancelled promptly when not needed. Similarly, temporary speed limits should be imposed as soon as a dangerous incident arises, and should be lifted as soon as the road is clear. Spot speed detection and point-to-point journey time measurements using probe vehicles are useful ways to recognize that everything is back to normal, as well as remote observation of traffic conditions using CCTV.

明确地证实事件结束和在事件早期检测事件一样重要。可靠地识别事件发生的开始和结束，这样我们就不会给驾驶员错误的通知，从而避免影响驾驶员对 ITS 系统的信心。需要 DMS 警示信息时应立即显示，不需要时应及时取消。同时，临时限速应在危险事件一出现就执行，且在事故现场清理后就马上取消限速。用探测车检测现场车速和测量点到点通行时间对于确定事态是否恢复到常态是一个有用的方法，就好像用 CCTV 远端监测交通状况一样。

2.3.3　Vehicle Location and Navigation　车辆定位与导航

```
┌─────────────────────────────────────────────────┐
│ 4 or more satellites are in line of sight from  │
│ in-vehicle receiver                             │
│ 车载接收器捕捉到4颗或4颗以上卫星                    │
└─────────────────────────────────────────────────┘
                        ↓
┌─────────────────────────────────────────────────┐
│ In-vehicle data processing is done based on the │
│ time of arrival (TOA) principle                 │
│ 通过时间差（TOA）原理在车内进行数据处理              │
└─────────────────────────────────────────────────┘
                        ↓
┌─────────────────────────────────────────────────┐
│ Receiver's three-dimensional coordinates        │
│ (longitude, latitude, and altitude) can be      │
│ determined                                      │
│ 确定接收器的三维坐标（经度、纬度和高度）             │
└─────────────────────────────────────────────────┘
                        ↓
┌─────────────────────────────────────────────────┐
│ The information of vehicle location is then     │
│ sent to the traffic center, the dispatch        │
│ center, or the bus stop, as needed              │
│ 车辆定位信息被发往交通中心、调度中心或公交车站等      │
│ 需要这些定位信息的地方                             │
└─────────────────────────────────────────────────┘
```

Figure 2.26　Flow chart of vehicle location and navigation
图 2.26　车辆定位与导航流程图

Figure 2.27　Global Positioning System (GPS)
图 2.27　全球定位系统（GPS）

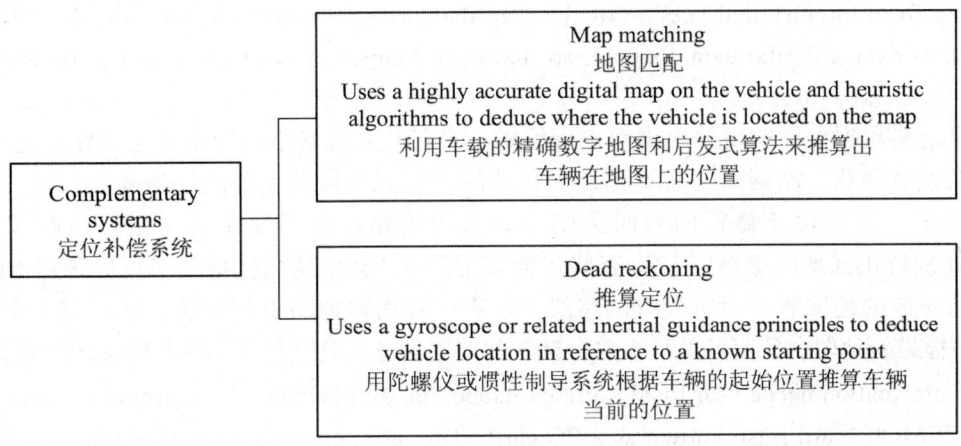

Figure 2.28　Complementary system
图 2.28　定位补偿系统

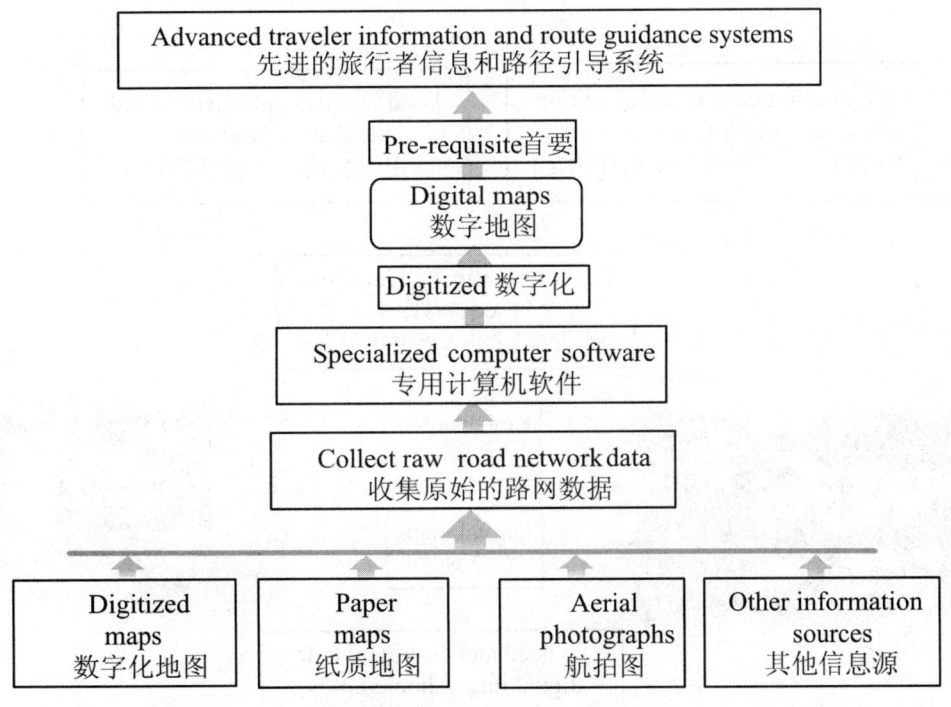

Figure 2.29　Advanced traveler information and route guidance system
图 2.29　先进的旅行者信息和路径引导系统

This data is compiled by the navigation hardware suppliers and there is a major ongoing effort to keep the data updated with the ever changing road network. Transport networks are evolving all the time. Some changes are permanent, like the opening of a new length of highway. Others, like the closure of a strategic link for bridge repairs, are temporary. Users can purchase or subscribe to regular map updates on CD-ROM, but some vehicles are equipped to "learn" road links which may be missing from the installed version of the map database. Another way is to broadcast the latest map updates over a digital data channel, so that even temporary road closures can be logged and stored.

数字地图数据由导航硬件提供商进行编辑，并有专人依据路网变化对这些数据进行更新。路网总在发展变化。路网的一些变化是永久性的，比如一段高速公路的新开通；而一些变化则是临时的，比如由于修桥而暂时关闭一条关键线路。路网变化时，用户可购买或预订 CD-ROM 进行正式地图更新。当然，有些车辆装配路线"学习"功能，该功能可以采用 CD-ROM 自学当前安装的地图版本中所没有的路线。还有一种用户地图更新方法，即通过一个数字数据信道广播最新地图，从而可以写入并存储新的路网信息，甚至包括那些临时关闭的道路信息。

For information needed for local route guidance, the digital map of a metropolitan area may be put in a PCMCIA card (also known as a PC card). Digital maps are also key enablers of location-aware.

城市区域的数字地图可以储存在一个 PCMCIA 卡（也称作 PC 卡)上，用于提供本地路径引导所需要的信息。数字地图同样也是位置感知和基于位置服务的关键因素。

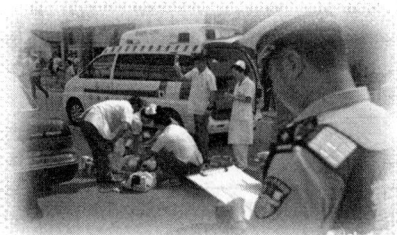

Figure 2.30 Application of digital maps
图 2.30 数字地图的应用

There are other methods for determining vehicle location, especially using cell phones. Such methods can be important for emergency calls from mobile with automatic indication to the rescue team where the caller is located, as well as to enable a host of location-specific ITS services.

还有其他确定车辆位置的方法，尤其是利用蜂窝电话的定位，这对于移动电话紧急呼叫很重要。紧急呼叫的同时可以向救援队伍自动告知呼叫者的位置，使得与位置相关的 ITS 服务成为可能。

2.3.4 Location-based Services　基于定位的服务

Among the host of potential and available location-based services, many customers (end users) put their the highest priorities on safety and security, which has led to the provision of rescue services as one of the earliest ITS offerings in the market place.

在基于定位的潜在和可用的服务中，许多消费者（终端用户）把安全放在了第一位，这使得救援服务成为 ITS 市场最早提供的服务之一。

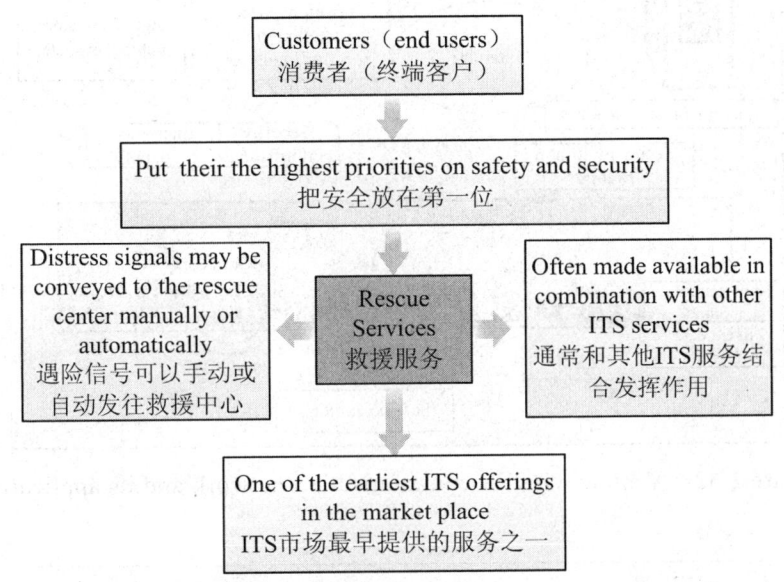

Figure 2.31　Rescue service system
图 2.31　救援服务系统

2.4　Communications and Data Exchange　通信和数据交换

2.4.1　Infrastructure-based Communications　基于基础设施的通信

In general, the communications cost of ITS is a significant portion (15% to 50%) of total ITS systems costs. When alternative communications means are compared, one should take into account both installation and operational costs. In general, stationary or wireline communications have relatively high installation costs due to high labor contents, whereas wide area mobile or wireless communications have relatively high operational (airtime) costs due to limited frequency spectrum.

Dedicated short range communications have no airtime cost but a relatively high installation cost of the equipment (roadside beacons). The specific choice of communications will depend on the specific ITS applications. A number of advanced technologies have been developed by the telecommunications industry and ITS professionals are rapidly taking advantage of these developments for high-speed, low-latency, multiplexing and switching networks.

通常，ITS 通信成本是整个 ITS 成本的重要部分（15%~50%）。比较可供选择的通信技术时，要考虑其安装和作业成本。一般，固定或有线通信的安装成本相对较高，主要是由于劳务费高。然而，广域移动或无线通信由于受频段限制，运行（空间时间）成本较高。专用短程通信没有系统作业成本，但是设备（路侧信标）安装费用相对较高。通信工业已经发展了许多先进的技术，并且 ITS 专业人员迅速掌握了这些高速率、低延迟、多路复用和交换网络上的进展。

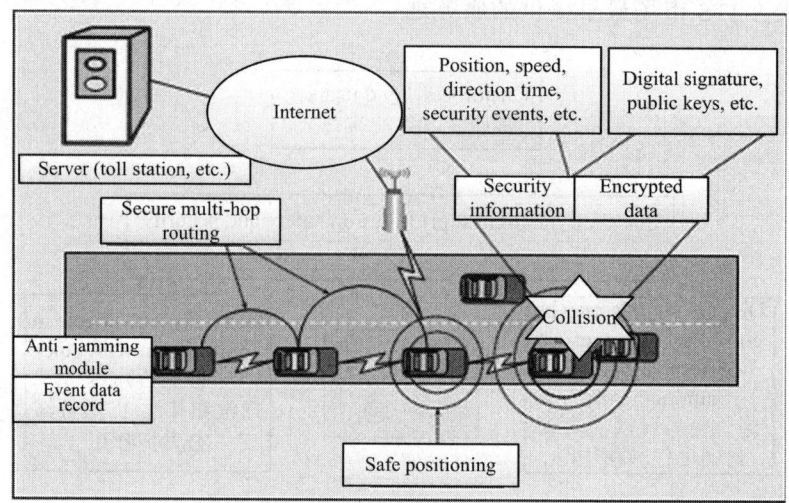

Figure 2.32　Vehicle wireless communication network and its application

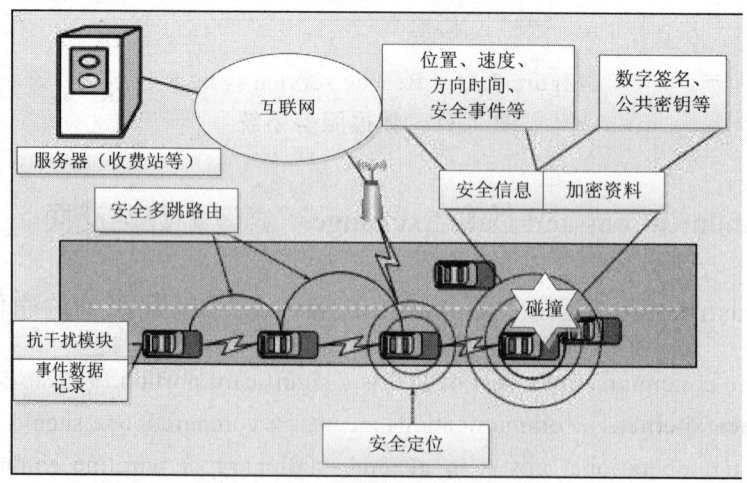

图 2.32　车辆无线通信网络及其应用

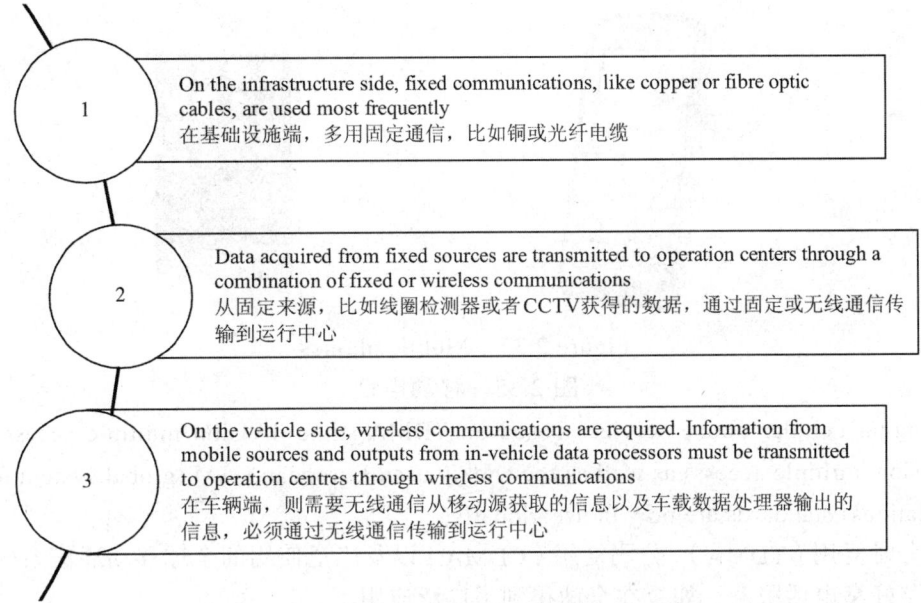

Figure 2.33　Applications of data communication
图 2.33　数据通信的应用

2.4.2　Mobile communications　移动通信

On the vehicle side, wireless communications play a vital part in various ITS functions.
在车辆侧，无线通信在各种 ITS 功能中起着至关重要的作用。

(1) Car phones were all analogue devices (a characteristic of first-generation, 1G, wireless communications) that were not suitable for data communications. Mobile digital terminals (MDT) used on police cars, trucks, and other special vehicles for data communications.

车载电话使用模拟设备（具有第一代无线通信特征），不适合数据通信。移动通信终端（MDT，Mobile Digital Terminals）在警车、卡车和其他特种车辆上用于数据通信。

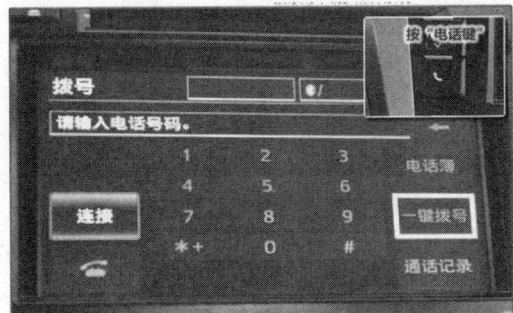

Figure 2.34　Car phone
图 2.34　车载电话

(2) Mobile phones and other personal communication systems are also digital (characteristic of second-generation, 2G, wireless communications) which opens the door to new possibilities for data transmission.
移动电话和其他个人通信系统采用数字设备（具有第二代无线通信特征），为数据传输提供了新的可能性。

Figure 2.35　Mobile phones
图 2.35　移动电话

(3) Digital cellular phone services based on TDMA (time division multiple access), CDMA (code division multiple access) as well as the widely used European GSM (global system for mobile communications) standards are now in use globally.

基于分时复用（TDMA）、分码复用（CDMA）以及广泛使用的全球移动通信系统（GSM）标准的数字蜂窝电话服务，如今在全球得到了广泛应用。

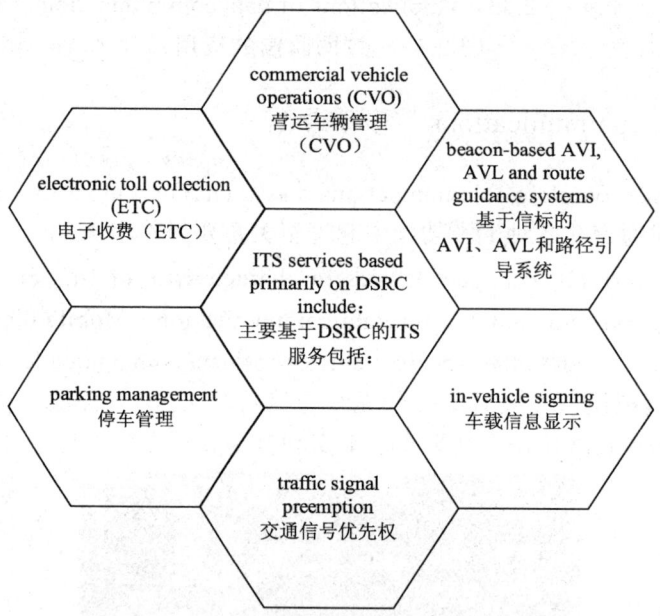

Figure 2.36　ITS services based on DSRC
图 2.36　基于 DSRC 的 ITS 服务

All three generations of wireless communications mentioned above are for wide area communications, ITS data or information managed by common carriers in the telecommunications industry.

上述三代无线通信都属于广域通信范畴，ITS 数据或信息和其他信息通信由电信业通过公用载体统一管理。

Dedicated short-range communications (DSRC) is the opposite and useful only for some dedicated purpose. Investors are public or private organizations interested in the specific ITS applications using DSRC.

专用短程通信技术（DSRC）属于短程通信范畴，用于某些特定用途。投资者是致力于使用 DSRC 开发特定应用的私营或公共组织。

2.4.3 Data Distribution 数据发布

(1) Private service providers:

民营服务提供商：

① Offer a value-added service by customizing traffic information to specific user needs;

依据特定的用户群需求定制相应的交通信息来提供增值服务；

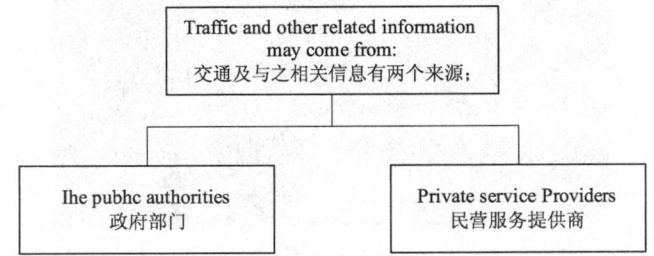

Figure 2.37 Source of traffic and its related information

图 2.37 交通及与之相关信息的来源

② Bundling it with other information services of general interest (e.g. news, sports, stock, and weather) for marketing reasons. Fixed equipment and mobile terminals are the two principal ways of distributing traffic and other relevant information. Fixed equipment, used on the infrastructure side, include regular telephones, conventional radio receivers, televisions, desktop computers, fax machines, information kiosks, and dynamic message signs (DMS).

为了营销目的把交通信息和其他信息绑定（如新闻、体育、股票和天气）。固定设备和移动终端是两个主要发布交通信息和其他相关信息的基本方式。基础设施一侧的固定设备包括电话、通用无线接收机、电视、台式计算机、传真机、信息亭和动态情报板（DMS）。

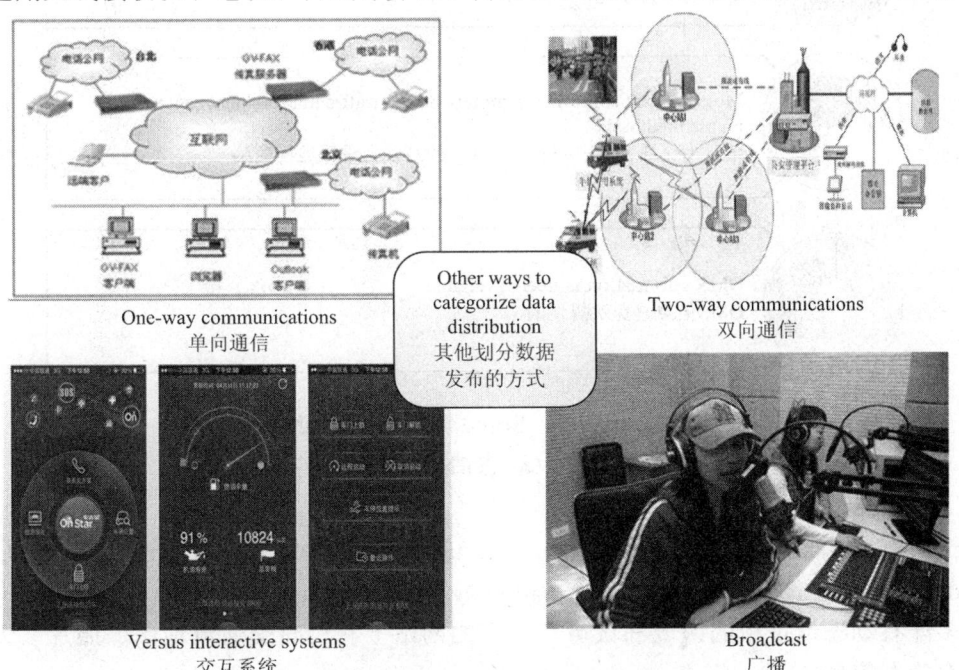

Figure 2.38 Other ways to categorize data distribution

图 2.38 其他划分数据发布的方式

Figure 2.39　Dynamic Message Signs (DMS)
图 2.39　动态情报板

As the name suggests, dynamic message signs (DMS) are road signs with messages that can be changed in real time.
动态情报板（DMS）是情报可实时变化的道路标志。

The messages may be activated automatically by nearby traffic and road sensorsto warn drivers of hazardous conditions ahead
交通和道路传感器自动触发动态情报板（DMS）显示信息告知驾驶人前方的危险情况

Messages are controlled remotely by the traffic management center on a preplanned basis
信息由交通管理中心在预先计划的基础上进行远程控制

DMS information is freely available
DMS信息是免费提供的

Figure 2.40　Some features of DMS
图 2.40　动态情报板的特征

（2）Internet　网络

Many regions and cities have made their real-time traffic flow maps, camera pictures, weather and road conditions, as well as static information available on their web sites.

很多配有动态情报板的区域和城市在它们的网站上有实时交通流地图、照片、天气和路况，还有静态信息。

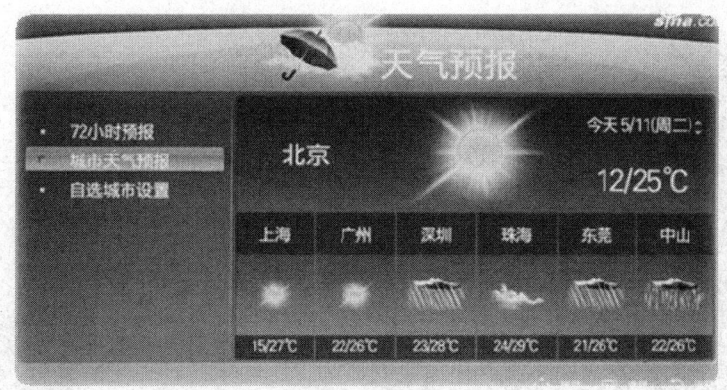

Figure 2.41　Weather forecast
图 2.41　天气预报

Within the vehicle, motorists have relied for years on car radios (both AM and FM) to receive traffic-relevant broadcasts which have brought great convenience to people. However, there are also some shortcomings.

车辆内，多年来驾车人依靠汽车收音机（AM 和 FM）来收听与交通有关的广播，这为人们带来了很大的便利，但仍然存在一些缺点。

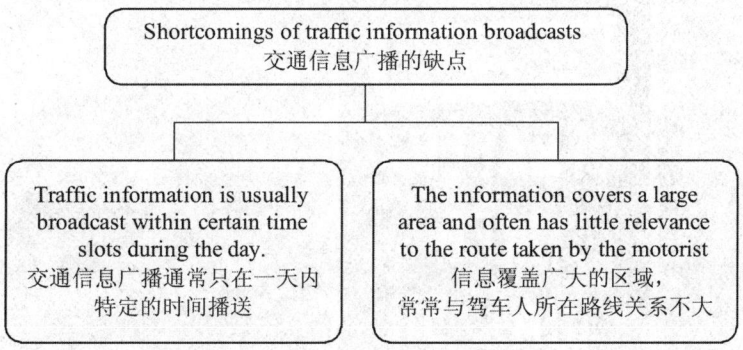

Figure 2.42　Shortcomings of traffic information broadcasts
图 2.42　交通信息广播的缺点

Ways to overcome these shortcomings:

克服这些缺点的方法：

① Low-power highway advisory radio (HAR) can be installed along the road segments;

在路段沿线安装低功耗公路路况广播（HAR）；

② High-quality voice recognition technology is adapted for handling telephone travel enquiries to provide traffic information specific to the user's route or location. The service can be highly automated, as described by the "511" service in the US, which is free to the public.

采用高质量声音识别技术处理关于出行的电话查询，提供针对用户特定出行路线和位置的交通信息。这个服务可以达到很高的自动化，就像美国"511"服务所描述的那样，其服务对于公众是免费的。

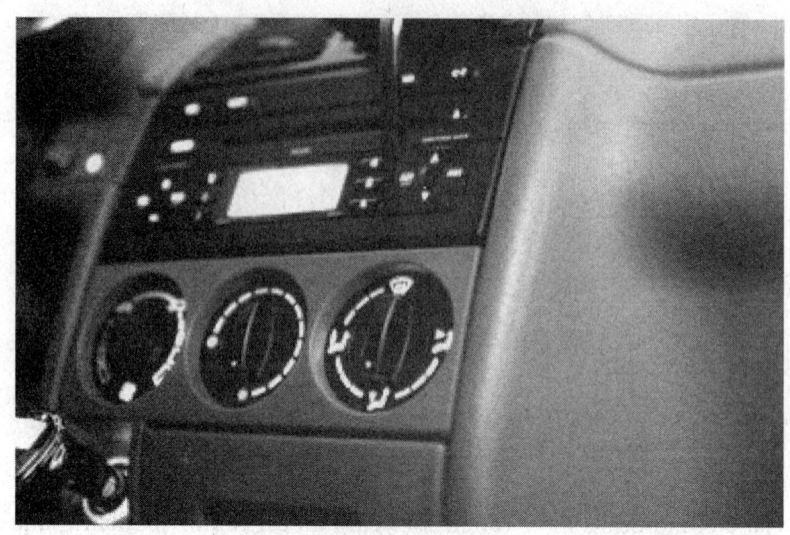

Figure 2.43 Car radios
图 2.43 汽车收音机

Figure 2.44 511sign (Artemis)
图 2.44 511 标志（Artemis）

2.5 Information Utilization 信息利用

Information utilization in ITS serves a number of primary functions, which are not mutually exclusive.

ITS 中的信息利用服务于很多基本功能，这些功能并不相互排斥。

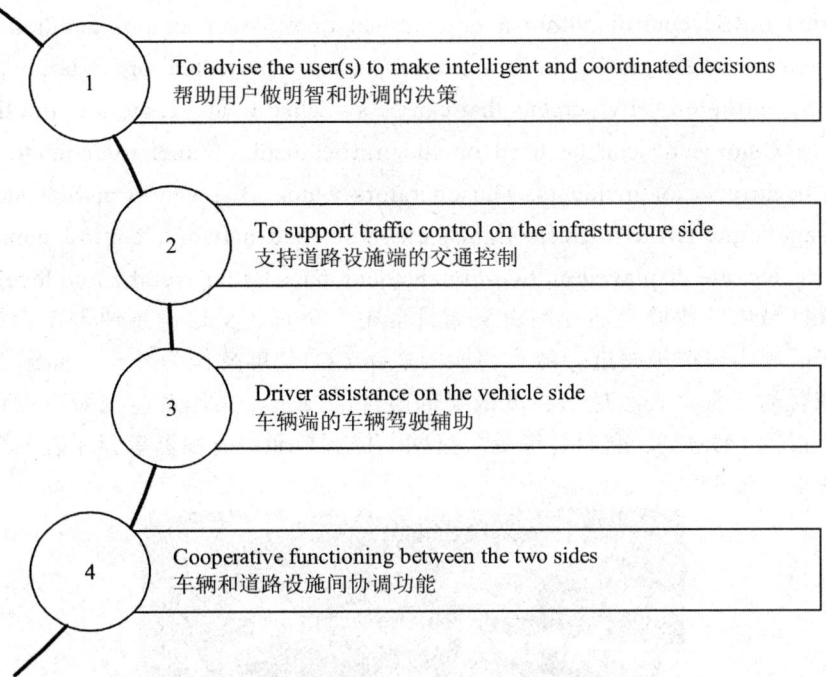

Figure 2.45　Information utilization of ITS primary functions
图 2.45　ITS 基本功能的信息利用

2.5.1　Decision Support and Traffic Control　决策支持和交通控制

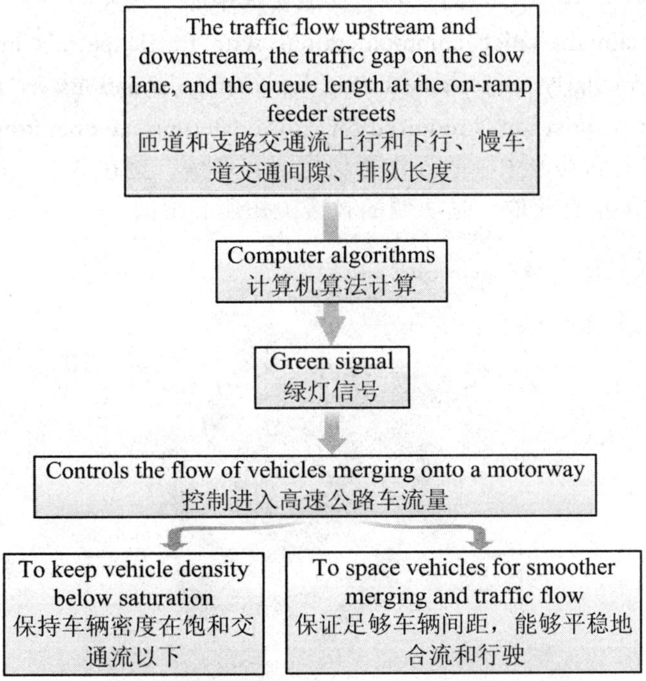

Figure 2.46　Coordinated traffic control
图 2.46　协调交通控制

Coordinated traffic control within a large urban or regional area is handled by the traffic management center, where traffic information is usually projected on a large display panel, supplemented by multiple CCTV screens that can be switched to any camera in the field (as shown in Figure 2.47). Color code can be used on the traffic display panel to indicate the degree of congestion or occurrence of incidents. The operators watch all the information and can operate dynamic message signs (DMS), traffic lights, etc. The road network, control elements (such as DMS), detectors, etc. are displayed on two-dimensional maps with several zoom levels.

大城市或区域内的协调交通控制由交通管理中心负责，交通信息通常投影在一个大的显示板上，可在区域内摄像机间进行随意切换的多路CCTV屏幕作为补充，如图2.47所示。用不同的颜色在交通显示板表示拥堵程度或交通事件的发生。操作者监视所有的信息，并且能够操作动态情报板（DMS）、交通灯等等。路网、控制单元、监视器等显示在具有多级缩放功能的二维地图上。

Figure 2.47　Traffic management center
图 2.47　交通管理中心

Operators also maintain voice communications with traffic patrols and operators in other centers, which is particularly important during emergency situations as timely, accurate, and interactive information acquisition is required for coordinated rescue operations.

操作者与交通巡警和其他中心的操作者保持语音通信，这在紧急情况下尤其重要，因为及时、准确、交互式的信息获取，是协调的救援工作所必须的。

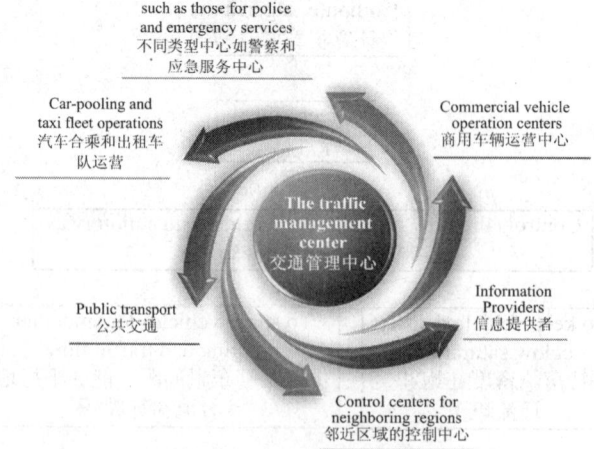

Figure 2.48　Schematic diagram of data network
图 2.48　数据网络示意图

For information integration and control coordination among transport centers (both public and private), there is a need to build a data network linking the traffic management center with other centers often operated by other agencies and organizations:

为了交通中心（公共和私营）间的信息集成和控制协调，需要建立一个数据网络将交通管理中心与其他机构和组织建立的中心连接起来：

On the vehicle side, traffic information terminals can provide route guidance or supplementary information to the driver, to support vehicle control, or speed advisory information for example.

车载部分，交通信息终端给驾驶员提供路径引导或辅助信息来支持交通车辆控制，或提供速度建议信息等。

> **例** **Berlin's traffic management center: Verkehrs Management Zentrale (VMZ)**
> **柏林的交通管理中心——沃克管理中心**
>
> Since the start of 2003 a fully operational, public-private transport management center (VMZ Berlin) has been monitoring, processing and disseminating information on Berlin's traffic and transport system to the general public and businesses. It provides basic mobility services for no charge and value-added services for a fee. Apart from some minor subsidy, VMZ's private operator will have to cover operating costs by developing commercial information services. VMZ is intended to influence travel demand through provision of appropriate information services. VMZ was set up as a public-private partnership with the investment costs for hardware and software borne by the Berlin government. Thus the system is owned by the state and operated on its behalf by the private consortium comprising DaimlerChrysler Services AG and Siemens AG.
>
> 从2003年年初开始，政府和私营企业合作的运输管理中心(柏林VMZ)，监控和处理柏林交通运输信息，并对公众和企业发布实时信息服务。该中心提供免费通信服务和有偿延伸服务。除了较少补助外，VMZ私营企业必须通过开发商业信息服务，筹集运行所需的费用。VMZ通过适当的信息服务来调整出行需求。柏林政府成立了政府和私营企业合作的VMZ并承担了软硬件的投资费。该系统的所有权属于国家，由DaimlerChrysler Services AG和Siemens AG运行该系统并从中获利。

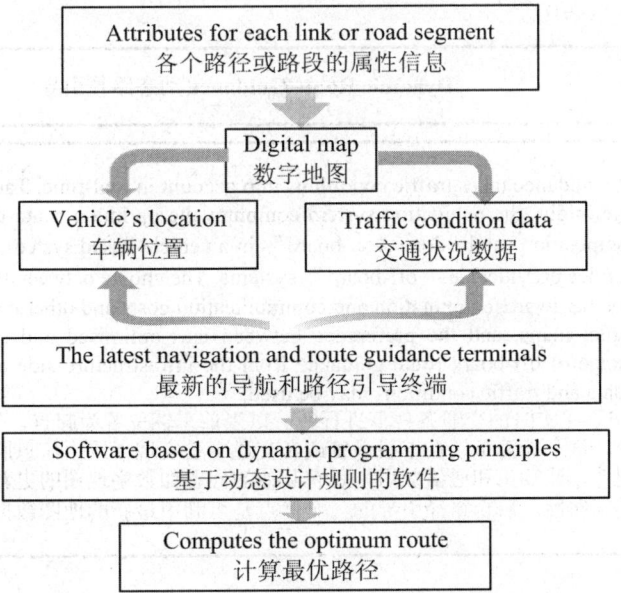

Figure 2.49　Optimum route computation processes

图 2.49　最优路径计算流程

2.5.2 Vehicle Control 车辆控制

While information technologies in ITS help the driver today to make strategic decisions through traffic information, navigation and route guidance on a minute-by-minute basis, control and sensor fusion technologies may in the future allow some degree of longitudinal and lateral vehicle control assistance to the driver.

如今 ITS 中的信息技术帮助驾驶者做出出行决策，提供时间精确到分钟的交通信息导航和路径引导，而控制和传感器融合技术未来也许可以在一定程度上应用纵向和横向车辆控制来辅助驾驶。

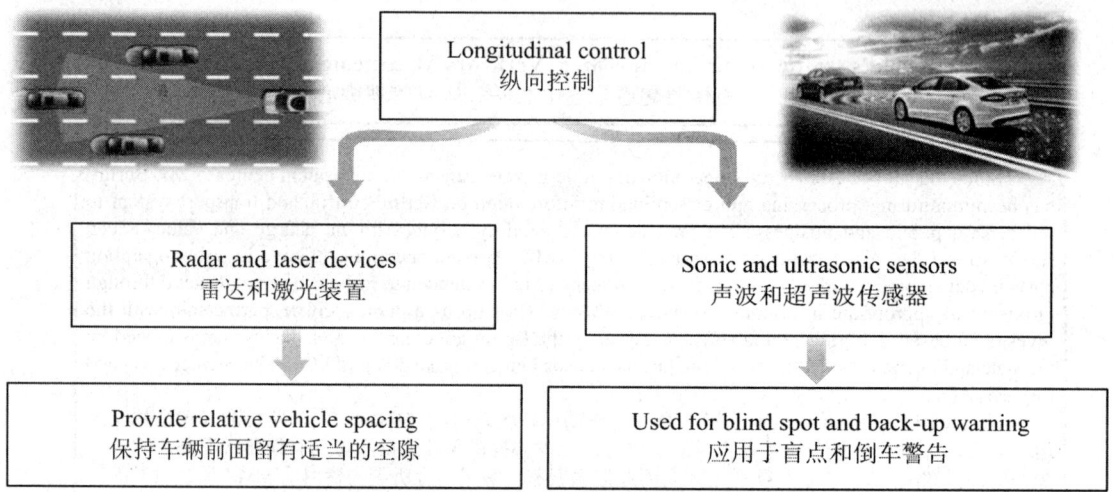

Figure 2.50 Vehicle longitudinal control block diagram

图 2.50 车辆纵向控制框架图

> **例**
>
> **Dynamic Route Guidance 动态路径引导**
>
> Dynamic route guidance takes traffic conditions into account in real-time. Taking the current location of the vehicle as the origin, the navigation system computes the optimum route to any given destination repetitively. The computation can be done "on-board" in a vehicle-based system, or at a traffic center (or at an information service provider) in "off-board" systems. The choice between these options depends on the trade-off between hardware, computation and communication costs and other considerations such as the need to update digital maps, and the preference between user-optimised and system-optimised traffic control. One advantage of off-board route guidance from the infrastructure side over onboard systems is that the latest map data and traffic conditions may be used.
>
> 动态路径引导是在实时的交通条件下进行的。以当前车辆位置为起点，导航系统反复计算到达终点的最优路径。这个计算可以在车载系统或者交通中心实现（或由信息服务提供商提供）。选择依据主要考虑硬件、计算量和通信费用，还有其他的问题如数字地图的更新，用户优化还是系统优化的交通控制的倾向性。后台路径引导的一个优点是可利用最新的地图数据和交通条件。

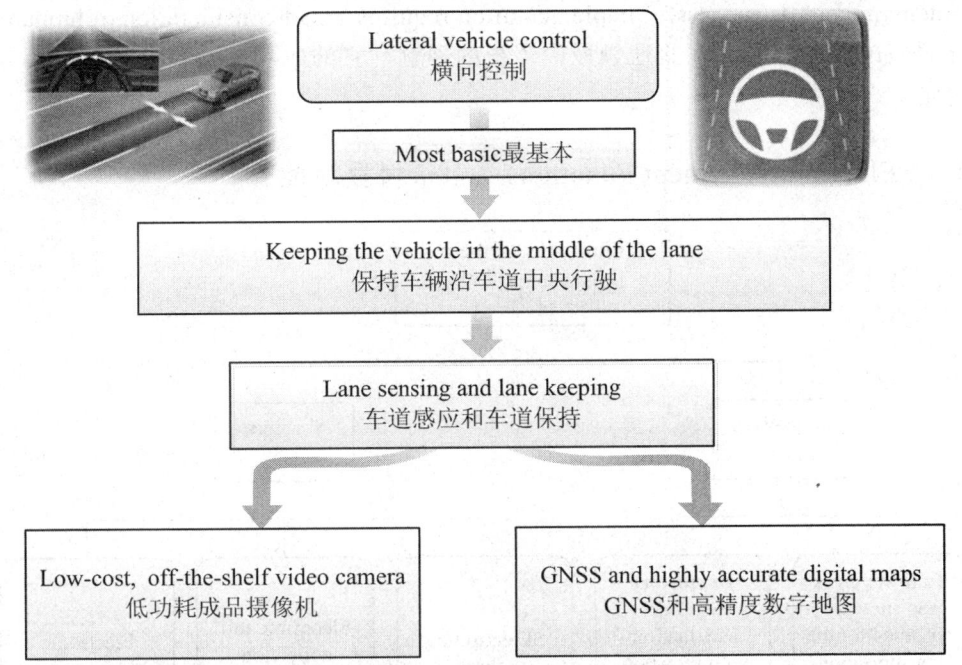

Figure 2.51　Vehicle lateral vehicle control block diagram

图 2.51　车辆横向控制框架图

Fully automated longitudinal and lateral vehicle controls may eventually lead to some degree of automated highway systems (AHS), which are defined as hands-off and feet-off driving.

全自动纵向和横向车辆控制发展到一定程度就形成了全自动公路系统（AHS），其定义是解放双手双脚的驾驶。

Figure 1.52　Unmanned vehicle

图 1.52　无人驾驶汽车

2.6　Electronic Payment　电子付费

Electronic payment's function extends beyond what is traditionally considered to be within the transport domain, and its successful implementation requires broad consideration of human factors.

电子付费的功能超越了在交通领域中传统的理解，它的成功实施要求对人为因素进行全方位的考虑。

2.6.1　Electronic Payment Functions　电子付费功能

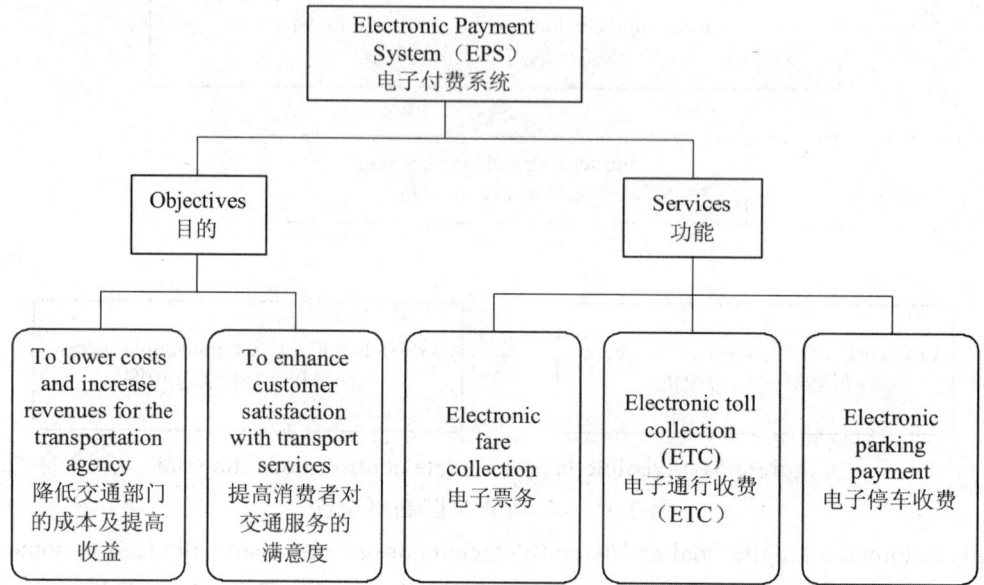

Figure 2.53　Objectives and services of Electronic Payment System (EPS)

图 2.53　电子付费系统的目的和功能

Figure 2.54　Dedicated channel of ETC

图 2.54　ETC 专用道

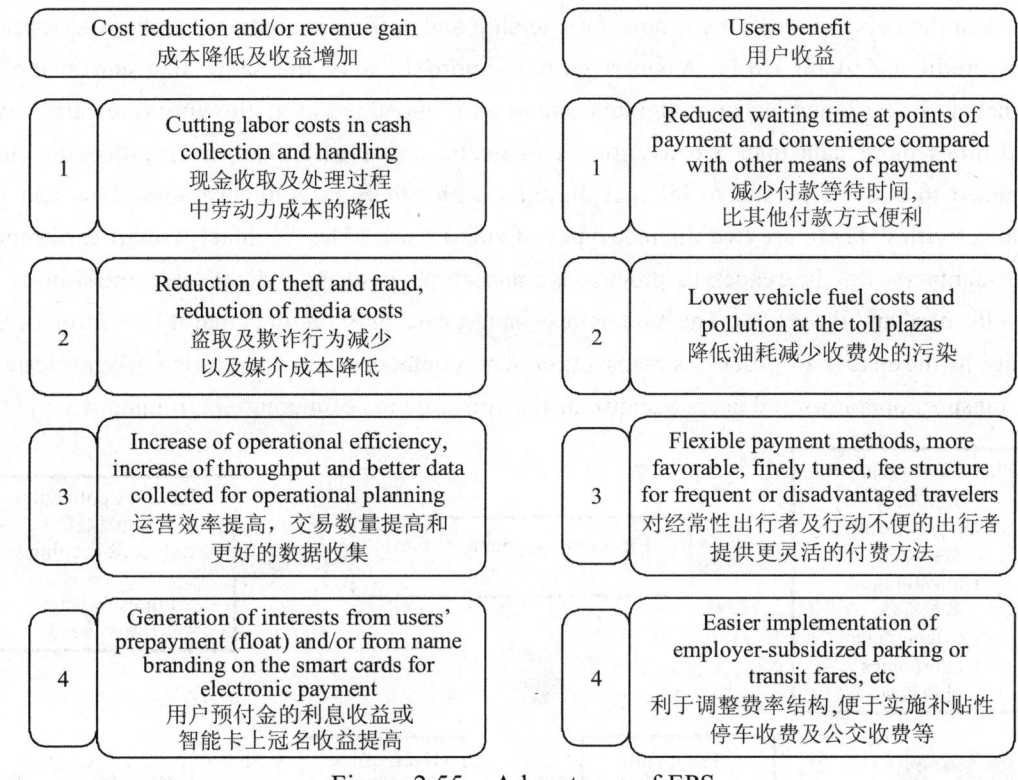

Figure 2.55 Advantages of EPS
图 2.55 电子付费系统的优点

From the customers' standpoint, once a universal electronic payment medium, such as the smart card, has become available, they would like to use it for other transport-related services such as paying for fuel at service stations, and even non-transport services-retail transactions for fast food, telephone, etc. Furthermore, the same smart card could be used not only for payment but also for other functions such as medical records, library lendings, identification for mobility allowance and social benefits.

从用户的角度而言，取得通用的电子付款媒介（如智能卡），他们可能将其用于与交通相关服务的付费，如加油站，甚至快餐及电话等零售服务付费。另外，同一张智能卡不仅可用于付款还可具有其他功能，如用于医疗记录、图书馆借记、机动补贴及社会福利的身份鉴别。

2.6.2 Electronic Payment Technologies　电子付费技术

The most common hardware options for EPS at the front end are smart cards, transponders and cellular telephones.

EPS 前台最普遍的硬件选择是智能卡、电子标签及蜂窝移动电话。

Smart cards are ideal for paying in transactions that are usually made in cash: phone calls, parking fees, transit fares, micro purchases and road tolls to name a few. These types of purchases are typically not attractive to credit or debit card companies because of the high volume of low-value transactions that are generated. With value stored on the card, this circumvents the problem and the delay in verifying proof of ownership and sufficient credit or funds experienced by users of credit and debit cards. A smart card is approximately the same size and shape as a traditional credit card, and has an integrated circuit chip imbedded in it, allowing it to carry several hundred times more data than a conventional magnetic stripe card. This microprocessor chip is programmed to allow a person to interact digitally with others to conduct transactions and other personal activities. There are two distinct types of smart cards. The "contact" smart card requires physical contact with the reader to process a transaction, assuring reliable transmission of data between the card and the reader. The "contactless" smart card only requires that it be within a certain proximity to the reader to process a transaction. The contactless card is particularly preferred by public transport operators and users because of the convenience of increased throughput.

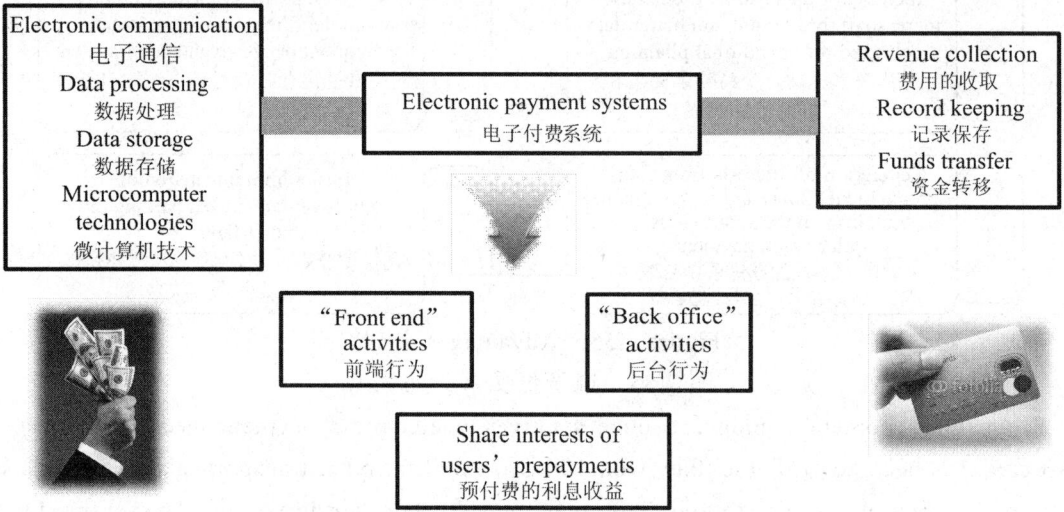

Figure 2.56　Electronic payment systems (EPS)

图 2.56　电子付费系统

Figure 2.57　Electronic payment

图 2.57　电子付费

智能卡是理想的付费方法，可替代传统的现金付费方式如：电话费、停车费、公交票，小额购物及道路收费。由于此类交易带来了大量低价值交易，通常对信用卡或银行卡公司没有吸引力。由于金额储存在卡里，智能卡规避了信用卡或银行卡用户会遇到的一些问题，比如：对拥有者身份进行辨识引起的延迟及核查是否有足够的信用及资金。智能卡与传统的信用卡大小及形状类似，里面有一个内嵌的集成电路芯片，可以比传统的磁卡多储存几百倍的数据。在微处理芯片上进行编程可让一个人与其他人进行电子交易及其他个人活动。智能卡分为两类，接触式智能卡要求在交易中与读卡器进行物理接触以确保卡与读卡器之间数据的可靠交换，非接触式智能卡仅要求在交易中智能卡距读卡器一定距离内即可。因为便于增加交易量，公共交通运营者和使用者一般倾向于非接触式智能卡。

Figure 2.58　Smart cards
图 2.58　智能卡

The transponder (also known as tag) operates as part of an EPS system as one of three main components: the transponder, the reader and the computer system for data processing and storage. The transponder, which is a little larger than a deck of cards, is usually secured to the vehicle in most toll applications and relies on RFID (Radio Frequency Identification) technology to operate. When it passes through the red zone (the area in which the reader signal is contained) it detects a signal and sends back identifying information to the reader. The reader sends information to the computer system for processing. Active transponders contain batteries to power their internal circuitry and transmissions. Passive transponders get their power from the radio frequency (RF) pulse they receive from the reader. Passive transponders have indefinite life, are less expensive, but operate within shorter range and transmit less information. Most transponders would rely on their readers to send data to the back office to settle the account. However, some newer transponders have built in slots for smart cards to allow immediate electronic payment through the smart card media.

无线应答器（一般称为电子标签）是 EPS 系统三个主要组成部分中的一个。EPS 系统的三个主要组成部分包括无线应答器、读取器及用于数据处理及储存的计算机系统。无线应答器比卡稍大，通常装在车里并依赖无线射频识别（RFID）技术用于道路收费。当车辆通过读取区（有读取信号的区域）时，它检测到信号并向读取器发送回识别信息，进而读取器向计算机系统发送信息进行处理。主动式的电子标签由电池向其核心电路和发射提供能源，被动式的电子标签从读取器发出的无线射频（RF）波中接受能源，被动式电子标签有无限次生命周期，价格低廉，但作用范围较短，传输数据较少。大多数的电子标签依赖读取器发送数据到后台进行财务分析。然而，一些新型的电子标签具有内置式智能卡插口，允许通过智能卡媒介进行即时的电子付费。

Figure 2.59　Radio Frequency Identification
图 2.59　无线射频识别

Cellular telephones have the potential of being a major EPS component of the 21st century's e-commerce system, which is already widely implemented through the Internet for users at their personal computers. This is because cellular telephones also contain an integrated circuit chip just as smart cards do, thus allowing the same functionality. Some cellular phones use the smart card as the enabling device. The chip, and/or smart card which is inserted into the phone, contains the user's pertinent information such as identification, phone book, billing information, etc. Cellular telephones can thus be used as an electronic payment media. They can also be used as an intermediary to access the Internet to purchase goods and services much in the same way that this process is done on a personal computer.

蜂窝式电话有可能成为 21 世纪电子商务主要的电子收费成员，目前已通过互联网在个人电脑上得以广泛应用。这是因为蜂窝式电话也像智能卡一样有集成电路芯片，因此具有同样的功能。有些蜂窝式电话用智能卡作为授权设备。芯片及（或）智能卡可内置在电话中，包含用户的相关信息，如身份、电话簿、收费单等。蜂窝电话因此也可用作电子付费媒介。它们还可作为中介像个人电脑一样通过互联网进行购物及服务交易。

Another component of EPS is the communication subsystem. The back office functions are performed with the aid of a host computer or a network of computers (for redundancy and reliability), to maintain all EPS databases, process and authorize different types of transactions for online systems, monitor status of EPS components, collect and process historical data, reconcile accounts, and facilitate other functions such as customer service.

EPS 的另一个组成部分是通信子系统。后台功能将通过以下工作实现：主计算机或计算机网络（见余性和可靠性）的协作、整个 EPS 数据库的维护，不同在线系统交易的处理及准许、EPS 各组成部分的状态监控、收集并处理历史数据、调节账户、推动其他客户服务功能的实现。

Depending on the specific application and hardware media chosen, a number of accessory technologies are necessary for EPS.

根据应用类别及硬件选择，EPS 还需许多辅助技术。

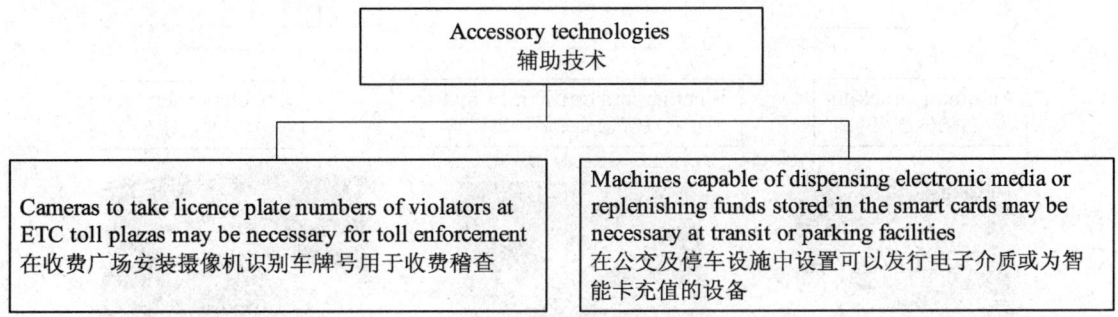

Figure 2.60　Accessory technologies of EPS
图 2.60　EPS 的辅助技术

2.6.3　Location Factors　位置因素

With decreasing costs and increasing power of technology, new options for EPS have emerged based on time and location.

由于成本的减低及技术的提高，基于时间及位置的 EPS 带给我们新的选择。

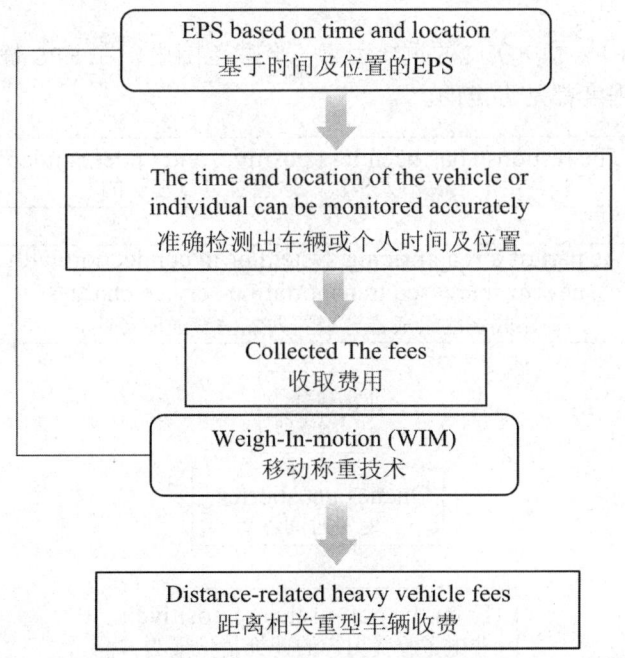

Figure 2.61　Applications of EPS based on time and location
图 2.61　基于时间及位置的 EPS 应用

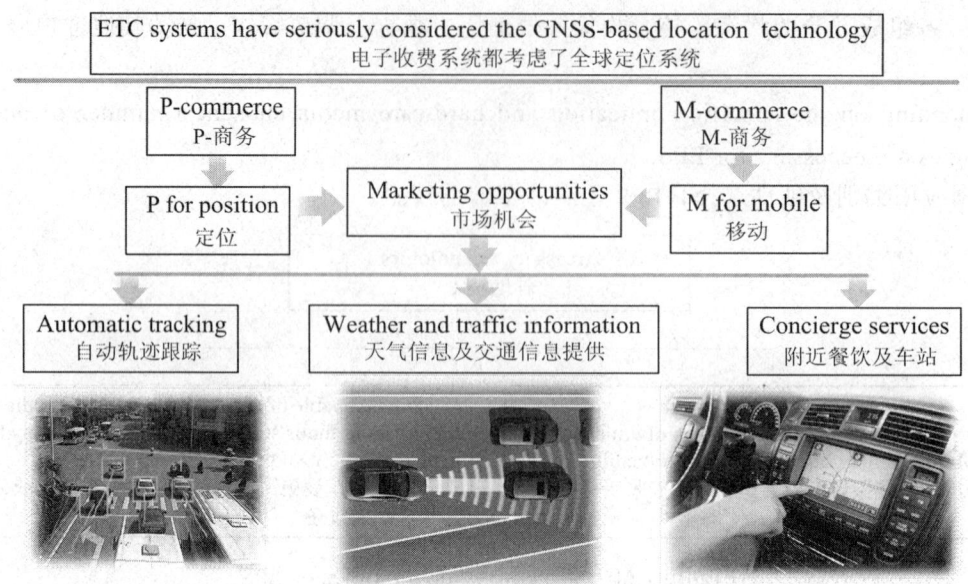

Figure 2.62　ETC systems that consider GNSS-based location technology
图 2.62　考虑了全球定位技术的电子收费系统

2.6.4　User Experience and Institutional Issues　用户体验及制度问题

User acceptance is understandably very important for successful implementation of EPS. Where EPS is implemented to replace the current means of payment, user acceptance around the world has been very positive.

用户的接受度是 EPS 成功实施的重要因素。全球范围内，在 EPS 替换现有付费方式的地方，用户对它的认可程度都是肯定的。

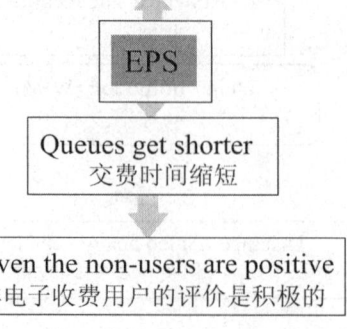

Figure 2.63　Significances of ESP
图 2.63　ESP 的作用

2.7 Human Factors 人为因素

Many of the important enabling technologies for ITS concern the human-machine interface (HMI): the way in which users interact with technology. Human beings are involved in ITS not only as drivers.

很多 ITS 重要的技术涉及到人机接口——用户和技术的交互。人类参与 ITS，不仅扮演驾驶者的角色。

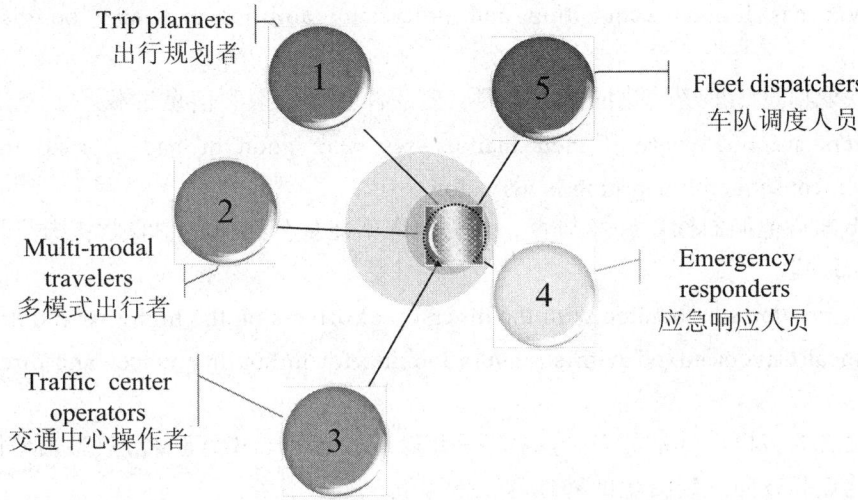

Figure 2.64 Roles of human beings in ITS

图 2.64 人类在 ITS 中扮演的角色

2.7.1 Human Factors on the Vehicle Side 车辆方面的人为因素

Human interaction with the vehicle is critical in the transport service domain, as mistakes or misjudgments in the primary driving tasks have clear safety implications.

人和车辆的交互在交通服务领域中显得尤为重要，因为行驶中的错误和误判与安全息息相关。

(1) Cell phone use as an alleged cause of accidents.

手机的使用导致事故。

(2) Some navigation units require the driver to stop the vehicle before entering destinations in the navigation.

一些导航单元要求驾驶者在导航设备上输入目的地时停车。

(3) Drivers can be similarly distracted by music, talking to passengers.

驾驶者同样也会被音乐和与乘客的谈话影响。

(4) Human-machine interaction, and the resulting human-machine interfaces (HMI), play an important role in imparting both functionality and user acceptance to ITS applications.

人机交互和随之而来的人机接口（HMI）在赋予 ITS 应用功能和用户认可上发挥了重要的作用。

There are many different types guidelines for "traditional" human factors and ergonomics work of support systems, and the resulting interfaces must be designed with great care on the basis of and/or the "rules of thumb" in the field of HMI design. Vehicle drivers require extra attention as their decisions and actions directly influence road traffic safety.

很多不同种类的支持系统和显示结果的接口必须依据"传统"的人为因素和人体工程学的指导方针以及在HMI设计中的"框架法则"进行认真设计,当车辆驾驶者的决定和行动直接影响到道路交通的安全时要格外注意。

The driver has limited acquisition and processing abilities and may be distracted and overloaded.

驾驶者获取信息、处理信息的能力有限,容易注意力分散和信息过载。

(1) Drivers are not aware if their manoeuvres were good or bad as road traffic is not self-instructive; consequently learning is very slow.

驾驶者不知道他们的操作好坏与否,因为他们不能从公路交通中自学提升,因此他们的学习进度非常缓慢。

(2) Safety problems associated with the diversity of drivers on the highway: old drivers mixed with young, local drivers mixed with strangers looking for unfamiliar places and direction signs, etc.

公路驾驶者的多样性带来的安全问题——年轻驾驶者和老年驾驶者,熟悉当地情况的本地驾驶者与对地点和方向感到陌生的外地驾驶者等混杂。

Figure 2.65　Dangerous roads
图 2.65　危险的公路

For this purpose, basic ergonomic design criteria for display, information, control and driver-assisting systems have been stated, and a number of basic guidelines appropriate to HMI system concepts were identified:

为了这个目的,这里描述了涉及显示、信息、控制和辅助驾驶系统基本的人类工程设计标准,确定了一些基本的适于HMI系统概念的指导方针:

| User Orientation 面向用户 | • Systems should avoid overloading and underloading the driver
• 避免使驾驶者压力过大或压力不足 |

| Task Orientation 面向任务 | • Allocation of tasks and resources should be performed efficiently by identification of the tasks that are best performed by the driver and those best suited for machines
• 通过确定驾驶者和机器分别最适合的任务来有效地进行任务和资源分配 |

| Technological Orientation 面向技术 | • Develop systems that appear to be simple to the driver
• 开发易于驾驶者操作的系统 |

| Procedural Orientation 面向过程 | • Ergonomists and psychologists need to be involved at the outset of the design process
• 生物工程学者和心理学者需要在设计过程的开始参与进来 |

Figure 2.66 HMI system concept

图 2.66 HMI 系统概念

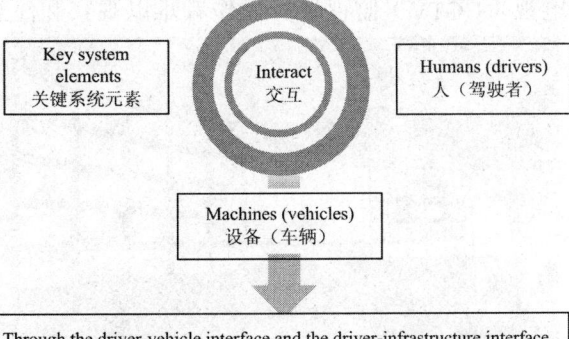

Figure 2.67 Components of road traffic

图 2.67 道路交通的组成

Road traffic is a multi-person, multi-machine process, organized by implicit and explicit rules, where the key system elements, humans (drivers) and machines (vehicles) interact. Interactions between these elements are performed through the driver-vehicle interface and the driver-infrastructure interface. The design of the driver-vehicle interaction is therefore not only a question of specification of displays and controls. The design must be related to the goal of the total human-machine system, i.e. to the context in which the system will operate and to the content of the information flow between use rand technical system.

道路交通是一个多人员、多设备的过程，由内在和外在的规则组织起来，其中关键的系统元素、人（驾驶者）和设备（车辆）进行交互。这些元素之间通过驾驶员与车辆接口和驾驶员与道路设施接口实现交互。驾驶者-车辆交互的设计不仅是显示和控制的问题，设计必须和整个人-机系统的目标相关，也就是系统运行应满足用户和技术系统之间信息流的传递。

Figure 2.68　Driver-vehicle interaction

图 2.68　人车交互

2.7.2　Human Factors on the Infrastructure Side　道路设施方面的人为因素

Human factors need to be considered for all users, not just vehicle drivers. For example, some of the modern traffic control centers have over 100 CCTV monitors on a wall, making it difficult for operators to detect and focus on critical sites.

人为因素需要考虑所有的用户，不仅仅是驾驶者。例如，一些现代交通控制中心在一面墙上有超过 100 个闭路电视（CCTV）监视器，操作者难以观察和注意重要的场景。

Figure 2.69　Traffic control centers

图 2.69　交通控制中心

One would expect the basic principles of human factors on the vehicle side to be just as valid on the infrastructure side. While this is generally true, the infrastructure side is complicated because of the large scale of its system and by the multiple organizations involved. Also, transport professionals have a more direct responsibility for employing best practice on the infrastructure side than they do on the vehicle side in order to enhance safety and user acceptance of ITS.

我们通常期望车辆方面的人为因素的基本原理在道路设施方面也有效。虽然这大体上是正确的，但由于系统的规模较大和多组织参与，道路设施方面通常很复杂。而且，为了加强 ITS 的安全和得到用户的认可，交通专业人员有更多的责任在道路设施方面比车辆方面做得更好。

Figure 2.70 Mont Blanc Tunnel: visible signs for evacuation routes
图 2.70 Mont Blanc 隧道——疏散通道的可视指示标志

The ultimate focus of ITS is on the end user, and human factors must be considered to enhance user acceptance.

ITS 关心的根本点在终端用户，因此必须考虑人为因素以提高用户的认可度。

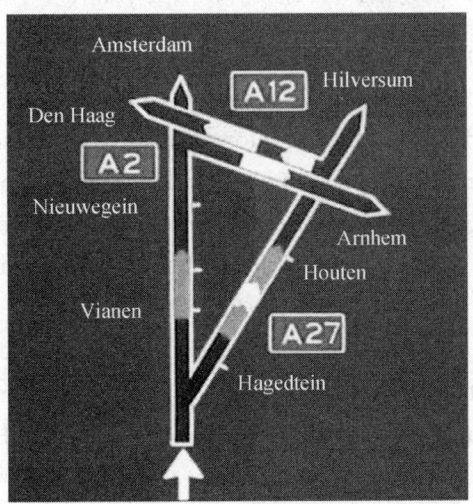

Figure 2.71 Route choice Variable Message Signs (VMS) graphic (Amsterdam)
图 2.71 提供路径选择的图形化可变信息板（阿姆斯特丹）

2.7.3　The Holistic Approach　整体分析

Focusing on user acceptance can help highlight all the diverging elements that could, would and should influence the design process. If desirable features are graded higher than costs (using a weighted criteria/cost function), the solution is accepted, will be purchased, and hopefully will be used.

关注用户的认可度可以揭示所有分歧产生的原因，由此将要或应该影响我们的设计方法。如果期望的性能高于花费（用加权标准费用函数），方案就会被采纳、购买和使用。

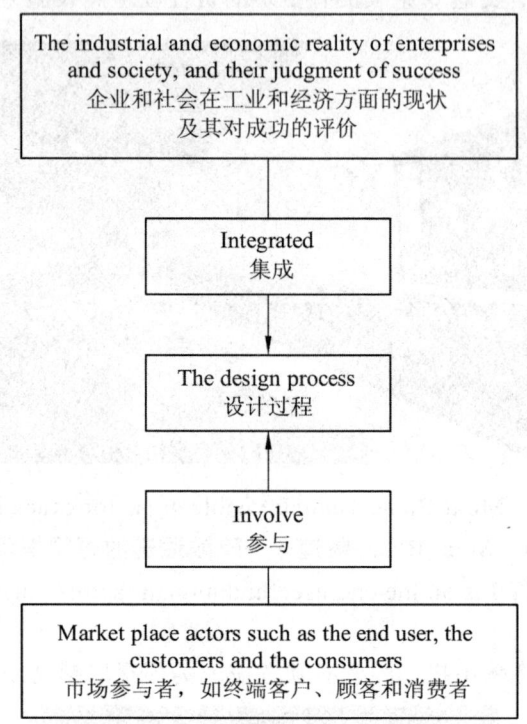

Figure 2.72　Design processes of solutions
图 2.72　方案设计过程

New products or solutions are seldom developed to solve or to meet completely new problems and needs. Very often a better performance of already existing solutions is the goal. It is also clear that old solutions and products should co-exist side by side with the new ones.

新产品或方案的开发不可能完全就决新的问题或满足需要，通常，将现有方案优化即是目标。很明显，老的解决方案和产品应该与新的一起存在。

A significant proportion of today's transport users are also technologically challenged. Elderly people with learning difficulties and those generally unfamiliar or uncomfortable with computer-based technology will have particular problems with poorly designed HMI for ITS systems.

当今相当比例的交通用户面临技术上的挑战，对学习新事物较慢的老年人和对以计算机为基础的技术不熟悉、不喜欢的人来说，使用设计欠佳的 ITS 系统的 HMI 会有困难。

In summary, human factors in ITS are both important and potentially complex. User-friendly ITS can be judged by its "usability, utility and likeability." When needed, the transportation professional should involve human factor experts at an early stage of design of ITS equipment and facilities. Doing it well does not have to be expensive if the human factors needs are kept in mind at the outset.

总之，ITS中人为因素既重要又具有潜在的复杂性。用户友好型的ITS由"可用性、有用性和似然性"指标来评定。当需要时，交通专家应邀请人因学专家参与到前期的ITS设备和设施的设计中。如果在开始就牢记以人为本，那么就有可能做出令人满意又经济实惠的产品。

2.8 Conclusions 结论

ITS is an important part of the digital revolution. The digital transformation of information and communication technologies has fueled major advances in areas such as satellite-based navigation, Digital Audio Broadcasting, third and fourth generation mobile phone networks, electronic payment, and smart cards. In Europe the combination of all these digital technologies applied to transport has attracted the generic term "Transport Telematics". Without these technological advances the opportunity for ITS would not exist at all.

ITS是数字革命的重要部分。信息和通信技术的数字化变革推动了诸如卫星导航、数字音频广播、第三代和第四代移动通信网络、电子支付和智能卡等领域的重大进步。在欧洲，所有这些数字技术结合在一起应用于交通，出现了一个专用术语"Transport Telematics"。如果没有这些先进技术的支持，ITS就不可能存在。

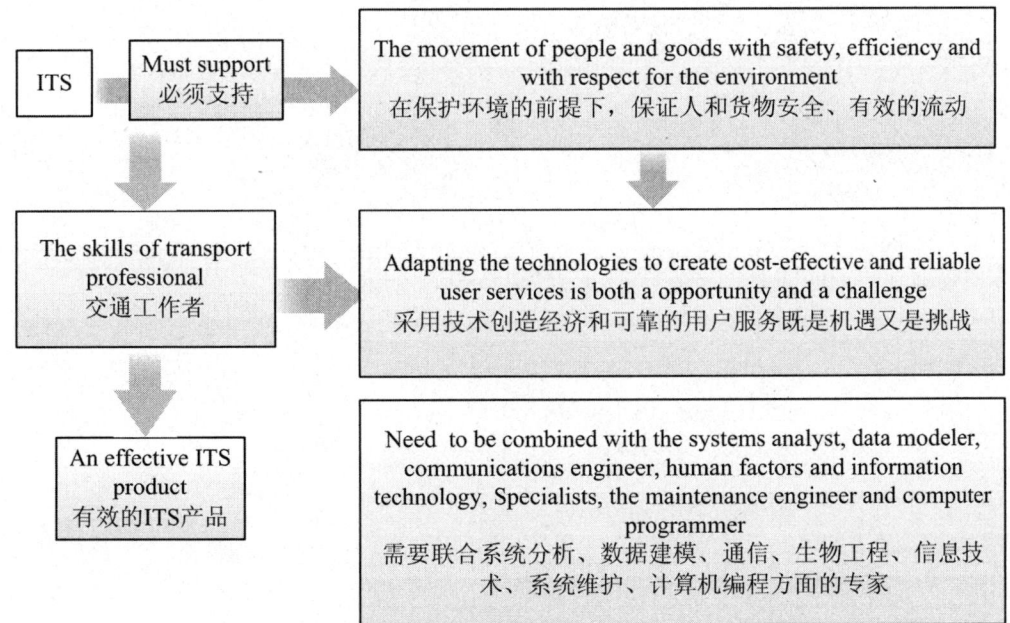

Figure 2.73　Requirements of ITS
图2.73　ITS的要求

Transport networks often have the requirement to operate through 24 hours a day, continuously seven days a week, and it follows that ITS must do the same, with only rare and occasional lapses tolerated. Readers of this book will therefore be engaged in the implementation of systems and services that are reliable and dependable for transport users and operators alike.

交通网络常常要求一天 24 小时运行、一星期连续 7 天，这就要求 ITS 达到同样的要求，当然极少和偶尔的差错也是允许的。所以本书的读者要为交通用户和相关的操作者实现可靠和可信赖的系统和服务。

 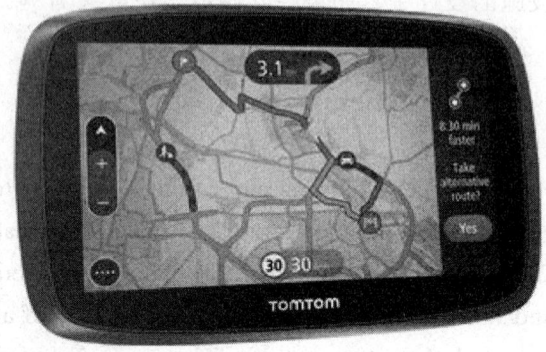

Figure 2.74　Satellite-based navigation
图 2.74　卫星导航

Chapter 3 What about ITS Architecture and Standards
第三章 ITS 体系框架和标准

3.1 ITS Architecture ITS 体系框架

3.1.1 Why is ITS Architecture important ITS 体系框架建设的重要性

（1）Shared Vision 共同愿景

The development of an ITS architecture usually begins with a consensus building process involving multiple stakeholders. Thus, the resultant architecture represents a consensus among the users, service providers, and transport agencies expressed in common terms, definitions, boundaries, priorities and expectations among the stakeholders who will later be making independent, but now consistent and mutually supportive, decisions.

ITS体系框架的开发通常始于这样一个共识，即建设众多利益相关者参与的一个进程。这样一个体系框架代表了用户、服务提供者和交通部门的共识，其表现于利益相关者接受的通用术语、定义、边界、优先权和期望。这些利益相关者以后会独立决策，但此时却必须相互一致、相互支持。

ITS architecture defines:
(1) The functions (e.g. gather traffic information or request a route) that are required for ITS;
(2) The physical entities or subsystems where these functions reside (e.g. the roadside or the vehicle);
(3) The information flows and data flows that connect these functions and physical subsystems together into an integrated system;

ITS architecture analysis provides other aides for planning and implementation of ITS deployments, including a deployment program, an organizational viewpoint, cost/benefit and risk analysis studies.

ITS体系框架定义了：
（1） ITS功能需求（如收集交通信息或路线请求）；
（2） 物理实体或子系统（如道路或交通工具），它们是ITS功能宿主；
（3） 连接各项功能或物理子系统形成集成系统的信息流和数据流。

ITS体系框架的分析为ITS发展的规划和实施提供了另外一些帮助，包括部署计划、机构的观点、成本效益和风险分析的研究等。

（2）Stakeholder Driven 利益相关者驱动

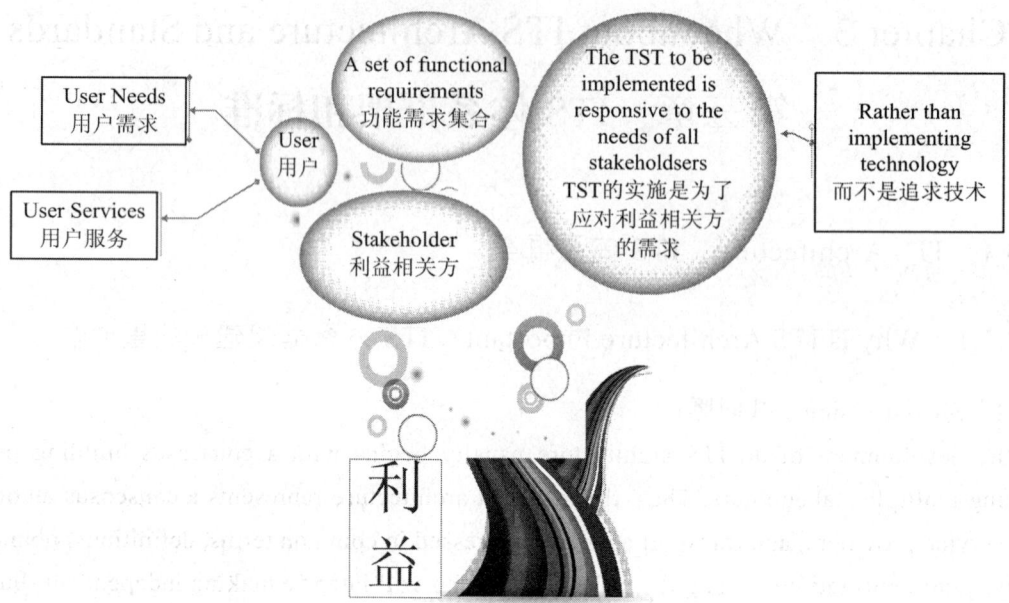

Figure 3.1　Stakeholder Driven
图 3.1　利益相关者驱动

（3）Promotion of ITS Standards Development 促进 ITS 标准发展

The ITS architecture will also show clearly and unambiguously the key processes which require a standardized interface, especially for communications and data exchanges. Based on the relevant interfaces and an analysis of operational needs, user requirements and hardware/software specifications, the architecture can help identify whether the various standards should be local, regional, national, or international.

ITS 体系框架还清楚表明需要标准化接口的关键过程，尤其是关于通信和数据交换的过程。基于对交互界面、实施需要、用户要求和硬件/软件规格的分析，体系框架可有助于区别各种标准是否可成为区域、地区、国家或国际等标准。

（4）Provision of Commercial Benefits 提供商业利益

Design and implementation of standardized ITS subsystems and components in conformance with the ITS architecture will stimulate an open market in equipment and software supply, permit economies of scale.

设计与应用标准化的 ITS 子系统以及与 ITS 体系框架相适应的组成部分，将刺激设备和软件供应市场的开放，发展规模经济。

（5）Risk Management 风险管理

A good ITS architecture will consider failure modes. The development of an ITS architecture also requires that transport policies and assumptions regarding who plays what role are made explicit. By facilitating the development of standards, the ITS architecture also reduces the risk of de facto or proprietary standards perpetuated by the dominant manufacturers.

优秀的ITS体系框架应考虑故障的状况。ITS体系框架的开发还需要了解交通政策和责任，以明确谁发挥什么作用。通过推动 ITS 标准的发展，体系框架还降低了占市场主要份额的制造商的已有或专有的标准可能面临的风险。

中国地图

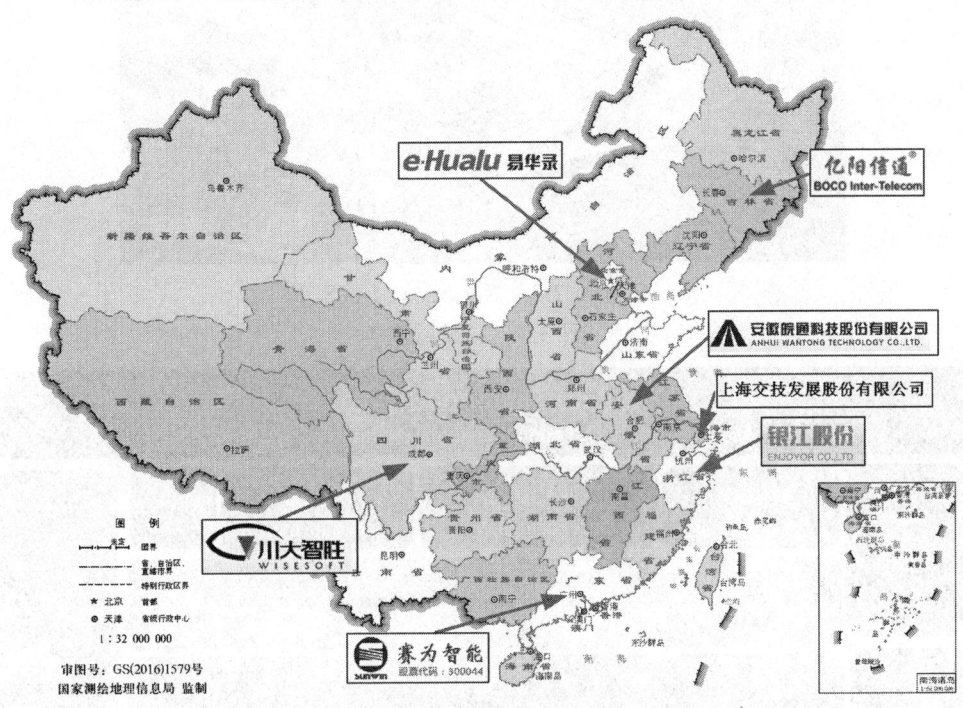

Figure 3.2　Equipment software supply market
图 3.2　设备软件供应市场

（6）Linking ITS to the Transport Planning Process　ITS 与交通规划程序相连接

ITS needs to be integrated into the local or regional transportation plan. An ITS architecture supports this integration by forcing all involved to identify the intended relationship between ITS and conventional transportation plans and solutions. It can also add substance to those plans through the definition of what is required to provide which services and the priority for their implementation.

ITS 需要与地方或地区的交通规划相结合。ITS 体系框架通过识别各项 ITS 内容和传统交通规划及解决方案的潜在对应关系来支持这种结合，它还可以从需要什么内容提供哪些服务和它们的实施顺序等方面为规划提供支持。

（7）Providing a Basis for System Development　为系统开发提供基础

The physical architecture and, if created within the architecture, a document describing the theory of operations, will provide a rigorous basis for defining the function of specific data processing modules, identifying where the processing should be carried out, and what data has to be acquired and shared between data processing units.

物理框架和描述运行理论的文档，将为定义特定数据处理模块的功能、识别应从何处执行数据处理、数据处理单元间需要共享什么信息等提供严格的基础。

Figure 3.3 Services of ITS

图 3.3 ITS 服务

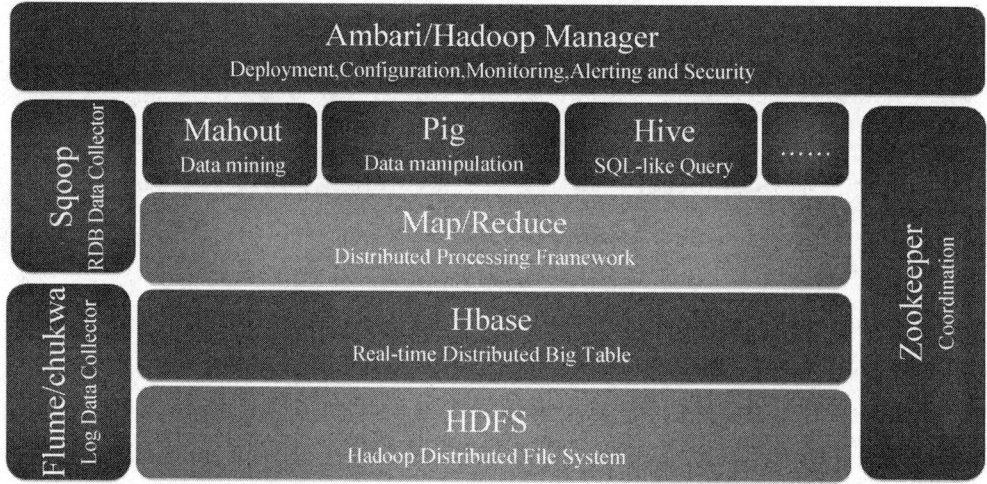

Figure 3.4 Data processing

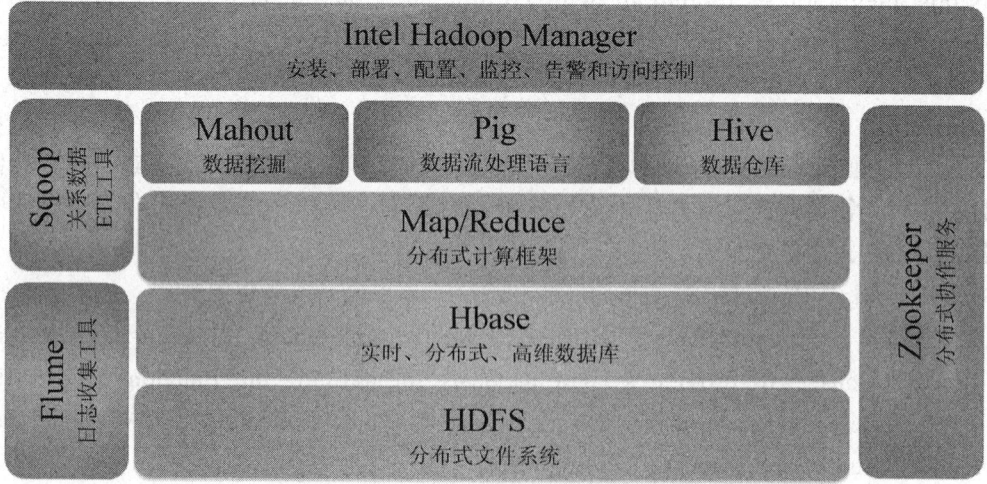

图 3.4 数据处理

（8）Provide a Framework for Future Expansion 为未来发展提供框架

ITS architecture provides a framework for system expansion and technological upgrades. By starting with a broadly-based architecture, one has a basis for evolution and expansion.

ITS 体系框架为系统扩展和技术升级提供框架。以基础广泛的体系框架为起点，便具有了变化与扩展的基础。

3.1.2　Level of ITS Architecture　ITS 体系框架的层面

Figure 3.5　Multi-level model for analysis of ITS architecture
图 3.5　ITS 体系框架分析的多层模型

Multi-level model for analysis of ITS architecture is primarily about information exchange and control between systems at various levels of abstraction. Traffic and transport managers lay down high-level properties, or policy, at Levels 3 and 2, and the architectural structure at Level 1 is then devised so that it conforms to these properties. Level 0 is not strictly part of the architecture. Level 3 architecture needs to reflect the real-world constraints that operate on transport agencies, and to reflect the requirements.

ITS 体系框架分析的多层模型主要关注的是系统间抽象出的各层的信息交换和控制。交通与运输管理者把高层特性或政策放置在第 3 层和第 2 层，第 1 层的框架结构被设计成适应这些特性。严格意义上，第 0 层不是体系框架的组成部分。第 3 层需要反映交通运输管理部门运转中的真实约束，并反映出系统特性需求。

The Level 3 architecture sets the framework within which the Level 2 architecture can be defined. Level 2 architecture defines the properties of those systems that operate under the aegis of a single agency, and it can take into account the characteristics of both existing "legacy" systems and future planned systems. The issues dealt with at Levels 2 and 3 are similar.

第 3 层框架设定了架构，在此架构下可进行第 2 层框架的定义。第 2 层框架定义了在单一机构中运行的各系统的特性，它可以把现有系统和规划系统的特性统一纳入考虑。在第 2

层、第 3 层处理的问题是类似的。

Level 1 architecture is primarily the concern of the systems engineers. At this level, the system structure will be defined so that ITS functions can be grouped together for cost-effective implementation and information systems can be logically decomposed into subsystems for design at Level 0.

第 1 层框架主要是系统工程师需要关注的。在这一层定义系统框架,这样 ITS 功能可根据实施中的成本-效益情况进行组合。同时,信息系统可按照一定的逻辑分解成多个子系统,便于在第 0 层进行设计。

3.1.3 User Need, Functional Requirement and Concept of Operations
用户需求、功能要求和操作概念

The first step in the establishment of an ITS architecture is the selection and prioritization of user services. The consensus view can then lead to the determination of functional requirements and a concept of operations that describes who provides and who receives which ITS service(s), and what interactions the providers must have in order to support the service delivery.

建立 ITS 体系框架的第一步是选择和确定重点的用户服务。取得共识即可确定功能需求、描述谁提供和谁接受哪项 ITS 服务的操作概念,以及提供方应如何合作以保证服务的提供。

Figure 3.6   Expressway
图 3.6   高速公路

(1) User Needs 用户需求

There are key actors and obvious stakeholder groups organized around domains (such as motorway networks, traffic control for medium-sized cities, and rural areas), and around areas of competence and responsibilities (such as road safety, public transport, fleet logistics, etc.). In addition to the more general objectives of improving safety, efficiency, environmental quality, etc. Following the principles shown in Figure 3.7, each interest group has its own policy goals.

在一些领域(如高速公路网、中等城市和乡村地区的交通控制)和在具有竞争和责任的区域(如道路安全、公共运输、货运物流等)周围聚集了相当重要的参与方和明显的利益相关方。除了提高安全性、效率、环境质量等大目标外,遵循图 3.7 所示原则,每个利益集团都有自己的政策目标。

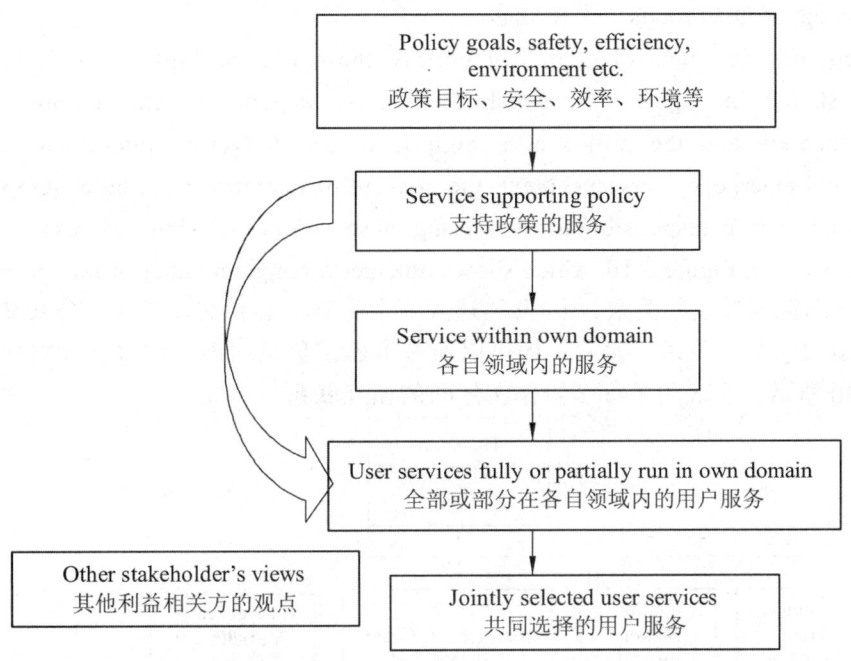

Figure 3.7 Policy implication of ITS service selection

图 3.7 政策影响 ITS 服务的选择

（2）Functional Requirement 功能要求

Once the services have been selected in figure 3.7, the functional requirements for providing these services must be determined. At this point, commonalities between domains may be identified. For example, the highway network operators may be planning to deploy ITS for electronic tolling (International Standard ETC System) and automatic incident detection. This functionality can be adapted to give high-quality traffic and traveler information, with point-to-point journey times.

图 3.7 中的服务一旦确定，提供这些服务的功能需求必须被确定下来。此时可识别出领域间的公共部分，比如高速公路网运营者可能计划实施 ITS 以实现电子收费（国际标准 ETC 电子收费系统）及事故自动检测等。这项功能适应于提供点对点旅行时间的高质量的交通和出行者信息。

Figure 3.8 ETC System

图 3.8 ETC 电子收费系统

（3）Concept of Operations　操作概念

A concept of operations diagram can portray these relationships. As exemplified by the architectural sketch in Figure 3.9, which graphically depicts the interactions among three management centers and the police at a high level for delivering intermodal transportation management and emergency services. Next, the concept of operations can be developed in greater detail to consider who is responsible for delivering these services to whom. An example of such an elaboration is given in Figure 3.10, which shows linkages among a number of interacting entities.

操作概念图能勾勒这些关系，图 3.9 描述了三个管理中心和交通警察在公共交通管理与紧急事件管理领域的交互关系。然后，还可以通过考虑谁负责向谁提供服务以更加细化操作概念，如图 3.10 所示，它表明了许多协作实体间的相互联系。

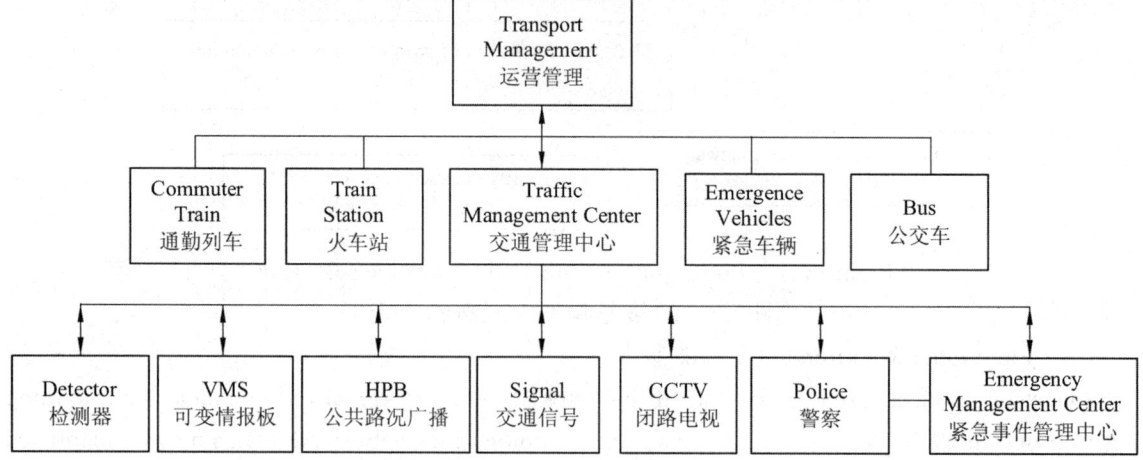

Figure 3.9　Architectural sketch
图 3.9　框架草图

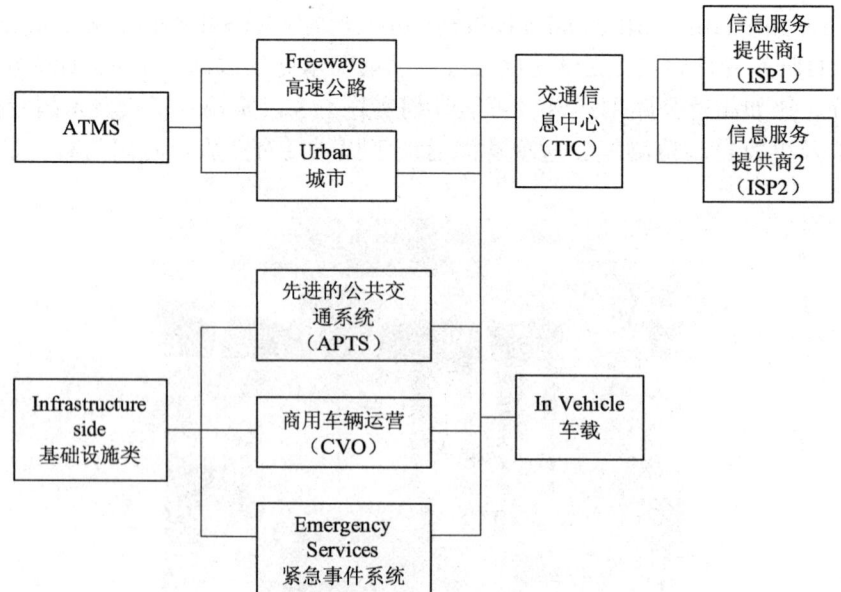

Figure 3.10　Conceptual relationships for ITS service delivery
图 3.10　ITS 服务传输概念关系

3.1.4　Logical or Functional Architecture　逻辑或功能框架

Logical or functional architecture is in the domain of Level 1 in Figure 3.5. The architecture depicts the processes and data flows between processes that are needed to meet the functional requirements previously determined. In developing the logical architecture, the common ground between the various user requirements and ITS services is examined, so that shared functions and common requirements can be grouped within the same set of processes.

逻辑或功能框架属于图 3.5 中第 1 层。该框架描述了为满足已确定了的功能需求所必须的功能模块和模块间的数据流。在逻辑框架的构建过程时，考虑了各种用户需求和 ITS 服务的共性内容，因此共享的功能和共性的需求可组合在同一功能模块集中。

In Figure 3.11, the simplified top-level logical architecture developed for USA is portrayed as a data flowdiagram. The arrows indicate directions of data flow that are needed to perform all the services selected by the national ITS community. The circles represent sets of processes that are broken down into more detail at subsequent lower levels of the logical architecture. At the lowest levels, the circles specify the data processing that is needed; for example, an algorithm for automatic incident detection.

图 3.11 以数据流图的形式给出了简化的美国国家逻辑框架顶层图。箭头表示完成所选定服务所必需的信息流动方向。圆圈表示可在更低逻辑框架层面上进一步细分的功能模块。在最底层面上，圆圈表示必需的数据处理过程，如事故自动检测运算。

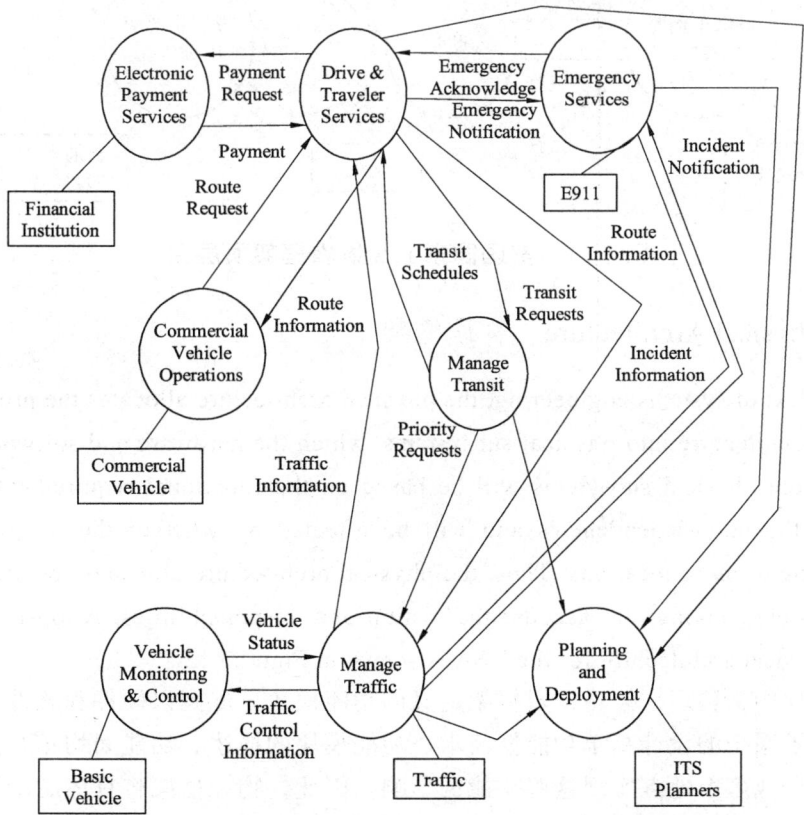

Figure 3.11　Top-level diagram of logical architecture for US ITS

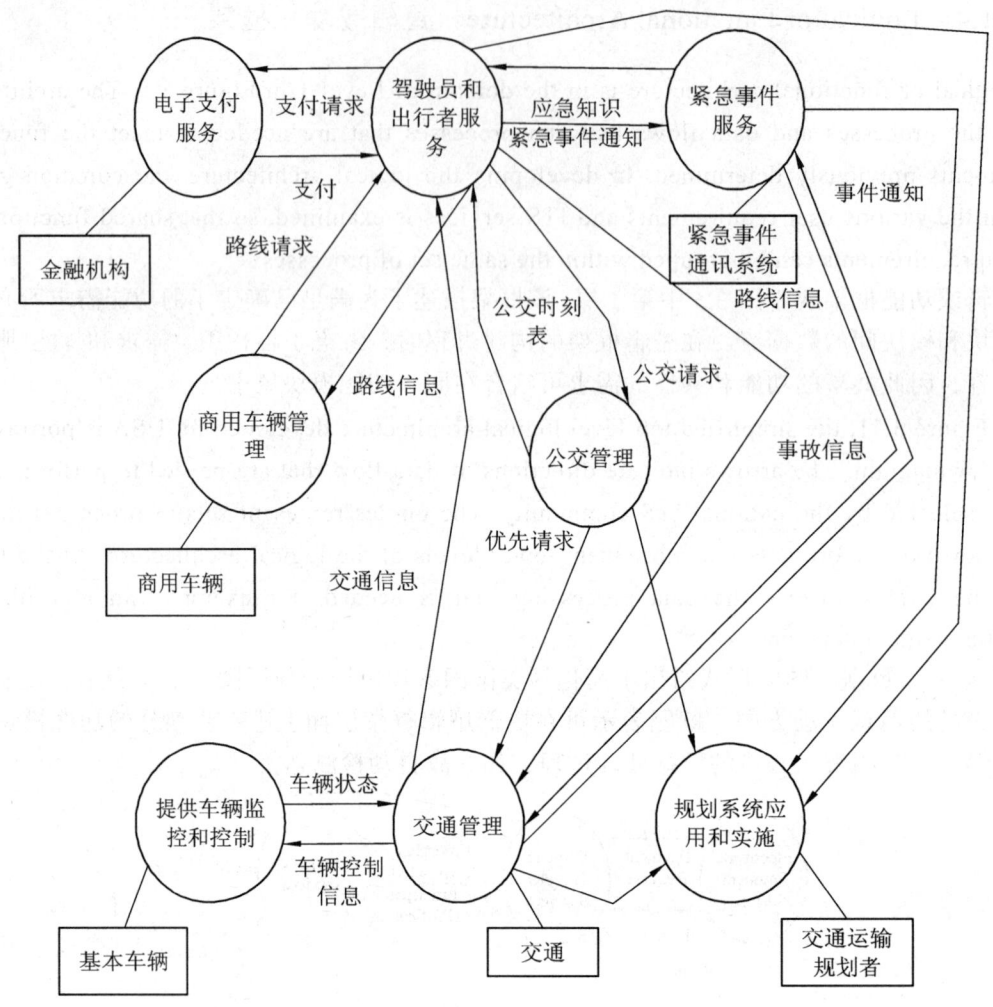

图 3.11　美国国家 ITS 逻辑框架顶层图

3.1.5　Physical Architecture　物理框架

In the context of systems engineering, the physical architecture allocates the processes defined by the logical architecture into physical subsystems, which the hardware and software will deliver. The design of the physical subsytems will be based on the functional requirements, the process specifications, the inter-dependencies and will be affected by whether the functions are to be performed in one or more locations. Thus, the physical architecture allocates specific processes to physical subsystems, taking into account the institutional responsibilities. A top-level diagram of the national physical architecture for the USA is shown in Figure3.12.

在系统工程中，物理框架将逻辑框架定义的功能模块分配到以硬件和软件体现的物理子系统中。物理子系统的设计基于功能性需求、功能模块的描述、功能间均相互依赖关系以及受到是否在一个或多个地点实现这些功能的影响。因此，物理框架将具体的功能模块分配到物理子系统时需要考虑制度因素。图 3.12 给出了美国国家物理框架顶层图。

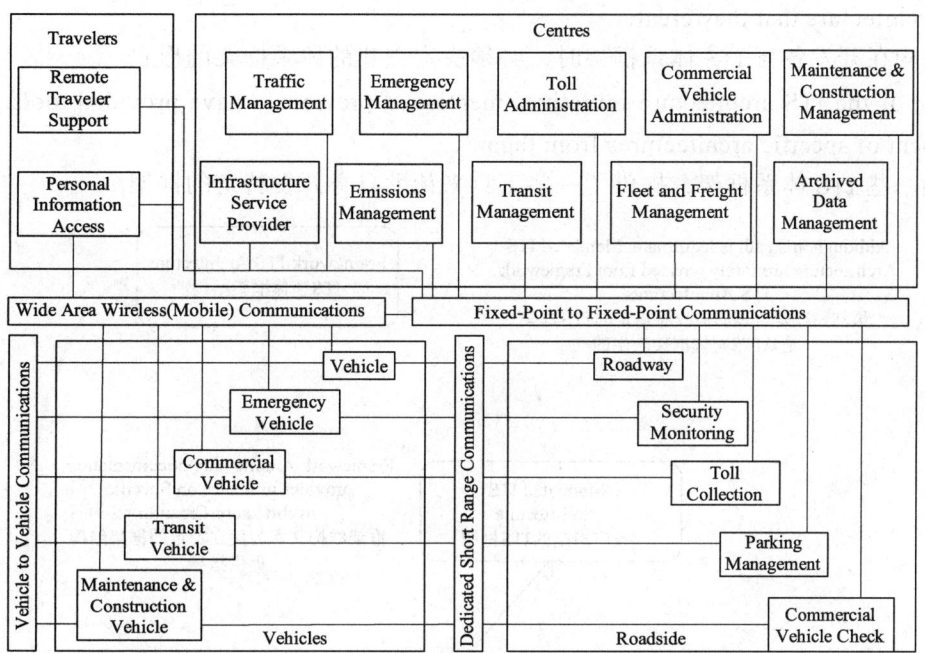

Figure 3.12   Top-level diagram of physical architecture for US ITS

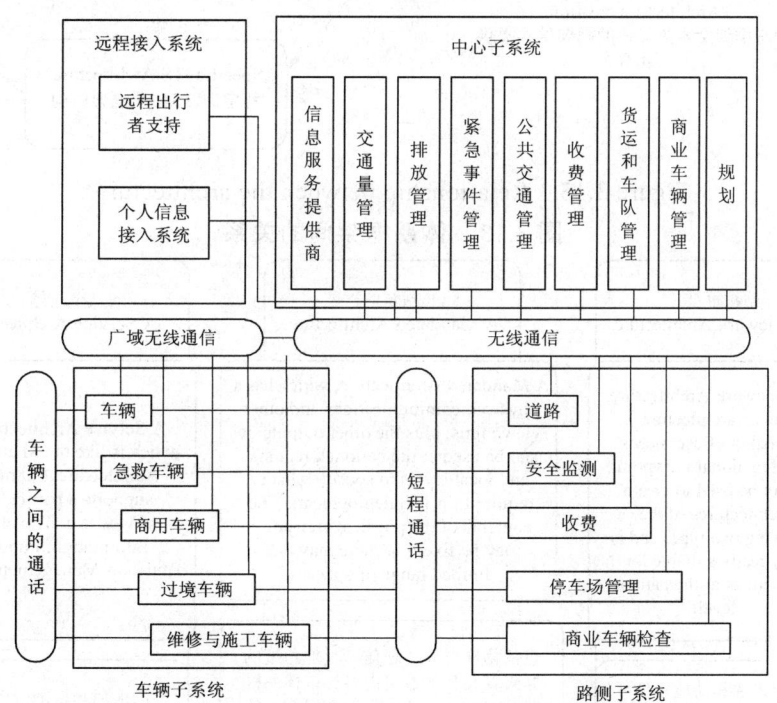

图 3.12   美国国家 ITS 物理框架顶层图

3.1.6   Regional Architecture and Turbo Architecture   区域体系框架和 Turbo 体系框架

When developing their own ITS architecture, organizations have to make decisions about the

121

form of architecture that they create.

各机构在开发各自 ITS 体系框架时，必须决定创建的体系框架的形式。

Some of the ITS architecture initiatives mentioned previously have provided tools to aid the development of specific architectures from them.

上述一些 ITS 体系框架，提供了一些工具来帮助自身开发特定的框架。

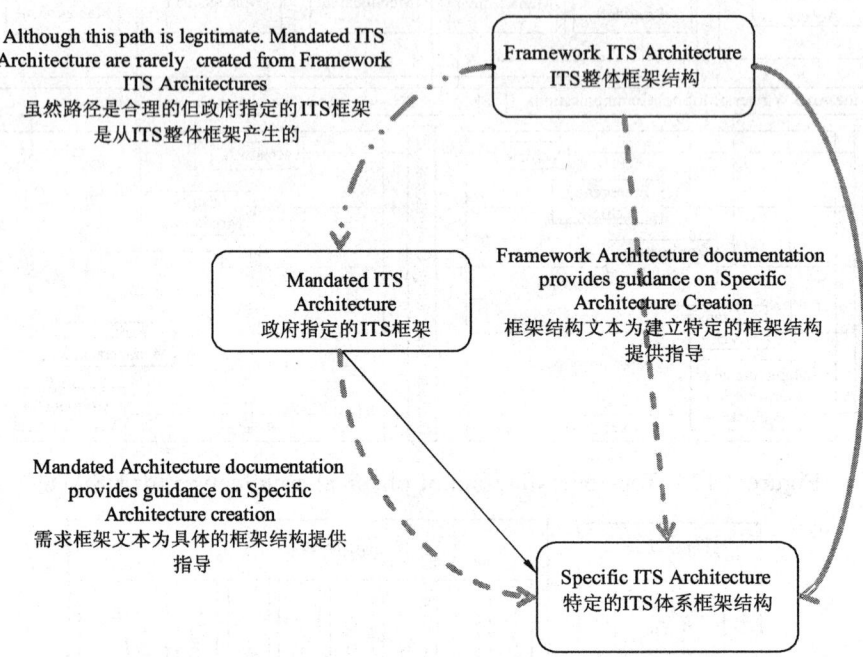

Figure 3.13　Relationship between the architecture

图 3.13　体系框架间的关系

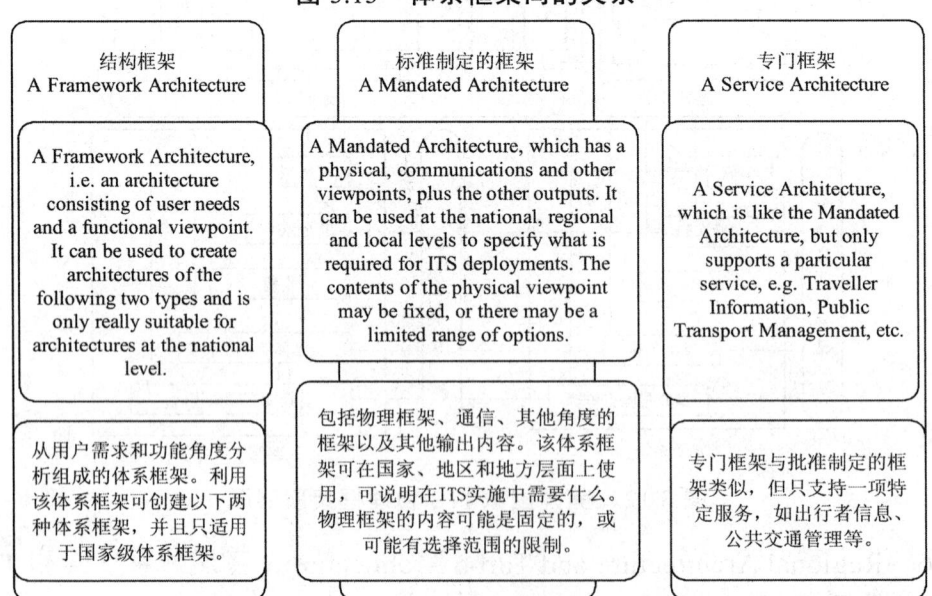

Figure 3.14　Different types of architecture

图 3.14　体系框架图的类别

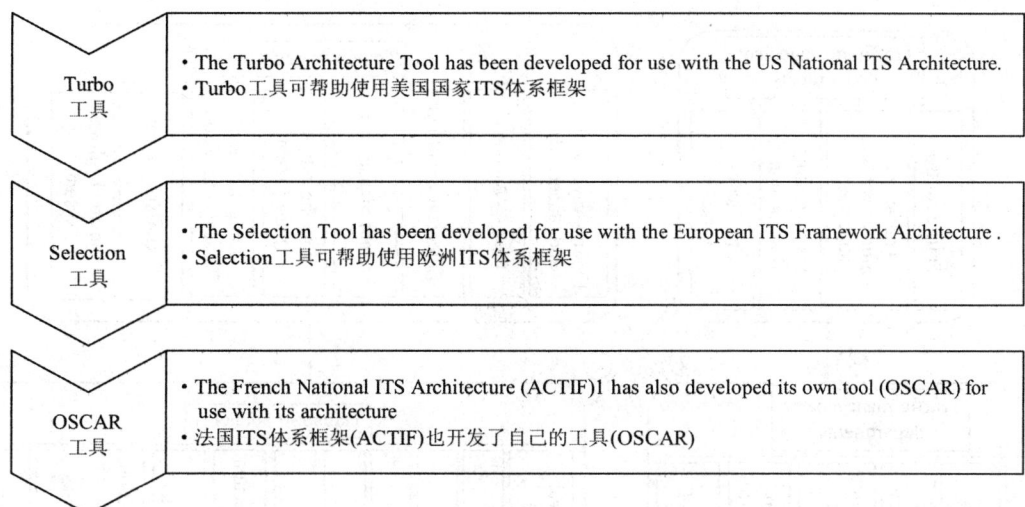

Figure 3.15　Tools are used for the ITS architecture.
图 3.15　用于 ITS 体系框架的工具

3.1.7　China ITS Architecture　我国的 ITS 体系框架

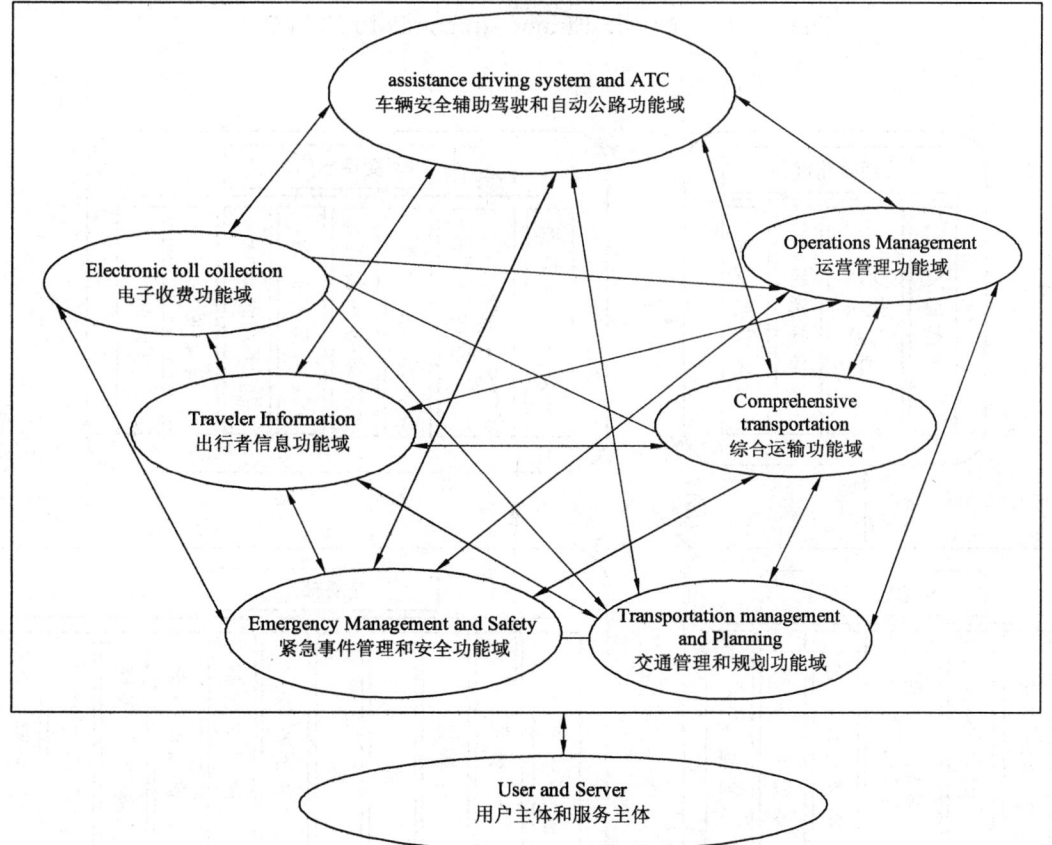

Figure 3.16　Top-level diagram of logical architecture for China ITS
图 3.16　我国国家 ITS 逻辑框架的顶层结构

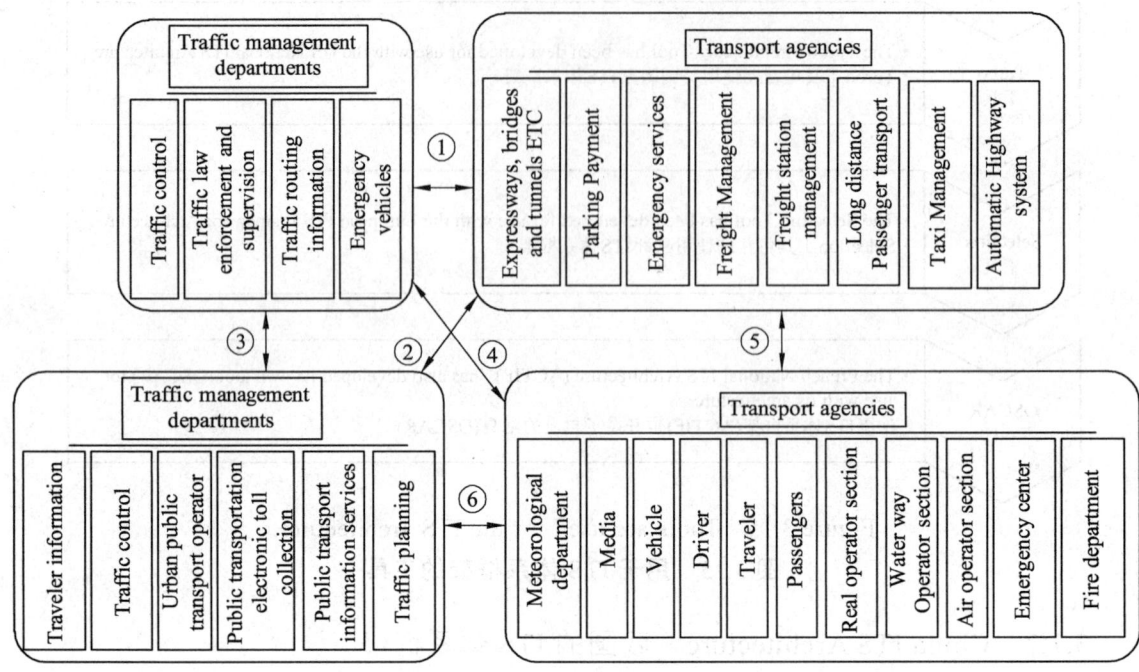

Figure 3.17　Physical frame structure of ITS in China

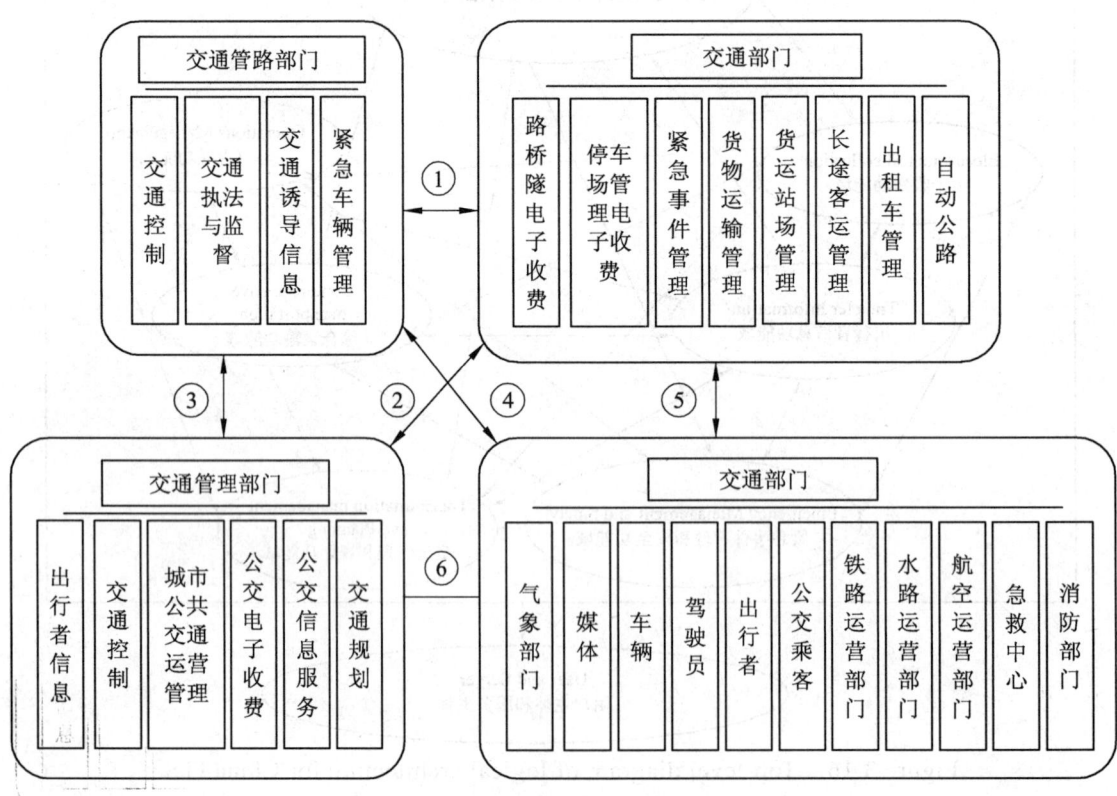

图 3.17　我国国家 ITS 物理框架结构

124

3.2 ITS Standards　ITS 标准

3.2.1 Types of ITS Standards　ITS 标准的类型

(1) Standards are needed in protocols and message sets to allow smooth data flow and information exchange among the subsystems.

协议和信息集需要标准，以保证各子系统间数据和信息的有效传输。

Standard message sets, usually defined in data dictionaries, are also needed to allow meaningful exchange of information between subsystems. For example, for information exchange related to incidents, there need to be standards for coding a certain number of message elements for unambiguous description of the location and the type of incidents. In case wireless communication is needed, the standardization of frequency and modulation technique is also implied.

各子系统间的有效信息传输，也需要标准信息集，通常在数据字典中定义。例如，紧急事件管理相关的信息交互，需要相当规模数量的事件相关信息的编码标准，包括位置的准确描述和事件类型。若需无线通信，还需要频率、调制技术等相关标准。

(2) Some standards may be needed only up to a certain level. For example, for most commercial vehicle operations, international standards may be needed for a given continent but global standards are not needed since lorries do not travel across continents. In contrast, standards for cargo identification should be global in order to facilitate freight identification, security checks, and movement between continents.

有些标准仅需要达到一定范围即可。比如，对众多商用车辆运营商而言，仅需要在特定的范围内制定标准，而不需在全球范围内制定，因为货车不会在各洲间行驶。相反，货物识别标准应在全球范围内制定，以促进货物辨识、安全检查以及各洲间的货物移动。

(3) Everyone follows the standards set by the dominant supplier, or consensus standards, which are arrived through procedures established by standard setting organizations. Standards may also be set by the government, usually as a last resort.

每个人所遵守的标准可由占市场主导地位的供应商制定，或是标准制定组织通过一定程序建立并得到一致认可的标准。标准也可由政府制定，但通常是不得已而采取的办法。

3.2.2 Motivation for Standards　制定标准的动机

Motivation behind standard setting includes safety, cost reduction, and market enhancement.

制定标准的动机包括保障安全、节约成本、扩大市场等。

From the perspective of suppliers, existence of common standards would lead to economy of scale in production and scale of the same equipment in a wider market. Companies in dominant market positions are reluctant to move away from the de facto standards of their own products, except perhaps in anticipation of a much larger market for everyone that would result from the establishment of new consensus standards.

从供应商的角度来说，现存的通用标准可使得产品规模效益和产品销售市场均有所扩大。在市场上占有主导地位的公司，不愿意抛弃他们自己产品的已有标准，除非一个统一的新标准的制定对每个人都意味着将拥有更大的市场。

From the perspective of the users, both public and private, there are two major motives in developing and adopting voluntary standards:

从使用者角度来说，不管是公共团体或私人，愿意开发和采用标准的动机主要有两个：

> Firstly, With established standards for ITS products and serxfces. the users can make their purchasing options from a range of competitive proxSders and do not get locked into a single one.
> 第一：随着ITS产品与服务标准的制定，用户可在具有一定竞争的供应商之间选择产品，而不局限于单一的供应商。

> Secondly, ITS standards support interoperability as well as system mtegation
> 第二：ITS标准支持互操作性以及系统集成

Figure 3.18　Two major motives of users in developing and adopting voluntary standards

图 3.18　用户开发和采用标准的两个主要动机

3.2.3　Current Status　现状

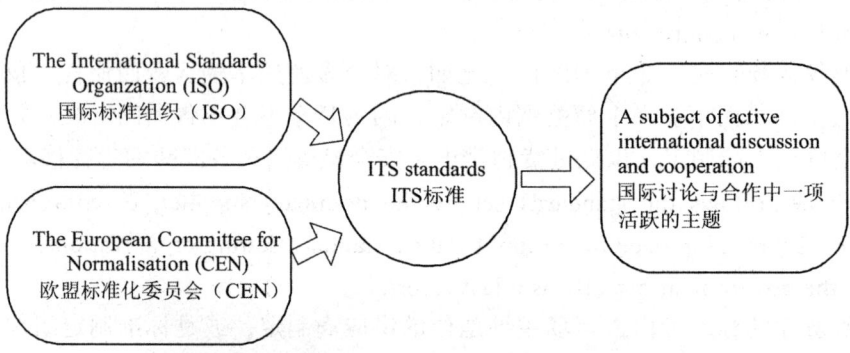

Figure 3.19　Current status of ITS standard

图 3.19　ITS 标准的现状

Particular interest to the traffic authorities are the National Transportation Communications ITS Protocol (NTCIP) in the US (Figure 3.22), these sets of standards are intended to facilitate data transfer between centers and roadside equipment as well as between control centers.

就交通部门而言，他们感兴趣的是美国国家 ITS 交通通信协议（NTCIP），如图 3.22 所示，这些标准集的目标是促进中心与路侧设备间以及控制中心间的信息传输。

ITS standards programmers around the world have matured from primarily development activities to deployment and support activities. Many industrialized countries have also been engaged in coordinating their own ITS standards with international standardization activities.

全世界的 ITS 标准项目逐渐走向成熟，从最初的开发活动到实施和支持各种活动。许多工业化国家已经着手于对本国 ITS 标准与国际标准化行动的协调。

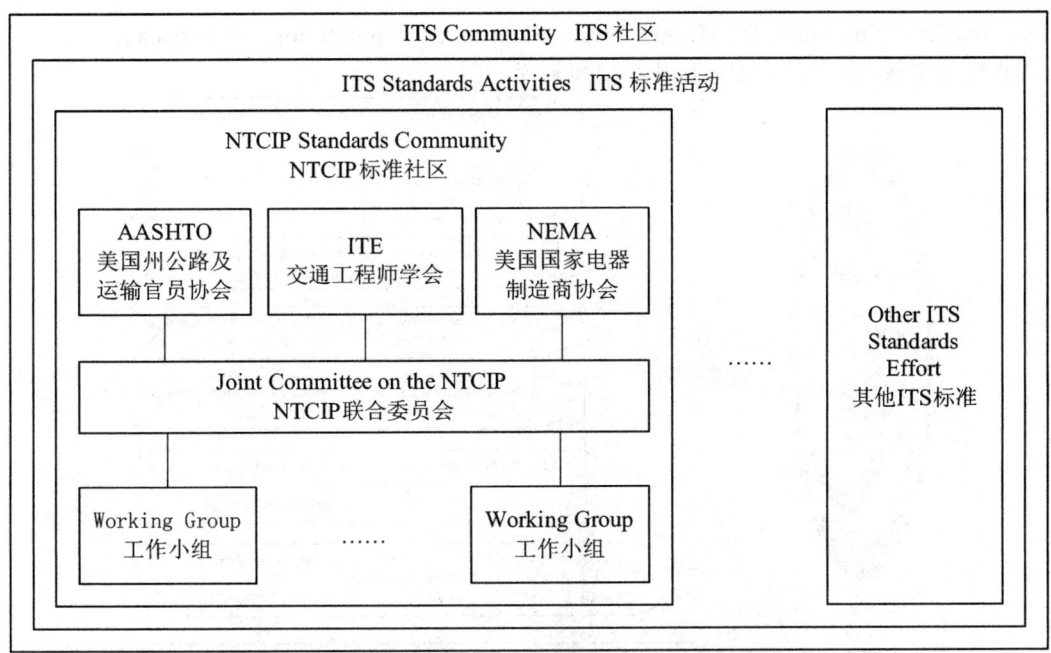

Figure 3.20 National Transportation Communications ITS Protocol for US
图 3.20 美国国家 ITS 交通通信协议（NTCIP）

For the rapidly developing field of ITS, the timing of standard setting is important. Even after standards are established, practical considerations must be given to acceptable migration paths for existing systems to move toward the new standards over a reasonable period of time.

对于发展迅速的 ITS 领域，制定标准的时点比较重要。即使在标准制定以后，还需要就一定合理时间内现有系统向新标准转化的可接受途径给予实际的考虑。

3.2.4 Planning for ITS Standards Application ITS 标准应用规划

What problems will be shown when planning for ITS standards adoption and application?
编制 ITS 标准的采用和应用规划会出现什么问题？

How do I start ITS deployment when different vendors offer products of different standards, none of which have been widely adopted? 当有众多不同的提供商提供不同标准的产品，却没有任何一个产品被广泛接受的时候，我们应该如何开展ITS应用？	A number of important ITS standards are, and will probably continue to be, uncertain moving targets？ 一些重要的ITS标准是否会存在下去仍是不确定的目标？
If so, do I miss out on the benefits of early ITS applications that are badly needed? 如果推迟ITS应用计划，那么是否会错过ITS早期应用所带来的效益？	Should I postpone ITS deployment indefinitely until consensus standards are firmly established? 是否应该推迟ITS应用计划直到制定了统一的、严格的标准？

Figure 3.21 Problems in planning for ITS standards adoption and application
图 3.21 编制 ITS 标准的采用和应用规划会出现的问题

This makes the planning for ITS standards adoption and application rather tricky.
这使得 ITS 标准的采用和应用规划相当棘手。

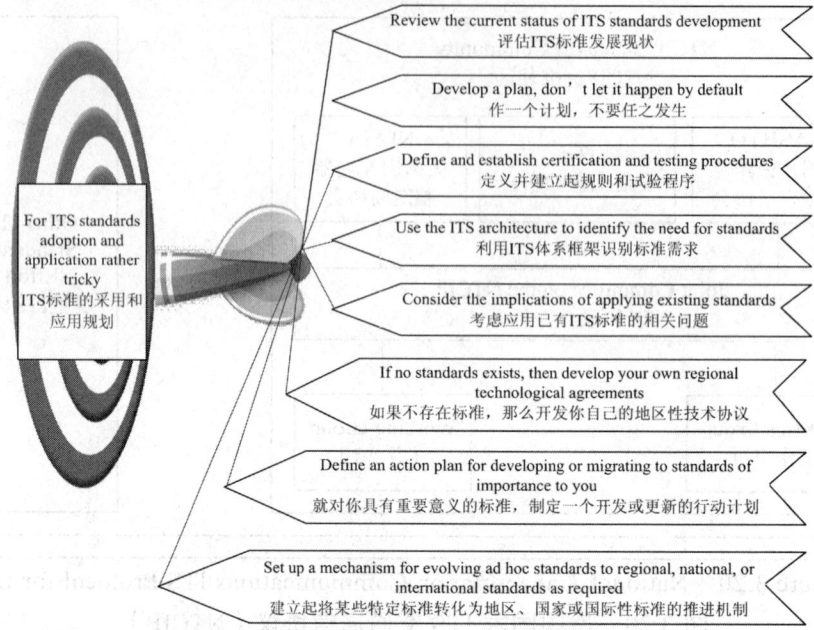

Figure 3.22　Suggestions on planning for ITS standards adoption and application
图 3.22　编制 ITS 标准的采用和应用规划时的建议

3.3　Conclusions　结论

ITS system architectures are being developed to fit all the ITS components into a systematic framework so that they will work in concert with one another to deliver the needed user services.	A specific architecture may be expressed in multiple forms. It is important that the decision makers should understand and endorse the concepts and functions that inform the development of ITS operations and organizational architectures. The systems engineers, for their part, need to work with the logical, physical, and communication architectures.	Based on system architecture, ITS standards are developed to ensure that all the hardware and software do fit together and can work in concert to deliver ITS user services. As new ITS standard will evolve continually with technology development, transportation professional can develop ITS effectively as long as they have a proactive strategy to deal with new standards.
ITS系统框架是把ITS各组成部分配合形成一个整体架构，以保证各部分相互协作来提供所需的用户服务。	一个详细的体系框架可以用多种形式来描述。对于决策者来说，理解和认可ITS操作和组织结构框架是非常重要的。对于系统工程师来说，他们应该在逻辑、物理和通信框架下开展工作。	基于系统框架，ITS标准保证所有的硬件和软件可配合工作，以提供各项用户服务。随着技术发展，ITS标准不断更新，只要交通专家用前瞻的战略去处理新标准，他们就可高效地推进ITS实施。

Figure 3.23　Conclusion on ITS architectures
图 3.23　关于 ITS 系统框架的结论

Chapter 4   What are the Benefits of ITS
第四章   ITS 的效益是什么

4.1　Who Benefits from ITS　谁能从 ITS 中获益

4.1.1　Road Users and Other Travelers　道路使用者和其他出行者

In the first instance, those who benefit from ITS are the road users and other travelers (often referred to as end-users).

首先，能够从 ITS 中获益的是道路使用者和其他出行者（通常称为终端用户）。

(1) Car users, truck drivers and delivery vehicles can all gain from ITS. For example, through greater safety, more certainty in their journeys, shorter journey times, more direct routes and easier access to parking.

小轿车用户、载货汽车驾驶员都能够从 ITS 中获益。例如，更加安全、增加行程的确定性、缩短行程时间、更直接的路线和更容易实现停车。

(2) Public transit users can have shorter journey times and rely on better information.

公共交通用户依赖于更可靠的信息能够获得更短的行程时间。

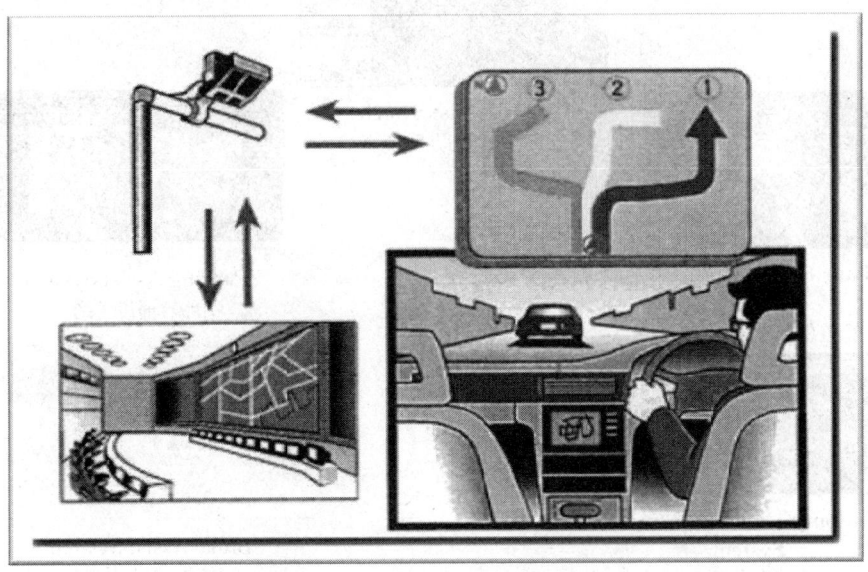

Figure 4.1　Travel route optimization
图 4.1　行程路线优化图

> **例** **Turin's 5T 都灵的5T**
>
> Turin's 5T (Telematic Technologies for Traffic and Transport in Turin) integrates nine ITS subsystems (including traffic control, traveler information, public transport management and parking management) under the Traffic and Transport Supervisor. Benefits come from shared communications, data exchange and close integration of functions.
> 在"交通与运输监视者"系统下,都灵的5T(都灵用于交通和运输的远程控制(Telematic)技术)集成了9个ITS子系统(包括交通控制、出行者信息服务、公共交通管理和停车管理),效益来自于共享通信、数据交换和功能的紧密集成。

(3) Some advantages of ITS come at a perceived cost to the user. There can be a trade-off. ITS 的一些优势也会让用户付出代价。用户需要做出权衡。

For example, safety, security and journey time predictability may come from tracking the location of the vehicle or controlling the driver's speed. Some will perceive this as an invasion of privacy, or unnecessary interference with the driver's control. Similar issues of perception come with in-car ITS. Driver aids can make driving safer for older people.

例如,安全、安保和旅行时间的可预测性可能来自于对车辆跟踪定位或控制驾驶员车速,有人会认为这侵犯隐私权或造成不必要的干扰。类似的问题也会发生在车载 ITS 上。驾驶员辅助系统可以使老年人安全的驾驶。

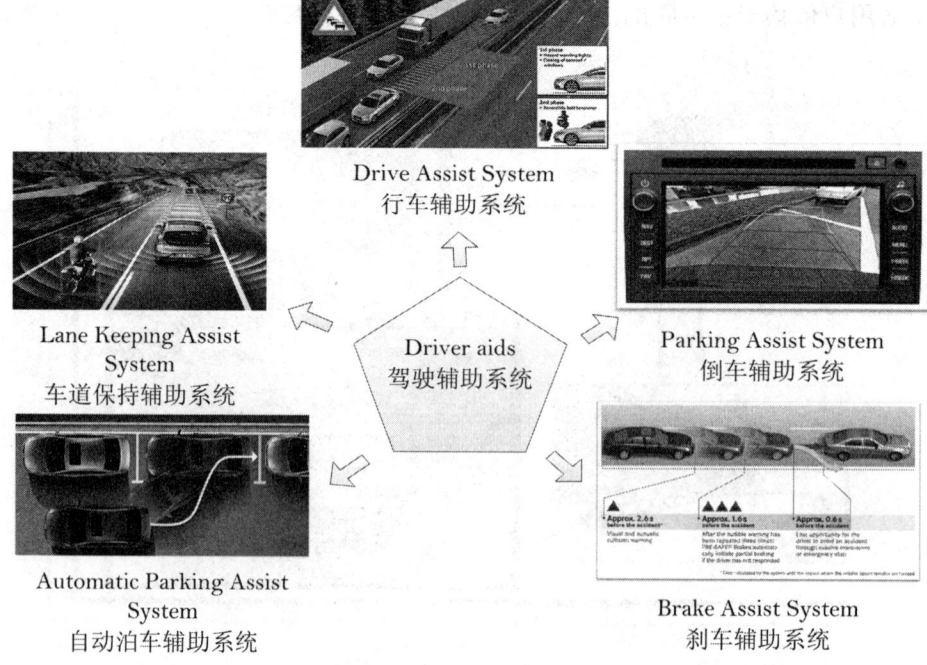

Figure 4.2 Driver aids system
图 4.2 驾驶辅助系统

(4) Pedestrians and other vulnerable road users can experience greater safety and a balancing of traffic priorities in their favor.

行人和其他弱势道路使用者能够感到更安全以及他们喜欢的各种优先通行的平衡。

(5) ITS can help in preventing incidents and delivering a faster recovery when things go wrong. ITS can bring benefits for emergency services and other agencies in their work to serve the needs of the travelling public.

ITS 能够帮助预防事件的发生，以及在事故发生后实现快速恢复。ITS 也可以给紧急事件服务和为出行的公众提供服务的其他部门带来效益。

4.1.2　Transport Professionals　交通专业人员

ITS can enable them to do a better job. An investment in ITS can help them to deliver safer and more reliable journeys, reducing the detrimental effect on the environment, giving priority to freight transport, commuter traffic, transit or pedestrians, whatever is the key market segment even the key market segment at a given time of day.

ITS 能使交通专业人员完成更出色的工作。不管是否有重要的市场区分，甚至在一天给定时间上的市场区分，投资 ITS 能够帮助他们实现更加安全和可靠的旅行，减少对环境的不利影响，赋予货物运输、通勤交通、公共交通或行人优先权。

ITS can help deliver many of the transport objectives set by planners, managers and politicians.

ITS 可以帮助实现许多规划人员、管理者和政治家设定的交通目标。

To restrain traffic, then ITS can give information to travelers about alternative modes and can help block access to key areas and collect the charges for access and the penalties for breaking the rules.

要限制交通，ITS 可以向出行者发布关于可选择的交通方式信息，以及可以帮助关闭进入重要地区的通道和收取通行费用，并对违反规则的行为罚款。

Figure 4.3　Electronic police
图 4.3　电子警察

4.1.3　Local Residents and Enterprises　当地居民和企业

(1) Local Residents　当地居民

ITS can deliver access control schemes, parking management, lorry routes and road user charges, all with substantial impacts. Streets may be quieter and safer, and in residential areas children may be able to play more safely. There may be reduced noise and emissions due to smoother traffic flows.

ITS 能够实现驶入控制方案、停车管理、货运路线和道路使用者收费，所有这些都有着重要的影响。街道变得更加安静和安全，居民区孩子们能够安全地玩耍。由于平滑了交通流，可以减少噪声和排放。

Figure 4.4　Parking management system

图 4.4　停车管理系统

(2) Local Enterprises　当地企业

Local enterprises can benefit from ITS providing more reliable deliveries and more reliable journey times for goods being dispatched. Local shops can benefit from ITS helping provide a better environment for visitors and shoppers.

当地企业能够从 ITS 中获益，是因为智能交通可以为配送的商品提供更加可靠的运送条件和行程时间。当地商店能够从 ITS 中获益，是因为 ITS 可以为游客和购物者提供更好的环境。

4.2　What are Specific Benefits　ITS 的效益是什么

4.2.1　Problems of Quantification　量化的问题

The benefits of ITS are varied and not always directly calculable. Real time information systems on public transport, for example, are often introduced at the same time as priority measures which make the service faster and more reliable, and often with new or refurbished vehicles. It can be difficult to separate the causes of the perception of improved service and the increase in patronage. In the opposite case, real time information on public transport may have no effect on patronage.

ITS 的效益变化范围很大，而且通常难以直接计算。公共交通上的实时信息系统通常与新车同时引入作为优先措施来提供更快和更加可靠的服务。因此很难将改进服务和增加优惠的感觉的原因分开。相反的情况，公共交通上的实时信息系统可能对优惠没有影响。

Figure 4.5 Beijing real-time bus APP
图 4.5 北京实时公交 APP

It is useful to consider both the aggregate and disaggregate benefits. Some benefits are in specific goal areas, such as safety. Others will be for specific groups of people, such as the rising population of mobile elderly and disabled people.

同时考虑整体和非整体的效益是非常有用的。一些效益是具体应用的目的领域，如安全性，其他效益则是针对具体的人群组成，如比例不断增加的老年人和残疾人。

4.2.2 Safety Benefits 安全效益

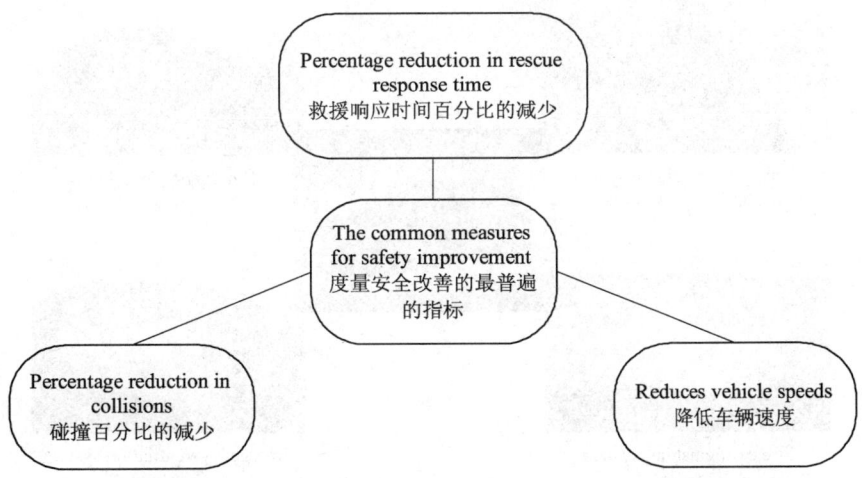

Figure 4.6 Common measures for safety improvement
图 4.6 度量安全改善的常见指标

(1) Percentage reduction in rescue response time 救援响应时间百分比的减少

The measure of percent reduction in rescue response time is not a direct indication of safety but is amenable to direct measurement in an operational test. Reduction in rescue response time would reduce the number of fatalities and the extent of injuries after an accident.

救援响应时间百分比减少并不是安全性的直接指标，但在运营测试中可处理为直接指标。减少救援响应时间可以减少事件后死亡人员的数量和受伤的范围。

The perception of personal safety is also important. The confidence that travel is safe does not come only from reducing accidents or collisions and their consequences. Many countries now have policy priorities relating to perceptions of personal safety.

个人安全的感知也是非常重要的，"出行是安全"的这种信心不仅仅来自于减少事故或碰撞以及它们的后果。许多国家已经有了关于个人安全感知的政策。

> **例** **HELP system　HELP系统**
>
> In Tokyo tests of the HELP system which sends location data from the vehicle to a control center in the event of an accident (e.g. if the airbag is activated), found that information from the in-vehicle system was received in the control center within 59 seconds on average, compared with 101 seconds from a mobile phone.
>
> HELP系统将车辆位置信息发送给控制中心，在东京HELP系统的测试发现，控制中心从车载系统接受到信息的平均用时在59s以内，与其对比的是移动电话为101s。

(2) Percentage reduction in collisions　碰撞百分比的减少

The measure of percent reduction in collisions is a direct indication of safety but difficult to obtain empirically from operational tests since real accidents are infrequent. Safety benefits of intelligent vehicles, cooperative vehicle-highway systems (CVHS), and active safety systems can be measured indirectly from test results on proving grounds away from public roads.

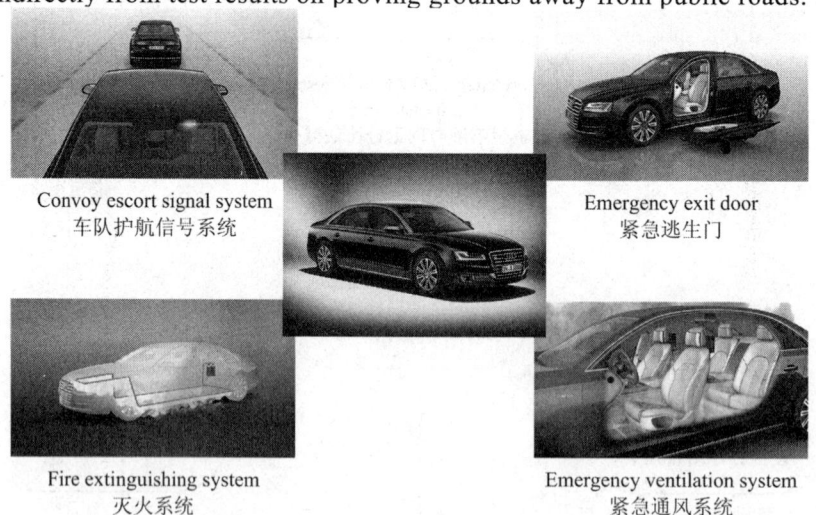

Figure 4.7　Intelligent vehicle
图 4.7　智能车辆

碰撞百分比的减少是安全的直接指标，但是由于实际中事故是偶发性的，因此很难从实际的运营测试中获取。智能车辆、车路协同系统（CVHS）和主动安全系统的安全效益可以间接从远离公共道路的测试结果中获得。

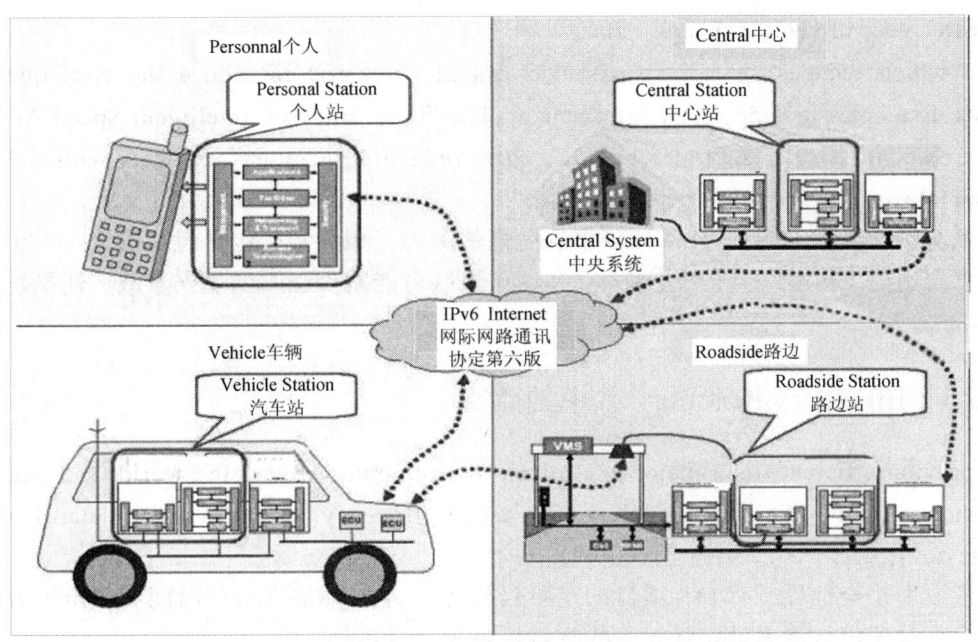

Figure 4.8　Cooperative vehicle-highway systems in European
图 4.8　欧洲车-路协同系统

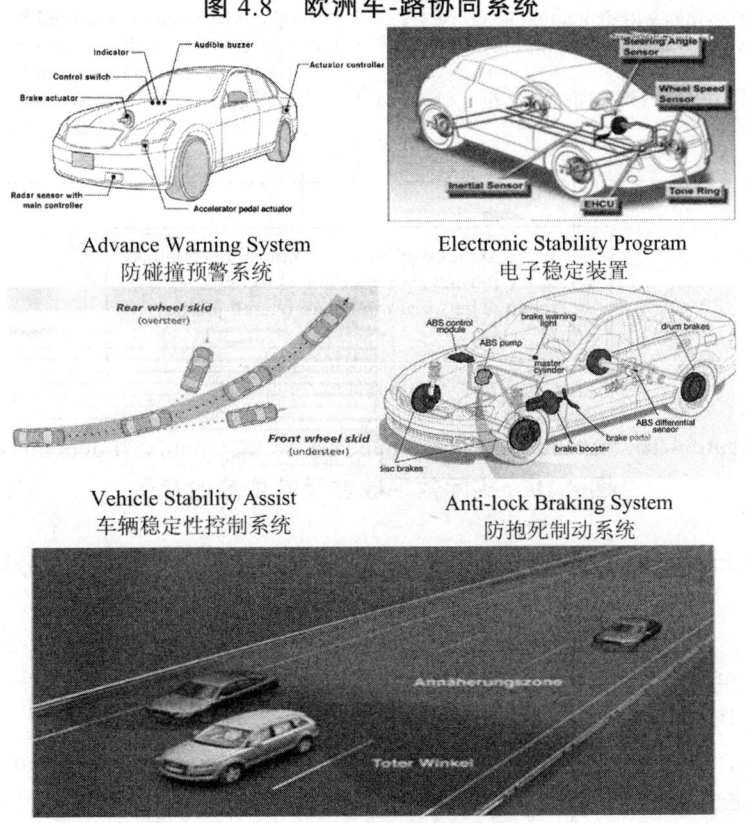

Figure 4.9　Active safety systems
图 4.9　主动安全系统

135

(3) Decrease of vehicle speeds　降低车辆速度

ITS which reduces vehicle speeds also has the potential to reduce the consequences of accidents. Examples include speed enforcement. The "Case Study on Intelligent Speed Adaptation (ISA) in Sweden" shows the potential for a 20% reduction in injury accidents with a 3%～4% reduction in average speeds in urban areas.

降低车辆速度的 ITS 也具备减轻事故后果的潜力，相关例子包括超速执法。关于瑞典智能化速度自适应（ISA）的研究表明，它在城市地区可能减少 20%的受伤事故，使平均速度降低 3%～4%。

4.2.3　Efficiency Benefits　效率的效益

Improving efficiency is a major goal of all ITS programs around the world. ITS can deliver efficiencies in journey time and certainty. The actual efficiency benefit to the traveler depends on the context.

改善效率是全世界所有 ITS 项目的主要目的之一。ITS 能够在行程时间和确定性方面实现效率提升，对于出行者来说实际效率的收益依赖于背景条件。

> Travel time savings will depend on levels of congestion and available opportunities for diversion.
> 旅行时间的节省将依赖于拥挤水平和可利用的转移机会。

> Improved vehicle control systems will increase throughput by reducing required headway. They will also reduce the number of collisions, thus further increasing throughput.
> 改进的车辆控制系统可以通过减少车头间距提高通行能力，它们也能减少碰撞的数量而进一步提高通过量。

> There are great benefits from improving certainty about the journey, whether that is routing, interchange between modes, or overall journey time.
> 从改善确定性中可以获得很多效益，无论是路线、交通模式间换乘或整个出行时间。

Figure 4.10　Actual efficiency benefit and the context it depends on

图 4.10　实际效率收益及其依赖的背景

4.2.4　Productivity and Cost Reduction Benefit　生产率和节省成本的效益

（1）Highways Management　公路管理

There are significant supply-side benefits of ITS in highways management.

在公路管理中，ITS 给供给方带来显著效益。

In Barcelona, the introduction of two lane management systems successfully increased the capacity of the road network, managing variations in demand at different times of day: a reversible flow lane and a shared lane for deliveries and traffic.

在巴塞罗那，两个车道管理系统的引入成功地提高了道路网的通行能力。这两个系统管理着在一天不同的时段内需求的变化：一个可逆车道以及一个用于送货和通行的共用车道。

> **例**   Highways management in Barcelona 巴塞罗那公路管理
>
> Barcelona has implemented various ITS-based services to manage the demand for travel in sensitive areas of the city since the early 1990s. These include a smart-card based access control system in the historic La Ribera zone, a tidal flow system and lane sharing for deliveries and traffic.
>
> Car-owners living within the area controlled by the access control system obtain an electronic permit in the form of a smartcard, to enter the zone. The smartcards are read at entry points to the zone and if validated, a retractable bollard is lowered automatically to allow entry to the zone. Other vehicles can obtain time-limited permits for access, for the time required.
>
> 20世纪90年代初期,巴塞罗那就开展了多种ITS服务来管理薄弱区域的交通出行需求。这些管理措施包括:在LaRibera古城区内安装基于智能卡的进出口控制系统、潮汐交通系统和交通运输的车道分配。
>
> 进出口控制系统辖区内的有车居民可以获得一张智能卡式电子特许证。当车辆进入该辖区的进口,系统会自动阅读电子卡。如果电子卡是有效的,那么障碍物会自动下降,允许车辆进入该辖区。其他车辆也拥有通行权利,但受到时间限制。

In the UK, the enforced variable speed limit and reduction in lane switching on the M25 "controlled motorway" has successfully improved the capacity of the motorway without increasing the number of traffic lanes.

在英国,在"受控制的高速公路"M25上的强制性可变速度限制和变换车道的减少在没有增加车道数的条件下成功地改善了高速公路的通行能力。

Figure 4.11   Ramp metering (UK Highways Agency)
图 4.11   匝道控制(英国高速公路控制机构)

(2) Cost Reduction   节约成本

While cost reduction is of interest to all road users, the associated benefits are most tangible to the operators of vehicle fleets and highway infrastructures. ITS productivity benefits have been assessed from the perspectives of fleet managers, transit authorities, and toll agencies.

虽然节约成本是所有道路使用者感兴趣的,但对于车队和公路基础设施的运营者来说,与成本相关的效益是最实际的。ITS生产率的效益是从车队管理者、公交负责人和收费部门的角度进行评估的。

> **例** **Real-Time Bus Information in Rural Gwynedd-Wals**
> **威尔士格温内思郡实时公交信息**
>
> Sponsored by the Welsh Assembly, Amserol ("timely" in Welsh) was launched in December 2002. It provides real-time information via onstreet displays at bus stops and on vehicles with scrolling displays. The information can also be accessed through the internet.
>
> The EU ARTS Project enables residents of most rural areas of Gwynedd to access Real-Time Information prior to setting out on their journey, simply by calling an enquiry number from their home telephone. Mobile telephone users can also receive similar information either prior to or during their journey, via an SMS message sent to them on request. The demonstration focuses on two local bus routes which operate daily and provide travel to work journeys and journeys for other local functions. "Amserol" is part of an integrated package of measures aiming to improve the experience of bus travel for people in rural areas of Gwynedd.
>
> 威尔士议会资助的AmseroL项目于2002年12月启动。该项目通过公交车站沿街显示屏和车内滚动屏,为公众提供实时服务信息。这些服务信息也可以通过因特网获得。
>
> 英国ARTS项目使Gwynedd乡村居民只需拨打咨询电话,就能够在出行前获得实时服务信息。当然,手机用户发送SMS请求,就能在出行前和途中接收类似的服务信息。在途经主要集散地的2条公交线上进行示范。Amserol项目旨在改善Gwynedd乡村居民的公交出行。

In freight transport, there are two separate streams of benefits available from ITS. The first is internal, improving the flow of supply chains through information and communication technologies ranging from control systems to vehicle and load monitoring. ITS can facilitate back-loads, port and customs preclearance and communications with the customer about the progress of the shipment. ITS can also monitor drivers' hours, alertness and driving performance.

在货物运输中,有两个单独的效益流可以从 ITS 获得。首先是内部的,通过从车辆控制系统到装载监视范围内的信息和通信技术而改进供应链的流。智能交通系统能够有助于装载、港口和海关的人员预清关,与顾客交流装船的进程。ITS 也能监视驾驶员的驾驶时间、机警程度和驾驶技能。

In Cologne, a series of services to support freight supply chain management, including multi-modal information service, electronic data interchange and smartcard pre-clearance improved business efficiency for 60% of the SME haulage companies involved, through time savings and faster handling of consignments.

在科隆,一系列服务支持货运供应链的管理,包括多模式信息服务、电子数据交换和智能卡预清关,通过节省时间和更快的托运处理,有 60%的 SME 货运公司提高了效率。

4.2.5 Environmental Benefits 环境效益

(1) ITS can help reduce emissions by smoothing traffic flows
ITS 可以通过平滑交通流等手段帮助减少有害气体排放

In most situations, local analysis and simulation are needed to estimate environmental benefits from a given project. It is difficult to measure air quality impacts on an entire region because of the large number of exogenous variables including weather, contributions from non-mobile sources, and the time-evolving nature of ozone pollution.

大部分情况下，需要当地的分析和仿真来估算给定项目的环境效益。由于大量的外部变量的存在，如天气、非机动车源的参与和臭氧污染时间变化特性，使得量化整个区域空气质量的影响非常困难。

Noise and vibration can be an issue, for example, when traffic control systems relocate traffic queues as part of a queue management strategy. Visual intrusion can be a problem where overhead gantry signs are required. In all these cases attention to the detail of location and design is required. Ozone message on VMS (Texas) is shown in figure 4.12.

当交通控制系统将重新配置交通排队作为一项排队管理策略时，噪声和振动也是一个问题。需要龙门架标志的地方，视觉干扰就成为了一个问题。在所有的情况中，需要对位置和设计的细节给予注意。图 4.12 是美国德克萨斯州用于环境显示的可变情况板。

Figure 4.12 Ozone message on VMS (Texas)

图 4.12 可变情况板上的环境信息（德克萨斯州）

（2）Environmental zones can be managed and monitored through ITS

环境区域可以通过 ITS 进行管理和监视

ITS can be used for signing the zone, especially if different regulations apply at different times. ITS can be used in air quality monitoring and in communicating air quality results to residents.

ITS 可以用于指示环境区域，尤其可以将不同的规则应用在不同的时间。ITS 能够用于空气质量监测，并将空气质量结果传达给居民。

A good example of this is in Queensland, Australia, where the South East Queensland Air Quality model uses GIS not only to map current air quality but to forecast the air quality implications of land use and transport planning decisions.

一个很好的例子就是澳大利亚的昆士兰州，昆士兰州东南部的空气质量模型应用于 GIS，不仅可以绘制当地的空气质量地图，而且可以预测空气质量与土地利用的冲突以及交通规划决策。

4.2.6　Benefits to People with Mobility Difficulties　对行动不便的人的效益

ITS can have significant benefits for people with mobility difficulties, for example, by improving access to public transport and making driving easier and safer. Information can be provided in many formats: sound for travelers whose sight is impaired and text for travelers whose hearing is impaired.

ITS 为行动不便的人带来重大的效益，比如在改善公共交通的可达性以及使驾驶更加容易和安全等方面。信息可以通过多种方式提供，比如给视力有问题的人提供声音，给听力有问题的人提供文本信息。

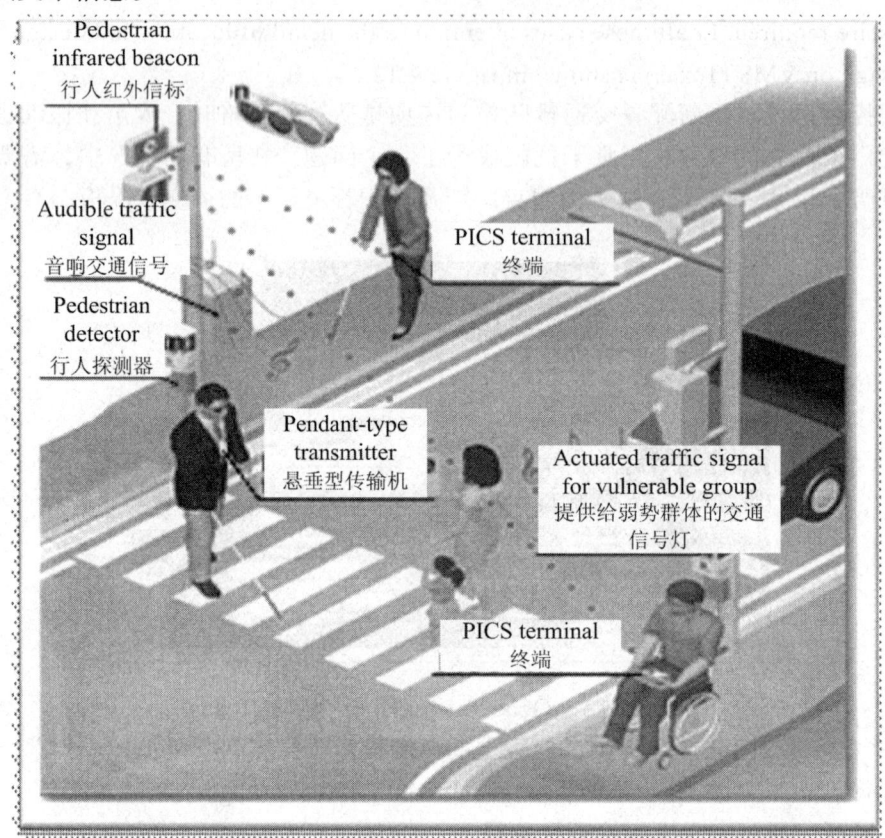

Figure 4.13 Working principle of blind pedestrian crossing system
图 4.13 盲人过街系统工作原理

An ITS application specifically designed to help visually impaired people has been developed in Japan. It is a navigation aid for pedestrians which uses dedicated infra red beacons for communications with a personal receiver. Voice instructions are transmitted by the beacons to help the user navigate on foot, and follow sometimes complex pedestrian routes.

日本发明了一种专门用来帮助视障人士的 ITS 工具。它为行人提供导航辅助，这种工具使用了专用的红外信标与个人接收器进行沟通。通过信标传输的声音指令用来帮助用户步行和跟随复杂的行人路线。

4.2.7　Benefits to Local Communities　对当地社会群体的效益

One of the significant beneficiaries of ITS is the community.

ITS 一个重要的受益群体是社会团体。

（1）Better freight management　更好的货运管理

The residential community has a better environment and improved road safety. 居民能够获得更好的环境和改善的道路安全。	The community of road-users has fewer delays and lower levels of risk and fear. 道路使用者可以有更少的延误，降低风险和担心的水平。
The manufacturing community has lower costs and provides more reliable services to customers. 制造业能够降低成本，给用户提供更可靠的服务。	The retail community can receive goods more efficiently, has lower delivery costs and provides a more pleasant environment for its customers. 零售业能更有效地获得商品，降低运输成本，并能为顾客提供更舒适愉快的环境。

Figure 4.14　Better freight management
图 4.14　更好的货运管理

（2）ITS which manages private traffic and ITS which manages public transport can both combine　管理私人交通的 ITS 和管理公共交通的 ITS 可以组合

例　Electronic Ticketing and Payment in Trondheim 特隆赫姆电子车票和支付

The Trondheim toll ring was set up in 1991 to improve traffic conditions in the city centre and provide a way to fund a package of major transport infrastructure improvements in the city. These include bus lanes, cycle routes, traffic calming and environmental improvements. Since the initial cordon was set up, the scheme has been developed into a sector pricing system, with additional toll stations added, bringing the total number of toll stations in 2003 to 23.

Toll stations and traffic management measures ensure that most drivers pass a toll station on their way into the city center. Tolls are levied on cars and goods vehicles on weekdays during the daytime, with a higher charge in the morning peak. Registered users obtain an electronic tag, mounted in their vehicle windscreen, enabling their account to be charged without having to stop at a toll station. Most toll stations have a separate lane for cash payments.

The system was one of the first in Europe to use short-range communications between the vehicle and equipment at the roadside as a method of charging against a registered account. In 2001, it was upgraded as part of a national strategy to create an interoperable system for all tolls in Norway (AUTOPASS). An electronic payment system was developed. One transport account can be used for toll charges and other transport costs including parking, public transport, cycle hire and taxis. The electronic card can be used for "contactless" payments or in contact mode, as a "stored value" card and a season ticket. Buses are equipped with electronic tags which enable them to pass the toll stations without payment, and also to obtain priority at traffic signals.

1991年特隆赫姆成立了"收费环"，改善市中心交通状况，并为城市交通基础设施改造提供资金支持。这些改造包括公交专用道、自行车专用道和交通环境改善。收费环建立后，收费方案被纳入行业价格体系中。2003年特隆赫姆"收费环"的收费站数量增至23个。

收费站设置和交通管理措施，确保大部分驾驶员由收费站进入市区。在工作日的早高峰时段，收费站对进入市中心的私家车和货车征收通行费。注册用户可获得一个电子标签，驾驶员将其安装在车辆挡风玻璃上。当经过收费站时，车辆无须停车，系统会通过电子标签自动扣除通行费。许多收费站还独立开设了现金支付通道。

该系统是欧洲较早运用DSRC进行车辆和路侧设备间通信的系统。为了建立全挪威收费互通系统，2001年挪威对该系统进行了升级（AUTOPASS），并作为国家发展战略的一部分。电子支付系统开发后，公众只需一个交通账户，就可以支付通行费、停车费、公交车票、自行车税和出租车费等。电子卡可以接触式或非接触式使用，也可以作为储蓄卡或季度卡。装有电子标签的公交车辆，通过收费站时不需要缴纳通行费，并具有信号优先权。

The UTC system introduced in Paris, France, included reducing the waiting time for pedestrians crossing at signals and extending crossing time, and adjusting signal times to suit cyclists. It has made the area safer for pedestrians and cyclists, and at the same time reduced the time which vehicles spend in traffic by 15%. This has wide community benefits, including giving freedom to some people (especially children) who might otherwise be unable to travel independently.

法国巴黎引进的城市交通控制系统，包括减少行人通过信号灯的等待时间、延长通过时间和调整适合于骑行者的信号时间。系统能够使该地区行人和骑行者更加安全，同时减少车辆在交通中花费时间的 15%。与此同时还具备更广泛的社会效益，包括给一些无法单独出行的人（尤其是小孩）一些自由。

（3）Traffic management and demand management 交通管理和需求管理

Electronic parking signs which help guide drivers to an empty space can ease queues, thereby reducing emissions and other environmental impacts of circulating traffic.

引导驾驶员寻找空位置的电子停车标志，能够减少排队，因此可以减少循环交通的有害气体排放和其他的环境影响。

Figure 4.15   Electronic parking signs

图 4.15   电子停车标志

4.3   Benefits to Roads Network Operations   对道路网络运营的效益

4.3.1   Application of ITS to Network Operations   路网运营中 ITS 的应用

From the perspective of road owners and operators, many ITS products and services improve efficiency by optimizing the use of existing facilities and rights-of-way. With these improvements, requirements for mobility and commerce can be met and the need to construct new or expanded facilities can be reduced. ITS maintain or expand the level of service whilst increasing throughput. ITS can also support management of infrastructure at times of extreme events, by providing high-performance real-time information to operators and users.

从道路拥有者和运营者的角度来说，许多 ITS 的产品和服务通过优化现有交通设施和路权来改进效率。通过这些改进，能够满足机动性和商业需求，减少新建和扩建基础设施的需求。ITS 通过增加通行能力来维持和提高服务水平。ITS 也能通过向运营者和用户提供高性能的实时信息，支持非常事件时期基础设施的管理。

> **例** **Icy road warning system (Denmark) 结冰道路预警系统（丹麦）**
>
> This system highlights icy driving situations before they actually arise, which enables preventative salting before the roadway becomes icy. For example, in Denmark, there are 290 recording stations along 11,000 km of Danish motorways and roads and a minor portion of the 60,000 km of local roads. Information such as road and air temperature, humidity, road resistance and freezing point is measured by sensors and transmitted via the telephone network and modem to 14 Winter Centers. The DMI (Danish Meteorological Institute) provides weather information. The information is processed and the VINTERMAN system assists decision making regarding salting actions. The system has provided the following benefits:
> - Opportunity to carry out preventative salting.
> - Avoidance of salting at unnecessary times.
> - Informing motorists of current icy road conditions.
>
> 这个系统在冰形成之前提醒结冰的驾驶情况，这能在道路结冰前就开展预防性的撒盐行动。例如，在丹麦，就有290个记录站点沿着11000km的丹麦高速公路和普通道路以及60000km的地方道路的很少部分布设。道路和空气温度、湿度、道路摩擦阻力和冰点信息可以通过传感器测量，并通过电话网络和调制解调器传送到14个冬季中心。DMI(丹麦气象研究所)提供气象信息。信息通过处理，然后VINTERMAN辅助决策制定撒盐行动。这个系统提供了以下效益：
> - 实施预防性撒盐的时机。
> - 避免在不必要的时间撒盐。
> - 现有结冰道路条件的监视。

The major functions of ITS-related network operations are :

ITS 相关的道路网运营的主要功能：

（1）Network monitoring　路网监视

Network monitoring, performs a key function in gathering prevailing road network information and providing support for other network operation activities. Thus although monitoring is an integral part of any ITS service, it does not usually provide any service on its own.

路网监视在收集主要道路信息和为其他路网运营活动提供支持方面起着重要的作用，因此，尽管监视是任何 ITS 服务不可分割的一部分，但它通常不会给自己提供任何服务。

Figure 4.16　Network monitoring center

图 4.16　路网监视中心

（2）Maintaining road serviceability and safety　维持道路的服务能力和安全

In order to improve road serviceability and safety, pro-active and re-active measures can be applied. Pro-active measures focus on the prevention of incidents/congestion and reactive measures focus on the detection/verification of incidents and unsafe road conditions, response and clearance, and recovery to normal operations.

为了提高道路的服务能力和安全性，可以运用主动和被动措施。主动措施关注事件和拥堵的预防，而被动措施关注事件、不安全道路条件、响应和清除以及恢复到正常运营的检测和证实。

（3）Travel aid and user information service　出行帮助和用户信息服务

Traveler information (ATIS) is a secondary preventative measure. Timely warning of unsafe road conditions and congestion reduces the occurrence of crashes. The traffic congestion that results from these incidents can lead to additional crashes and cause delayed response to emergency situations. According to one study, for every minute an incident remains on the roadway, it causes an additional five minutes of delay after the incident is cleared.

出行者信息服务（ATIS）是一种辅助性预防措施。及时的不安全道路条件和拥堵的警示能够减少碰撞的发生。事件引起的交通拥挤能够导致额外的碰撞并延误对紧急情况的响应。根据一项研究，事件在道路上每停留一分钟，就能导致额外五分钟的延误。

4.3.2　Benefits From Traffic Control　交通控制带来的效益

Advanced systems make use of up-to-date communication and real-time software technologies to enhance safety and improve traffic flow. Solutions include ramp metering, speed control, tidal flow systems, adaptive signal control, collective and individual route guidance and freight access control.

先进的系统使用最新的通信和实时软件技术来提高安全性和改进交通流。解决办法包括：匝道控制、速度控制和潮汐流系统、自适应信号控制、群体和个人路线导航以及货运通道控制。

Figure 4.17　Tidal lane
图 4.17　潮汐车道

4.3.3　Benefits from Traveler Information　出行者信息带来的效益

Traveler information services are complementary to the traffic control functions of network operations.

出行者信息服务是路网运营中交通控制功能的一项补充。

(1) They aim to provide high quality, real-time, detailed information on transportation system operational conditions, including weather, so that individual travelers can make informed decisions regarding whether to make a trip, when to make it, what mode to take, and what route to take.

它们旨在提供关于交通系统运营条件包括天气在内的更高质量、实时和详细的信息，以使出行者做出关于是否出行、什么时间出行、采用什么方式出行、走哪条路线的明智决策。

(2) Traveler information can be provided in a number of ways.

出行者信息可以通过多种方式提供。

The Internet is a popular method of conveying pre-trip traveler information. Commercial broadcast media, including radio, cable television, commercial television, and teletext services are also popular methods of dissemination. Changeable Message Signs (CMS) are also being used to disseminate en-route traveler information.

因特网是一种十分流行的传达出行前信息的方法。商业广播媒体，包括广播、有线电视、商业电视、图文电视服务，也是流行的发布方法。可变信息标志（CMS）也被用于发布途中出行信息。

(3) En-route information provided through in-vehicle navigation systems is increasingly available.

通过车载导航系统提供的途中出行信息越来越多。

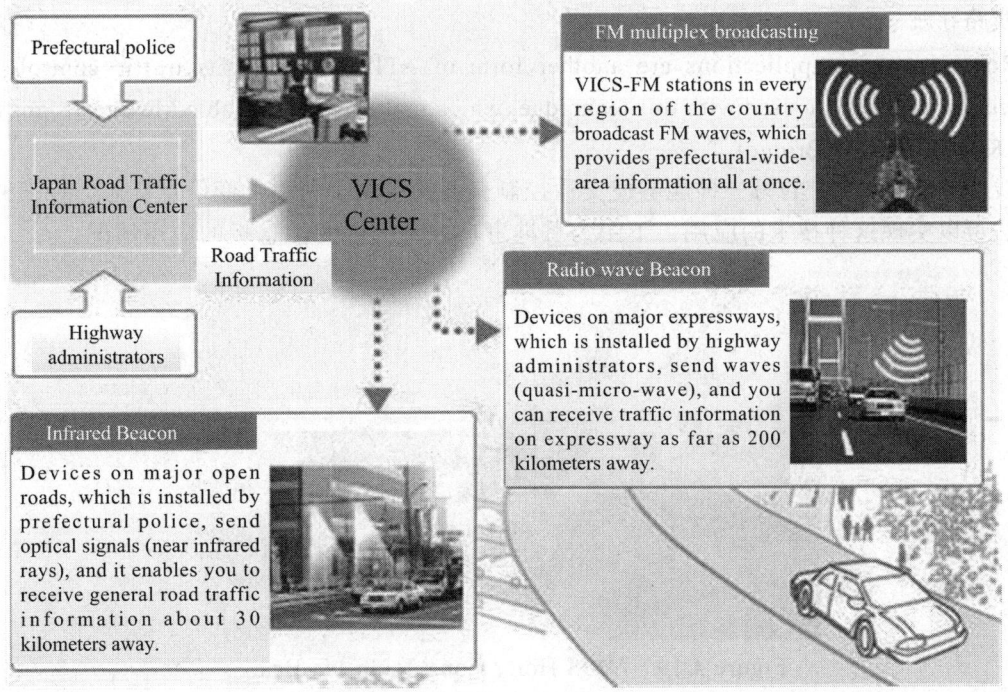

Figure 4.18　VICS system in Japan

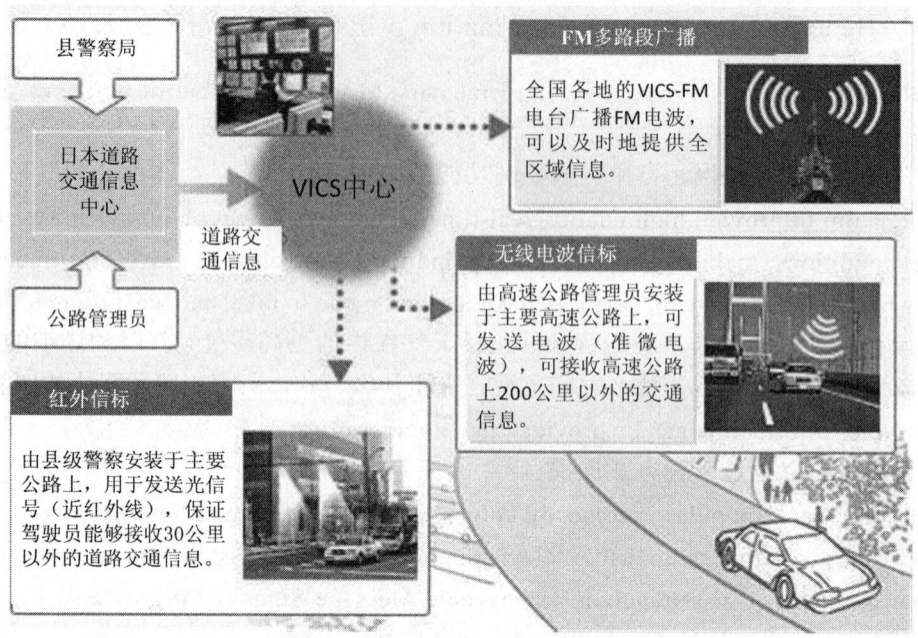

图 4.18　日本的 VICS 系统

The Vehicle Information and Communication System (VICS) system in Japan, enables drivers to select the shortest, most convenient routes available and ensures that traffic is distributed smoothly, further improving road safety and the flow of traffic.

日本的道路交通情报通信系统（VICS）系统能够使驾驶员选择最短和最方便的路线且可以确保交通合理的分布，进而改善道路安全和交通流。

（4）Route Guidance

线路导航

Route guidance applications are another form of ATIS that benefits traffic control. Three different approaches are used with this technique, which make use of Variable Message Signs (VMS Hong Kong Tsing Ma Bridge).

线路导航是 ATIS 的另一种能够使交通控制获益的应用。利用可变信息标志，有三种不同的方法可以实现这种技术的应用，下图为香港青马大桥的可变信息板的应用情况。

Figure 4.19　VMS Hong Kong Tsing Ma Bridge

图 4.19　香港青马大桥的可变信息板

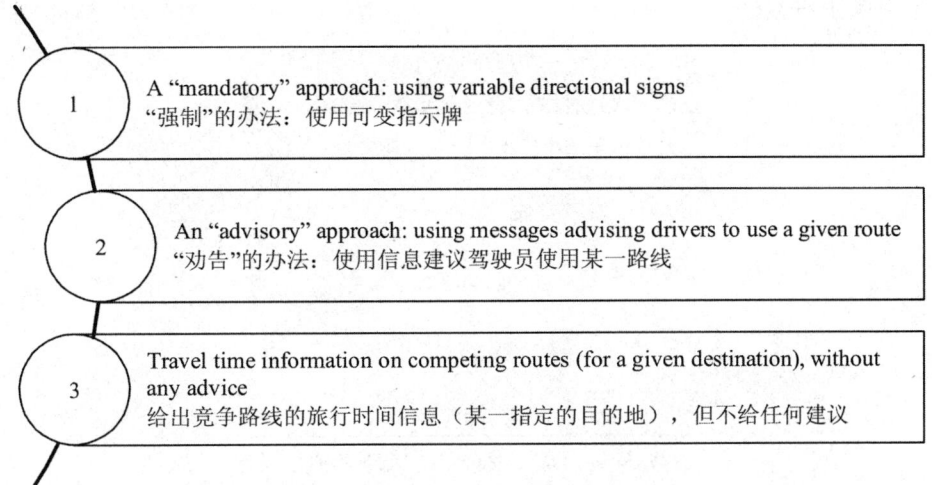

Figure 4.20　Three methods of using variable message sign

图 4.20　可变信息标志的三种使用方法

4.3.4　Inter-modal integration, Intra-modal integration　交通模式间和交通模式内的整合

(1) Inter-modal integration, Intra-modal integration

交通模式间整合，交通模式内的整合

① Inter-modal integration　交通模式间整合

Inter-modal integration means switching between different forms of transport. It applies to switching between car, cycle, walk, bus, rail, coach, tram etc. or from land transport to air or sea.

不同交通模式间的整合是指不同交通方式间的转换。它主要应用于小轿车、自行车、步行、公共交通、铁路、巴士、电车等，或从地面到空中或海上运输之间的转换。

② Intra-modal integration　交通模式内整合

Intra-modal integration is when people switch from one vehicle to another but on the same mode, changing from bus to bus or parking the car to join a car-share.

交通模式内整合是指人们从一辆车转移到另一辆车，但却是在同一种方式之内，从公共汽车到公共汽车间的换乘或停车后加入合乘车。

(2) Some of the most significant ITS impacts on inter- and intra-modal transfer

ITS 对交通模式内和模式间转换的一些重要影响

Some of the most significant ITS impacts on inter- and intra-modal transfer have been from information systems. For example the real time bus information by telephone and cell phone in North Wales. ITS also provide integrated information for different networks. Examples include the 511 National Travel System.

ITS 对交通模式内和模式间转换的一些重要影响来自于信息系统，比如在北威尔士可以通过电话和手机获取实时的公交信息。ITS 也能够为不同网络提供整合的信息，相关的例子包括美国的 511 全国出行系统。

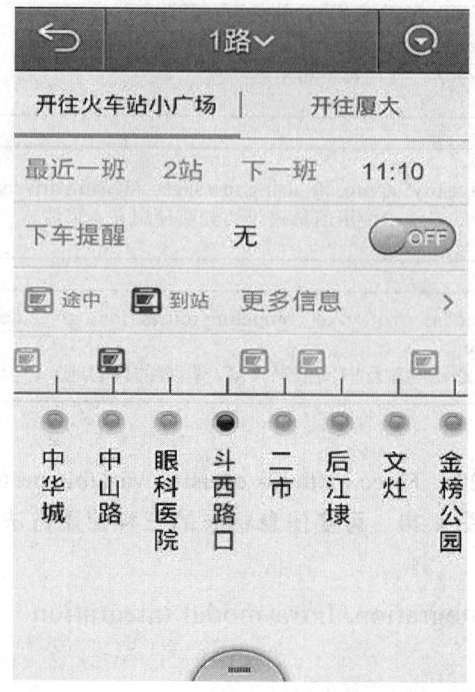

Figure 4.21　Obtained real-time transit information via mobile phone
图 4.21　通过手机获取实时的公交信息

(3) Guaranteeing connections helps users have confidence to use the public transport system
保证连通性能够帮助用户有信心使用公共交通系统

In the US, "Connection Protection" is being tested: this ensures that connections between different forms of transit work smoothly i.e. the bus waits an extra three minutes to pick up passengers from late-running rail. There are also small system applications. For example, Corlink, in the English County of Cornwall, guarantees rail to bus transfer.

在美国，对"连通性保护"项目进行了测试——这可以确保不同公共交通方式间的顺畅连通比如……。还有一些很小的系统应用，例如在康沃尔郡的英国县中，Corlink 能够保证铁路到公共汽车间的换乘。

Corlink is a demand responsive service for very rural areas, which takes the passenger to a main bus route to connect into the rail system. The Corlink driver is given real time information on the operation of the main bus service and the rail service. ITS also provide door-to-door journey planning for multi-modal journeys, both on-system and via the Internet, for example OVR and Eurotel.

Corlink 是一种用于偏远地区的需求响应服务，它可以将乘客送到与铁路系统连接的主要公共汽车线路上。Corlink 驾驶员被给予了一些关于主要公共汽车服务和铁路服务的实时信息。ITS 也为多模式出行提供了门到门的计划，可以通过车载系统和因特网，比如 OVR 和 Eurotel。

| 例 | Door-to-door Journey Planning OVR　门到门出行计划 |

> OVR is a private sector company providing a national public transport information service for the Netherlands. All public transport operators are obliged to supply OVR with details of their services. Funded by public transport operators, OVR provides high quality accurate information for the whole journey, disseminated through a telephone enquiry service and a well-used Internet service.
>
> Eurotel, a mobile phone company in the Czech Republic has developed an inter-modal traveller information service providing a high quality service for door-to-door public transport and walking information, as part of a "Mobile Guide" package, including retail and leisure information.
>
> OVR是一个提供荷兰全国公共交通信息服务的私营公司。所有的公共交通运营者都有义务为OVR提供他们服务的详细信息。在公共交通运营的资助下，通过电话咨询服务和广泛使用的因特网服务，OVR为整个行程提供高质量的精确信息。
>
> Eurotel，捷克共和国的一个移动电话公司，已经开发了多模式间出行信息服务，可以提供用于门到门的公共交通和出行信息的高质量服务，作为"移动指南"套餐的一部分，包括零售和休闲信息。

(4) Integration within and between modes will increasingly be facilitated by electronic payment

不同模式间的整合通过电子支付变得越来越方便

It should be noted that urban and interurban applications are different. The management of interfaces in urban areas can be complex, whilst the scope of a charging system on an interurban network is vast. Apart from revenue collection, ITS can help implement payment systems which encourage a reduction in distance travelled on the roads.

应该指出，城市和城市间的应用是不同的。城市地区的接口管理是非常复杂的，而同时城市间路网上的收费系统的范围是非常大的。除了收费外，ITS能够帮助实现一个鼓励人们减少在道路上的出行的支付系统。

4.3.5　Synergy Benefits　协同效益

(1) ITS can also create synergies with non-transport services
ITS也能与非交通服务协同

Figure 4.22　Highway ambulance service
图 4.22　高速公路救护服务

One example is the application in Arizona for the motorway ambulance service. Another example is the use of dynamic message signs to help find kidnapped children; the AMBER Alert system has proven effective in California and is being adopted by other States in the USA.

其中一个例子就是在美国亚利桑那州用于高速公路救护服务的应用，另一个例子是使用动态信息标志帮助寻找被绑架的儿童。AMBER 警报系统在加利福尼亚已被证明是行之有效的，目前正逐渐被美国其他地区采用。

(2) The functional synergies within ITS are also valuable

ITS 中功能协同是非常有价值的

The benefits of common data dictionaries are great and the applications very varied. There are large scale applications such as the common dictionary for radio data systems in Europe. Common digital road and street information systems and maps also support information services. National applications can help with the implementation of an integrated information system through "Electronic Government".

共同的数据字典效益巨大而且应用广泛。这里还有更大范围的应用，如用于欧洲广播数据系统的公共字典。一般数字化的道路和街道信息系统及地图也支持信息服务，且通过"电子政府"，国家层面的应用可以帮助实施整合的信息系统。

(3) ITS can also facilitate integrated transport and spatial plans

ITS 能够促进综合运输和空间规划

It is easier to manage innovations such as selective time-sharing and multiple use of infrastructure with ITS. ITS can give information on the regulations in force at different times and can monitor the effects of the time-sharing, as in Barcelona, where the tidal flow system is managed by ITS, and variable message signs informs drivers of the current status of the shared lane for deliveries and traffic.

应用 ITS 使管理创新变得非常容易，如选择性时间分配和基础设施的多重使用。ITS 可以在不同时间提供有效的法规信息，能够监视时间分配的作用，如在巴塞罗那通过 ITS 管理的潮汐交通流管理系统，以及可变信息标志告知驾驶员送货和交通共享车道上的现状。

(4) One of the long-term real advantages of ITS is that one system can support another

ITS 的长期优势之一是一个系统能够支持另一个系统

Once truck, buses and vans are equipped with Automatic Vehicle Location, it becomes possible to use them as mobile sources of data about journey times, congestion and real-time localized weather conditions. Once traffic monitoring is in place for the road network, real-time data can be fed to the logistical support systems used by vehicle fleet managers, to assist scheduling and service reliability .They can reduce the environmental impacts of increased traffic and they can provide "windows" (opportunities) for freight and other essential traffic in areas largely given over to pedestrian movement.

一旦载货汽车、公共汽车和旅行车安装了自动车辆定位系统，以此作为行车时间、拥挤和实时地方天气的数据来源就成为可能。一旦交通监视用于道路交通网络实时数据采集，这些数据可以用于车队管理者使用的物流决策支持系统，协助运行时刻和服务的可靠性。它们能够减少增加的交通带来的环境影响，也能给货物运输和其他重要的交通提供机会。

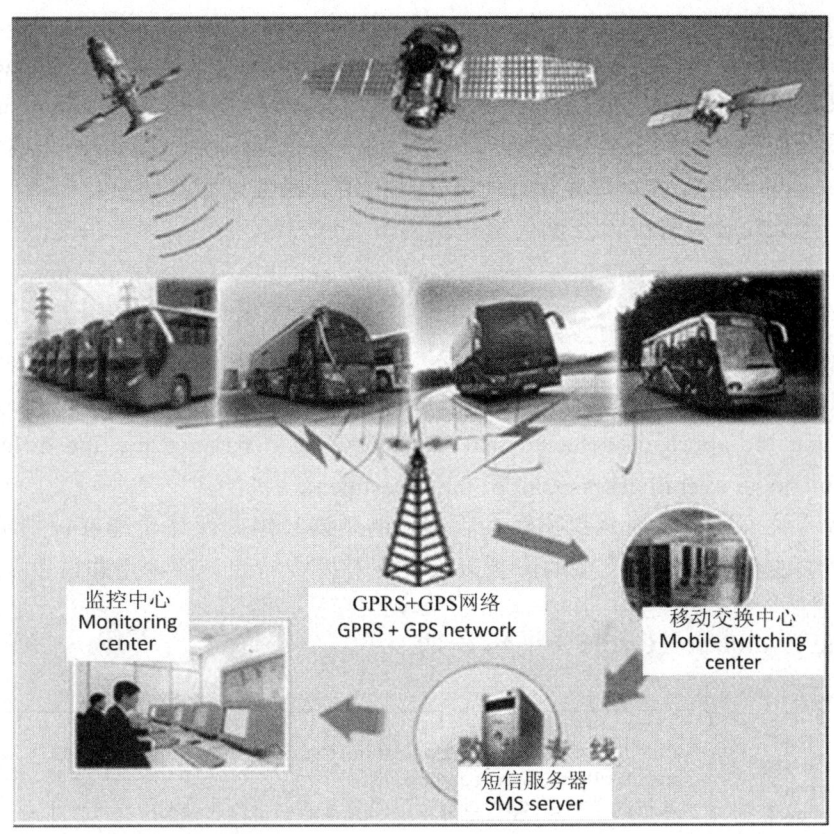

Figure 4.23 Vehicle management system
图 4.23 车辆管理系统

4.4 How are Benefits Evaluated 如何进行 ITS 效益评价

4.4.1 Why Evaluate 为什么要评价

(1) Evaluation is important for determining future investments and for checking the cost-effectiveness of existing systems

评价对于决策未来的投资与核对现有系统的成本效益很重要

Evaluation is never simply a matter of "justifying" investment. ITS must be a response to a need, not something we want in order to keep up with trends. It follows that all evaluation must start by a definition of the problem or opportunity.

评价决不仅仅是简单地"判断"投资。ITS 必须是一种对需求的反应，而不是我们为了顺应趋势的需要。由此得出结论，所有的评价必须从问题或机会的界定开始。

(2) The same fundamental systems can serve different policy goals and deliver different ITS products and services

同样的基础系统可以服务于不同的政策目标，提供不同的 ITS 产品和服务

It is therefore essential to design the system to deliver what is needed. A properly structured approach to the assessment of the problems to be solved and to the evaluation of the options will ensure that the right ITS are used in the best way. A critical factors analysis will help determine which business objectives or policy goals are served by ITS and how delivery can be measured.

因此，设计能够满足需求的系统是必要的。用于评估待解决问题和评价选择方案的适当的结构化方法，可以确保 ITS 能够以最佳方式被使用。对关键因素的分析有助于确定 ITS 服务于哪些商业目标和政策目标以及如何量化输出。

(3) ITS investment can result in benefits in one area and disbenefits in another

ITS 投资在一个领域可以产生效益而在另一个领域却产生弊端

For example electronic payment systems can reduce vehicle delays at payment points dramatically, it is important to ensure that evaluation is comprehensive enough to identify all major impacts, and that the approach selected makes it possible to balance out the different types of impact and come to an overall assessment of the investment.

电子收费系统可以明显地减少车辆在收费点的延误，但确保评价能够识别出所有的主要影响，选择方法能够平衡不同类型的影响以及实现对投资的综合评价是非常重要的。

4.4.2 The Evaluation Cycle 评价周期

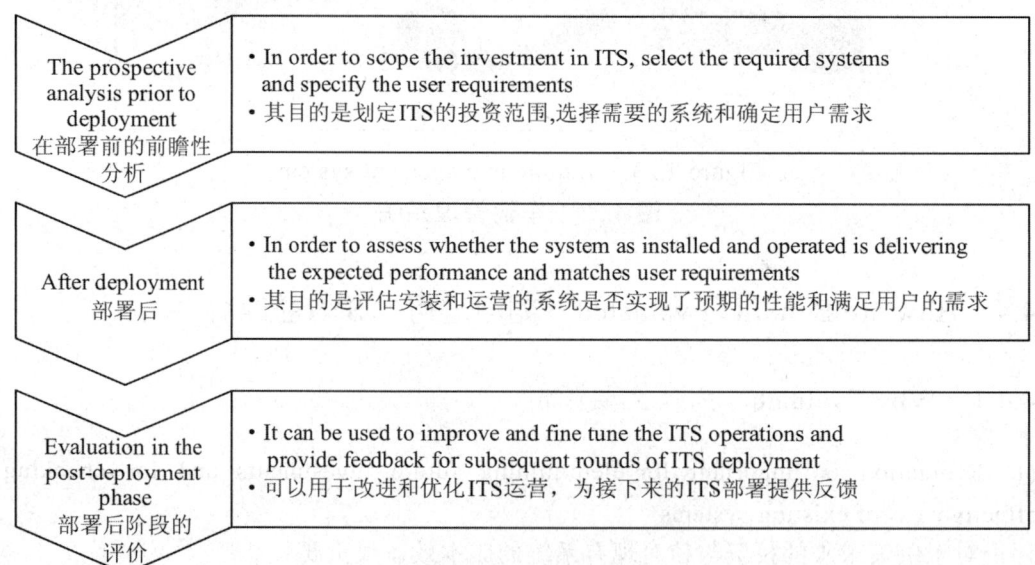

Figure 4.24 Evaluation Cycle
图 4.24 评价周期

The evaluation process is cyclical: positive results can be built on, and less positive results can be analyzed to ascertain what went wrong and what can be done to remedy the situation in hand and to improve the results of similar applications in the future. This cycle is illustrated in Figure 4.25.

评价的过程是周期性的：如果是正面的结果就继续，如果是负面的结果则需加以分析从而确定什么地方出了错，可采取何种补救措施，从而改进将来的相似应用的效果。评价周期如图 4.25 所示。

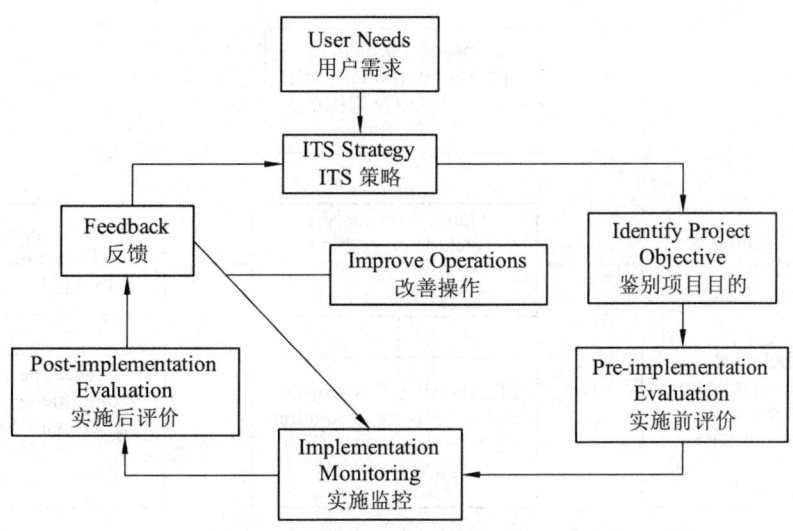

Figure 4.25   ITS evaluation cycle
图 4.25   ITS 评价周期

4.4.3 Pre-implementation Analysis: Making an Informed Choice   实施前分析：做出明智的选择

(1) The potential impacts of the proposed ITS will have to be set against the costs of procurement system build, maintenance and operations

ITS 的潜在影响需要与系统的建设、运营和维护成本进行比较

There are always choices to be made, so it is important to consider the relative merits and costs of the different options. This requires a systematic approach and careful judgment, including political judgment.

因为总要在方案间进行选择，所以考虑不同方案相对优点和成本是很重要的。这就需要有系统的方法和谨慎的判断力，包括政治判断力。

① Keep the transport policy objectives firmly in mind.

将交通政策目标牢记在心中。

② Choose evaluation measures relevant to the key issues for decision or debate, and which will be understood by the decision-makers.

为了决策或商讨，选择与主要议题相关的评价指标，并且这些指标要易被决策者理解。

③ Evaluate the "do nothing" or "do the minimum" option and any non-ITS alternatives, as well as the ITS options that are being considered.

评价"什么也不做""做最少的事"、任何非 ITS 的可选方案和正被考虑的 ITS 方案。

④ Think about possible side effects and the secondary or unintended impacts of ITS, such as the impact of public transport priority on private traffic, or the need to increase public transport supply to meet demand.

考虑 ITS 可能的副作用和次要作用或意外的影响，如公共交通优先或为满足需求而增加的公共交通供给对于私人交通的影响。

153

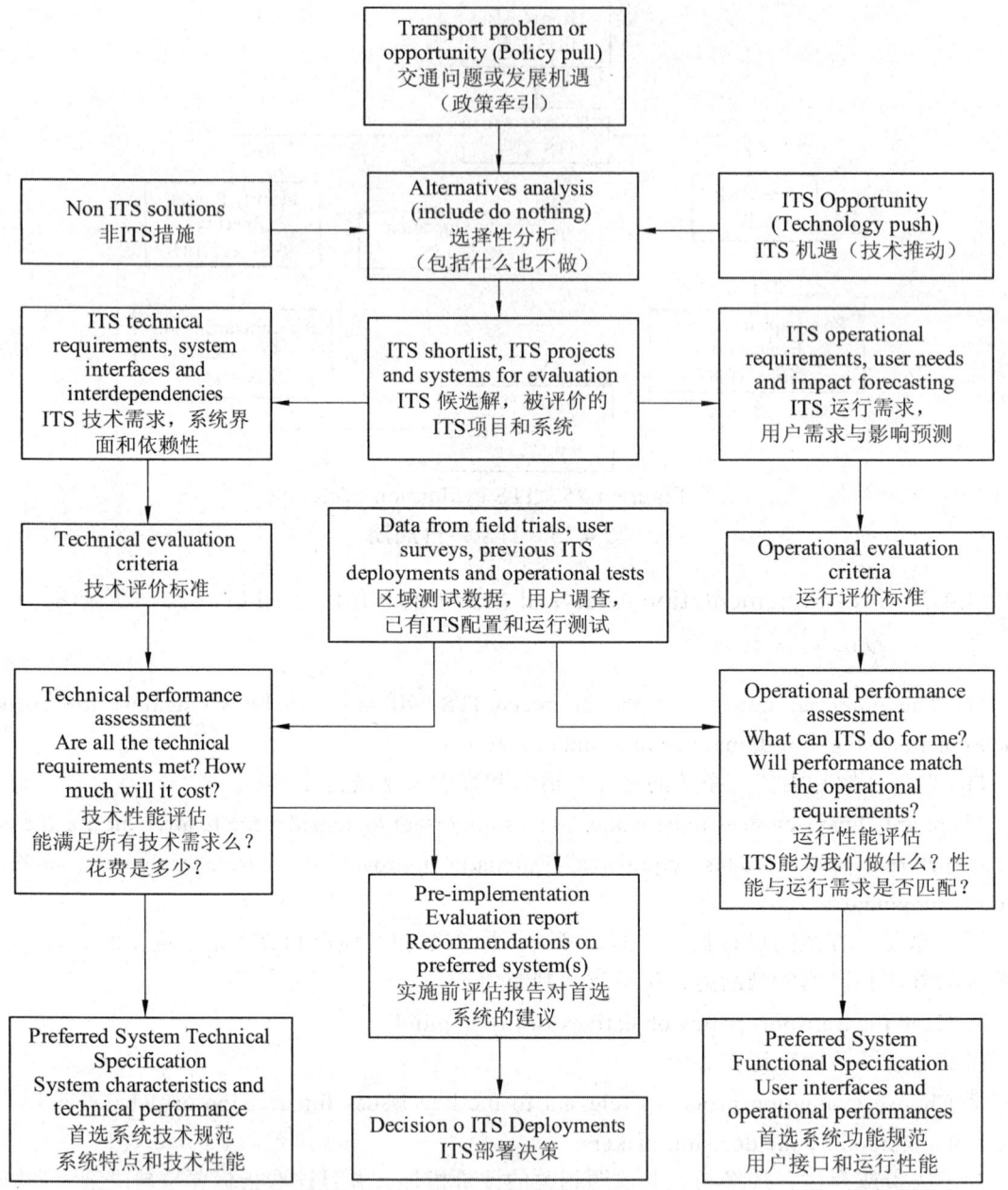

Figure 4.26　Flowchart for pre-implementation evaluation of ITS projects
图 4.26　ITS 项目实施前评估流程图

⑤ Cost-benefit calculations should be based on empirical data as much as possible.
成本-效益计算应该尽可能基于经验数据。

⑥ If limited data or resources mean that test results from one experiment are being scaled up or scaled down to form the basis of a new evaluation, use only valid empirical data and take great care.
如果仅有有限的数据或资源，意味着从一次试验得到的结果可能被放大或缩小构成一个新的评价基础，只使用有效的经验数据并要十分小心。

(2) What ITS can do is related in a systematic way to the problem or opportunity being

tackled.

ITS 能够做的是以系统的方式去处理需要解决的问题和机遇。

Traditionally the forerunners to ITS, computer-controlled traffic systems, have been built to a definitive design as specified by the client. In today's world the systems are more complex. Close attention is needed to the user requirements and the development of a detailed functional specification. In practice the separate, often parallel, streams of technical performance and impact evaluation feed into a practical choice about whether to use an ITS solution or a different solution, or do nothing.

ITS 的先驱——计算机控制的交通系统，是按照用户指定的设计方案进行建设的。在今天的世界，该系统越来越复杂。需要对用户的需求和详细功能说明的开发给予密切关注。在实际中，分开的或并行的技术性能和影响评价反馈到实际的选择中，以确定是否使用 ITS 解决方案或其他的解决方案，或什么都不做。

4.4.4　Post-implementation Analysis: Monitoring and Improving Performance
　　　　实施之后的分析：检测和改进性能

After an ITS solution has been implemented, monitoring and evaluation are used to learn lessons and improve performance in the future. Does the solution meet its objectives? Are the outcomes as intended? Monitoring the impacts can identify the range of benefits achieved, and these can be quantified with data from the internal monitoring.

在实施 ITS 解决方案之后，监测和评价可以用于学习经验教训和改进系统性能。这种方案是否满足目标？产生的效果是否是最初设想的？监测影响可以确定获得效益的范围，并且可以由内部检测数据定量化。

A systematic approach is needed to ensure that the different types of impacts are identified and in this case, measured. The principles listed earlier for making an informed choice apply, with modifications, to post-implementation analysis:

需要一个系统的方法以确保有不同类型的影响被识别，并在这种情况下被量化。前面列出的用于做出明智选择的应用原则，修改后可以用于实施后分析：

(1) Establish a base scenario for comparison of results. (Often the "before" situation or an extrapolation to current situation.)

建立一个用于进行效果对比的基础场景（通常是"事前"情形和现状外推）。

(2) Select evaluation measures relevant to the transport policy objectives.

选择与交通政策目标相关的评价指标。

(3) Experimental design principles should be considered, such as the comparison of performance between experimental group (experiencing the ITS) and the control group (similar in all possible respects but not experiencing the ITS).

应考虑实验设计原则，比如对实验组（实验 ITS）和控制组（在所有可能的方面相似但不进行 ITS 实验）的性能进行比较。

(4) Ensure that the experimental design will identify unintentional side effects in case they

occur.

确保实验设计能够识别意想不到的副作用的发生。

(5) If practical, multiple approaches should be used to confirm test conclusions.

如果是可行的，应该用多种方法测试得出的结论。

(6) If practical, multiple test sites should be used to compare test results.

如果是可行的，应该用多个测试点来比较测试结果。

(7) Both positive and negative results should be reported as useful data and lessons learned.

不论正面或负面的结果都应作为有用的数据及经验教训记录在报告中。

(8) Ensure that the evaluation takes place over a long enough time period for the full impacts of the scheme to be identified.

确保评价持续足够长的时间，以便识别所有对方案的影响。

(9) Report both the positive and the negative results.

给出含正面和负面结果的报告。

The results of post-implementation analysis should be fed into the evaluation cycle, improving operations and monitoring and also influencing ITS strategies for the future.

实施后的分析结果应该被纳入评价周期之内，改善运行和监测以及影响未来的ITS战略。

4.4.5 Role of Public Consultation 公众咨询的作用

In many ways ITS are "halo" products and services:

在许多方面，ITS是"光环"产品和服务系统：

Some communities have greeted so-called "smart" traffic control systems with great suspicion because of worries about the consequences of traffic being re-routed onto unsuitable roads.

一些团体已经质疑这种所谓的"智能"交通控制系统，他们担心交通被导向不适宜的路段。

Transport professionals increasingly need to be aware of the value of public consultation as part of the evaluation process, and what lies behind a successful consultation with users and stakeholders.

交通专家正逐渐意识到公众咨询作为评价工作一部分的价值，以及与用户和投资者的成功咨询能够带来的效果。

(1) Consultation has several very different uses 公众咨询有很多不同的用途

① The primary use is to ascertain what is needed: is there a market?

第一个用途，确定需要什么——有市场么？

② The secondary use, which is critical in many areas of public policy, is for influencing thought and changing behavior.

第二个用途，在很多涉及公共政策的地方很重要，因为它对人们的思想和行为的改变有所影响。

Road user charging and demand management are likely to be delivered through ITS. If people are to accept this, real dialogue is needed about the trade-offs between increasing travel, reducing congestion and the demands for safe neighborhoods and clean air. In Trondheim, public information was similarly important to the success of the shared lane and access control schemes in Barcelona.

道路使用者收费和需求管理可能通过 ITS 来实现。如果人们接受 ITS，那么真正的问题就是关于增加旅行、减少拥挤、安全空间和良好环境需求间的权衡。公众的信息和媒体活动是 ITS 在特隆赫姆实施成功的关键。在巴塞罗那，公众的信息同样对成功分配道路和驶入控制方案起了重要作用。

(2) Application of consultation is citizen involvement. 调查询问应用是公民参与

In research for the UK Highways Agency, Social Research Associates drew out distinct areas of community and market consultation and influence. These were:

英国社会研究委员会为英国公路部门研究划分了社区地点，做市场调查询问并给予指导。如下：

① Telling: Leaflets, newsletters, videos, media, awareness campaigns, marketing.

告知——广告传单、新闻、录像、媒体、宣传活动、销售行动。

② Asking: Driver education, attitude surveys, community workshops / round tables, Delphi sessions, combining with existing consultations, Citizens' Panels, discussion groups, mystery shoppers, direct comment lines for feedback.

询问——驾驶员教育、态度调查、社区工作坊/圆桌会议、希腊古都式会议，结合现有的调查询问、市民平台、讨论组、秘密购物者，将反馈意见排序。

③ Discussing: Travelling exhibitions, "Passing the Public Involvement Parcel", public meetings, visual approaches, websites, travel diaries, journey merging studies, capacity building, small area consultation, stakeholder involvement.

讨论——巡回展览、"经过公众参与地点"、公众的会议、可视途径、网站、旅行日记、旅程综合研究、接受能力培养、小区调查、利益相关方的参与。

④ Deciding: Audits and observations, referenda, "Planning for Real", temporary infrastructure, Citizens' Juries, performance indicators, targets and community indicators, visioning exercises, outreach to socially excluded groups, value management.

决定——监督和观察、投票、"实际的计划"、临时的设施、市民的陪审团、性能的说明者、目标和社区的说明人、可视化的练习、扩展到社会上的其他团体、评价的管理。

(3) The task is to match 工作任务

The task is to match the technique to the purpose of the consultation. In assessing demand, we rely on the "asking" and "discussing" techniques. The results from this can be used in models or can stand alone. Where consultation is trying to change behavior or attitudes, it is necessary to combine the "telling" and "discussing" techniques with two phases of "asking" to gauge attitudes to a question before the work and afterwards.

工作任务是使技术手段和调查目的相匹配。在评定需求时,我们依赖"询问"和"讨论"的手段。因为这种方法的结果可以被用于模型也可以单独应用。而当调查询问要影响和试图改变人们的行为和态度时，则有必要把"叙述"和"讨论"的手段与在事前和事后"询问"问题观察态度两个阶段联合。

(4) Some key cautionary notes 注意事项

There are some key cautionary notes on public involvement. It can be difficult to get reliable opinions on some ITS applications. In trying to forecast likely take-up and use of a system or application, the halo effect of new ITS products and services can lead to over-optimistic forecasts. That does not mean that the response should not be believed. It does mean that a strategic consultation would focus on the outcome or on the measure of progress towards the outcome, rather than on the means of achieving it.

在公众参与中有一些主要注意事项。首先，在 ITS 应用中得到一些可靠性意见是困难的。当试图预测可能使用的一个系统或应用时，新 ITS 产品和服务的光环效果导致过于乐观的估计。这不是说这种反应不可靠，而是说一个有策略的咨询应该关注目标或关注实现目标的过程，而不是关注实现目标的方式。

4.4.6　Quantifying the Costs　计算成本

(1) Cost data for ITS installation and operations are often difficult to assess. Estimates for ITS costs must be made in the local context to support local project decisions. ITS cost data are available at various levels of aggregation. The costs to be considered in planning are capital costs, unit costs, whole system costs and lifetime costs.

获得 ITS 设施的安装和运营成本数据通常是很难的。估计 ITS 成本必须是在当地从上到下的对工程的支持工作中进行。ITS 成本数据是各种不同标准的数据集合。在规划中考虑的成本有资本成本，单元成本，整个系统成本和系统生命周期成本。

Comprehensive unit cost data for planning purposes are described in the US database of ITS costs and benefits and Appendix 2 is drawn from this database. However, the unit cost of equipment and installation may vary from country to country and the cost figures for each ITS product and service should be used with caution.

美国的 ITS 成本和效益数据库，以及从中摘录的附录 2 记录了为规划目标服务的复杂的单元成本数据。然而，这些单元成本和安装成本各国之间不同，在应用每一项 ITS 产品和服务的成本数字时应该特别谨慎。

单元成本分为资本成本、运营成本和维护成本三部分。准确的运营和维护成本众所周知是难于获得的，因为它来源于一般的经营组织成本中。

Installation costs will vary between regions, depending both on the terrain and the availability of skills to work on and manage the project. Software development, testing and installation can be major and difficult to predict. Similarly the task of developing databases and data dictionaries for ITS is very labor intensive. A pre-existing data dictionary and database will save on development costs, but only if data quality is adequate for the purpose, meaning that data are accurate, up-to-date and coded in sufficient detail.

安装成本各地不同，主要依据为地域不同、工作可达到的技术水平不同以及对于工程的管理不同。软件开发、安装和测试在预测方面是最主要和困难的，我们共同的任务是建立 ITS 数据库和数据词典，而此项工作是需要付出相当劳动的。已有的数据词典和数据库只有在数据质量符合实验目的的情况下，即在数据是精确的、最新的和有足够详细编码的情况下才会节省开发成本。

(2) There can be substantial cost reduction through integration of ITS components.

通过对 ITS 部件的整合而减少的成本是可观的。

Care should therefore be taken when using any unit cost data. It would be a mistake to add up the unit costs without considering possible cost savings through integration and good system design.

应用任何单元成本数据时，都应认真谨慎，没有考虑可能通过系统整合和改良设计节省成本的情况而把单元成本盲目累加有可能是错误的。

(3) The life-cycle cost of ITS includes maintenance costs, operations costs and the cost of periodic refurbishment and replacement.

ITS 生命周期成本包括维护成本、运营成本、周期更新和重置成本。

Careful monitoring of lifetime costs is needed to build up information on the real costs of ITS maintenance and operations. Maintenance costs can be quite high with ITS, by comparison with, say, roads and bridges. The equipment may be sensitive and is often exposed. Refurbishment and replacement should be planned in the initial budget. Technological advances may mean rapid obsolescence of ITS hardware and software, which means more frequent replacement and higher costs.

认真监测整个过程成本需要得到实际的 ITS 维护和运营成本信息。与道路和桥梁的维护成本相比，ITS 维护成本相当高，因为设备时常是暴露在外面的而且是敏感的。更新和重置成本应该写在最初的预算中。技术的进步、ITS 硬件和软件的迅速淘汰，意味着我们需要更快的更新和更高的成本。

4.4.7 Summarizing Benefits and Costs 效益和成本小结

Specific benefits and costs vary greatly from one location to another. The context is always a key determinant of both costs and benefits. For specific projects simulation techniques may be useful for estimating the likely benefits. For example, the US Federal Highway Administration has developed the ITS Deployment Analysis System (IDAS) that can be used in planning for (ITS) deployments. There are several factors which might influence the cost:

不同地方的某种特定设备的成本效益有很大的不同，这个背景对费用和效益的确定也是关键的。针对特定的项目，模拟技术能够有效地估测可能的效益。比如，美国联邦公路局已经开发的 ITS 评价软件 IDAS，该系统可以应用于 ITS 部署规划。以下是一些可能影响成本的因素：

First, the size of a scheme: 500 CCTV cameras have a lower unit cost than five cameras.

第一，方案的规模：购买 500 台 CCTV 摄像机的单元成本低于购买 5 台摄像机的单元成本。

Next, the location: terrain may be difficult or easy. Communications links may already be in place or they might be a special requirement. The existing investment in ITS technology can be a factor: adding new features into an existing traffic control system may be cheaper than installing an entire new system.

第二，位置：地形条件可优可劣，通信线路可能已经安置好或者有特殊的需求。现有的

ITS 投资可能也是一个因素：在现有交通控制系统上加新的装置比重新安装完整的新系统可能要便宜。

It is necessary to have some idea of the likely costs and benefits of ITS during planning, especially for the cost-benefit analysis, public consultation and decision-making phases. A useful reference for current costs and benefits gives detailed unit costs and benefits, largely for specific ITS in the US, as well as case studies of whole system applications.

在 ITS 规划过程中，尤其是成本效益分析、公众调查咨询和决策实施阶段，有必要了解可能的成本效益。一本有实用价值的关于当今的效益成本参考文献给出了美国大部分 ITS 的详细单元成本和效益，同时还有对整个系统应用的案例研究。

4.5 Advice on ITS Evaluation 关于 ITS 评价的建议

4.5.1 Approach to Evaluation 评价方法

(1) Description 概述

Whatever the motive for doing ITS evaluation work, it has to be well thought through and properly targeted if it is going to be useful. The methodology needs to take account of the ITS scheme objectives, user needs and stakeholder expectations of the project.

无论进行 ITS 评价工作的动机是什么，如果想取得有用的成果，都应该彻底考虑并确定适当的目标。评价方法需要考虑 ITS 方案的目标、用户需求和利益相关方对项目的期望。

(2) The people who execute the work of evaluation 执行评价工作的人

Whoever commissions evaluation work needs to be clear about the reasons for making the evaluation, and who is going to use the results. It is important to establish the basis on which those groups will judge the success or failure of the scheme and plan the evaluation exercise accordingly. An evaluation exercise that is not properly planned carries with it a risk that what is measured will not be what is considered important – it may even fail to measure the things changed by the ITS.

执行评价工作的人需要明确评价的前提，即要清楚评价的原因以及评价的结果为谁所用。在建立评价小组的基础上来判断项目的成功或失败，以及有依据地计划评价工作是非常重要的。一个没有计划好的评价工作，将会伴随着所观测到的并不是我们认为的重要信息的风险——甚至不能检测出由 ITS 带来的改变。

(3) Factors influencing evaluation level 影响评价水平的因素

The level of evaluation depends on a number of factors, including the scale of the project, the specific policy goals the investment is designed to serve and the transport development objectives that apply. The balance of objectives is likely to vary from one scheme to the next. Another factor is whether the technology or type of service to the end user is new. A new or innovative use of ITS may justify more effort in evaluation as compared with an ITS technique that is well proven.

评价的水平受许多因素的影响，包括方案的规模、投资想要实现的具体政策目标和交通发展目标。不同方案目标间的平衡可能差别很大。另一个因素是技术和服务的类型对于用户来说是否是新的，一个新的或创新的 ITS 应用与已经充分证实有效的 ITS 技术相比需要在评价中付出更多的努力。

4.5.2　Evaluation Checklist　评价列表

(1) The importance of socio-economic as well as technical evaluation.
社会经济评价和技术评价的重要性。

(2) The detailed breakdown of impacts as well as breadth of multiple impacts.
影响的详细分类和复合影响的广度。

(3) Need for large-scale as well as small-scale evaluation.
大范围评价需求与小范围评价需求。

(4) Variances as well as expected values of impacts.
影响与期望值的差额及影响的期望值。

(5) Indirect as well as direct impacts.
间接和直接的影响。

(6) Unintended as well as intended effects.
意料之外的作用和意料之中的作用。

(7) Long-term as well as near-term consequences.
长期和近期的结果

(8) Gradual adaptation as well as immediate responses in human behaviors.
人类行为的逐渐适应与即时反应。

(9) Multiple as well as single (most important) impacts.
复合影响和单个（最重要的）影响。

(10) Private as well as public sector concerns.
私营部门和公共部门的考虑。

(11) Interests of third parties as well as those of major stakeholders.
第三方的利益和主要利益相关方的利益。

(12) Distributive as well as aggregate costs and benefits.
分项的成本和效益以及整体的成本和效益。

4.5.3　Practical considerations　实际考虑

Before an evaluation is started, there are some practical considerations to be taken into account. In planning a major ITS investment, a budget should be planned for evaluation before and after implementation to confirm value for money and to provide feed-back when planning further projects.

在评价开始之前，需要进行一些实际的考虑。在规划一项主要的 ITS 投资时，应该包括用于前后对比评价的预算，以确保将来项目成本的评估为将来的项目提供反馈。

Affordability will often be an issue. Whichever evaluation method is used, there often will not be a sufficient budget to answer all the questions around an investment. It then becomes necessary to priorities. The template in Table 4.1 will help decide the issues on which to focus the evaluation budget.

负担能力将经常成为一个问题。无论使用什么评价方法，通常没有足够的预算回答关于投资的所有问题，因此有必要对问题进行排序。表 4.1 将有助于我们确定评价预算关注的问题。

Table 4.1　Issues focused on the evaluation budget

表 4.1　评价预算关注的问题

目标区域 Goal Area	指标 Measure
安全 Safety	碰撞/死亡 Crashes/fatalities
效率 Efficiency	通行量/旅行时间节省/可靠性 Throughput/travel time savings/reliability
机动性 Mobility	可达性/模式间的连接 Accessibility of opportunities/inter-modal connections
生产力 Productivity	成本节约 Cost savings
能源和环境 Energy and the environment	排放和燃料消耗 Emissions and fuel consumption
用户满意度是底线 Customer satisfaction is the bottom line	

The systems themselves should be programmed to provide data which will monitor the impact they have. An example: real-time information at bus stops provides information on bus headways. Storing this information gives a record of service intervals, which are a key aspect of reliability as perceived by the passenger.

系统本身应能够提供用于监视它们所产生影响的数据。例如：公交车站的实时信息能够提供关于公共汽车车头间距的信息。储存这些信息提供了服务间隔的记录，该记录是乘客能感觉到的服务可靠性一个重要的方面。

Figure 4.27　Real-time information of the bus station in Singapore

图 4.27　新加坡公交车站的实时信息

Evaluation is specialist work. That does not mean that it always needs to be complicated, nor even to be carried out by specialists. Where data need to be collected, this can be done in-house, provided that it is done credibly, using an objective approach and sound methods. For most evaluations, it is a good idea to use specialists the first time a task is carried out. That way, the in-house staff can learn how the evaluation should be done. Formal training should enhance this learning. As well as bringing in specialists the first time a job is done, it is worth employing specialists from time to time to ensure that up-to-date methods are introduced.

评价是专业的工作，但这并不意味着评价有多复杂，也不意味着一定要由专家执行。在需要收集数据的地方，假如使用客观和合理的方法且确保评价是可信的，评价工作就能够成为一项内务工作。对于大部分评价工作来说，使用专家执行第一次的任务是个很好的主意，那样内部的职员就可以学习如何进行评价，正规的培训将强化这一学习过程。除了引进专家进行第一次工作外，经常雇用专家以确保不断引进最新的方法也是非常值得的。

4.5.4　Some useful indicators　一些有用的指标

1. ITS can contribute to a variety of objectives　ITS 可实现许多目标

```
┌─────────────────────────────────────────────────────────────┐
│ Maximise use of existing networks  现存路网使用效率最大化      │
└─────────────────────────────────────────────────────────────┘
┌─────────────────────────────────────────────────────────────┐
│ Reduce operational costs  减少运营成本                        │
└─────────────────────────────────────────────────────────────┘
┌─────────────────────────────────────────────────────────────┐
│ Improve efficiency and safety  改善效率和安全                 │
└─────────────────────────────────────────────────────────────┘
┌─────────────────────────────────────────────────────────────┐
│ Help protect and enhance the environment  有利于保护和改善环境│
└─────────────────────────────────────────────────────────────┘
┌─────────────────────────────────────────────────────────────┐
│ Reallocate space to prime users at different times of day or year │
│ 在一年或一天中的不同时段,重新给主要的用户分配空间                │
└─────────────────────────────────────────────────────────────┘
┌─────────────────────────────────────────────────────────────┐
│ Make public transport easier to use  使公共交通使用更方便     │
└─────────────────────────────────────────────────────────────┘
┌─────────────────────────────────────────────────────────────┐
│ Improve end-users' satisfaction  改善最终用户的满意度         │
└─────────────────────────────────────────────────────────────┘
┌─────────────────────────────────────────────────────────────┐
│ Help shift people from traditional car use to less intrusive modes │
│ 促使人们使用轨道交通等无干扰的交通模式                         │
└─────────────────────────────────────────────────────────────┘
┌─────────────────────────────────────────────────────────────┐
│ Reduce the amount of new capacity that needs to be added     │
│ 减少需要增加的通行能力的数量                                  │
└─────────────────────────────────────────────────────────────┘
┌─────────────────────────────────────────────────────────────┐
│ Make public transport more reliable (and be perceived as more reliable, which │
│ encourages people to switch to public transport)             │
│ 使公共交通更可靠(使人们感觉到更可靠,鼓励人们使用公共交通)      │
└─────────────────────────────────────────────────────────────┘
```

Figure 4.28　Objectives that ITS can contribute to

图 4.28　ITS 可以实现的目标

(2) Many templates exist for critical factors analysis　关于关键因素分析的模板

Many templates exist for critical factors analysis. The template shown as Table 4.1 is adapted from the approach given by Peters, 1999.

有很多用于关键因素分析的模板，表 4.1 重要因素分析模块中显示的模板采用的是 1999 年 Peter 给出的方法。

This template provides a good basis for expressing what end result or outcome is being sought and what visible results or measures are expected if ITS has the desired effect. The "goal area"/"measures" categorization approach can be applied to the full range of objectives for ITS. These can be very wide. Safety improvements might include benefits in perceptions of personal safety. Environmental benefits will often include noise reduction and might include community benefits. In each of these cases, it is possible to define a "goal area" or "outcome" and to agree the "measures" by which progress can be monitored.

这个模板为表述产生明显的结果或期望得到 ITS 设计效果的手段提供了良好的基础。"目标区域"/"指标"的分类方法可以应用于整个 ITS 的目标范围，这个范围非常广泛。安全性改善可能包括个人安全的感觉；环境效益时常包括噪声的减少，也可能包括社区效益。这其中的每种情况都可以定义一个"目标区域"或"指标"，并且同意使用这个"指标"来监测取得的进步。

4.5.5 Summary of Evaluation Methods 评价方法小结

In Europe, the CONVERGE guidelines developed for the European Commission's Fourth Framework R&D Program set out systematic guidance on planning ITS evaluation and reporting results. This approach has subsequently formed the basis of other national and European guidance.

在欧洲，由欧盟第四框架研发计划开发的 CONVERGE 指南列出了规划 ITS 评价和报道结果的系统指导，这个方法后来逐渐成为了其他国家和欧洲的指南的基础。

In the USA, the ITS Joint Program Office provides guidelines for before and after evaluation of ITS and the ITS Deployment Analysis System provides software for cost-benefit analysis.

在美国，ITS 联合计划办公室提供了关于 ITS 事前和事后评价的评价指南，而且 IDAS 提供了用于成本效益分析的软件。

Given the great diversity of possible responses to users and their needs, ITS can be adapted to serve widely different policy objectives. Politicians like to be seen to be pro-active, and may be happy to invest in ITS which are visible, regardless of whether the systems are strictly appropriate. The five tests below represent a way of formalizing political considerations, not a new task. In the political context, any scheme has to be seen to be:

考虑到用户和其需求做出的可能反应的多元化特点，ITS 可以服务于更为广泛的不同目标。政府官员喜欢自己被认为是积极主动的，愿意投资产生看得见效果的 ITS，而不管该系统是否是真正合适的。下面 5 个检验指标代表了一种政府考虑的形式，而并不是一个新的任务。在政治背景下，任何方案必须体现出以下特点：

- Deliverable 可实施的
- Acceptable 可接受的
- Affordable 可负担的
- Measurable 可测量的
- Electable 可选择的

4.6 Conclusions 结论

ITS investments provide a wide variety of benefits: reduced accidents, less severe injuries, improvements in journey times, reduced congestion, greater productivity for transport operators and better environmental quality, to name but a few. These benefits are valued by the travelling public, professionals, communities, businesses and service providers.

ITS 投资能够产生各种各样的效益：减少事故，减少受伤的严重性，改善行程时间，降低拥挤程度，提高运输操作人员的生产率，改善环境质量等等。这些效益对于出行的公众、专业人员、社区、商业和服务提供者都有价值。

Evaluation is a key part of the ITS deployment process. It is not an optional add-on, nor is it a pass/fail "test". Its purpose is to ensure that the systems deployed are the most appropriate ones, to ensure that investment is targeted towards areas and applications that will bring the most benefits. If the evaluation is well-structured, it gives a clear framework for assessing any new ideas or problems identified after consultation, or during project development.

评价是 ITS 部署过程中的一个重要组成部分，它既不是可选择的附加测试，也不是通过或不通过的测试，它的目的是确保部署的系统是最合适的，确保投资是针对地区和应用的，并且能够带来最大的效益。如果评价有良好的结构，它给出了一个用于评估在咨询后或项目进展过程中出现的任何新观点或问题的条理分明的框架。

In summary, evaluation enables those involved in funding and deploying ITS to:

总之，评价能够使参与投资和部署 ITS 的人们：

➢ Understand the impacts of the proposed ITS system or service. 理解所提出的 ITS 系统或服务的影响。

➢ Give confidence in the planned scheme. 建立对计划方案的信心。

➢ Quantify the benefits and justify the expenditure. 量化效益和判断费用的合理性。

➢ Help make future investment decisions. 帮助制定未来的投资决策。

➢ Learn lessons for the future. 为了将来学习经验教训。

The benefits and limitations of each option should be considered, as well as the costs, before a program or project investment decision is made. Each roads manager must make an informed decision

在计划和项目投资决策做出之前，每一个备选方案的效益、局限性以及成本都应被考虑。每一个道路管理者都必须做出明智的决策。

Chapter 5 How do I Plan and Finance ITS
第五章 如何进行 ITS 的规划和投资

5.1 Context for ITS Deployment ITS 实施背景

5.1.1 Policy Context 政策背景

Across the globe, the deployment of intelligent transport systems has been somewhat slower than anticipated. This has not been caused by technological limitations. It is rather because of nontechnical concerns such as institutional issues and commercial considerations. Although the vision for the role of ITS may be clear, the path to deployment in practice is often problematic. For example, ITS may require organizations to develop an operational capability that was not required before. ITS may also require a heavy investment in "hard" and "soft" ITS infrastructure and "info structure" involving the use of fast developing technologies. This can raise major public policy considerations, not least the appropriate level of public finance, or the terms and conditions to be placed on private sector promoters of ITS.

因为某些原因,全球范围内 ITS 的实施都有些滞后于预期,这不是因为技术上的限制,更多的是因为非技术因素,如制度上的问题和商业化的顾虑。虽然 ITS 所扮演的角色可能已经很清楚,但实际中的实施过程却常常问题众多。比如 ITS 可能会需要一些组织来开发以前不需要的运行能力,ITS 也会需要在"硬的"和"软的"ITS 基础设施及使用快速发展的技术的"信息基础设施"上进行重大投资。这些可能主要需要增加公共政策方面的考虑,不仅仅包括公共财政的适当水平,或者是针对私营部门的 ITS 开发者的条款和条件。

ITS needs to be considered in the context of overall transport services and hence must contribute to transport policy goals The factors of successful ITS deployment is that a systematic planning and design process that can respond to user needs, it is consistent with national or international requirements for inter-operability of systems and equipment, recognize market opportunities and technology developments, integrated with any previously installed "legacy" systems. The factors of successful ITS deployment is mentioned in figure 5.1.

ITS 需要在整个运输服务的背景下进行考虑,因此必须对交通运输的政策目标有所贡献。成功的 ITS 部署有如下要素:系统化的规划和响应用户需要的设计过程,国内及国际上对系统及设备互操作性的要求相一致,认识市场机遇、技术、发展、系统规范与标准,能与任何以前安装的"既有"系统相集成。ITS 成功部署的要素如图 5.1 所示。

A systematic planning and design process that can respond to user needs 系统化的规划和响应用户需要的设计过程	It is consistent with national or international requirements for inter-operability of systems and equipment 国内及国际上对系统及设备互操作性的要求相一致
Recognizes market opportunities and technology developments 认识市场机遇、技术、发展、系统规范与标准	Integrated with any previously installed "legacy" systems 能与任何以前安装的"既有"系统相集成

Figure 5.1　Factors of successful ITS deployment
图 5.1　ITS 成功部署的要素

Current thinking is that ITS should be considered as service driven. The systems aspects of ITS are important but only in the context of the services they deliver. However, ITS services do not stand alone. They are linked with other infrastructures such as mobile communications, smart cards, automated payment clearance systems and in-vehicle electronics. The availability and stability of these supporting infrastructures have a profound influence on the cost and risk profile of ITS services and products. An ITS service which has to finance a major infrastructure may fail because of the financial barriers and technical risks. If the cost regime or longevity of the supporting services is uncertain then the venture may be judged too risky. As with any other enterprise, promoters will be looking for a clear path to successful and profitable delivery. The infrastructure of ITS is mentioned in the figure 5.2.

目前的观点是，ITS 应该被看作是由服务驱动的，ITS 系统的各个方面是重要的但仅仅在它们所提供的服务背景下才是这样，但 ITS 的服务并不能独自存在。它们要与其他基础设施相连接，如移动通信、智能卡、自动支付结算系统及车载电子设备等，这些支撑设施的可用性和稳定性对 ITS 服务和产品的成本和风险有重大影响。一个必须在主要基础设施上投资的 ITS 服务有可能因为资金障碍和技术风险而失败。如果成本构成或者支持服务的持续时间不确定，投资也会被断定风险较大。对于任何企业而言，开发者都会寻找有把握的途径去获得成功和利润。ITS 所需要的基础设施内容如图 5.2 所示。

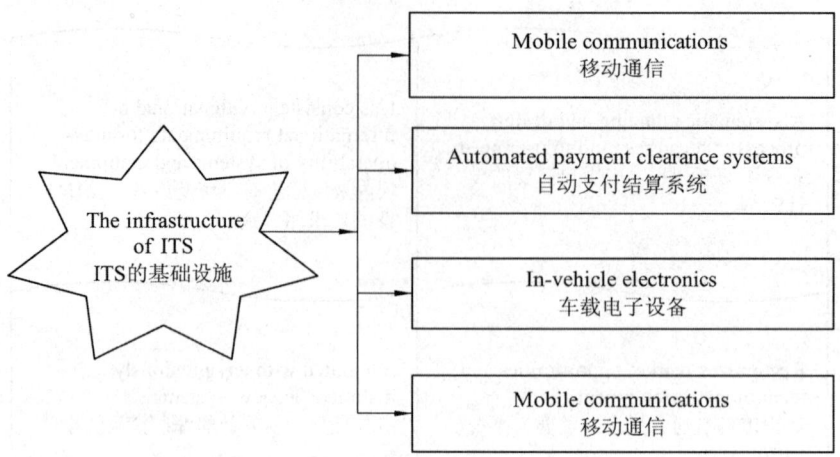

Figure 5.2　Infrastructure of ITS
图 5.2　智能交通系统的基础设施

The key to success can be summed up in four simple rules: ITS should be incorporated into the mainstream transportation planning and investment cycles. Project finance needs to be on a whole-life basis, including maintenance and operational costs as well as the capital for start-up investment. Use innovative procurement methods in the public sector, involving multiple evaluation criteria to secure best value (i.e. a move from awarding a contract solely on the basis of lowest cost). Where appropriate, the private sector can be involved in partnerships and out-sourcing, both for the investment in ITS infrastructure and for ITS operations and delivery of ITS Services.

成功的关键可以概括为以下四个简单原则：ITS 应与主流交通规划和循环投资周期体系合为一体。项目投资要基于全寿命周期，既包括初始的投资，也要包括维护和运营成本。在公共部门使用创新性的采购方法，采取多重评价准则以确保最大利益（例如，不再全然基于最低成本原则签订合同）。机会适宜时，私营部门能被吸纳为 ITS 基础设施投资、运营和提供 ITS 服务的合作伙伴及外包商。

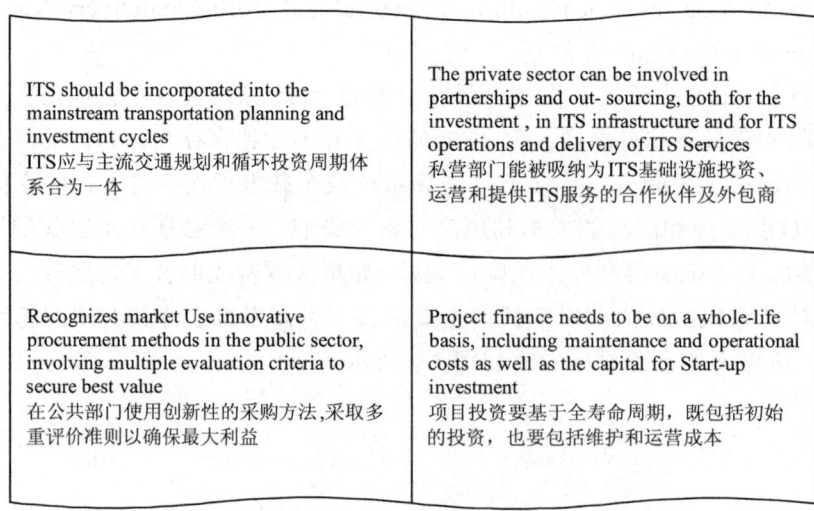

Figure 5.3　Four simple rules of ITS
图 5.3　ITS 的四项简单原则

The figure 5.4 illustrates the different dimensions that a city or region will need to consider when embarking on a program of ITS deployment.

下图描述了城市和地区着手进行 ITS 实施计划时需要考虑的不同因素。

Figure 5.4　Factors be thought of ITS deployment

图 5.4　ITS 实施需要考虑的因素

5.1.2　Public Policy Issues　公共政策问题

At the local level, policy relates to those subjects within the political control of regional, metropolitan, rural and other non-national government bodies, e.g. local road and public transport network management, parking, environment, travel information. The public authorities need to create a framework for analysis and assessment of ITS services, both from the point of view of individual ITS applications and, at a more general level, from the perspective of the urban planning and transport authorities in a city or region. A good example is the imbedding of the Japanese ITS policy under the 1995 Basic Guidelines on the Promotion of Advanced Information and Telecommunication Society announced by the national government of Japan.

在本地范围内，政策与以下这些有关：区域、都市和农村的行政控制，以及其他非中央的政府实体，如本地道路和公共交通网管理、停车、环境和出行信息服务等。公共机构需要建立能分析和评估 ITS 服务的框架，包括从单个 ITS 服务的角度以及在更普遍意义上从城市或地区的城市规划和交通管理部门的角度。日本政府曾颁布 1995 年度先进信息与通信的社会基本推进计划，日本 ITS 政策包含其中，这就是一个很好的例子。

ITS technologies are now developed to the stage where they offer a range of applications that can be tailored to provide a variety of services in support of local transport policy. Transportation goals and objectives are not the only consideration, because ITS is an important component in the development and exploitation of Information and Communication Technologies (ICT). ITS may therefore be subservient to ICT policy goals and priorities.

现在 ITS 各项技术已发展到了这样的地步，它们可以提供广泛的应用，这些应用是可调整的，以便提供不同的服务以支持地方运输政策。由于 ITS 是信息和通信技术（ICT）开发和应用的重要组成部分，因此交通目标和对象已经不是唯一考虑的因素，所以 ITS 有可能受到 ICT 政策目标和优先项目的影响。

5.1.3　Regional ITS Infrastructure and Info Structure　区域 ITS 基础设施和信息设施

The infrastructure for ITS is made up of a number of different features. For the systems to work, ITS services need all the basic components in place, fully and reliably operational. For example a lack of basic infrastructure affecting any part of the information supply chain will lead to poor-quality information services. The infrastructure of ITS is shown in figure 5.5.

　　ITS 的基础设施特征各异，数量众多。系统想要正常运作，需要 ITS 服务的基础组件全部就位并可靠运行。例如，一旦某个影响到信息供应链的基础设施缺乏就会导致信息服务的质量低下。ITS 的基础设施如图 5.5 所示。

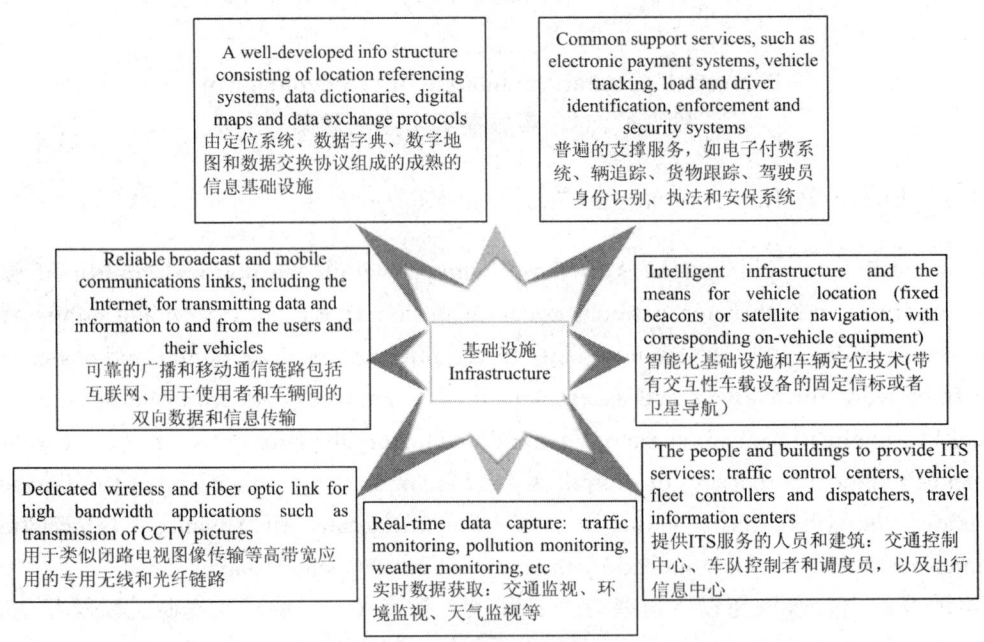

Figure 5.5　Infrastructure of ITS
图 5.5　ITS 基础设施

5.1.4　ITS Service Characteristics　ITS 服务特征

These concern the features of the selected ITS services that are planned or desired, the service profiles and the levels of service to be offered. There are many options, such as the extent and detail in transport network coverage, whether it is single travel mode or multi-modal coverage, or for general or specialist use. The notices of ITS service characteristics are shown in figure 5.6.

　　本节关注于被选定的 ITS 服务的特性，它们是已经规划的或希望提供的，可以提供这些服务的概貌和层次。这里涉及许多选择，例如交通覆盖网络中的程度和细节，不论是单出行模式还是覆盖多模式出行，或者是一般应用还是特殊应用。ITS 服务特征注意事项如图 5.6。

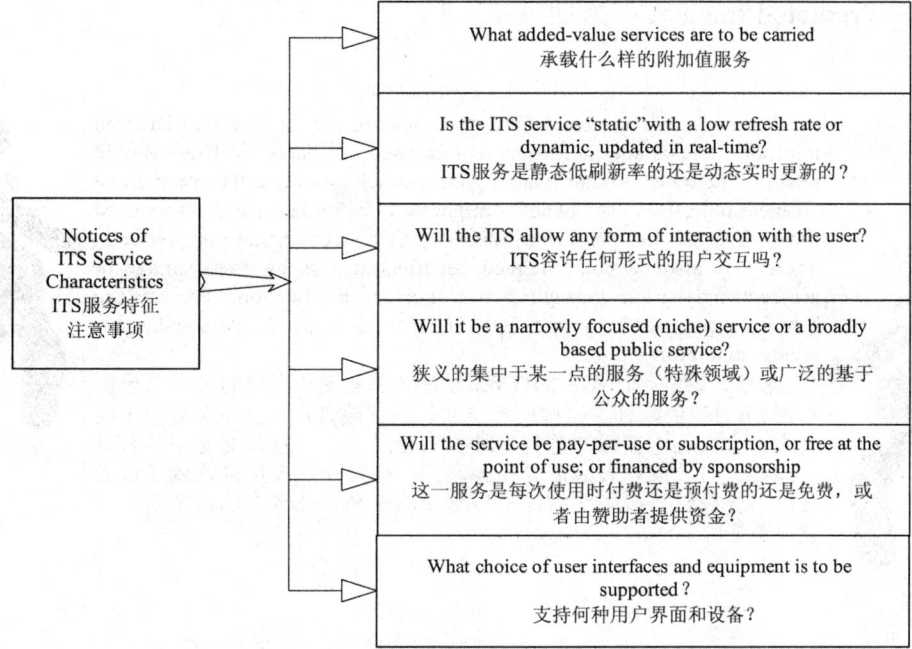

Figure 5.6　Notices of ITS Service Characteristics
图 5.6　ITS 服务特征注意事项

5.1.5　Operating Context　运营背景

Operating context is about the basic organizational, regulatory and institutional framework for deployment and the service set-up. A suitable service set-up will improve the commercial and public sector cases through suitable risk distribution, cost sharing, service pricing and higher quality delivery. The methods of the appropriate service structure to improve the investment effects are shown in figure 5.7.

运营背景部分阐明了用于部署和服务结构的基本组织形式、规章和制度框架。适当的服务结构将通过分散风险、分担成本、服务定价和高质量的传递，改善商业和公共部门的投资效果。适当的服务结构改善投资效果的方法如图 5.7 所示。

Figure 5.7　Methods of the appropriate service structure to improve the investment effect
图 5.7　适当的服务结构改善投资效果的方法

171

5.1.6 Predicted Impacts 预期影响

These are the forecast effects the proposed ITS service will have on transport systems and their users as discussed in Chapter 4. These should relate to the transport and related public policy goals and the commercial business objectives. The benefits might be to individuals, such as reduced travel time and the perceived reliability of collective transport services. There may also be policy-related benefits, such as improved image or accident prevention through better incident notification. The service benefit experienced by the individual might include personalize or preferential information.

这里讨论的是已确定的ITS服务对交通系统和用户的预期效果，如第4章讨论的那样。这些应和交通、公共政策目标及商务对象关联起来。个人可能获得的益处有减少旅行时间，对整体交通服务有可靠感等。与政策相关的益处也会存在，如提高图像质量，或通过更好的事件警告来预防事故。个体感受的便利之处也应包括个性化或优先服务的信息。

5.1.7 Public Sector Business Case 公共部门的业务问题

This deals with the desirability or feasibility of the service as seen from the authorities' perspectives. Funds made available from public sources, such as local, regional or national taxation, have to be justified.

从政府部门的观点来看，服务应具有预期目标和可用性。来自公共资源，如来自本地、地区或全国税收方面的投资等公共资源，必须正确使用。

The decision on funding ITS take into account the ongoing operating and maintenance costs as well as the capital investment required.

ITS 的投资决策应把运营维护成本和资本投资需求置于同等重要的地位。

5.1.8 Commercial Business Case 商业项目

The commercial business case rests on the return on investment and the profitability of the operation as a whole, including any monies received as a subsidy or through sponsorship. A decision to progress the project will depend on a risk assessment of all the uncertain factors. The uncertain factors of ITS is shown in figure 5.8.

商业项目依赖于投资的回报和整体运营的盈利能力，包括所有补贴和捐赠的资金收入。是否投资项目取决于对所有不确定因素的风险评估。ITS 的不确定因素如图 5.8 所示。

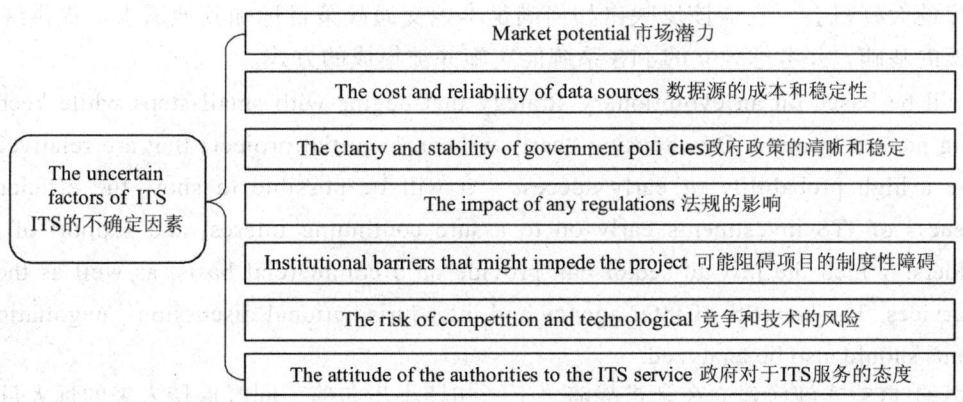

Figure 5.8 Uncertain factors of ITS
图 5.8 ITS 的不确定因素

5.2 The ITS Framework Plan ITS 框架规划

5.2.1 High-level Deployment Strategy 高层次的实施战略

A mature, integrated ITS system is something that can only evolve over a period of time. Cities and regions can lay the foundations for this by developing a strategic framework and an ITS architecture to provide direction to local ITS deployment. High-level deployment strategy of ITS is shown in figure 5.9.

一个成熟的、集成的 ITS 系统必须在一个时期内逐步形成。城市及地区可以通过开发一个战略框架和一个 ITS 体系框架为地区的 ITS 发展提供方向，并为此打下基础。ITS 高层次实施战略组成部分如图 5.9 所示。

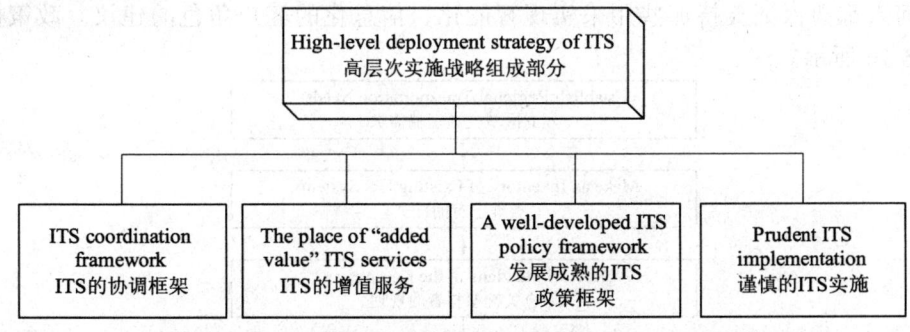

Figure 5.9 High-level deployment strategy of ITS
图 5.9 ITS 高层次实施战略组成部分

A national, regional or local ITS policy framework is an opportunity to analyse the requirements for deploying ITS, and assign roles and responsibilities, budgets and priorities. It should reflect what needs to be done to meet the local transport policy objectives and other requirements. Provide the basis for specifying ITS system architecture and consider the ways in which individual ITS systems can be brought on stream and integrated.

国家、地区或本地的 ITS 政策框架是分析 ITS 实施需求、确定角色和责任、制定预算及发展次序的大好机会，它应该反映出如何满足本地交通政策目标和其他需求。提供细化 ITS 体系框架的基础，并考虑独立的 ITS 系统能实施并被集成的方式。

It will be based on an evolutionary strategy that begins with small steps while keeping the future big picture in mind. By choosing "early winners"– initial projects that are relatively small and have a high probability of early success – it will be possible to show the efficiency and effectiveness of ITS investments early on to assure continuing interest and support of the key stakeholders. Which the private sector can provide on a commercial basis, as well as the public sector services. The benefits of inter-agency and inter-jurisdictional discussions, negotiations, and agreements should also be analyzed.

谨慎的 ITS 实施应建立在渐进战略之上，初期小步向前，同时保持未来的远大目标。选择"早回报"项目，相对投资较小，早期成功机率高，就可以显示其投资的效率和效益，也能得到持续投资和主要出资人的支持。私营部门和政府部门可以为此提供商业基础。对机构间利益和跨辖区的协商、谈判与协议也应加以分析。

5.2.2　Steps in Policy Framework Analysis　政策框架分析中的步骤

The process of developing a framework plan will bring together the main actors and agencies involved in deploying future ITS systems. In winning their support, it is helpful to have a clear vision of how ITS should develop. The ITS needs technical support and political support. Whoever champions the realization of that vision will need to secure supporting advice to fulfill the intelligent informed customer role in the face of rapidly changing technological capabilities. Steps in policy framework analysis are shown in figure 5.10.

框架规划的制定过程将把主要参与者和未来实施 ITS 的有关机构结合起来，有助于明确 ITS 的发展远景，这一远景需要技术和政治的支持。面对日新月异的科技能力，支持实现这一远景的任何人都要保证支持那些用来实现智能化、信息化的客户角色的建议。政策框架分析步骤如图 5.10 所示。

Figure 5.10　Steps in policy framework analysis

图 5.10　政策框架分析步骤

(1) Establish Regional Transportation Needs　建立区域交通运输需求

Ideally, this will be based on a survey of the needs of the users: shippers, carriers, distribution companies, bus and coach operators, commercial activities, private individuals, and national and regional governmental organizations. The framework needs to respond to current policy issues such as environmental sustainability, economic development, safety and security, for example the European eSafety initiative and the USA Homeland Security.

理想情况下，从调查使用者的需求起步：船主、运输公司、分销公司、客车和货车经营者，商业机构，个人、国家和区域政府机构。这一框架需要反映如环境可持续性、经济发展、安全和安保等政策主题，例如欧洲的 eSafety 初期规划和美国 Homeland Security 规划。

(2) Make an Inventory of Existing ITS Systems　整理已有的 ITS

An important input to the ITS framework plan is an inventory of existing ITS systems and services that are either already operating or under development. The future of these "legacy systems" must be addressed specifically in the ITS Framework Plan. Decisions will be needed on whether to retain and upgrade them or to invest in new systems that have improved capabilities and performance.

对 ITS 框架规划而言，其中一项重要的来源是清理现有的 ITS 系统和服务，包括已经运营或正在开发的。在 ITS 框架规划中，这些"已有系统"的将来必须给予特别的强调，需要决定是保留和升级这些项目，还是投资新系统以改善系统能力和业绩。

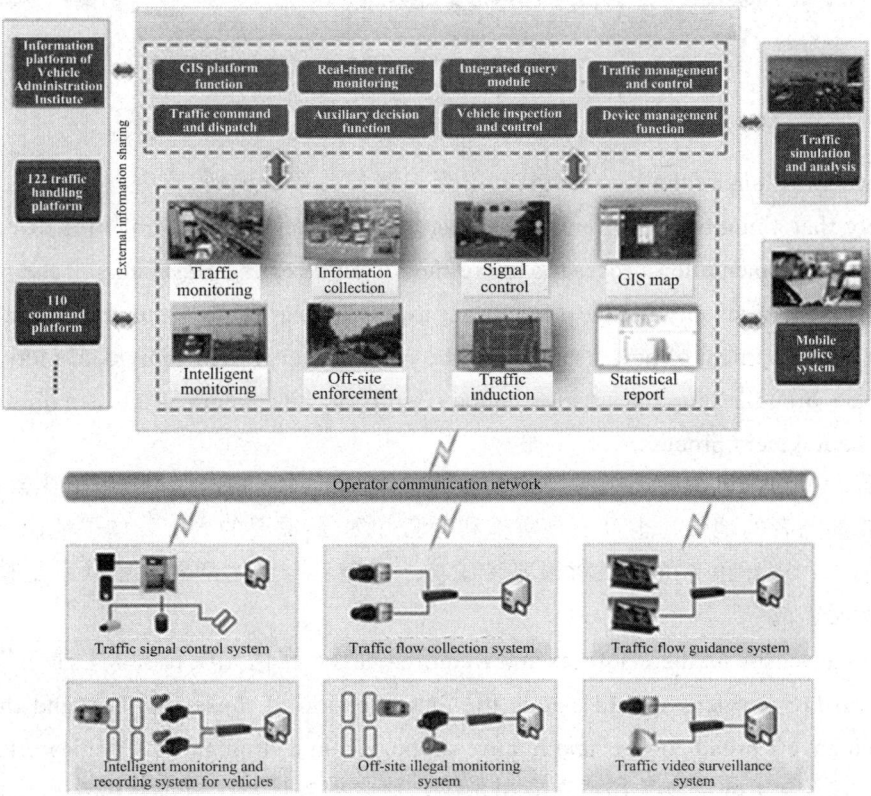

Figure 5.11　ITS Framework

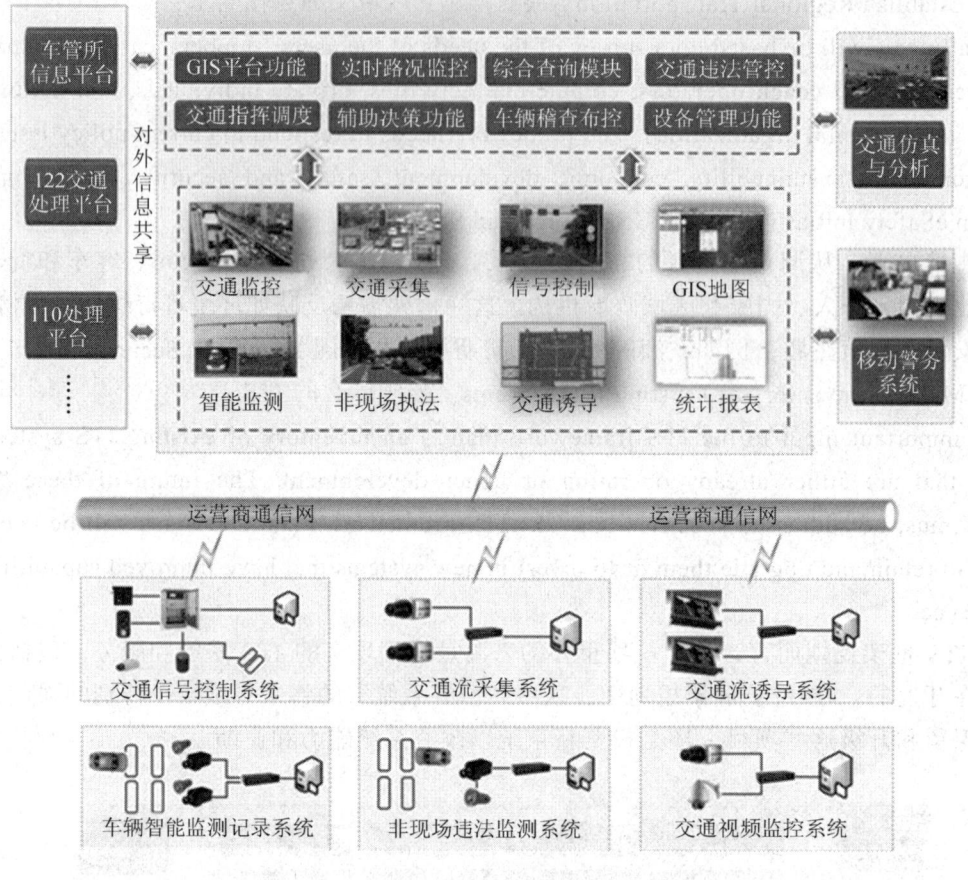

图 5.11 ITS 框架

(3) Review the Plans of the Key Actors　审查关键参与者的规划

It is likely that a number of different organizations will need to "buy in" to the overall vision for ITS and the implementation process to make the vision a reality. Harmonizing the positions of the principal actors is probably the most important aspect for the deployment and operation of ITS. The successful development of new services will be much easier if their individual motivations and interests can be brought into line. Close contact with the key actors is needed throughout the planning and deployment process.

很可能若干不同的组织会需要参与到 ITS 的总体愿景和实施过程中，以使愿景成为现实。协调各个主要参与者的地位，也可能是实施和运营 ITS 最重要的方面。如果他们单独的动机和利益能够纳入，则新服务的开发将很容易成功。关键参与者之间的紧密联系是整个规划和实施过程中所必需的。

(4) Build consensus on the Priorities and Requirements　在优先项和需求上建立共识

A focus on ITS services should enable the identification of those services, and the enabling systems, which have a broad context and require support from a strategic ITS framework.

ITS 服务应着重于确定服务和建立应用系统，使之内容广泛，并能从战略框架得到支撑。

(5) Analysis Roles and Responsibilities　分析承担的角色及责任

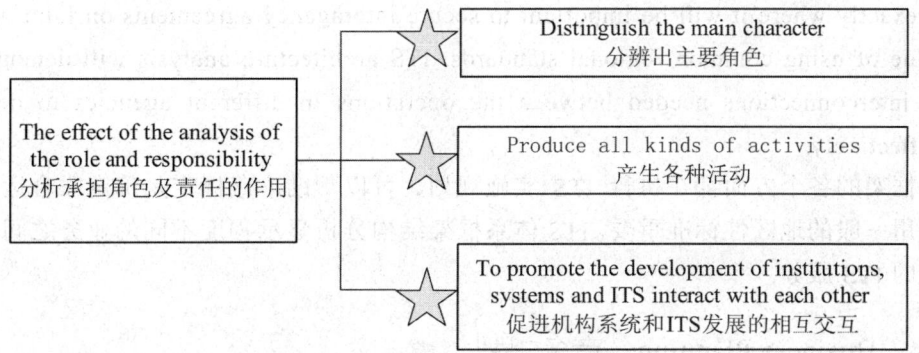

Figure 5.12　Effect of the analysis of the role and responsibility

图 5.12　分析承担角色及责任的作用

(6) Documentation　文档

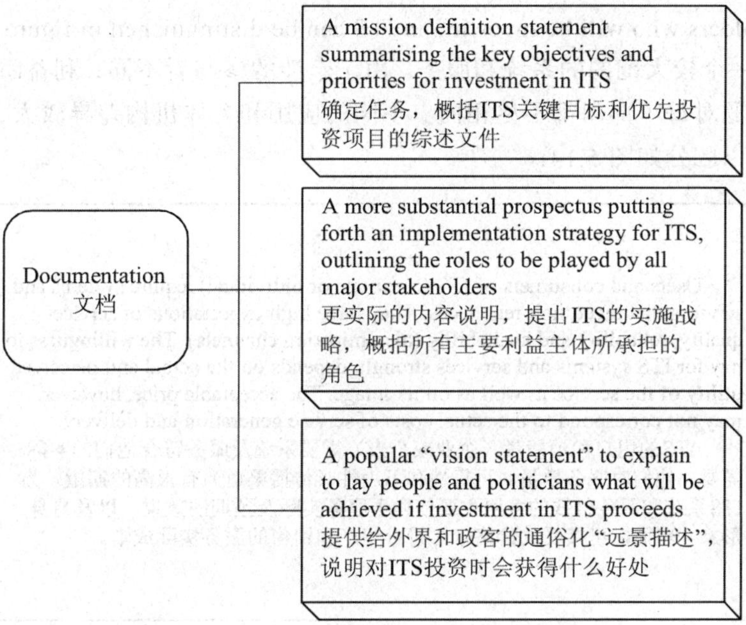

Figure 5.13　Inclusions of ITS documentation

图 5.13　ITS 文档所包含的内容

5.2.3　ITS Architecture　ITS 体系框架

A number of countries are developing their own national ITS architectures following the lead given by the US National ITS Architecture. When doing so, it is important to identify local operational priorities and institutional structures that are significantly different from the US.

一些国家遵循美国国家 ITS 体系框架所给出的指导，正在开发自己的国家 ITS 体系框架。重要的是，必须找出本土的优先项和制度结构，这些都和美国截然不同。

Each aspect of architecture has a bearing on ITS implementation plans and can help to pin-point exactly where it will be important to secure interagency agreements on joint operations, or the value of using common regional standards. ITS architecture analysis will demonstrate the extent of interconnections needed between the operations in different agencies to deliver ITS services effectively.

体系框架的各个方面都在执行 ITS 实施规划，可以帮助准确标定是确定联合运营协议重要还是使用一般的地区性标准重要。ITS 体系框架结构分析显示程度不同的业务之间需要相互提供有效的 ITS 服务。

5.2.4 Business Planning　商务规划

ITS covers a wide range of systems and services. Because different players are involved, stakeholder roles and attitudes and the legal and institutional issues vary for each sector. Whilst there will be wide variations between different applications and individual institutions, three broad groups of stakeholders who will be investing in ITS can be distinguished in figure 5.14:

ITS 涵盖了一个较大范围的系统和服务。由于牵涉的参与者不同，利益团体角色、态度以及法律、体制问题对每个部门都不尽相同。不同的应用和个体机构差异较大，投资于 ITS 的三大利益团体可以区分如图 5.14：

> Users and consumers of ITS (corporate or individual) require systems and services that meet their real needs. They have high expectations of service quality, reliability and availability (dissemination channels). The willingness to pay for ITS systems and services strongly depends on the actual and perceived utility of the service as well as on its image. The acceptable price, however, may not correspond to the actual costs of service generation and delivery.
>
> ITS的用户和消费者（企业或个人）需要系统及服务符合他们的实际需要。他们对服务质量、可靠性和可用性（传播渠道）有很高的期望。为ITS系统和服务付钱的意愿主要依靠于服务实际及预期的效果，以及自身形象。然而，可接受的价格未必符合生产和销售的服务实际成本。

> The public sector will adopt ITS to deliver various public services, objectives and strategies. Where these are made explicit, as advocated in Chapter 4, public interests in ITS service development are usually justified by positive impacts on traffic management and modal shift, economic development, business location, image and social inclusion. Public authorities then seek to involve the private sector in order to exploit the enterprise culture, limit public expenditures and increase efficiency.
>
> 公共部门将通过ITS提供各种公共服务、目标和战略。如第4章所提倡的，这些都明确表明了ITS服务发展中的公共利益，常常被证明对交通管理模式转变、经济的发展、企业经营地点、企业，形象和社会包容性上均有积极影响。公共机构则寻找私营部门参与，可以弘扬企业文化，节省公共开支和提高效率。

> Private sector players share the objectives of marketing their products/ services through ITS, entering a future growth market and/or developing a new profitable business area. In this, private sector actors depend heavily on the framework conditions established by the public sector, which they often see as an obstacle to the free market. On the other hand, differences between various private sector players imply differing orientations and priorities when defining new ITS service delivery models. This will require different strategic agreements.
> 私营部门参与者拥有共同的目标，即营销他们的产品/服务，进入正在成长的市场，同时也可以开发新的有利可图的业务领域。在这里私营部门参与者强烈依赖公共部门建立的体系框架条件，而他们常常认为那是自由市场的障碍。另一方面，不同私营部门参与者的差异意味着他们在确定新的ITS服务传递模式时，有着不同的倾向和优先项。这将需要不同的战略协议。

Figure 5.14　Three broad groups of stakeholders
图 5.14　三大利益团体

When different groups considering whether the distribution of their budgets to the ITS, there are three distinct evaluation system in operation.

不同的团体在考虑是否分配他们的预算给ITS时，有三个截然不同的评估系统在运行。

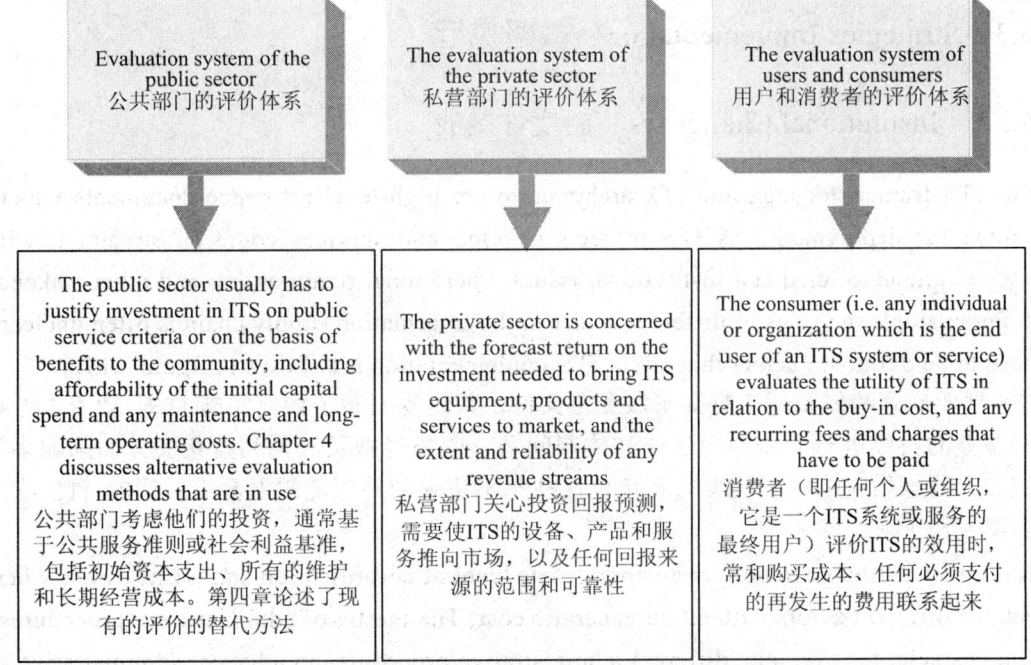

Figure 5.15　ITS's three different evaluation system of business planning
图 5.15　ITS商务规划的三个不同的评估系统

ITS projects will frequently require justification against at least two, if not all three of the underlying business models. Failure to meet one or other of the investment tests will produce a classic "chicken and egg situation" – who goes first, the supplier or the purchaser in making a commitment to the system or product?

ITS项目往往需要对至少两个或三个基本的商业模式进行验证。不符合一个或其他的投资测试，将产生经典"鸡和蛋困境"：谁先行，是供应商或买方，做出系统或产品的承诺？

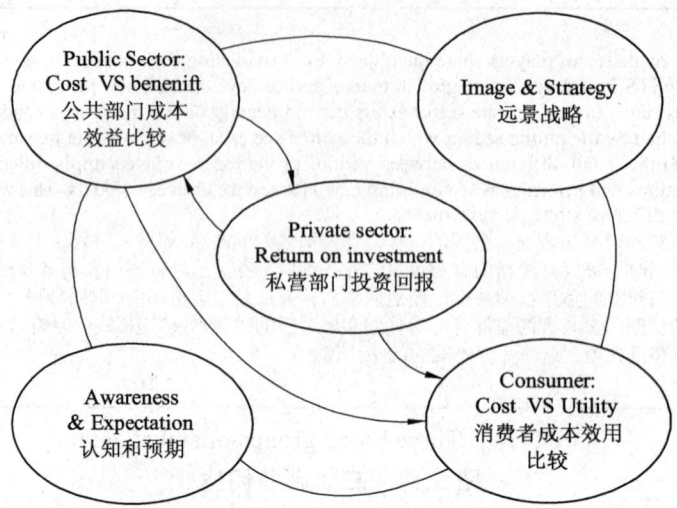

Figure 5.16 Inter-dependencies between the public sector, the private sector and consumers
图 5.16 公共部门、私营部门和消费者之间的相互依存关系

5.3 Strategies Implementation 战略执行

5.3.1 Institutional Challenges 制度性挑战

The ITS framework plan and ITS architecture are high-level reference documents which set the context for deployment. As ITS projects develop and services come on stream, it will be necessary to attend to legal and institutional issues, operational requirements and other stakeholder issues. For example the roles of different actors in the information supply chain is often unclear and may need to be defined. Factors that affect ITS implementation are shown in figure 5.17.

ITS 框架规划和体系框架是高等级参考文件，其内容明确了如何实施 ITS。随着 ITS 项目开发和服务的持续进行，需要对法律和体制问题、业务经费及其他利益相关方面问题多加关注。例如，信息供应链中不同参与者角色往往是不清晰的并可能需要界定。影响 ITS 实施的因素如图 5.17 所示。

It is a real challenge to deliver an appropriate level of co-ordination and create synergy benefit between the different actors without bureaucratic cost. The inertia of administrative procedures can be a real obstacle, for example, different administrative procedures in adjacent administrative areas which have to be harmonized. Examples are the installation and maintenance of roadside detection equipment, or a detailed local operating agreement, if there is a need for new safety or operational procedures this can also take up valuable time. ITS operational requirements are frequently geared to an operations or control center at the hub of the ITS service.

提供适当层面上的协调并且形成不同参与者之间的共同效益而无官僚成本，这是一个真正的挑战。行政程序的惯性或许是真正的障碍，例如毗邻行政区域的不同行政程序就必须进行协调。诸如安装和维修检测路边设备或细化本地经营协议，如果有新的安全需求或操作程序的需要，也要为之付出相应的时间。ITS 的运营需求往往侧重 ITS 服务枢纽的某个运营或控制中心。

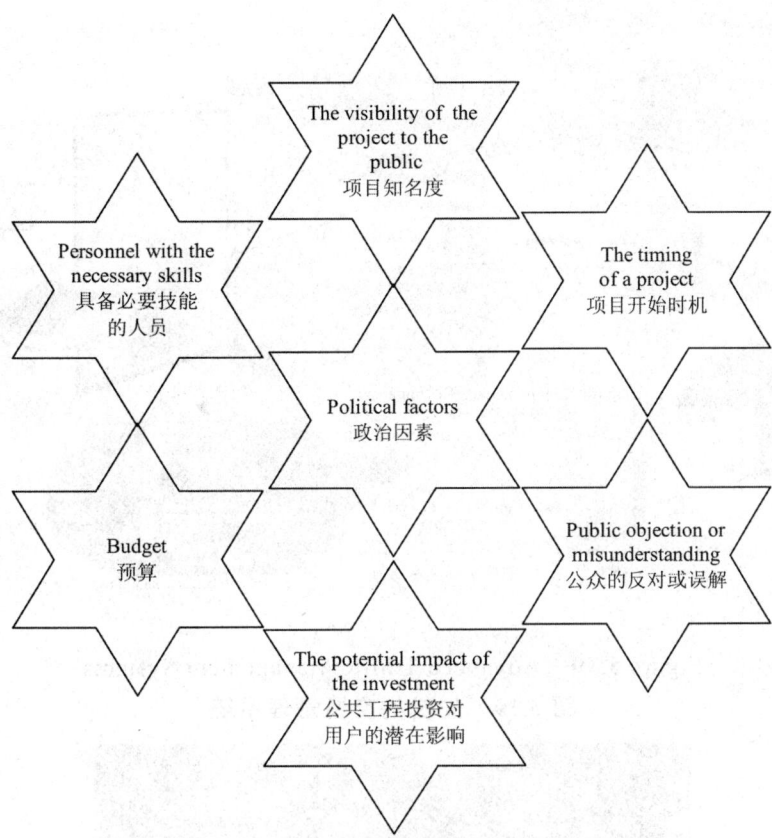

Figure 5.17 Affect factors of ITS implementation

图 5.17 ITS 实施的影响因素

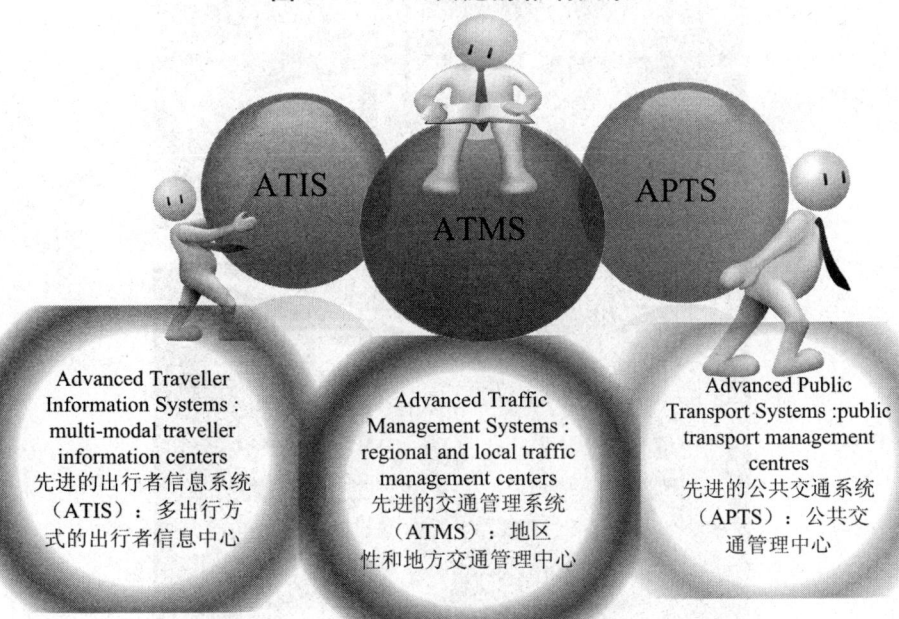

Figure 5.18 Control center at the hub of the ITS service

图 5.18 ITS 服务枢纽的控制中心

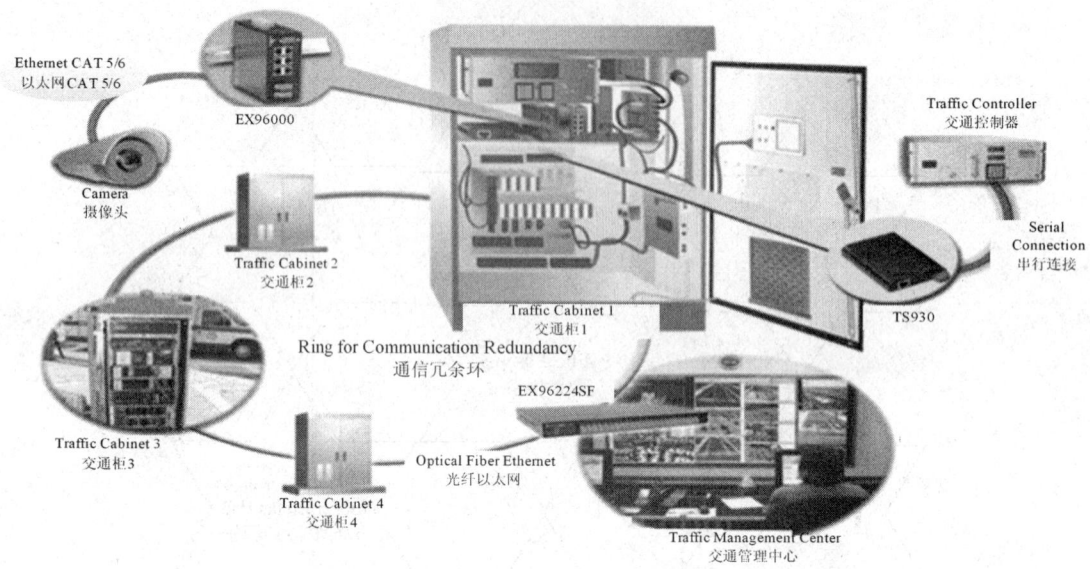

Figure 5.19 Advanced Traffic Management Systems
图 5.19 先进的交通管理系统

Figure 5.20 Advanced Public Transport Systems
图 5.20 先进的公共交通系统

5.3.2 A "Route map" for ITS deployment ITS 实施的路线图

Resolving the institutional issues needs to proceed in parallel with the technical aspects of ITS project planning. The specific ITS development must be checked for its feasibility and desirability in the local context, from both technical and non-technical perspectives. There is usually more than one way to carry out ITS implementation; for example, rapid versus gradual introduction, home-grown versus imported systems, public versus private initiatives, etc. Implementation of ITS analytical framework is shown in figure 5.21.

解决体制问题需要与技术方面的 ITS 项目规划同步进行。无论是从技术和非技术观点上，具体化的 ITS 发展必须检查其在本地的可行性和需求状况。通常有一个以上的途径来进行 ITS 实施，例如快速或逐步引进，采用国产或进口的系统，从公共或私营部门来着手等。ITS 的实施分析框架如下图 5.21。

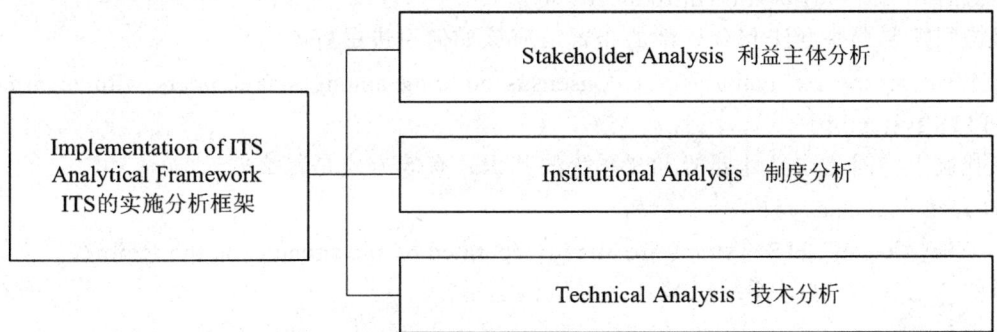

Figure 5.21 Implementation of ITS analytical framework
图 5.21 ITS 的实施分析框架

(1) Stakeholder Analysis 利益主体分析

① Who are the major stakeholders in this domain?
谁是这个领域的主要利益主体？

② What impact would the proposed development of ITS have on each stakeholder?
预定的 ITS 发展可能对每一个利益主体有哪些影响？

③ What ITS systems does each stakeholder have now; i.e. legacy systems?
每个利益主体现在都有什么 ITS 系统，如遗留系统？

④ What plans does each have to develop ITS, short term and long term?
每个利益主体的长期和短期的 ITS 发展计划是什么？

⑤ What aspects of the planned ITS system would each stakeholder view positively and/or place as high priority?
已计划的 ITS 系统哪些方面能让每个利益主体看好并（或）作为重点项目？

⑥ What aspects of the planned ITS system would each stakeholder view negatively and/or place as low priority?
已计划的 ITS 系统哪些方面能让每个利益主体不看好并（或）不作为重点项目？

⑦ Are there ITS functions that all the key stakeholders would buy into?
有没有 ITS 功能是所有的关键利益主体都愿意支付的？

(2) Institutional Analysis　制度分析

① Which organizational units are in a position to provide leadership in developing ITS for this domain?

哪个组织单位在本领域发展 ITS 中承担领导地位？

② What organizational models are suitable for operating ITS in this domain?

什么组织模式适合本领域的 ITS 运营？

③ How well do existing institutional arrangements match these models?

现存的制度布置能够在多大程度上匹配这些模式？

④ Are there any obvious organizational gaps or weaknesses? How might these be rectified?

有没有可见的组织性隔阂和脆弱点？如何进行调整？

⑤ What legal, contractual, and other organizational arrangements are required between agencies? How can they best be introduced?

机构间需要哪些合法和合约性的布置？应该如何引进最好？

⑥ What means are available for consensus building among stakeholders with regard to the planned ITS systems?

在利益主体间建立已计划的 ITS 系统的共识，有效方式是什么？

(3) Technical Analysis　技术分析

① What "legacy" ITS systems are already operated by the agencies in the region?

哪些"已有的" ITS 系统已被本区的机构运用？

② What are the requirements for interoperability, both now and in the near-term/ medium-term future?

现在和短/中期内互操作性的需求是什么？

③ Where is it necessary to achieve compatibility and where is it optional?

哪里需要达到兼容？哪里是可选？

④ What communications infrastructure is available for ITS?

哪些通信基础设施是 ITS 可用的？

⑤ Where would data or information need to be exchanged between agencies?

哪里的机构之间需要交换数据或信息？

⑥ Are digital mapping and location referencing systems in place?

数字地图和定位参考系统就位了吗？

⑦ What data dictionary and data exchange standards have been adopted? Would data dictionary and data exchange standards need to be developed?

采用了哪些数据字典和数据交换标准？是否需要开发数据字典和数据交换标准？

The ITS Route Map is a means of translating concepts and plans into reality. It assigns roles and responsibilities and specifies how the stakeholders can organize themselves to implement the recommendations of the Framework Plan.

ITS 的路线图是一种将规划和观念变为现实的方式，它确定角色和责任人，并指明如何才能使利益主体自我组织来落实框架规划。

5.3.3 Effective Coordination Mechanisms 有效的协调机制

Effective dialogue between the key actors is the means of transforming the organizational arrangements from concept into reality. A task force of the major players can help to develop voluntary agreements and memoranda of understanding (MOUs) between the actors on matters of common concern. Examples from Europe are the two fora which give life and substance to the MOUs on cross border data exchange and on the provision of the language-independent Radio Data System / Traffic Message Channel (RDS/TMC) on FM radio. The fora create the opportunity for all interested parties to discuss problems together and agree on practical solutions. The body charged with high-level coordination of ITS development must have sufficient standing to be able to influence the decisions of key actors regarding conformance to the ITS architecture, data exchange formats and use of standards. The roll-out of ITS services may require voluntary cooperation agreements. An example is the National Economic Forum for Transport Telematicconvened at the federal level in Germany and chaired by the Federal Minister for Transport.

> **例**
>
> **German National Economic Forum on Transport Telematics (ITS)**
> **德国关于"运输的远程信息处理"的经济论坛**
>
> 1. Members of the Public/Private Partnership
> (1)Administration (Bund, Federal Lander, Cities)　(2)Service providers
> (3) Public transport companies　(4)Automotive industries
> (5) Private transport companies　(6)Electronics industries
> 2. Basic Agreements
> (1)Competition of technologies and services　(2)Devices for multiple intermodal applications
> (3)Priority for private services　(4)no new legal regulations
> (5)Interoperability of applications　(6)public/private partnerships for management of traffic data
> 3. Fundamental Experiences
> (1)The Forum gives partners the opportunity to discuss problems.
> (2)Private operators provide individual traffic information and guidance systems.
> (3)Framework for private ITS services must be created early on.
> (4)Transport sector needs a global satellite navigation system under civilian control.
> (5)ITS is in practice today in the public sector.
> (6)Services and systems should be interoperable.
>
> 1.公共/私营成员
> （1）管理机构（盟国、联邦、城市）　（2）服务提供者
> （3）公共运输公司　（4）汽车产业
> （5）私营运输公司　（6）电子产业
> 2.基本的协议
> （1）技术和服务的竞争　（2）多式联运应用的设施
> （3）私营服务的重点项目　（4）没有新的法律规则
> （5）应用系统的互操作性　（6）公共/私营参与者对交通数据的管理
> 3.基础性经验
> （1）给合伙人讨论机会的论坛　（2）私营运营者提供的个人交通信息和导航服务
> （3）私营ITS服务必须提前完成的框架　（4）运输部门需要的民用全球卫星导航定位系统
> （5）公共部门当前实施的ITS　（6）服务和系统应具有互操作性

关键参与者之间的有效对话是将概念转化为现实的组织性行为手段。任务组的主要参与

者能帮助起草自愿协议和谅解备忘录（MOU），体现参与者之间的共同关注之处。例如在欧洲，有两个论坛提供涉及跨境数据交换和提供在调频电台中发布的独立于语言的数字广播系统/交通信息频道（RDS/TMC）的基础性的备忘录。这些论坛创造机会让所有相关的各方展开讨论，并探寻实际问题解决方法。负责 ITS 发展高级协调的机构，一定要有足够的权威，能够促成主要参与者就 ITS 体系框架、数据交换格式、标准使用等达成一致。将 ITS 服务首次推向市场需要自愿合作协议。例如，主题为交通运输通讯的国家经济论坛在德国联邦召开，由联邦运输部长主持。

A national or regional steering committee with high-level political backing can be very effective in bringing together all the main actors to focus on achieving a common goal. It requires the support of a dedicated interagency coordination unit or some kind of technical panel drawn from the participating authorities. International, national, and regional public/private partnership organizations(figure 5.22), like ITS America, ITS Canada, ITS Europe (ERTICO), ITS United Kingdom, ITS Australia and ITS Japan (VERTIS) can play a useful part in setting up this consultation machinery.

具有高层政治背景的国家或区域执行委员会，可以非常有效地召集所有主要参与者集中实现一个共同的目标。这需要一个专门的在各支持单位间进行协调的组织或由某种机构联合成立的技术组织。国际的、国家的、区域性和公共/私营合伙组织（图 5.22），比如美国 ITS 协会、加拿大 ITS 协会、欧洲 ITS 协会（ERTICO）、英国 ITS 协会、澳洲 ITS 协会、日本 ITS 协会（VERTIS），在建立这一协商机制时可以发挥自己的作用。

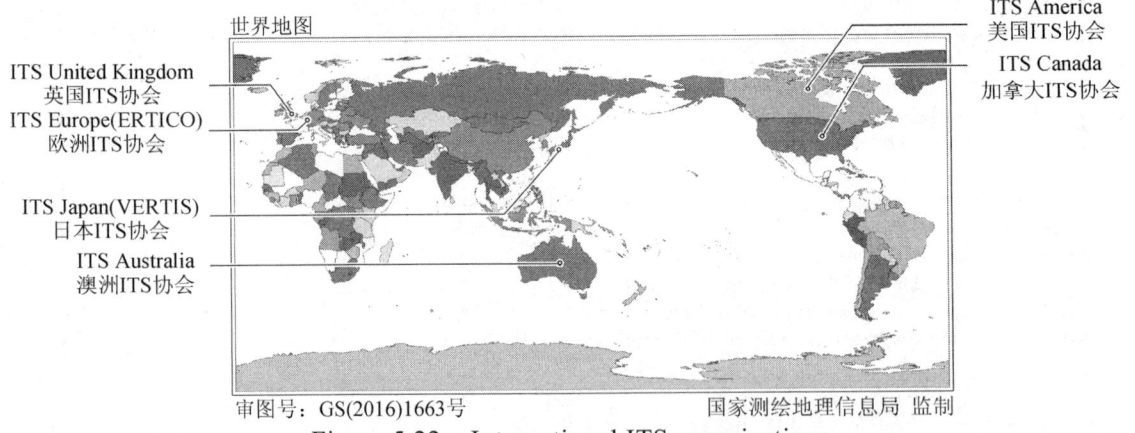

Figure 5.22　International ITS organizations
图 5.22　国际 ITS 协会

At the national or regional level, it may also be useful to create an advisory panel of other major stakeholders in ITS, including any significant private-sector actors, for consultation and advisory purposes.

在国家或区域性层面来说，建立一个 ITS 主要参与者的咨询组织也很有用处，为了达到咨询和顾问目的，应包括重要的私营部门参与者。

5.3.4　Operating Agreements　运行协议

Inter-agency and inter-company cooperation requirements may need to be formalized.

Inter-agency and inter-company cooperation requirements may need to be formalised. Public/public, public/private, and private/private collaboration agreements and contracts are often needed. These agreements can range from informal agreements between the parties to cooperate on day-to-day operational tasks, to more ambitious and formal contracts and memoranda of understanding (MOU), involving sharing of common systems. Midway between these two are the agreements on data exchange, specifying the agreed data formats and minimum data quality requirements (e.g. accuracy, timeliness, and extent of data consolidation or editing). The contractual relationships and information flow involved in delivering ITS-based information services can be quite complex. For example, a private sector service provider may need to secure contracts at five levels.

机构之间和公司之间的合作应要求正式化。公共/公共、公共/私营、私营/私营的合作协议和合同往往是很有需要的。这些协议可包括诸如当事人之间的非正式协议、合作的日常业务工作以及涉及共同系统分享的更为目标远大的正式合同和谅解备忘录（MOU）。介于二者之间的是数据交换协议,包括具体商定的数据格式、数据质量最低要求（例如准确性、及时性、数据整理或合并的程度涉及到以 ITS 为基础所提供的信息服务的协议关系和信息流会相当复杂。例如，一个私人服务提供商可能需要取得 5 个级别的协议：

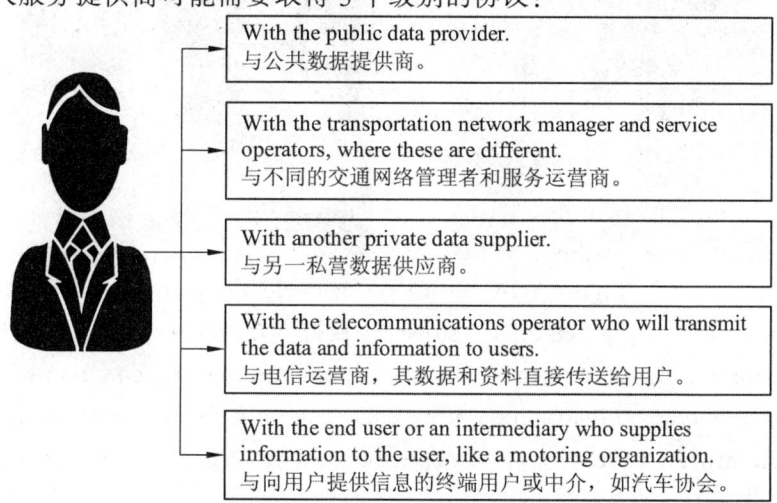

Figure 5.23   ITS operating agreements
图 5.23   ITS 的运行协议

It is likely that no two actors will have precisely the same set of requirements, since each has individual needs and resources. If it is appropriate, the details can be made the subject of contracts or formal agreements so that the receiving party can rely on a minimum performance specification from the sender, and there is a means of redress if this minimum is not achieved.

正是由于个性化的需要和资源，任何两个参与者的要求都可能会有不同，如果条件适宜，可以细化合同或正式协议，这样接收部分就能保证从发送端提出的最低性能规格，如果没有达到最低要求，还有补救的方法。

5.3.5   Communications Plan   通信规划

A good communication and public information strategy, and subsequent attention to it during project management are very important. Neglecting to take the communication strategy into account in due time has been a source of failure for some projects, but special attention to it brings success to others. The Trondheim Toll ring gained public support in part because of the positive publicity it received. Similarly the original California Smart Corridor is an example where adequate communication measures were taken and the project was successful. The story might have been different because of the number and the level of concerned entities, but all parties combined around a common mission.

良好的沟通和公共信息战略，以及随后的项目管理中保持关注是非常重要的。疏忽在合适的时候采取沟通策略是某些项目失败的根源之一，而关注这一点的项目获得了成功。特隆赫姆收费环路赢得公众的支持，部分是因为它的正面宣传。同样原加州智能走廊更是一个充分沟通后获得成功的案例。由于所考虑的实体的数量和层次不同，故事也不尽相同，但各方在共同的使命下联合起来。

Figure 5.24　Norway - Bicycle elevator
图 5.24　挪威——自行车电梯

Where possible, a program manager should be appointed to bring communication, attention to detail and energy to overcome institutional problems. The program manager can provide drive and co-ordination from project start through to deployment. The responsibility of program manager is shown in figure 5.25.

如有可能，应任命一个项目经理来促进沟通，注重细节，克服体制问题。项目经理可以从项目开始到实施，给项目提供驱动力并相互协调。项目经理的职责如图 5.25 所示。

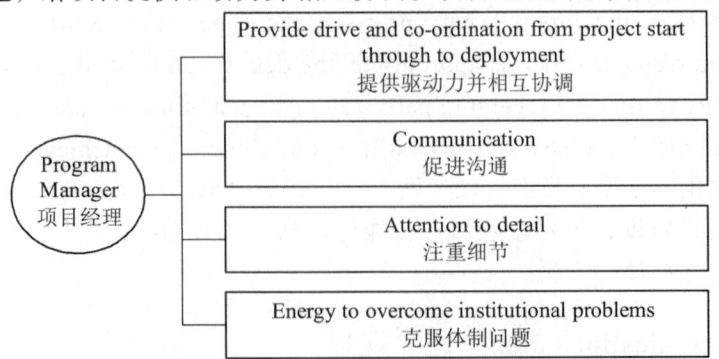

Figure 5.25　Responsibility of program manager
图 5.25　ITS 项目经理的职责

5.4 Financing and Contracts 投融资与合同

5.4.1 Budget planning 预算规划

The budgetary environment and the need to finance capital and operating costs are often cited among the major difficulties met during the deployment of ITS projects. Not least is the importance of getting firm spending commitments into budgets where more than one agency is involved. Where multiple agencies are jointly responsible for developing a project, careful coordination of budgets and other funding inputs will be essential.

预算环境、融资需求、运行费用等困难是在 ITS 项目实施过程中经常遇到的。从不止一家机构获得稳定资金相当重要。对于多家机构共同负责开发的项目，细致地调整预算和其他资金投入是最基本的要求。

To avoid the situation where funding problems are the source of indefinite delays, an integrated and evolutionary approach to project finance should be promoted so that significant returns can be generated earlier. Transparency of costs may also improve willingness to pay. Special attention is needed over the technical choices to ensure they are sound and will minimize investment risks, taking into account the constraints on budgets on the one hand, and the need to achieve early benefits such as increased highway throughput or environmental improvements on the other.

为避免资金问题成为拖延的根本原因，应采用一种能尽早见到收益的新的项目融资方式。透明的成本花销也能够增强人们投资的愿望。要特别关注技术选择，以保证技术合理性，并把投资风险降至最低，一方面要考虑预算限制，另一方面还要考虑通过提高道路通行能力或者改善环境等措施以尽早获益。

5.4.2 Innovative Forms of Contract 合同形式的变革

New forms of contracts have been developed to minimize the risk of project failures, control development costs and secure effective risk management. The following are six alternative scenarios, each featuring an innovative approach to financing and procurement. None of these scenarios is absolutely definitive, and various hybrid options exist.

现在已有一些新型合同形式，它们能把项目失败的风险降至最小，有效控制开发成本，并确保有效的风险管理。下面给出 6 个可选方案，每一个均在融资和资金获取等方面有所创新。下述方案并不是完全确定不能改动的，可存在多种方案并存的情况。

(1) Build, Operate, and Transfer 建设、运营、移交
(2) Design to Cost 成本设计
(3) Franchise 特许经营权
(4) System Leasing 系统租赁
(5) Procurement Agent Role 采购代理
(6) System Manager Approach 系统管理者的方法

5.4.3 Public Agency Procurement Procedures 公共机构采购程序

The innovative forms of contract described in Section 5.4.2 allow a great deal of flexibility in how the public sector shares risk with the private sector. Since these innovative contracts are relatively new, the negotiations also raise unprecedented issues. Public agencies and authorities are therefore employing specialist legal advisors, private finance advisors and commercial advisors, in addition to their technical advisors, to assist in the contract negotiations. Contracts are awarded against multiple evaluation criteria to secure the best value, in a move away from accepting lowest cost tenders. An objective evaluation of bids against pre-determined selection criteria is the norm. The criteria to be used for evaluating the bids should be made available to the bidders at the time that tenders are requested, common procedures are shown in figure 5.26.

5.4.2 部分描述的合同创新形式为公共机构和私立机构分摊风险提供很多灵活度，因为这些创新的合同相对较新，所以谈判中也带来一些意想不到的新问题。因此公共机构会雇用很多专业的法律顾问、私人财务顾问、商业顾问以及技术顾问帮助合同谈判。根据多评估标准，只有那些能够确保达到最佳效果而不是花费最少的合同才能得到批准。每个标书都要根据以前设置好的标准进行目标评估，用于评估标书的标准应该让每个申请者及时获得，共同过程如图 5.26。

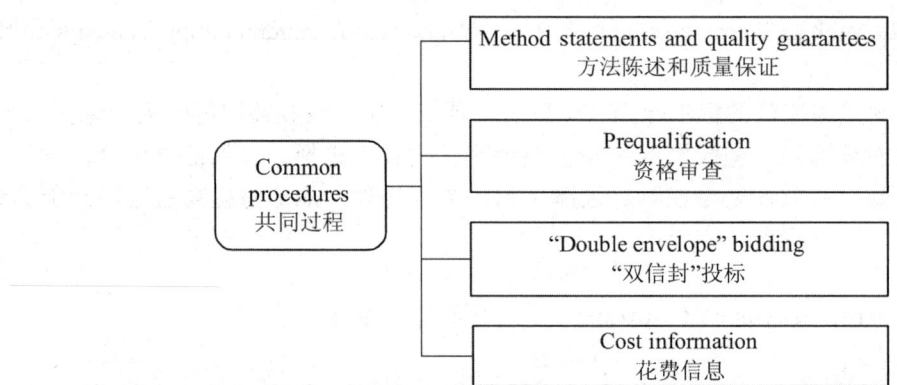

Figure 5.26　Public agency procurement common procedures
图 5.26　公共机构采购共同过程

(1) The public sector issues that have been identified with these innovatory contracts include the following: the latitude allowed to the supplier to adopt technical solutions of their own choosing, and the impact this might have on other ITS contracts. Cost recovery at the end of public/private partnerships: ownership, licensing, or leasing of equipment, buildings and other facilities. Criteria for analyzing "best value" especially with respect to different kinds and degrees of risks need to ensure transparency and propriety in the use of public funds. The amount of information sharing allowed and/or required between potential contractors at the bidding stage. The justification and acceptability of single-source procurement under various circumstances. Contingent liability: e.g. who should be held responsible for bugs in the off-the-shelf software chosen, but not developed, by the selected contractor.

与新合同有关的公共部门问题如下：允许的范围和影响：允许供应商采取技术方案的范

围,以及对其他 ITS 合同可能带来的影响;在公私合作末期的成本回收:所有权、许可权、设备建筑及其他设备的租用;分析"最好价值"的标准,特别是针对不同风险种类和程度的分析标准;在使用公共资金时,需要确保透明度和适当性;在投标阶段竞标公司之间允许和/或要求共享的信息量;在不同的环境下,单一来源采购的正当性及可接受性;可靠性:比如谁应该对投标人选择的非定制的软件缺陷负责。

(2) The private sector issues which surface in contract negotiations include the following: Latitude in developing "expedited" procedures that are different from the traditional procedures used by the public partner. Required surety, bonding, and guarantees. Measures to be used to determine acceptable performance. Cost recovery implications. Commercial confidentiality of proposal and cost information. Tradeoffs between use of public funds, risks, and resale value. Costs of early termination, should it occur. Procedure for handling disputes between public and private partners.

私营部门涉及合同谈判的问题如下:开发"加速"程序的范围,这些程序与公共部门使用的传统过程不一样;要求的保人,联结及保证书;用于确定可接受性能的措施;成本回收的含义;建议的商业机密和成本信息;在公共资金使用、风险以及再销售价值之间的平衡;可能发生的合同提前中止的成本;处理公私合作伙伴之间分歧的程序。

(3) The practice is developing of negotiating with a preferred bidder with a second choice in reserve in case the negotiations fail. Procurement in this way can be costly in terms of staff time (also for the bidders), especially if there are disagreements and the negotiations become protracted. Good preparation pays off. It is helpful to all concerned if the ITS functional requirements, the service performance requirements and the contract freedoms are well thought through and made as explicit as possible in the tender invitation documents.

与首选的投标人协商时,必须留一个备选投标人,以防谈判破裂。这种方式的采购在人工时间上的成本可能较高(对投标人也一样),特别是当存在分歧并且谈判延长之后。做好准备工作可以克服这些不足,如果 ITS 的功能需求、服务性能需求以及合同自由空间都经过仔细考虑,并且在投标邀请文件阶段准备得尽可能清晰,那么对所有相关方都有帮助。

5.4.4　Handling of Risks　风险处理

With an unproven market for ITS, an exclusive agreement–even for a few years–means a more secure revenue base for the promoter and provides a degree of comfort if the start-up costs are high. The lack of such assurances may cause the market to fail.

针对没有验证的 ITS 市场,专用协议——哪怕只用几年——对促进者来说,意味着更安全的财务基础,并且如果启动资金过高的话,可以提供一定程度的缓解作用,缺乏这样的保证措施有可能导致市场失败。

There is growing expertise in risk assessment and allocation methods. Public agencies will find themselves involved in negotiations with private sector actors on risk valuation and mitigation. In addition contracts will need to describe what the adjudication procedures are if things go wrong.

风险评估和分配方面逐渐积累了很多经验。公众机构将会与私营部门进行风险评估和减轻的谈判。另外,合同还要描述如果事情进展不顺,需要用到什么仲裁程序。

The varied risks involved in setting up ITS services will inevitably be reflected in contract negotiations. First, there are inherent technical risks associated with such systems, and the risk of innovation, An innovative ITS system can only be proven beyond doubt at the time of implementation.

设置ITS服务时涉及的各种风险不可避免地反映在合同谈判中 首先，这些系统有一些固有的技术风险以及改进风险，新的ITS系统只能在推广应用后才能消除人们的怀疑。

A contractor will only contemplate the development of an ITS system if there is a good chance of making a reasonable profit. With some ITS operations the contractor will wish to insure against failures that are not under its direct control, particularly those operations which have to interface with pre-existing (legacy) systems belonging to the public agency, or some other party. The contractor may therefore seek guarantees and assurances from third parties in order to underwrite these risks.

承包人只有在获取相当利润的机会存在时，才愿意开发ITS系统。对ITS的某些业务，承包人只希望确保工作就可以了，特别是那些必须与属于公共部门或其他团体的现有系统进行业务交互的功能。因此承包人可能会从第三方寻找担保，以规避这些风险。

Figure 5.27　Handling of Risks

图 5.27　风险处理

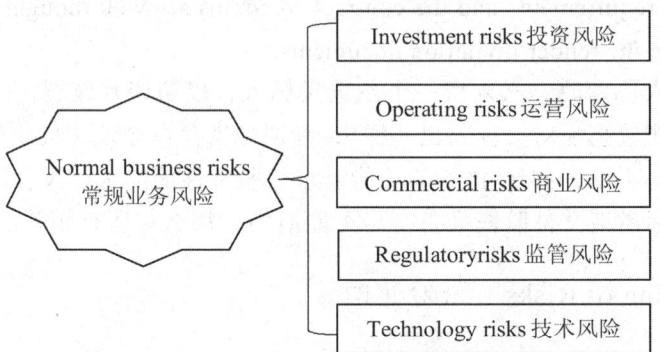

Figure 5.28　Normal business risks

图 5.28　常规业务风险

5.4.5　Single Supplier or Competition　唯一提供商或者竞争

As ITS services move from experimental to operational, the issue of competition becomes progressively more important. It will be necessary to strike a balance between policy and business requirements in ITS and create mutually beneficial partnerships between customers and suppliers, service providers and their users. Also it may be desirable to get small and medium-sized enterprises more involved in development of ITS services to develop local capability. Central to this is how the supplier recovers the cost of ITS system and product development, especially when the public sector is the major – and sometimes the only – customer. Early customers – the pioneers – may be paying for development work and problem-solving which will benefit later customers, without necessarily being able to share the development costs with these others.

随着 ITS 服务从实验到运营的转变，竞争的问题逐步变得重要起来，因此很有必要在政策和 ITS 行业需求方面进行平衡，并且在顾客和供应商、服务提供者和用户之间建立双赢的合作关系。另外，需要使中小型企业更深入地介入 ITS 服务开发、满足当地需求。该问题的核心是供应商如何回收 ITS 系统及产品开发的成本，特别是当公众部门是主要的，有时甚至是唯一顾客的情形。早期的先驱顾客，可能为后期顾客收益的开发和解决问题方案买单，前期顾客也不必和其他人共同承担这些开发花销。

A difficult issue for the public agencies is whether to opt for single or multiple sourcing of the systems, hardware, software and communications for ITS. The issue is particular to large contracts for traffic control and freeway management systems (ATMS), electronic payment systems (EPS), vehicle fleet management systems etc. it is easier to maintain supplier independence if open architecture and standards, and non-proprietary systems are specified. Strategies that encourage multiple sourcing and price competition will offer protection for the agencies against becoming bound by a single monopoly supplier.

公众机构面临的一个难题是对 ITS 是否选择单源或多源的系统、硬件、软件及通信，该问题对于大合同，如交通控制、高级公路管理系统、电子收费系统、车队管理系统等更适用。如果指定开放的结构、标准、非专有系统，那么维持供应商的独立性更容易。鼓励多源和价格竞争的战略有助于防止由一个垄断供应商把所有机构变为一体。

5.5 Public-Private Partnerships 公共-私营合作

5.5.1 Working with the Private Sector 与私营部门合作

Road network operators have provided all infrastructure systems as part of their networks. These have included systems such as traffic signals, dynamic message signs, and toll collection. Telecommunications and broadcast radio have also provided systems and networks for their services. The automobile industry has produced systems for use in the vehicle including a range of radio and mobile communication equipment.

路网运营者提供所有的基础设施系统作为道路网络的一部分，其中包括交通信号、动态情报板、收费系统。电信和广播电台也为他们提供了相应的系统和网络服务。汽车行业已制作车载系统，包括一定范围的广播和移动通信设备。

Private sector involvement, often in some form of public/private partnership, poses new issues of financing and procurement that are unprecedented, knotty, and not yet completely resolved. Private financing has been proposed for ITS projects because of the potential to combine public benefits with commercial opportunities. The project of cooperation with private sector is shown in figure 5.29.

私营部门通常以某种形式的公共-私营合作关系参与进来，并带来新的财政问题，以及前所未有的、棘手的且尚未完全解决的融资和采购问题。由于受到公共利益与商业机遇相结合的潜在影响，私人筹资计划已被提出用于 ITS 项目。与私有企业的合作案例如图 5.29 所示。

Figure 5.29　Project of cooperation with private sector
图 5.29　与私营部门的合作案例

Four principal motivations of private sector are shown in figure 5.30.
私营部门合作的四项主要基本动机如图 5.30 所示。

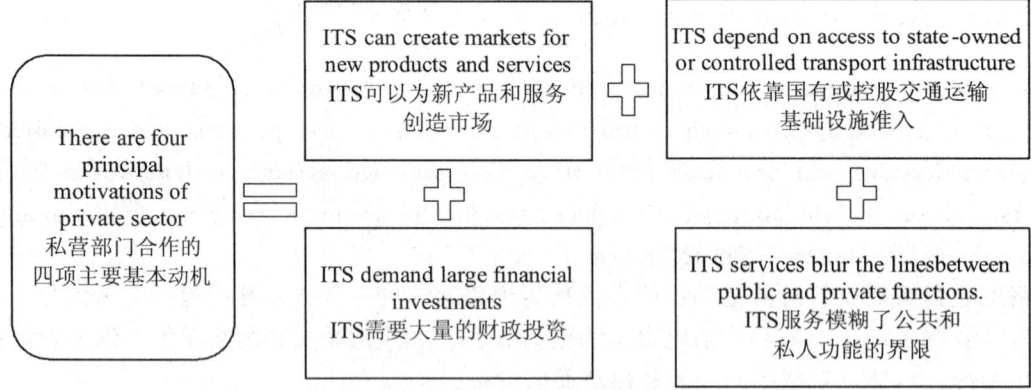

Figure 5.30　Four principal motivations of private sector
图 5.30　私营部门合作的主要四项基本动机

As we have seen, the ITS world is distinguished by the high investment often needed to achieve acceptable results. Investment cycles differ for public investment and commercial business. Moreover, the opportunity cost of private sector capital is much higher than public sector. Financial incentives that are underwritten by the public authorities may be appropriate where the socio-economic benefits are likely to be very high. As with other major infrastructure investments, the return on investments may be long-term, whereas private sector finance normally requires a short or medium payback period. This phenomenon may be an inhibiting factor for the projects where private and public sectors must cooperate. Opportunities for private sector participation may be hampered by other factors.

我们已经看到，ITS 的世界往往需要高投资来达到可接受的效果。公共投资和商业经营的投资周期不同。此外，私营资本的机会成本远高于公共部门。社会经济利益很高的地方，财政激励由公共当局负责应该是合适的。由于与其他主要的基础设施投资一样，投资回报率可能是长期的，但通常私营部门需要短或中等的回报期。这种现象可能是私营部门和公共部门进行项目合作的一种内在原因，私营部门参与的机会可能受到其他因素的阻碍。

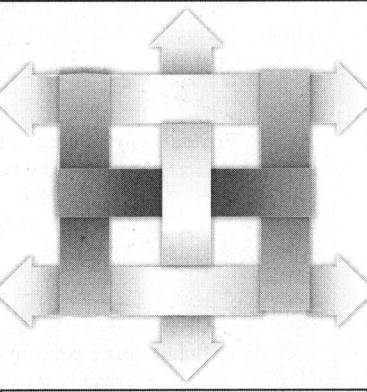

Figure 5.31　Hampered factors of opportunities for private sector participation
图 5.31　私营部门参与机会的阻碍因素

Notwithstanding these difficulties, public/private partnerships have the potential for creative synergy between the public sector culture and the entrepreneurial approach. Both parties in the partnership can bring their own skills and expertise to the combined operations. The public sector can provide a stable regulatory framework covering safety, technical standards and open systems, system effectiveness, and environmental impact. Five Points for Successful Public/Private Partnerships is shown in figure 5.32.

尽管面对这些困难，公共-私营合作关系具有在公共部门文化和企业方式之间建立协调的潜力。合作伙伴的双方可以利用自己的拿手技能和专业知识，携手经营。公共部门能够提供稳定的制度框架，涵盖安全、技术标准、开放系统和系统的有效性，以及环境影响。成功的公私合作关系的五个要点如图 5.32 所示。

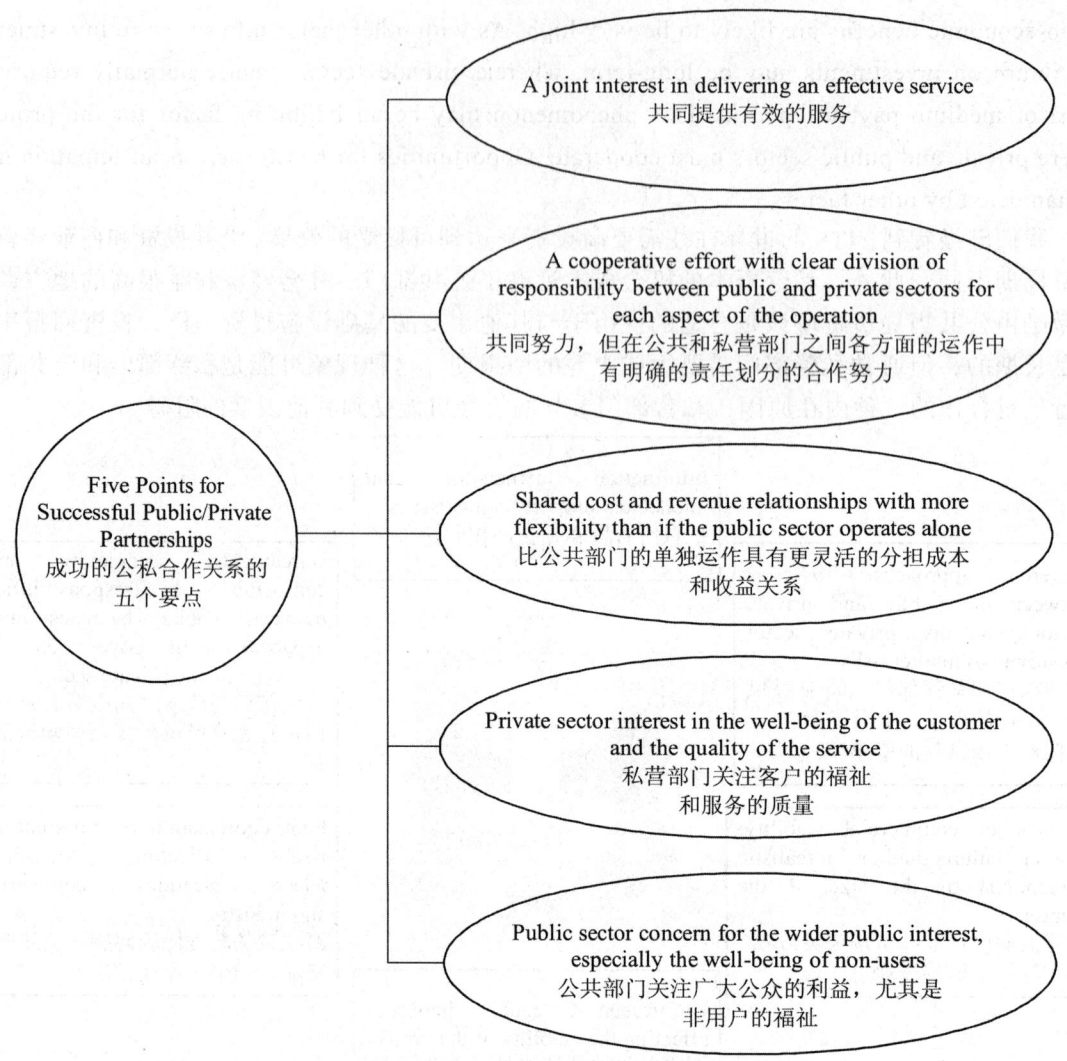

Figure 5.32　Five Points for Successful Public/Private Partnerships
图 5.32　成功的公私合作关系的五个要点

5.5.2　Creating the Conditions for Private Sector Investment　创造私营部门投资环境

　　Building partnerships requires trust, understanding, commitment, and communication. When any of these ingredients is missing problems will arise, and when all of them are compromised, severe difficulties are inevitable. Without trust, achieving consensus on project direction and resolving technical issues becomes very difficult. Trust is built by working together toward common objectives and seeing that the team members live up to their commitments. Understanding of the roles and responsibilities, and commitment to mutual goals, keeps the project moving toward deployment. Setting a framework of rules and guidance, and removing institutional barriers to new and high priority ITS are among the critical roles that public authorities must assume. These institutional arrangement flow from the Framework Plan. Typically, in the area of commercial traffic and traveller information services, the private sector is asking the public agencies to authorize some or all of the following:

建立合作关系需要信任、理解、承诺和沟通。任何一点的缺失都会产生问题，而当一切都严重受损时困难就不可避免。没有信任，达成对项目目标的共识和解决工程技术问题就变得很困难。相互信任就是在为共同的目标而努力、合作伙伴兑现其承诺中建立起来的。认识到自身的角色和责任，并承诺共有目标，推动项目朝着实现逐步前进。对新的和优先的 ITS 而言，设定框架规则和指导并消除体制障碍，公共部门必须承担关键角色。这些体制安排由框架规划给出。通常，在商业和旅游交通信息服务领域，私营部门要求公共机构给予以下的部分或全部授权：

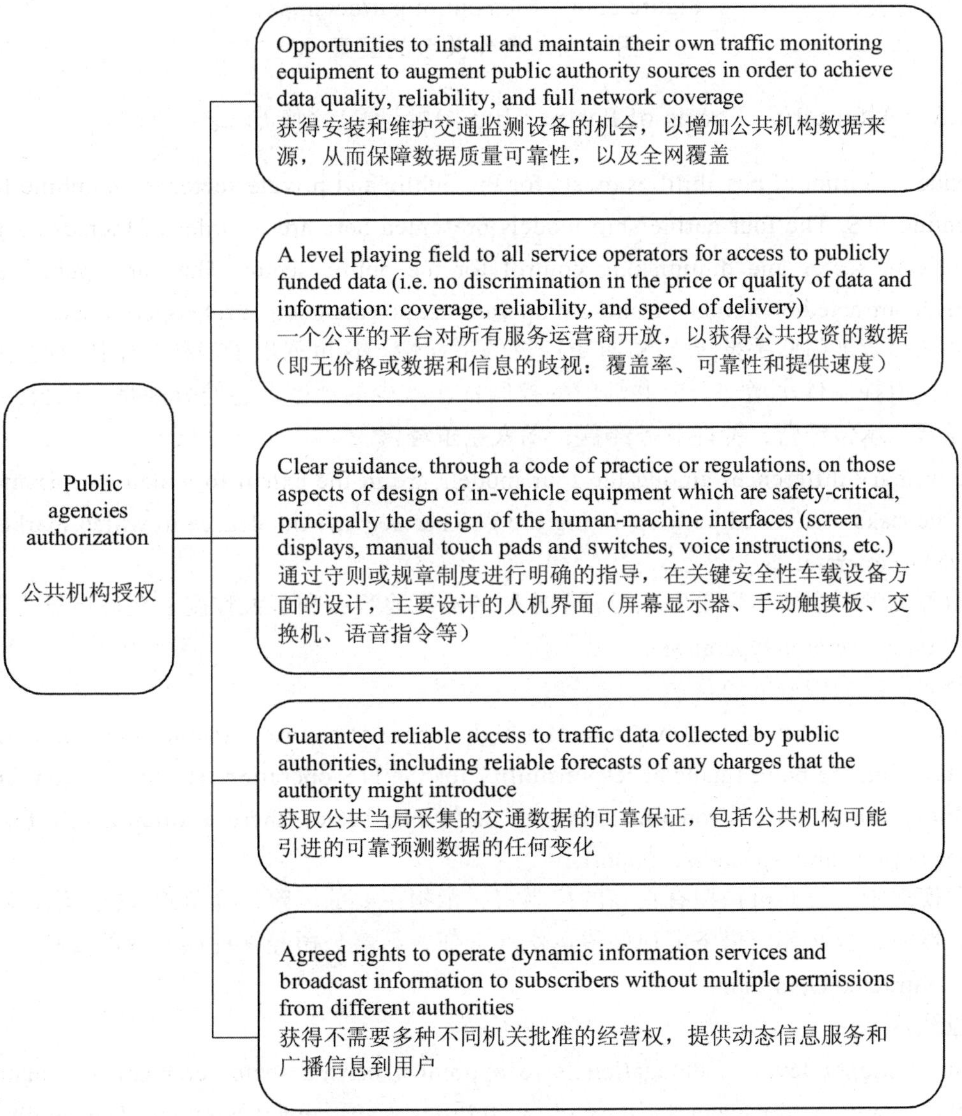

Public agencies authorization 公共机构授权

- Opportunities to install and maintain their own traffic monitoring equipment to augment public authority sources in order to achieve data quality, reliability, and full network coverage
  获得安装和维护交通监测设备的机会，以增加公共机构数据来源，从而保障数据质量可靠性，以及全网覆盖

- A level playing field to all service operators for access to publicly funded data (i.e. no discrimination in the price or quality of data and information: coverage, reliability, and speed of delivery)
  一个公平的平台对所有服务运营商开放，以获得公共投资的数据（即无价格或数据和信息的歧视：覆盖率、可靠性和提供速度）

- Clear guidance, through a code of practice or regulations, on those aspects of design of in-vehicle equipment which are safety-critical, principally the design of the human-machine interfaces (screen displays, manual touch pads and switches, voice instructions, etc.)
  通过守则或规章制度进行明确的指导，在关键安全性车载设备方面的设计，主要设计的人机界面（屏幕显示器、手动触摸板、交换机、语音指令等）

- Guaranteed reliable access to traffic data collected by public authorities, including reliable forecasts of any charges that the authority might introduce
  获取公共当局采集的交通数据的可靠保证，包括公共机构可能引进的可靠预测数据的任何变化

- Agreed rights to operate dynamic information services and broadcast information to subscribers without multiple permissions from different authorities
  获得不需要多种不同机关批准的经营权，提供动态信息服务和广播信息到用户

Figure 5.33　Public agencies authorization

图 5.33　公共机构授权

The elements of a successful cooperation relationship between the private sector and public sector are shown in figure 5.34.

私营部门与公共部门建立成功合作关系的要素如图 5.34 所示。

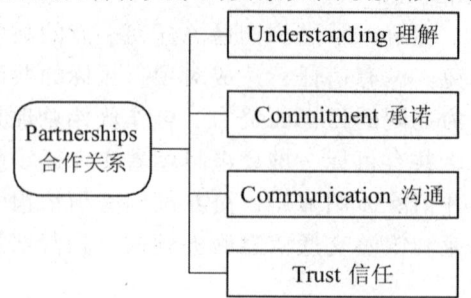

Figure 5.34　Element of partnerships

图 5.34　合作关系的要素

5.5.3　Alternative Forms of Partnership　可选的合作形式

A wide spectrum of possibilities exists for the public and private sectors to combine forces in implementing ITS. The four partnership models presented here are in order of increasing freedom for the private sector and diminishing control for the public sector. They are: public centered operations; contracted operations; franchise operations; private competitive operations.

公共和私营部门联手推行 ITS 有更广泛的可能性。这里列出了四种合作伙伴类型，按照私营部门自由控制依次增加，公共部门的控制依次减少的顺序，它们分别是：以公共部门为中心的经营；承包经营；特许业务经营；私人竞争经营。

The primary differences among the four models are in the extent to which the private sector takes on the risks associated with operating the ITS service and the degree to which market forces are allowed to operate.

这四种类型的主要区别是私人运营 ITS 服务的风险程度和多大程度上允许市场力量运作。

(1) Public Centered Operations

以公共部门为中心的经营

In this model, the public agency retains a high degree of control, assumes the major burden of risk and takes on the main financial responsibility for the ITS operation. However, even where the responsibility for operations remains firmly in the public sector, there is often a role for private companies in providing specialist support.

这一模式中，公共机构拥有很高的控制权，承担主要的风险，并负责 ITS 运作主要的融资工作。然而，公共部门仍坚定地保留运作的责任，私营公司经常提供专业的支持。

(2) Contracted Operations

承包经营

A much higher level of delegation is to appoint a private sector company to manage and service the operation, for example, through a facilities management contract. The public agency retains control of operational policy and gives direction but the private company runs the everyday operation and maintains the ITS services.

更高级别的授权是指定一个私立部门公司来管理和提供这些服务业务，比如通过资源管理合同。公立机构保持对业务政策的控制并给出方向，但私立公司运营日常业务并维护 ITS 服务。

(3) Franchise Operations

特许业务经营

Under the franchise model, management of the entire operation of the ITS service or facility is handed over to the private sector with a very high level of delegation over its development. The public sector agency will specify the terms on which a private company can take on the franchise, but it stands back from day-to-day involvement in the operation. Its role is mainly to see that service standards are maintained and service users are not subjected to unfair pricing.

在特权模式下，ITS 服务或设施的整个业务管理转移到私营部门手中，并对其开发有很高级别的授权。公立部门代理机构将规定一些术语，指定私营公司能够享有这些特权，但公立部门不参与日常运营，其主要任务是监督服务标准能够维持，并且服务用户不遭受不公正价格的待遇。

(4) Private Competitive Operations

私人竞争经营

It is most clearly seen with driver information services that depend on public information or access to highway infrastructures. The data, information, and other facilities controlled by the public sector are provided to more than one company in order to encourage competition, as exemplified by the market for driver information services that is emerging in the UK.

显然，驾驶员信息服务依靠公共信息或通过公路基础设施获取信息。为了鼓励竞争，数据、信息以及其他有公共部门控制的资源要提供给多个公司，例如提供驾驶员信息服务的市场已出现在英国。

Four types of partners is shown in figure 5.35.

四种合作伙伴类型如图 5.35 所示。

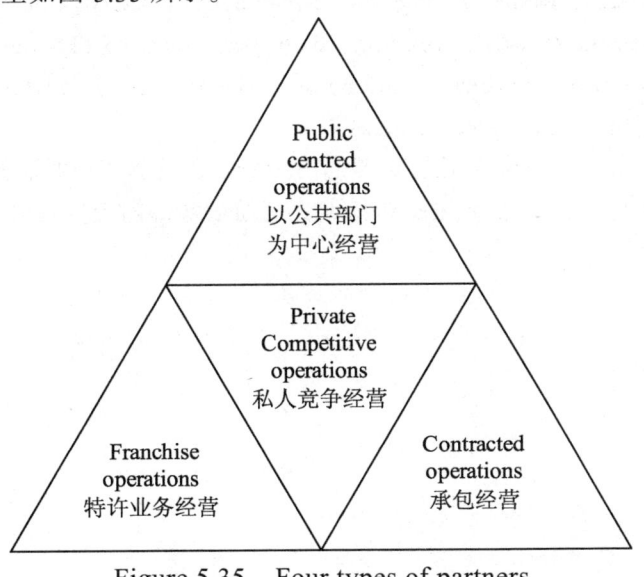

Figure 5.35　Four types of partners

图 5.35　四种合作伙伴类型

5.6 Conclusions 结论

The crucial institutional issues in ITS are: deployment planning; working with the private sector; and financing and procurement. Transportation professionals involved in ITS must become familiar with alternative and innovative ways to resolve these institutional issues.

ITS 中的关键体制问题在于：实施规划、与私营部门合作、融资及采购。涉及到 ITS 的交通专业人士必须熟悉这些可选的和创新的方式来解决体制问题。

Practitioners wishing to invest in ITS systems are strongly advised to go through a comprehensive planning exercise in consultation with key stakeholders. This chapter emphasizes the value of having a well-researched and well-structured ITS framework plan, which can inform the preparation of a ITS implementation plan, followed by the development of a detailed program plan.

欲投资 ITS 的从业者最好与主要利益方协商，进行全面的规划。本章的重点在于一个被深入研究和良好搭建的 ITS 框架规划的价值，并能为 ITS 实施规划的准备提供信息，然后建立一个详尽的计划方案。

Interagency agreements are an important means of securing integrated ITS operations. When a partnership is formed among multiple organizations, especially if some of them are in the private sector, the role of each partner and its measure of success must be absolutely clear to all parties, preferably documented in memoranda of understanding early on.

机构之间的协议是保证集成 ITS 运营的一个重要手段。当多个组织之间形成合作关系，尤其是部分包含私营部门的情况，每个合作伙伴的角色，及其衡量成功的方式，对各方都必须绝对明确，最好早就记载在谅解备忘录中。

For effective implementation of ITS, the public sector is advised to consider close cooperation with private sector organizations, taking full advantage of the distinct contributions to ITS deployment that can be made by each sector. Given the nature of ITS business and its systems characteristics, transportation agencies should be open toward, and innovative about, new forms of public procurement and financing arrangements.

为有效实施 ITS，公共部门应考虑与私营部门组织密切合作，同时充分利用每个部门对 ITS 实施的不同贡献。由于 ITS 的业务性质和特点，交通运输部门应实行开放的、创新的、新形式的公共采购和融资计划。

Chapter 6 How do I Launch ITS
第六章 如何启动 ITS

6.1 Launching ITS at the Program Level 在规划层面开展 ITS

Early ITS research and development activities began as isolated pilot projects, but racially all countries engaged in ITS deployment now have formal ITS programs. This is to ensure consistency and synergy among ITS projects, continuity of funding, and the systematic development of public support and new resources so that ITS can be relied upon as effective tools for solving transportation problems.

早期的 ITS 研究和开发活动都始于孤立的示范项目，但现在所有致力于 ITS 开发的国家都建立了正式的 ITS 规划，以确保 ITS 项目之间的一致性和协同性、投资的连贯性、公众服务和新资源的系统性发展，使 ITS 成为可靠的解决交通运输问题的有效工具。

6.1.1 National ITS Program Formation 国家 ITS 规划构成

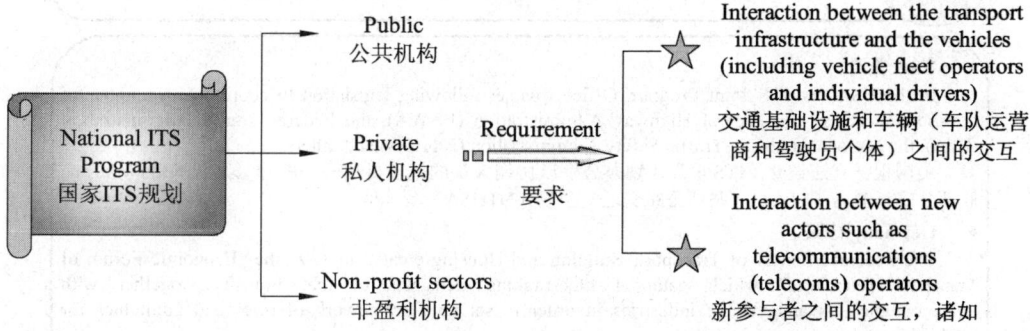

Figure 6.1 National ITS program formation and requirements
图 6.1 国家 ITS 规划构成及要求

The establishment and maintenance of an ITS program can be greatly facilitated by national legislation and/or high-level government leadership, especially funding. Without this a host of completely new ITS activities would be difficult, if not impossible, to launch.

一个 ITS 规划的建立和维护可以通过国家法律或者高层政府推动，尤其是投资方面。否则，许多全新的 ITS 行动将是困难的，启动也是不可能的。

The results of enabling legislation include fundamentally new policies to introduce ITS as a way to augment road capacity, as well as to enable new incentives for the private sector to enter the ITS market. Enabling legislation can also encourage the creation of new organizational frameworks so that multiple public agencies at various levels can work closely together, as well as providing multi-year funding for ITS activities. Good examples of such legislation are the 1989 Driver

Information Systems Act of the UK, the 1991 Intermodal Surface Transportation Efficiency Act (ISTEA) of the USA, and the 1995 Basic Guidelines on the Promotion of Advanced Information and Telecommunication Society announced by the national government of Japan.

授权的立法效果包括介绍ITS是提高道路通行能力的方法的基本新政策，也包括激励私营企业进入ITS市场的新政策。授权的立法鼓励新组织框架的产生，这样不同层面的公共机构可以紧密合作，还可以为ITS领域提供多年的资助。这类立法方面的案例包括英国1989年的驾驶员信息系统法案、1991年美国的综合地面运输效率法案（ISTEA）和1995年日本政府的推动先进的信息和通信社会基本指南。

Figure 6.2　Legislation and funding
图6.2　立法与投资

例　Examples of National Coordination 国家协作的范例

- **USA 美国**
  In the USA, the ITS Joint Program Office was set following legislation to coordinate a number of transport agencies—the Federal Highway Administration (FHWA), the Federal Transit Administration (FTA), the National Highway Traffic Safety Administration (NTHSA), and others.
  美国根据立法设立了ITS联合计划办公室以协调大量的运输机构——联邦公路局（FHWA），联邦公路运输局（FTA），联邦公路交通安全局（NTHSA）及其他。

- **Germany 德国**
  The Federal Ministry of Transport, Building and Housing created in 1995 the "Economic Forum of Transport Telematics" which gathered high-ranking delegates of that ministry, together with telecommunication and vehicle industries in order to set up a framework of rules and guidelines for establishing telematics services.
  联邦运输、建筑和房地产部于1995年创建"交通通信与控制经济论坛"，该论坛聚集了该部高级别的代表，与通信和车辆制造商一起为建立远程服务而设立规则和指南的框架。

- **Japan 日本**
  In Japan five (later consolidated to four) national ministries involved in ITS have worked together through ministry liaison conferences and in concert with ITS Japan.
  5个与ITS相关的国家省（后合并为4个）通过省际联席会议共同工作，并与ITS国家中心相呼应。

After the enabling legislation is in place, continuing cooperation and coordination among relevant government agencies is essential to carry out the legislative intent. Any significant legislation and policy pronouncements usually represent the fruition of a long process of consensus building among major ITS stakeholders or interest groups. Some stakeholders may actually take a negative position initially and need to be won over.

授权立法后，相关政府机构之间的继续合作和协调是实现立法意图的基础，任何重要的立法和政策宣言通常代表了 ITS 利益团体间或利益群体间达成共识的漫长过程的一个成果，需要争取一开始可能持反对立场的利益团。

Both international cooperation and international competition have encouraged ITS programme formation.
国际合作和国际竞争都促进了ITS机制的建立。

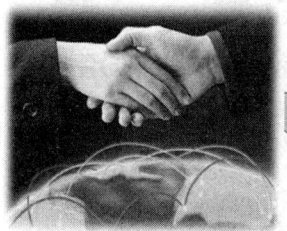

Relationship between ITS and International development
ITS与国际发展的关系

International competition has also led to the support for ITS programmes within individual countries which wish to keep pace with the growing international ITS market.
国际竞争使追随国际ITS市场的国家为ITS项目提供支持。

International linking of ITS services and mutually beneficial exchange of ITS experience has also been an important stimulus. Interestingly. ITS服务的国际链接以及互惠互利的ITS成功经验交流也是一个很重要的激励。

Figure 6.3　Relationship between ITS and International development
图 6.3　ITS 与国际发展的关系

6.1.2　ITS Program Development　ITS 规划发展

In parallel with developing the ITS policy framework analysis, experience shows that ITS program development must be accompanied by maintaining effective liaison and institutional arrangements with all potential interested parties and stakeholders. One necessary step at this strategic level involves a process of education and training, in the broadest sense, of both technicians and decision makers (including the statesmen) about ITS.

经验表明，在开发 ITS 政策框架分析的同时，ITS 计划的开发要与各潜在的感兴趣单位和利益团体维持有效的联络并且在制度上予以合理的安排。在战略层的一个必要步骤就是开展教育和培训工作，广义上，既要针对 ITS 相关的技术人员也要针对决策者（也包含政治家们）。

There is a great variety of ITS technologies, choosing where to start depends on the problem to be solved. At the ITS program level, some technologies are more basic in the sense that they form part of the ITS info structure, and their introduction enables further ITS applications to be developed. For example, without digital maps, drivers would not be able to know readily where they are with respect to their destinations. Thus, digital maps are an enabling technology for vehicle navigation, and must be in place before navigation and route guidance services can begin.

存在众多的 ITS 相关技术，选择从哪里开始启动 ITS，取决于需要解决的问题。在规划层面，非常基本的技术构成了 ITS 基础设施的一部分，并且使得即将开展的 ITS 应用成为可能。例如，如果没有电子地图，驾驶员将无法容易地获知相对于目的地的位置。电子地图是车载导航的基础技术之一，并且是必须在导航和路线引导服务开展前就位的技术。

Figure 6.4　Education and Training
图 6.4　教育与培训

Figure 6.5　Application of digital maps
图 6.5　电子地图的应用

ITS will inevitably use leverage on the existing and growing computer networks and telecommunications infrastructure. These take a tremendous amount of capital to build for all services—not just transportation- related services.

ITS 将不可避免地在现有的与成长中的计算机网络以及通信基础设施技术之间利用杠杆效用进行选择，这使得需要有巨大的资金来建立各种服务——不仅仅是运输相关的服务。

National ITS programs differ around the world because of the differences in transportation needs and legacy systems in different countries or regions. The three major ITS continents (Europe, North America, and Asia-Pacific) have all tended to focus on different implementation priorities.

Countries on the verge of launching their ITS programs should note the varying emphases among different countries with ITS experience while selecting the best partner(s) for international cooperation.

由于不同国家和地区运输需求和传统体系的不同，各国的 ITS 规划不尽相同，在欧洲、美洲、亚太这三个发展 ITS 的大陆，往往关注不同的执行优先级。即将启动 ITS 规划的国家，在选择最好的国际合作伙伴过程中应注意有 ITS 发展经验的不同国家各有侧重。

Figure 6.6   Computer networks and telecommunications infrastructures

图 6.6   计算机网络以及通信基础设施

Figure 6.7   SWOT of ITS

图 6.7   ITS 战略分析

In the absence of a national plan dedicated to ITS, some countries with accelerated programs of motorway construction have included the basic ITS infrastructure in their motorway investment plans. In this way the motorway can be operated efficiently, basic ITS services can be offered immediately to the users, and the investment paves the way for developing additional ITS applications when the future national ITS plans are in place.

没有 ITS 专项规划的国家，在发展高速公路基础设施的投资预算中包含 ITS 基础设施的建设。这种方式可以有效运营，基本的 ITS 服务可直接提供给用户，当国家 ITS 规划制定后，这些投资为附加的 ITS 应用的开展铺平了道路。

6.2 Launching ITS at the Project Level 项目层面启动 ITS

As ITS implementation moves from program to project level, project planning comes into focus. This should include the consideration of institutional pre-conditions, financial commitments, enabling technologies, early actions, and precautions. On the basis of pooled experience from around the world, a set of common advice is offered to all ITS services at the project level (in subsection 6.2.1), while additional advice will be categorized in subsequent subsections according to six established application areas:

当 ITS 的实施由规划层面转到项目层面时，项目的计划就成为焦点。项目计划需要考虑制度前提、财务承诺、可行的技术、先期的行动以及防范机制。基于全世界汇集起来的一些经验，本章 6.2.1 节针对所有 ITS 服务在项目层面的开展给出了一系列通用的建议，后面的各节分为六个应用领域给出附加的建议：

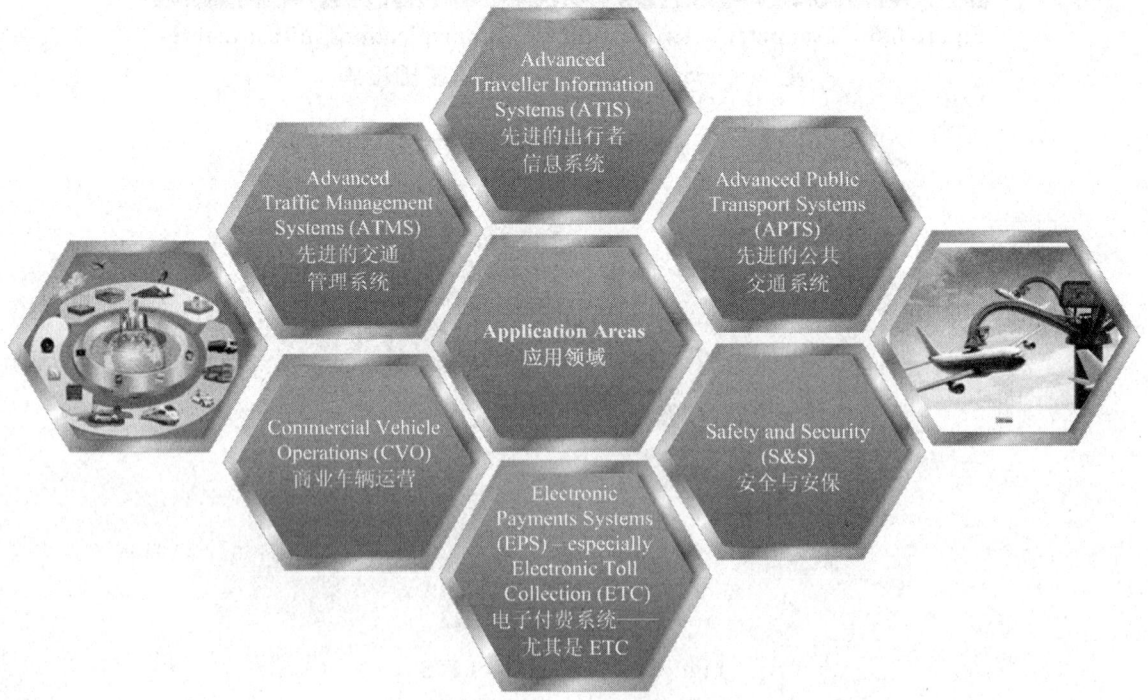

Figure 6.8 Application Areas of ITS Services
图 6.8 ITS 服务的应用领域

6.2.1 Common Advice to All ITS Services 对所有 ITS 服务的通用建议

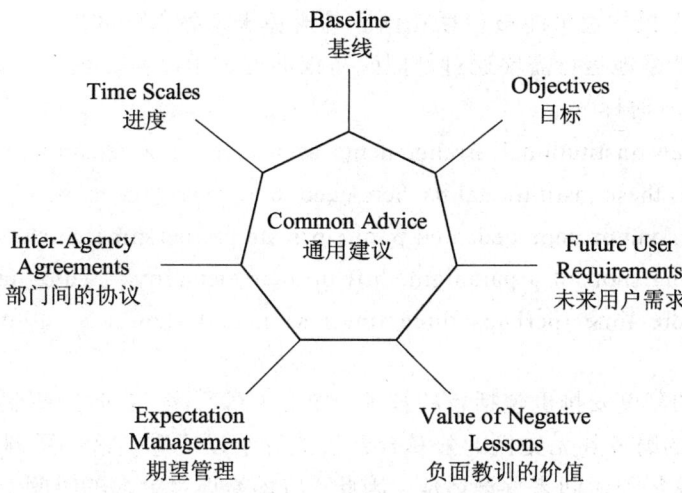

Figure 6.9　Common advice on ITS services
图 6.9　对 ITS 服务的通用建议

(1) Objectives　目标

As the first step in basic project planning, clear objectives and targets of ITS services need to be defined, taking into account the specific local requirements and whether different systems will be required to interoperate, now or within the planning horizon. These objectives need to be agreed by all actors involved. This is the basis for all other steps, like the definition of evaluation criteria, the interagency agreements, time scales and expectation management.

作为基本的项目计划的第一步，需明确定义 ITS 服务的目标和对象，需要考虑当前或未来规划层面上特殊的本地需求和不同系统对协作的需求。这些目标需要由各利益团体共同认可：这是评价标准定义、机构间的协议、进度和期望值管理等步骤的基础。

(2) Baseline　基线

Establish the baseline of current system performance before launching any ITS service so that the new service can be evaluated by comparing it with the baseline scenario. While this is an obvious first step in any approach to evaluation, a common mistake in many ITS projects has been to take this step later than it should have been, or not collecting sufficient data to establish a robust baseline.

在启动 ITS 服务之前，需建立当前系统性能的基线以对此新服务与该基线设定的场景进行评价。虽然这是所有评价中的第一步，但是很多 ITS 项目拖后执行该步骤或者不收集足够的数据以建立一个鲁棒的基线。

(3) Inter-Agency Agreements　部门间的协议

Practically all ITS services involve the cooperation and/or coordination among multiple transportation agencies. Even in the case of single-mode management, multiple agencies under different jurisdictions may be involved. Exactly how each agency is supposed to operate in the new cooperative manner needs to be documented in the form of interagency agreements in order to avoid misunderstanding in the future (Section 5.3.4 Operating Agreements).

实际上，所有的 ITS 服务都涉及多个运输机构间的协调和合作。即使是单一管理模式，不同管辖区域的多个机构也可能被包括在内。为避免未来各部门间的误解，在新的协作方式中，每个机构如何严格地运行需要通过部门间协议的方式予以明文规定（见 5.3.4 合作协议）。

(4) Time Scales 时标

ITS involves new institutional arrangements as well as new technologies. As discussed in Chapter 5, sometimes these institutional barriers need to be overcome by new planning approaches, innovative financing, and/or unprecedented public/private partnerships. Such a barrage of changes often demands nothing short of a paradigm shift in their mentality – which takes time to evolve. Therefore, much more time (perhaps three times as much) should be allowed than originally expected.

ITS 既包括新的制度安排也包括新的技术。如第 5 章所述，有时这些制度障碍需要通过新的规划方法、创新的财务和无先例的公私合营模式等予以规避。这一系列改变恰恰要求心态上的范式转移——这需要时间来逐渐适应。因此，应该给项目更多的时间（也许应该是原来预期的时间的三倍）。

(5) Expectation Management 期望管理

Public expectations of ITS, particularly on the part of politicians and the media, may be unrealistically high. Although this has largely been overcome as the field of ITS matures, it is important to manage expectations carefully. It is prudent to take an evolutionary approach to ITS deployment and not try out too many new devices or new approaches simultaneously.

ITS 的公共预期，尤其是政治和媒体，有可能不切实际得高，但是随着 ITS 领域的成熟可以在很大程度地被克服。谨慎的预期管理是很重要的，将进化方法引入到 ITS 发展中需要格外谨慎，不能同时试验太多新技术和设备。

(6) Value of Negative Lessons 负面教训的价值

Negative lessons are part of the cost of living at the cutting edge of new ideas and technologies. Although unfortunate, they should not be considered as failure. Negative lessons learned can be useful not only as advice to avoid mistakes in future projects, but also as feedback to promote corrective measures in the current project.

负面教训是生活在新的技术和方法前沿的代价之一。负面教训虽然不幸，但是不应该当作是失败，负面教训是很有用的，不仅可看作避免未来项目犯错的建议，也可以看作当前项目推进正确措施的反馈。

(7) Future User Requirements 未来用户需求

Because of the lengthy time needed to implement some ITS projects, systems should be planned to anticipate changes in user requirements over time; e.g. how information will be accessed by users in the future, say five years after initial implementation. For example, next-generation cell phones will enable transit riders to obtain travel information interactively, on the move, as an alternative to using kiosks at the transit stations or their computers at home or office.

由于需要执行很长的时间，一些 ITS 系统需要预测用户需求随着时间推进而产生的改变，诸如系统开始应用 5 年后，未来的用户如何访问信息等。例如，下一代手机可以使驾驶者和转乘者在移动中通过交互方式获取出行信息，可以作为车站的信息亭、办公室或家用电脑的重要补充。

6.2.2 Advice on Advanced Traffic Management Systems 对先进的交通管理系统的建议

Advanced traffic management systems (ATMS) are the base for launching many other ITS user services.

先进的交通管理系统（ATMS）是启动许多其他ITS用户服务的基础。

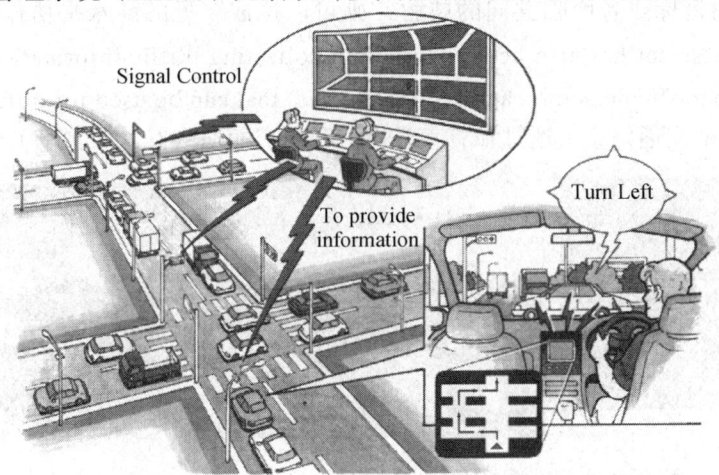

Figure 6.10 Traffic management system (Source: Japanese Highway Development Organization)

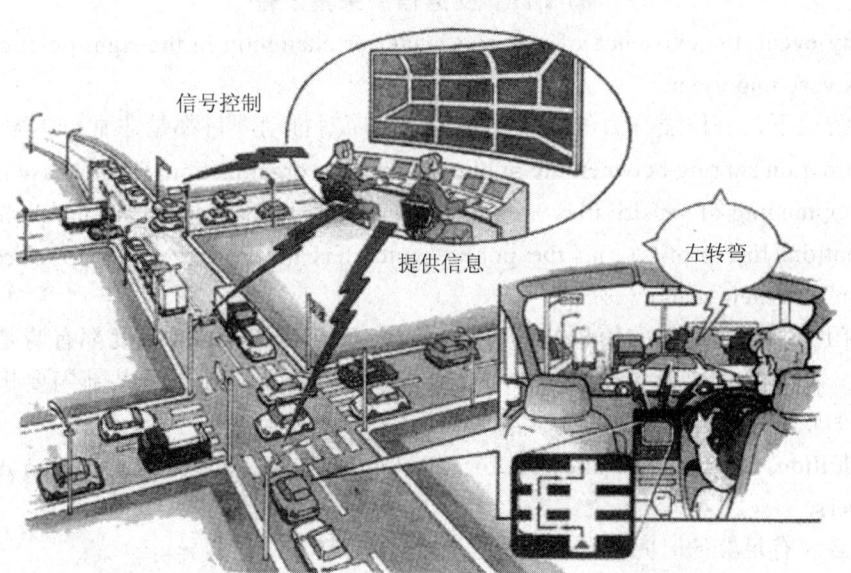

图6.10 交通管理示意图（来源：日本高速公路发展组织）

(1) Inter-Agency Cooperation 部门间协作

① Bureaucratic inertia and fear of change are often barriers to the interagency cooperation needed for ATMS services.

官僚惯性和对改变的恐惧往往阻碍 ATMS 服务所需的部门间合作。

② An inter-agency agreement can be developed in parallel, so that each party can retain its own responsibility to serve the public as before, without surrendering control of its own systems and information.

部门间的协议可以使各团体保持与之前一样的各自为公共服务的职责,不丧失对各自系统和信息的管理权。

③ Unusually high levels of cooperation can be achieved if there is a common goal or a common threat.

如果有共同的目标或者面临共同的威胁,则可以达成罕见的高水平协作。

④ The private sector has also been involved in collecting traffic information (through private helicopters, private traffic detectors, and probe vehicles) that can be used for traffic management.

私营机构收集的交通信息(通过私有直升机、私有交通检测器、探测车)可用于交通管理。

Figure 6.11 Traffic information collection equipment

图 6.11 交通信息采集设备

⑤ In any event, the existence of a strong leader or champion in the right position to promote the project is very important.

在任何情况下,一位强有力的主管领导者或主席对推动项目都是非常有重要的。

⑥ Information sharing between the public and private organizations in this case must be based on clear understanding of sensitivities on both sides: the private partner has shareholders to worry about (i.e. bottom line profits) and the public sector has the voting public to worry about (i.e. statesmen can lose their seats).

公共部门和私营部门间的信息共享必须建立在双方对各自的敏感度都有清楚的理解这一基础上,如:私营合作伙伴要担心利益相关方(如利润底线)以及公共部门要担心具有投票权的大众(如政治家可能因此丧失权利)。

⑦ In addition, time must be allowed for adjusting cultural differences between the public and private partners.

另外,必须有足够的时间允许公、私营参与者调节其文化差异。

(2) Technology Standards for Electronic Information Sharing 电子信息共享的技术标准

① Timely sharing of traffic and transport information through electronic systems is frequently the technical cornerstone of ATMS projects.

及时通过电子系统共享交通和运输信息通常是 ATMS 项目的技术基石。

② Software models and communications protocols are also crucial, but are driven by much larger markets than ITS, which needs to follow these non-transport-related developments.

软件模型和通信协议也是至关重要的，它们由比 ITS 更大的市场来驱动，交通运输领域需遵循这些非运输相关领域的软件模型和通信协议。

(3) Adequate O&M Staff and Budget 足够的运营/维护人员和预算

① Design and cost calculation for ATMS must be done on the "lifecycle" basis.

ATMS 的设计和成本计算必须基于生命周期原则。

② ATMS deployment planning must therefore take into account the need for training and the cost of supporting the existing operation and maintenance (O&M) staff, which may also need to be expanded.

ATMS 的发展规划必须考虑相应的培训需求，现有的以及未来扩展的运营、维护团队所需的成本。

③ If adequate staff and budget do not exist, the ATMS deployment should be postponed or downscaled.

如果没有足够的人员和预算，ATMS 的发展可能会被拖延或缩减 。

6.2.3 Advice on Advanced Traveller Information Systems 对先进的出行者信息系统的建议

Advanced traveller information systems (ATIS) involve the end users and often the private sector in the supply chain.

先进的出行者信息系统（ATIS）包括终端用户，通常也包括供应链中的私营机构。

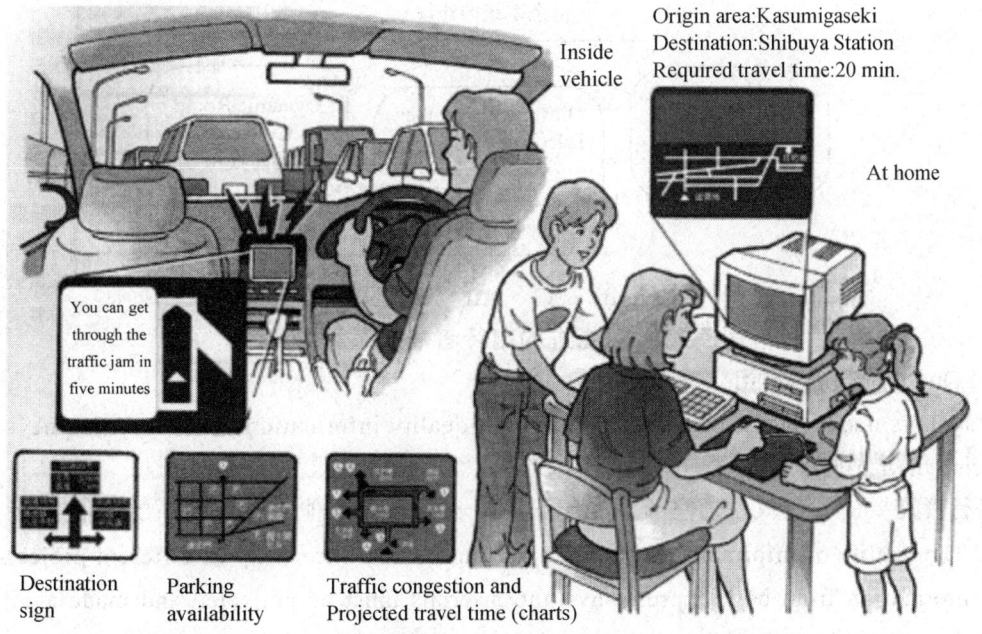

Figure 6.12　Route guidance and navigation
(Source: Japanese Highway Development Organization)

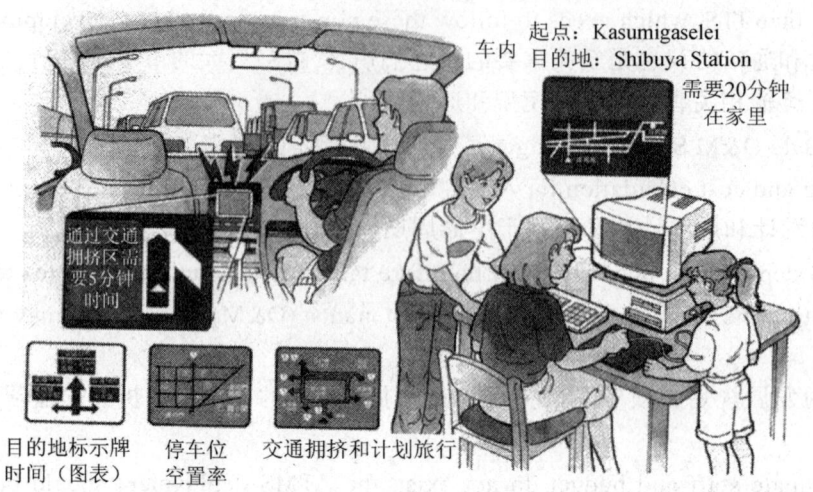

图 6.12 路线指导和导航示意图（来源：日本高速公路发展组织）

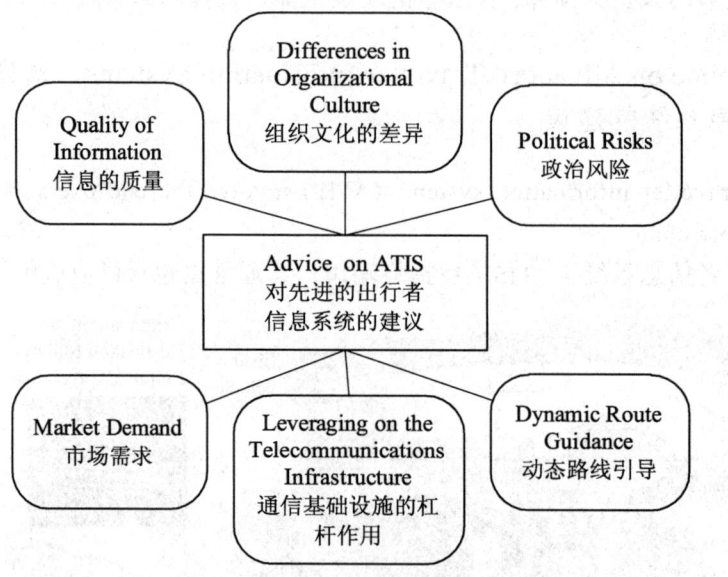

Figure 6.13　Advice on ATIS

图 6.13　对先进的出行者信息系统的建议

(1) Quality of Information　信息的质量

Travellers need not just information, but high-quality information about their journeys, before and during their trips.

出行者需要的不仅仅是信息，而是出行中、出行前关于他们行程的高质量信息。

① The quality of information is defined or emphasized differently in different projects. Thus, traffic information from both expressways and arterials must be collected and made available 24 hours a day, seven days a week.

不同项目中信息的质量界定或重要程度将有所区别。不完整的信息价值不大，因此，应该完整地收集一天 24 小时、一周 7 天高速公路和主干道的交通数据。

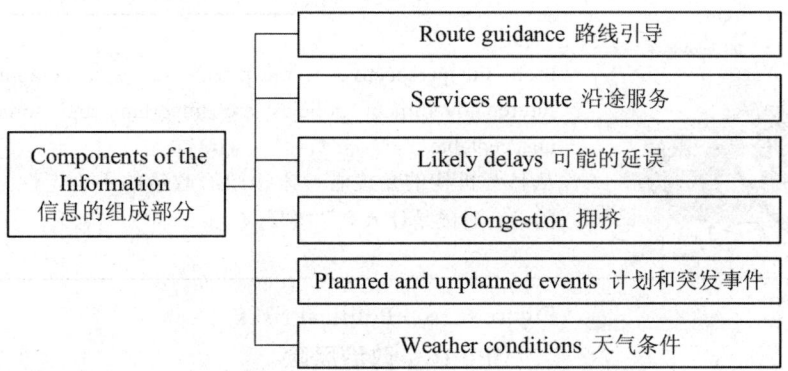

Figure 6.14   Components of the Information

图 6.14   信息的组成部分

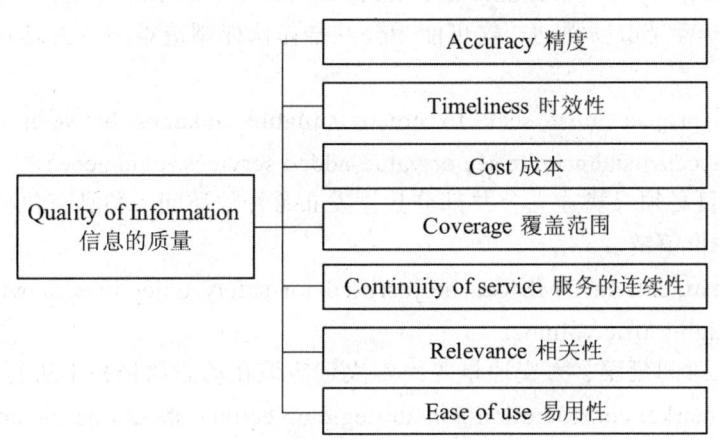

Figure 6.15   Quality of Information

图 6.15   信息的质量

② Create added value to satisfy the paying customers.

满足付费用户对附加值的需求。

③ As part of the process of ensuring information quality, maintenance regimes for ATIS equipment must also be in place and adhered to.

作为确保信息质量过程的一部分，ATIS 设备的维护体制一定要就位并一贯坚持。

(2) Differences in Organizational Culture   组织文化的差异

① Public/private partnerships have the potential for creative synergy between the public sector culture and the entrepreneurial approach.

公私合作有可能实现公共部门文化和企业家实现手法之间的创造性协同配合。

② What is needed is extra effort to communicate and build mutual trust and understanding among the organizations from the different sectors, countries, and cultures.

来自不同部门、不同国家和不同文化的各组织机构间进行沟通并建立相互信任和理解需要付出格外的努力。

(3) Political Risks   政治风险

From the perspective of the private sector, uncertainties in future government policies are important and sometimes unacceptable.
从私营机构的角度看，未来政府政策的不确定性是重要的，有时候是让人无法接受的。

Figure 6.16 Political risks
图 6.16 政治风险

(4) Market Demand   市场需求

① ATIS private partners are understandably market-driven. This can create problems for the public partners, especially in operational tests that may last for several years.

ATIS 私营参与者受市场驱动，这可能为公共合作伙伴制造难题，尤其是对需要持续数年的运营测试。

② Any ATIS project must seek to create suitable linkages between public-sector data distribution (open access) and private sector value-added services (paid access).

任何 ATIS 项目必须寻找建立公共部分数据发布（开放访问）和私有机构增值服务（付费访问）之间适当的价值链。

③ Public investments in DMS can be justified for safety objectives or when there are long traffic delays and high traffic volumes.

安全目标、长时间延误、大交通量等因素决定应该在动态情报板上进行公共投资。

④ Therefore, market consideration and strategic objectives should be included early on in the design of large-scale operational tests involving the private sector, and should be reviewed periodically throughout the tests.

因此，包括私营机构在内的大范围的运营测试的设计应该尽早地考虑市场需求和战略目标，并在测试的整个过程中进行周期性的评价。

(5) Leveraging on the Telecommunications Infrastructure   通信基础设施的杠杆作用

① The communication needs of ATIS services should gain leverage from the fixed and mobile telecommunications infrastructure that is already in place.

ATIS 服务的通信需求应在固定和移动通信基础设施之间寻找平衡点。

② The rapid growth in cell-phone networks for wide area mobile communications has weakened the case for beacon technology. Cellular telephones have advantages over beacons by providing bidirectional communications, anytime and anywhere, without the need for new and dedicated infrastructure. On the other hand, cellular networks have less capacity for high-speed data transmission, as compared with dedicated short range communication beacons (infrared or microwave).

大范围移动通信的手机网络快速发展，弱化了信标技术，蜂窝移动电话在任何时间、任何地点都可以提供双向通信，无需新的和专门的基础设施，另一方面，蜂窝网络高速数据传输的能力偏低，而专用短程通信信标（红外或微波技术）则具备高速数据传输能力。

③ The boom in ATIS to distribute traffic information through telephones (both wireline and wireless) and the Internet rests primarily on the expanding telecommunications infrastructure.

ATIS 在通过电话（有线或无线）和 Internet 发布交通信息方面的快速扩展主要依赖于通信基础设施的扩展。

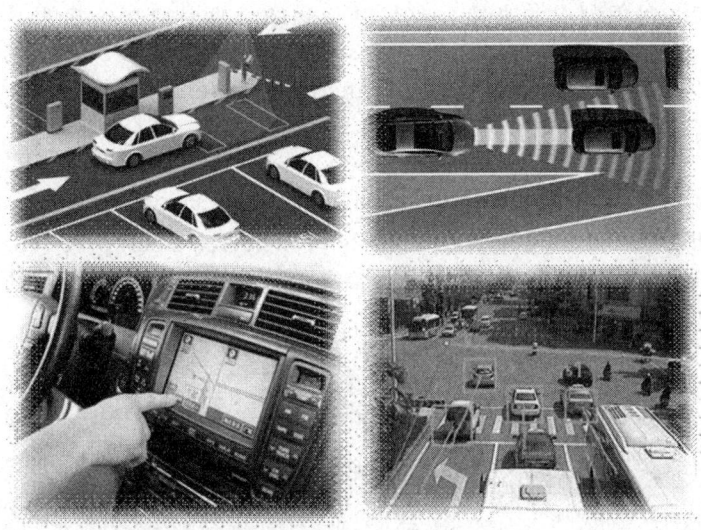

Figure 6.17　Telecommunications infrastructure

图 6.17　通信基础设施

(6) Dynamic Route Guidance　动态路线引导

① Dynamic route guidance has turned out to be more challenging than originally expected. Data collection, processing, and distribution, as well as institutional barriers have all proved to be more complex than was first thought.

动态路线引导比原先预想的更具挑战性。数据收集、处理和发布以及制度上的障碍都比原先预期的更加复杂。

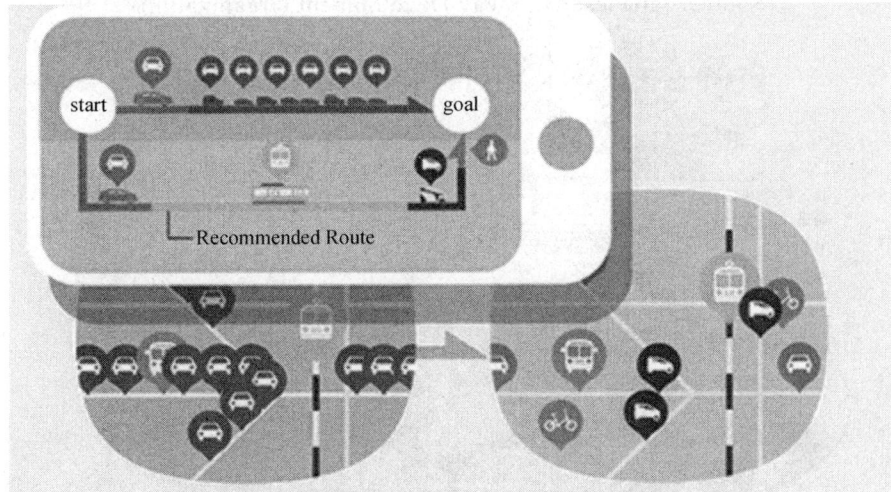

Figure 6.18　Dynamic Route Guidance

图 6.18　动态路线引导

② The system needs to take account of the current location of the driver or passenger, his and her travel preferences (e.g. fastest route, least cost route, truck route when required) and take account of restrictions (e.g. no expressway driving), as well as the ever-changing traffic conditions.

系统需要统一考虑驾驶员或乘客当前的位置、出行偏好（时间最短、费用最省、货车路线等），并需要考虑各种限制（非高速公路驾驶）和随时改变的交通条件。

6.2.4　Advice on Advanced Public Transport Systems (APTS)　对先进的公共交通系统（APTS）的建议

APTS includes all collective transport management and shared transport management. Thus, the management of high occupancy facilities is often considered a part of APTS services.

APTS 包括所有集中运输管理和共享运输管理。因此，高占有率设施的管理包括在 APTS 服务中。

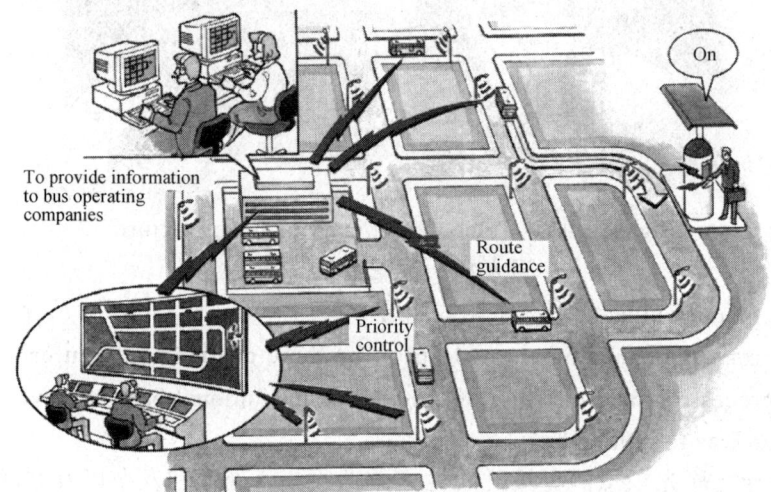

Figure 6.19　Public transport operations
(Source: Japanese Highway Development Organization)

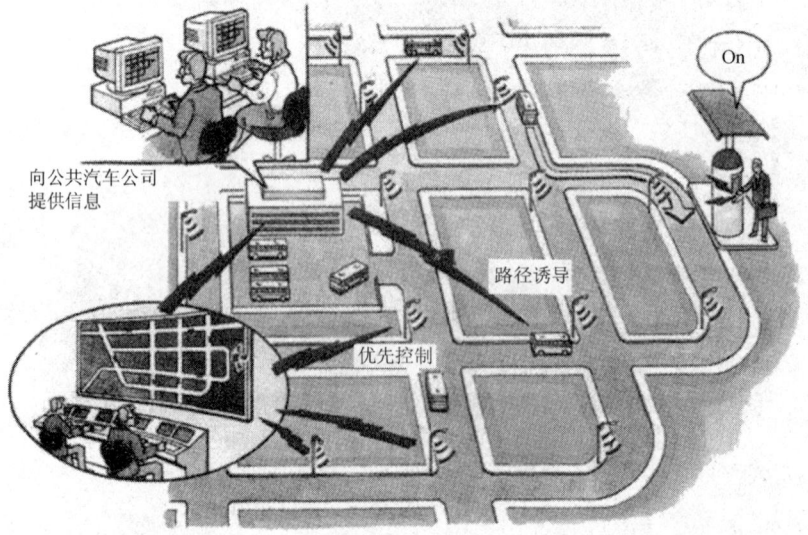

图 6.19　公交运营管理示意图（来源：日本高速公路发展组织）

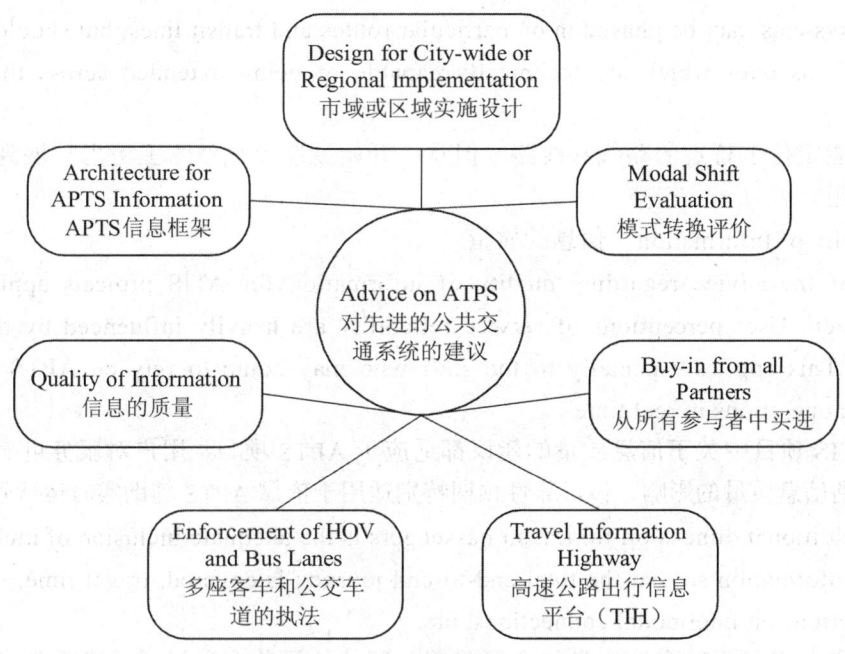

Figure 6.20　Advice on ATPS
图 6.20　对先进的公共交通系统的建议

(1) Design for City-wide or Regional Implementation　市域或区域实施设计

① APTS systems often begin with an investment in vehicle locations systems that bring immediate benefits to transit operations.

城市或区域 APTS 系统的设计往往从对给运营管理带来直接利益的车辆定位系统进行投资开始。

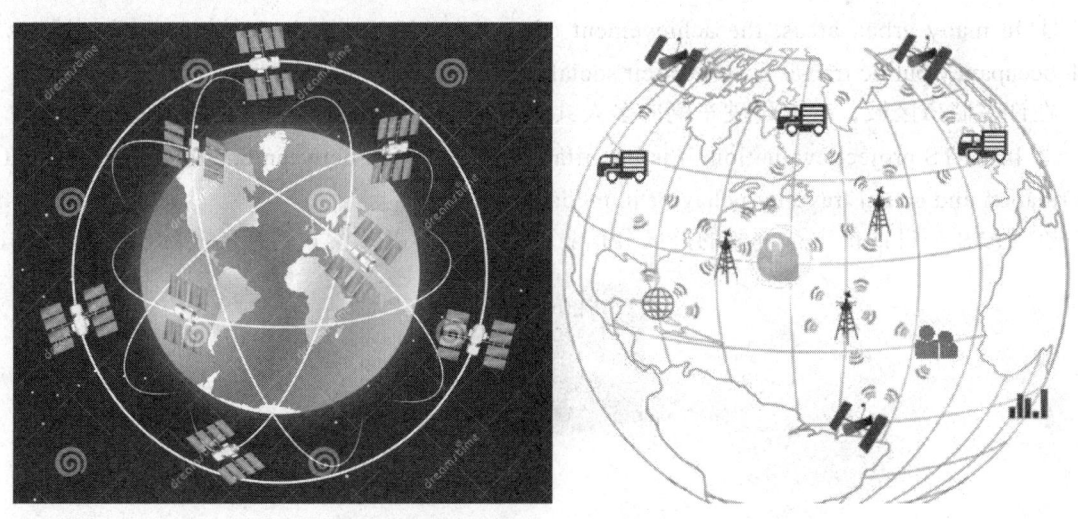

Figure 6.21　Vehicle locations systems
图 6.21　车辆定位系统

② Real-time information and other sophistications (like sensors which measure passenger numbers boarding and alighting at each stop) build on this.

实时信息和其他复杂信息（如用来获取乘客上下客数量的传感器）都是基于此建立起来的。

217

③ The systems may be phased in on particular routes and transit lines, but should be designed from the start as ones which are technically capable of being extended across the full transit network.

系统可能定位于特定的路线和线路,但从一开始就应该从技术上考虑扩展到整个路网运营管理的问题。

(2) Quality of Information 信息的质量

① All of the advice regarding quality of information for ATIS projects applies to APTS projects as well. User perceptions of service reliability are heavily influenced by the quality of information. This applies especially to the staff who may come to rely on APTS as an aid to managing the operations in real time.

所有 ATIS 项目中关于信息质量的建议都适应于 APTS 项目。用户对服务可靠性的预期很大程度上受到信息质量的影响,该可靠性预期特别适用于依靠 APTS 辅助实时运营管理的人员。

② An additional dimension for transit passengers is the adequate inclusion of multi-modal and interchange information so that the total end-to-end journey is covered: travel time, the total cost, detailed directions on intermodal connections, etc.

为确保点到点的运输乘客信息的全面覆盖,额外的涵盖多种模式、换乘信息在内的旅行时间、总的费用、多模式换乘节点处的详细方向指引等多元信息也需要包括在 APTS 系统中。

③ Since information about multi-modal transport can be complicated, and transit users often include elderly people and people with a disability, ease of use is particularly important.

由于多模式运输的信息复杂度较高,而且运输使用者包含了老年人和残疾人,因此,信息的易用性尤其重要。

(3) Modal Shift Evaluation 模式转换评价

① In many urban areas, the achievement of modal shift from single occupancy vehicles to high occupancy public transit is an explicit social objective.

在许多城市区域,单人驾驶车辆向多人共乘车辆的模式转换已经成为明确的社会目标。

② In APTS project evaluation, it is important to distinguish between tangible improvement in information and actual traveller behavior in modal shift.

在 APTS 项目评价中,重要的是区分信息的切实改善以及模式转换的实际出行者行为。

Figure 6.22 Modal Shift
图 6.22 模式转换

(4) Buy-in from all Partners 所有合作伙伴的认可

The primary purpose of many APTS projects is to provide management information for the operator rather than information for the traveller.

很多 APTS 项目的主要目的是为运营者提供管理信息而不是为公众提供信息。

Figure 6.23　APTS projects provide management information

图 6.23　APTS 项目提供管理信息

(5) Enforcement of HOV and Bus Lanes　多座客车和公交车道的执法

```
Enforcement of
HOV and Bus Lanes  ──┬── Bus lanes and high-occupancy-vehicle (HOV) lanes are widely used
多座客车和公交         │    to implement bus priority or demand management for congestion relief.
车道的执法            │    公交车道和多座客车(HOV)车道广泛用于实施公交优先和
                    │    缓解拥堵的需求管理过程中。
                    │
                    ├── Lack of adequate space for the HOV lanes and the lack of cost-effectiveness
                    │    enforcement technologies have been a disincentive.
                    │    缺乏足够的HOV车道空间和成本效益比高的稽查技术是一大障碍。
                    │
                    └── Careful planning of bus and HOV lanes is needed for maximum effectiveness
                         and camera-based enforcement should be considered.
                         细致规划公共汽车和HOV道以实现效率最大化,
                         而且考虑基于视频的稽查手段。
```

Figure 6.24　Enforcement of HOV and Bus Lanes

图 6.24　多座客车和公交车道的执法

(6) Architecture for APTS Information　APTS 信息框架

① APTS often requires close collaboration and information exchange between multimodal agencies, such as between bus operators, a transit management center, a traffic management center, and in many locations rail, ferry and airport operations as well.

APTS 经常需要多运输模式机构间进行紧密的合作和信息交换，这些机构包括公交运营商、运输管理中心，交通管理中心以及本地火车站、摆渡站、机场之间等。

② One way to assure this relationship is by selecting a client-server architecture for the technical implementation of information sharing.

一种确保这种关系的方法就是选择适用信息共享技术应用的 C/S 框架。

(7) Travel Information Highway　高速公路出行信息平台（TIH）

① The TIH model uses a distributed set of data services published on a common bearer. Users can gather data from a number of sources by selecting them from the published list of services and registering to receive some or all of the data.

TIH 模型使用一个发布在通用模板上的分布式数据服务集，用户可以通过从已发布服务列表中选择数据源并进行注册登记以接受部分或全部数据。

② Multi-modal travel information sharing is essential for such projects as Transport Direct, which aims to provide travellers with all the information they need before and during a journey anywhere in the UK and with the ability to buy the associated tickets.

对于类似 Transport Direct 的项目，多模式出行信息的共享是基础，该项目旨在在英国任何地点为出行者提供出行前、出行中所需的所有信息，并使出行者具备购票能力。

6.2.5　Advice on Electronic Payment Systems (EPS)　对电子付费系统（EPS）的建议

EPS included electronic toll collection (ETC) applications、smart cards for other applications, and electronic payments to facilitate implementation of demand management.

EPS 包括电子不停车收费系统（ETC）、智能卡以及促进需求管理实施的电子付费等。

(1) Dedicated Short Range Communications(DSRC) Standards　专用短程通信技术（DSRC）标准

The most common electronic payment service to date has been electronic toll collection (ETC). There are two basic types of DSRC systems for ETC: active and backscatter.

最通用的电子付费服务就是 ETC。ETC 有两种类型的 DSRC 技术：主动式和被动式。

Figure 6.25　Dedicated Short Range Communications
图 6.25　专用短程通信技术

① DSRC supports parking payment, in-vehicle information systems, CVO, electronic commerce, and other services.

DSRC 支持停车付费、车载信息系统、CVO（商用车辆管理）、电子商务以及其他服务。

② Also required is a plan for migrating toward new standards that are still evolving. Alternative approaches to ETC other than DSRC (e.g. use of GPS/GSM or automatic license plate readers) should also be considered.

同时应考虑如何跟上不断改进的新标准，也应考虑基于非 DSRC 技术的 ETC 系统（GPS/GSM 或牌照识别系统）。

Figure 6.26　Services Supported by DSRC

图 6.26　DSRC 支持的服务

(2) Other Enabling Technologies　其他需要的技术

However, there are other enabling technologies for ETC that should not be neglected. For example, toll charges usually vary from one type of vehicle to another. Thus, automatic vehicle classification (AVC) is needed to determine the amount that should be collected. In addition, violators must be identified and penalized in order to enforce payments through ETC.

然而不应该忽视运用 ETC 的其他可行技术，例如，电子收费通常按照车型收费，需要以自动车辆识别（AVC）技术确定收费额度。另外，识别任何情况下的违规车辆，对违法者进行身份识别并处罚，以保证 ETC 系统的强制收费。

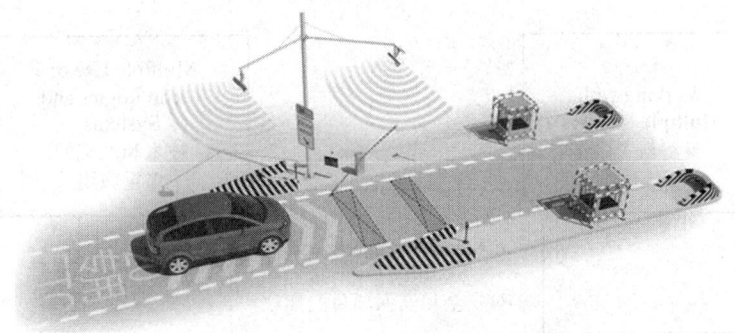

Figure 6.27　Schematic of ETC

图 6.27　ETC 自动收费站示意图

(3) The Broader Aspect of Electronic Payments　电子付费的延伸应用

① Electronic payment is frequently considered as a means to carry out innovative financing to enable or accelerate highway construction.

电子付费通常被看作筹措资金和加速高速公路建设的有效方法。

② Electronic payment has also enabled or facilitated the implementation of road pricing.

电子付费也为道路拥挤收费和浮动费率道路收费的实施提供了可能和刺激。

③ Electronic payment has been used as the broader term to encompass electronic payments, which can facilitate implementation of transportation economic policies, as well as electronic fare collection for transit operations and toll collection for tunnel, bridge, and road usage.

电子付费能够促进交通运输经济政策的实施，还包括公共交通电子付费系统和隧道、桥梁、道路使用收费。

6.2.6　Advice on Safety and Security Projects　对安全和安保项目的建议

Figure 6.28　Safety and Security
图 6.28　安全和安保

Transportation professionals are increasingly faced with the challenge of taking or sharing responsibilities in new projects related to safety and security, ranging from handling traffic incidents, enhancing road safety in cooperation with intelligent vehicles, to reducing the threat and damage caused by terrorist attacks.

运输专业人员越来越需要在安全和安保相关的项目中承担或分担责任。这些安全和安保项目包括处理交通事故、在智能车辆协作中提高道路安全、减少由于恐怖袭击引起的威胁和损害等方面。

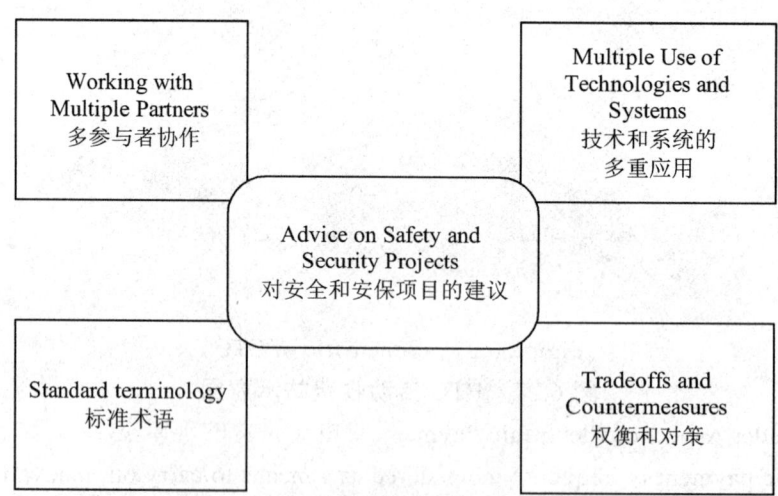

Figure 6.29　Advice on Safety and Security Projects
图 6.29　对安全与安保项目的建议

(1) Working with Multiple Partners　多参与者协作

① Most transportation professionals have experience working with police, fire, and emergency medical services in handling traffic incidents and should work with existing incident management and emergency planning groups wherever possible.

大多数运输专业人员在处理交通事故方面拥有与警察、火警、急救中心合作的经验，他们应与现有事故管理部门、紧急事件计划编制部门共同工作。

② Their close coordination is helped if they can be co-located. The traffic agency may also need to work more closely with transit and train agencies under emergency situations as the City of New York discovered on September 11, 2001 for rapid evacuation of a large population.

位置上的一体化（同址办公）有助于他们的紧密合作。紧急情况下，交通部门也需要与运输和铁路机构紧密合作，以应对如2001年9月11日纽约恐怖袭击等紧急情况下大量人员的快速疏散。

Figure 6.30　Cooperation

图 6.30　协作

③ Transportation professionals in the public sector are used to working with actors in the private sector to research the frequency and negative consequences of vehicle collisions. Such public/private partnerships can be effective in dealing with security issues, but only if the partners fully understand each other's roles, and avoid future misunderstandings through written agreements.

公共部门的运输专业人员习惯于与私营部门的人士共同工作，研究车辆碰撞的频率和负效应。当公、私参与者理解各自的职能并通过协议的方式避免未来的误解，则能共同有效地处理安全事件。

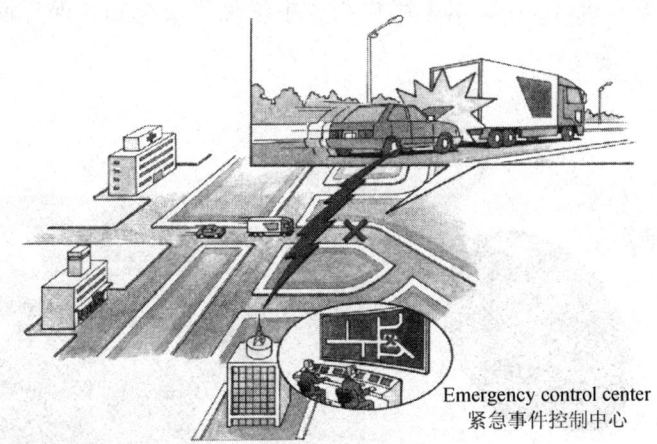

Figure 6.31　Automatic emergency notification

(Source: Japanese Highway Development Organization)

图 6.31　自动紧急事件提示系统示意图（来源：日本高速公路发展组织）

(2) Multiple Use of Technologies and Systems 技术和系统的多重应用

① ITS have proved to function well in redirecting traffic during emergency situations serendipitously.

在偶发性紧急情况下，ITS 在改变交通流方向方面起到了较好的作用。

② ITS and operational procedures can be designed in such a way that they can function well in dual or multiple modes – managing traffic in routine situations and work effectively in emergency situations (natural disasters or terrorism).

ITS 及其运作过程可以设计成双模式或多模式工作方式，在日常情况下用来管理交通，紧急情况下有效处置事件（自然灾害或恐怖活动）。

(3) Standard terminology 标准术语

① Development of common terminologies helps the coordination between traffic management and public safety.

通用术语的发展有助于交通管理和公共安全之间的协调。

> **例**
>
> **Standard terminology 标准术语**
>
> The IEEE 1512 Family of Standards specify digital message sets for transportation incident management by laying out a framework for digital communications that bridge ITS systems such as ATMS, public safety systems such as fire, police and EMS, and public works.
>
> IEEE 1512标准族通过发布数字通信框架的方式规定了交通运输事件管理的数字报文集，这个数字通信框架为诸如ATMS等在内的ITS系统与诸如火警、警察、EMS和公共事务等公共安全系统之间搭建起沟通的桥梁。

② The new US National ITS Architecture (Version 5.0) has included the new user service of "Disaster Response and Evacuation".

新的美国 ITS 体系框架（5.0 版本）用户服务中增加了安全和安保方面的服务——灾难响应和疏散用户服务。

Figure 6.32　Application of smart cards

图 6.32　智能卡的应用

③ ITS technologies are already deployed for dual or multiple purposes. Smart cards have been used for identification and access control of transport personnel.

ITS 技术基于多种目的得到应用。智能卡已经广泛应用到运输人员的识别和门禁管理中。

(4) Tradeoffs and Countermeasures 权衡和对策

① The increase of safety and security comes with a cost, and there are various tradeoffs in the choice of technologies and maintenance options.

伴随着安全和安保措施的加强随之而来的是成本的增加，在技术选择和维护选择方面有很多权衡考虑。

② Operational and maintenance contracts must specify maximum call-out times for responding to an emergency. Contracts with suppliers of power and communications should specify maximum recovery periods in the event of a supply failure.

运营和维护协议必须规定紧急情况最大响应次数，与电力和通信供应商的协议应规定故障情况下的最大修复时间。

③ A security risk assessment should evaluate the vulnerability of key ITS.

必须针对 ITS 关键系统的弱点进行安全风险评估。

④ There are politically sensitive tradeoffs between security and privacy, such as in the choice of an appropriate level of surveillance, and between security and transport efficiency (productivity).

在安全和隐私方面也有一些政治上敏感的折中，诸如，监控的级别之间以及安全和运输效率（生产力）之间的选择等方面。

⑤ Instead of backing up all the ITS equipment and info structure at critical points, one would make a higher-than-normal investment in mobile ITS equipment (cameras, variable message signs, etc.) that has maximum flexibility for contingency deployment at unpredictable locations during emergencies.

在移动 ITS 设备（照相机、可变情报板等）方面给予高于以往的投资，而不是在所有 ITS 设备和信息结构的关键点提供支持。这些移动 ITS 设备在紧急情况下，在不可预见地点的紧急调度方面具有最大的灵活性。

6.3　Regional ITS Deployment　区域 ITS 部署

Experience in ITS implementation over recent years indicates that transportation professionals are faced with several special challenges that are common to most if not all ITS projects. This section discusses four of these regional challenges: regional deployment strategies, technology and operations, enforcement and communications.

近年 ITS 实施经验表明，运输专业人员必须要面对一些并非 ITS 项目本身，而是所有项目共同面临的挑战。本部分讨论区域 ITS 发展面临的四个挑战：区域部署战略、技术和运营、执法和通信。

Figure 6.33 Advice on Regional ITS Deployment

图 6.33 对地区 ITS 部署的建议

6.3.1 Advice on Regional Deployment Strategies 对区域部署战略的建议

The full benefits of ITS can be realized only if the many stand-alone traffic and travel information systems are integrated within a region. However, integration is not as straightforward as some might expect.

ITS 整体效益的显现需要许多孤立的交通和出行信息系统整合在一起,然而集成并不像期望的那样容易。

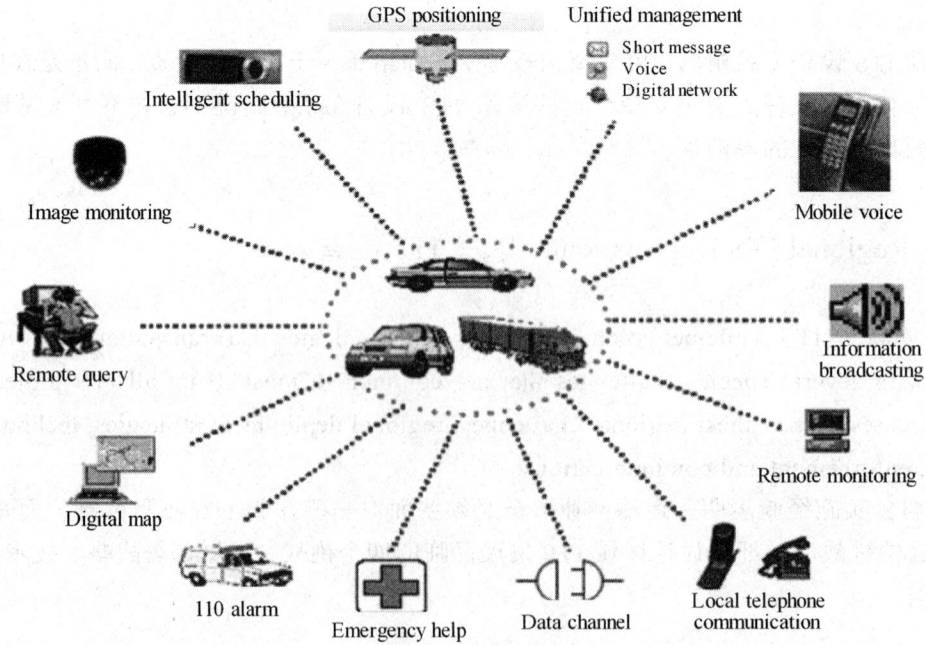

Figure 6.34 Travel information system

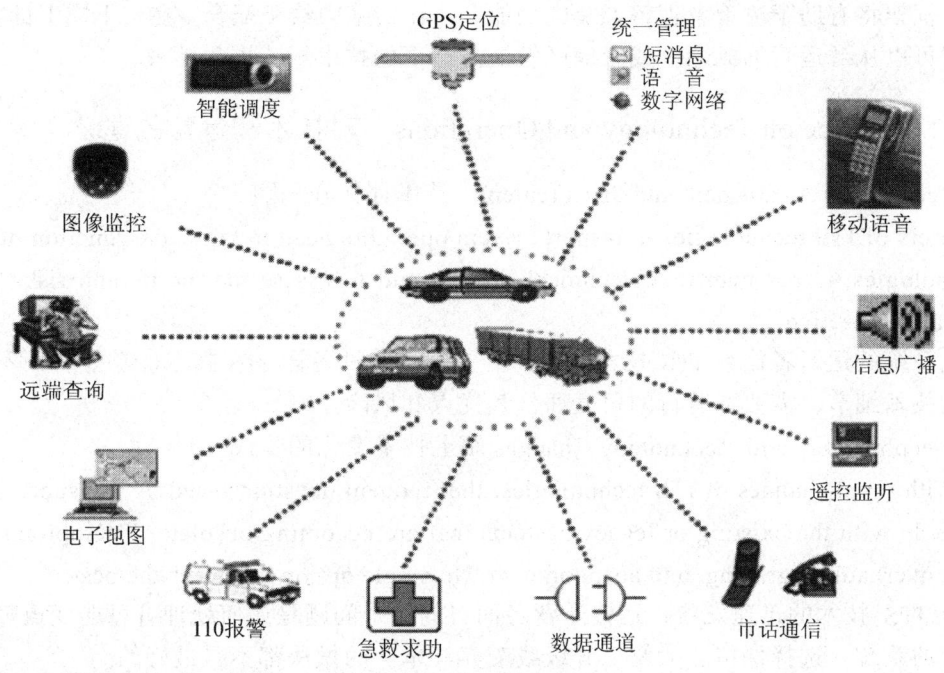

图 6.34 出行信息系统

(1) Dimensions　尺度

① The first practical issue in regional deployment has to do with its dimensions.

在地区范围内部署 ITS 时，很重要的一个难题就是确定它的尺度。

② In order to define a "region" in which ITS applications are to be integrated, one has to consider integration at different levels – domestic integration within a country, international integration with trade partners or with geographical neighbors.

要定义开展 ITS 应用集成的"地区"，必须考虑不同层次的整合——国家范围的整合，贸易伙伴或者相邻国家之间的跨国整合等。

③ The size of the region will determine the level of interoperability that is required. The appropriate scale of deployment depends on specific applications.

区域的大小决定了所要求的互操作性的层次，部署的范围取决于特定的应用。

④ This has led to the suggestion of ETC based on GPS for trucks and DSRC for cars.

建议 ETC 系统基于在货运车辆上安装 GPS 而在小汽车上安装 DSRC 设备。

(2) Techniques to Encourage Success　促进成功的技术

① People and organizations have different objectives, motivations and attitudes. Although most of these institutional problems could be alleviated by legal and contractual arrangements, building consensus requires seed funding.

个人和组织具有不同的目标、动机和态度。大多数制度上的问题可以通过立法和契约安排，以及建立共识需要种子资金的方式予以解决。

② System architecture can help high-level decision makers understand the functioning of ITS and cooperate in its deployment. In this bottom-up approach, a regional architecture can evolve from a "concept of operations" or from technical specifications based on regional objectives.

体系框架将有助于决策者理解 ITS 的功能，并在实施中给予配合。在自下向上的方法中，地区框架可以从"运营的概念"或者地区发展目标下的技术规范进化而来。

6.3.2 Advice on Technology and Operations 对技术和运营的建议

(1) Technology Assessment and Procurement 技术评估和采购

As users of ITS technologies, transport system operators need to know the function of various ITS technologies, rather than their technical details, and to assess the merits and risks from an operational perspective.

运输系统的运营者作为 ITS 技术的用户需要知道各种各样 ITS 技术的功能，而不需要了解它们的技术细节，需要从运行的角度评价其优点和风险。

(2) Keeping Pace with Technology Changes 跟上技术变化的步伐

① With rapid changes of ITS technologies, the frequent question faced by transport operators is what to do with the existing or legacy systems that are becoming obsolete? The options include retention, overhaul, upgrading, and abandonment. No single option is always the best.

随着 ITS 技术的迅速发展，运输运营者面对的一个问题是如何处理有可能变成障碍的现有或遗留的系统。选择保留、大修、升级或废弃等单一的做法都不是最好的。

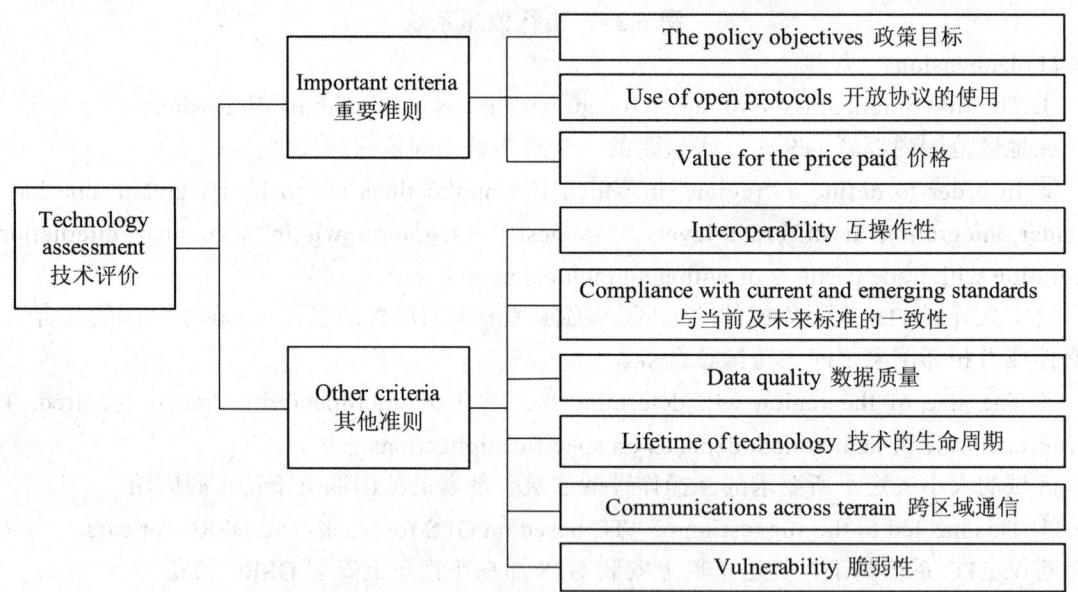

Figure 6.35　Technology assessment criteria
图 6.35　技术评价准则

② In general, one should go for generic devices and abandon special ones in order to lower cost and to gain flexibility for future upgrading and easier integration with other ITS devices.

通常，从未来升级、集成和降低成本的角度考虑，ITS 设备应该尽量选用通用设备，放弃专用设备。

③ There is no lack of ITS vendors who are willing to educate and train management and staff before and after system procurement.

不乏 ITS 提供商乐意在系统采购前、后教育和培训管理者和工作人员。

④ For in-depth learning, participation in discovery or scan tours to peer organizations domestically or overseas has proved effective if advance preparation is made prior to taking these tours.

要深入学习，提前做好参观考察准备，事实证明参观学习国内或者海外同行也是有效方法。

⑤ Sponsoring and participating in test projects are very good ways to keep pace with new developments.

发起和参与一些测试项目也是很好的跟上新技术的方法之一。

6.3.3　Advice on Enforcement　对执法的建议

Many ITS applications, such as access control, electronic payment, non-stop tolling and ATMS rely on camera-based automatic enforcement systems.

许多 ITS 应用如入口控制、电子支付、不停车收费和 ATMS 等都需要依靠自动摄像执法系统。

Automatic enforcement always consist of at least three different procedures

自动执法至少包括如下过程：

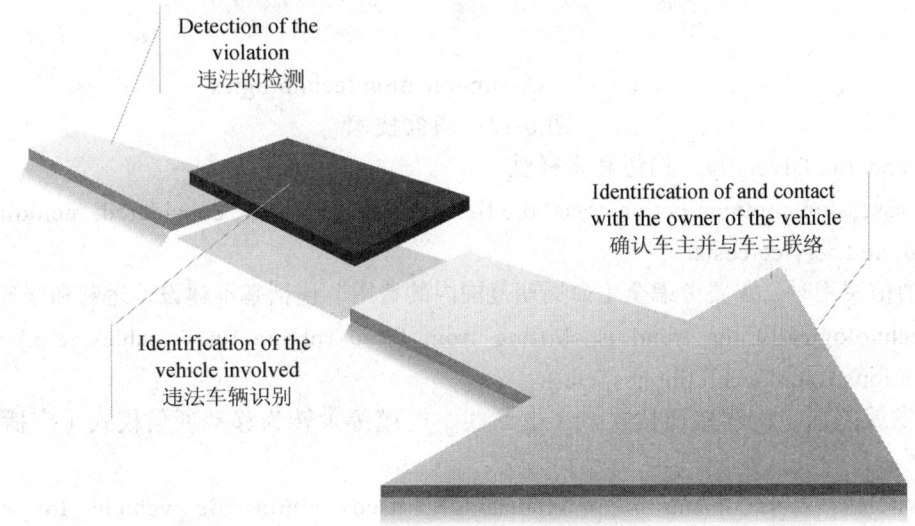

Figure 6.36　Procedures of automatic enforcement

图 6.36　自动执法的过程

In order to combine these procedures into one system the aim is to create a fully automatic system. The strategy for automatic enforcement varies between countries depending on detection technology used, the organization of policing and vehicle records, traffic legislation and system of sanctions. An important prerequisite for an efficient automated enforcement system is the availability of a centralized register of vehicles and their owners at a national level.

应建立全自动化系统将上述处理过程集成在一个系统中。根据所使用的检测技术、警察和车辆档案管理部门、交通立法、制裁系统的不同，不同国家的自动执法策略多种多样，有效的自动执法系统的先决条件是国家级的中央车辆、车主登记库的建立。

6.3.4　Advice on Communications　对通信的建议

Communications are a crucial element in ITS deployment, playing an increasing role as system integration and regional deployment are emphasized. At the same time, communication technologies are becoming more sophisticated, resulting in higher capabilities and lower costs.

通信在 ITS 应用中是关键因素，随着系统整合和地区推广策略的强化，通信将扮演越来越重要的角色。同时，通信技术也越来越复杂，随之而来的是通信能力的提高、费用的降低。

Figure 6.37　Communication technologies

图 6.37　通信技术

(1) Trend and Diversity　趋势和多样性

① In assessing communication costs, the life-cycle cost must be considered, including capital, operational, and service costs.

评估通信费用时，需要考虑全生命周期范围内的费用，包括基本建设、运营和服务的费用。

② Technologically the trend is shifting from fixed (phone lines, cables, etc.) to mobile communications (radios, cell phones, etc.).

技术发展趋向于由固定通信模式（电话线、电缆等）转为移动通信模式（广播、蜂窝电话等）。

③ Wireless communication is increasingly used within the vehicle for convenient interconnections between laptop computers and many other digital devices such as navigation units.

无线通信越来越多地应用于车辆上以促进便携式电脑和诸如车载导航单元等其他数字化设备之间的通信。

④ Local area networks (LAN) based on wireless "Bluetooth" standards, and mobile access to the Internet, are now available. For pre-trip planning, access to the Internet still relies heavily on wire line communication (phone line and cable at the home base).

基于无线"蓝牙"标准的局域网（LAN）和移动访问 Internet 已经可用。出行前规划，大部分还依赖有线通信的方式接入到 Internet（家庭的电话线或网线等）。

⑤ However, with more LAN using wireless connections in buildings, and more cell phones accessing the Internet through the wireless application protocol (WAP), the question of whether the

Internet at home and in the office uses wire line or wireless communications has become moot.

随着楼宇无线局域网接入、基于 WAP 的手机用户接入,使得有线还是无线接入到 Internet 的讨论变得没有意义。

(2) 3G Wireless Communications　3G 无线通信

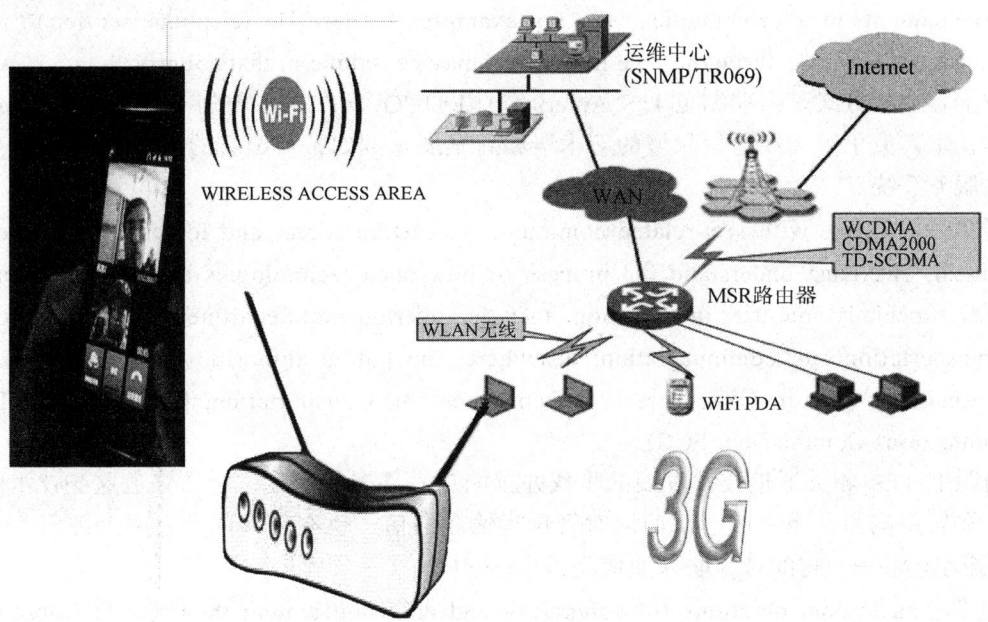

Figure 6.38　3G wireless communications

图 6.38　3G 无线通信

Third-generation (3G) wireless technologies promise higher bit rates (upwards of 2 Mbps) and other capabilities (e.g. roaming), as compared to the first-generation of analogue wireless communication and the second generation of early versions of digital wireless communication.

相对于第一代模拟无线通信和第二代数字无线通信来说,第三代无线通信技术(3G)将提供更高的传输速率(高达 2Mbps)和其他功能(如漫游)。

Figure 6.39　Hand-held wireless device for vulnerable road users

(Source: Japanese Highway Development Organization)

图 6.39　弱势群体用户的手持式无线设备(来源:日本高速公路发展组织)

(3) Keeping Up with Communication Technologies　跟上通信技术

① A recommended good practice is to periodically scan for new developments on the web pages of such organizations as ITS America and ERTICO. There are also web pages that are helpful to both technical and non-technical people who want to just understand the new terminology and new developments in telecommunications. For example, the new 511 telephone service to get free traffic information in US through voice interaction may be unique in that country.

被推荐的好方式是定期浏览 ITS America、ERTICO 等 ITS 组织的网页。这些网页适合技术和非技术人员了解无线通信领域的新术语和新发展。例如，美国新的 511 电话免费交通语音信息服务系统。

② To keep pace with ITS-related communication technologies and forecast the rate of their deployment, one must understand the process of how such technologies are regulated. In many countries, especially countries in transition, a single governmental department has jurisdiction over both transportation and communication; elsewhere, the public authorities over these two areas reside separately (e.g. in USA there is a Department of Transportation, USDOT and a Federal Communications Commission, FCC).

为跟上 ITS 相关通信技术发展的步伐并预测未来部署的速度，必须知道这些技术的管理体制。在转型国家，单一政府部门同时管理运输和通信，也有一些国家，两个部门分别管理（如美国运输部——USDOT，联邦通信委员会——FCC）。

③ The basic considerations for comparing and choosing among them for ITS applications remain the same-namely, in addition to cost-benefit analysis, one should consider the criteria of range, coverage, latency, directionality, one-way versus two-way communications, reliability and vulnerability to natural versus man-made disasters, sabotage, etc.

ITS 应用中通信技术的比较和选择的基本考虑是一样的——即注意成本效益分析，应考虑距离、覆盖范围、响应时间、方向性、单向和双向通信、可靠性、抗灾性（自然灾害和人为灾害、故障率等方面的标准）。

④ This last point also suggests that a technology scan should include monitoring of military technologies. It is widely recognized that two of the most important ITS technologies originated from the US defense enterprise; viz. GPS and the Internet.

最后的建议是应该同时关注军事技术的发展，普遍认为 ITS 技术中 GPS 和 Internet 两项技术都是来自于美国国防部门。

6.4　Conclusions　结论

Many countries have established national ITS programs and supported ITS projects. Their cumulative experience has provided the basis for the advice given in this chapter for transportation professionals who are about to launch ITS programs and various kinds of ITS project.

许多国家建立了国家 ITS 规划，并支持 ITS 项目的建设。他们的经验积累形成了本章中给即将启动 ITS 计划和各类 ITS 项目的运输管理者一系列建议的基础。

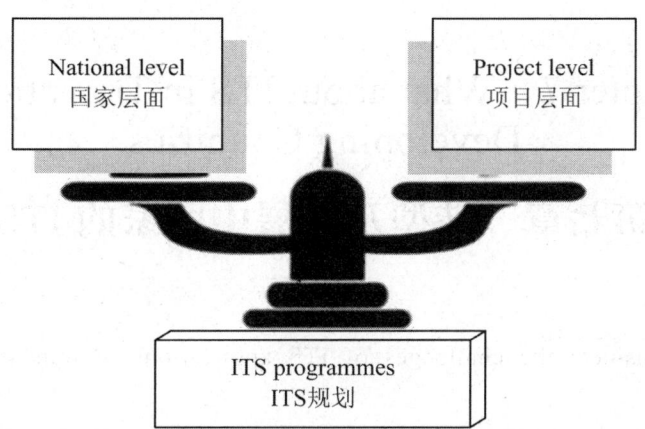

Figure 6.40　Establishment of ITS programs
图 6.40　ITS 规划的建设

(1) National level　国家层面

Most countries start their ITS programs with an assembly of interest groups across the transport and telecommunications sectors, that include actors from the public, private, and nonprofit sectors. Their consensus leads to the formation and maintenance of national programs facilitated by legislation and/or high-level government leadership.

大多数国家都是将包括公、私、非盈利机构在内的运输和通信领域的部门和利益团体联合起来，共同启动他们的 ITS 计划。他们的共识导致通过立法或更高层面的政府领导层来推动国家框架的建立和维护。

(2) Project level　项目层面

All projects should begin by setting clear objectives and targets for the ITS services, taking into account specific local requirements and the need for interoperability. Planning for ITS projects should include the establishment of current baseline for comparison with performance of future ITS services, careful management of expectations, adoption of an evolutionary approach to get early winners, and a process for learning from both positive and negative lessons.

所有项目应该从设定清晰的 ITS 服务的目标和对象开始，需考虑本地的特殊需求和协作的需求。ITS 项目的计划应该包括建立为对比评价未来 ITS 服务所需的当前基准线、系统预期的有效管理、吸取先前成功者的革新方法、从正面和负面的教训中学习的方法。

Chapter 7 What about ITS in Transitional Developing Countries
第七章 转型及发展中国家的 ITS

This chapter considers the challenges of ITS applications to transitional and developing countries.

本章介绍转型及发展中国家 ITS 的应用所面临的挑战。

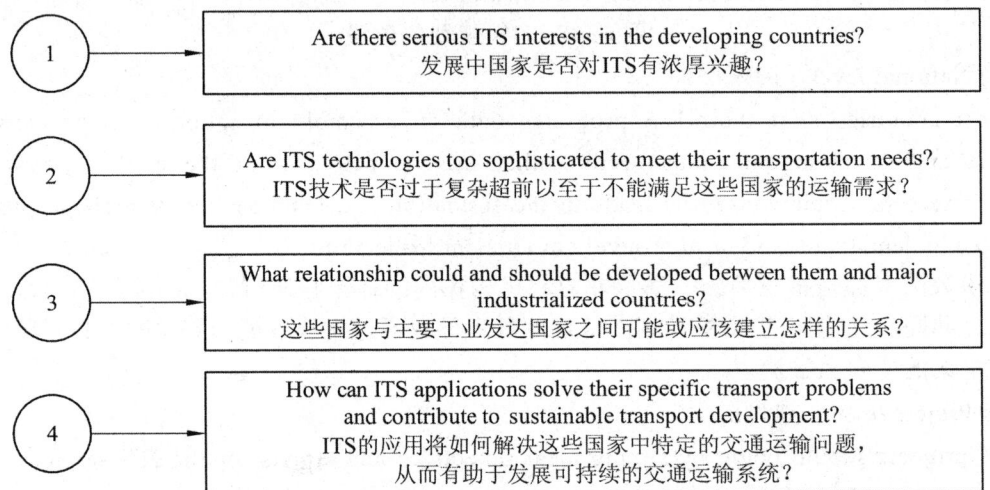

Figure 7.1 Challenges of ITS applications to transitional and developing countries

图 7.1 转型及发展中国家 ITS 应用所面临的挑战

Transitional and developing countries represent such a wide range of conditions that this chapter is intended only as a general guide to help analyze ITS issues in these countries. The situation in three different regions of the world – Asia, Central and Eastern Europe and Latin America – is described. Advice is offered to decision-makers and transportation professionals in all countries.

转型及发展中国家代表了范围相当广阔的地区，本章的目的仅为帮助分析这些国家的 ITS 问题提供一般性指导。本章主要介绍三个地区——亚洲、中欧及东欧、拉丁美洲的情况。同时，为所有国家的决策者和交通运输专家们提出一些建议。

7.1 Special Considerations 特殊的考虑

ITS technology transfer and mutual learning between regions are now commonplace in the major industrialized countries of Europe, North America, Japan and Australia. However, this is not necessarily true with transitional and developing countries since the special requirements of these countries must be considered in many ITS applications. Practitioners in these countries are advised to make use of the World Bank series of Technical Notes on ITS, in addition to the material in this book.

目前在欧洲、北美、日本和澳大利亚等主要工业发达国家，不同地区间的 ITS 技术转移和相互学习是很平常的事情。然而，由于必须要考虑转型及发展中国家在许多 ITS 应用中的特殊需求，所以在这些国家采取这种方式未必正确。建议转型及发展中国家从事 ITS 的先导者充分利用世界银行关于 ITS 的技术资料以及本书中的一些材料。

7.1.1　The Transportation Challenge and Motivating Questions　交通运输的挑战和启发性问题

As standards of living increase, there is an even more rapid growth of demand for transportation capital – for highways and railways, cars and trucks – in the transitional and developing countries. Often, therein lies the problem – the capital required to make such a transformation in these countries probably exceeds the combined resources from all existing sources that can be devoted to transportation on any reasonable basis. In the face of this limitation, many transportation professionals are turning to ITS as a means of squeezing more efficiency and productivity out of a given transportation investment, whether it is the infrastructure or the vehicle fleet.

随着生活水平的提高，转型及发展中国家对交通运输投资的需求越来越大，包括公路、铁路、小汽车和货车。通常，这种情况下会出现一个问题：在这些国家，转型需要的资金可能超过现有资源中可以以任何合理的理由提供给交通运输系统的所有资源的综合。面对这样的局限性，很多交通运输专家开始转向 ITS，把 ITS 看作是在给定的交通运输投资下获得更多的收益和产出的方法，而不管这种投资是针对基础设施还是针对车辆。

Figure 7.2　Transportation investment
图 7.2　交通运输投资

Given this special situation, the motivating questions behind this chapter are:

在这种特殊背景下，本章所关注的问题是：

(1) Which ITS applications are particularly helpful to transitional and developing countries?

哪些 ITS 应用对转型及发展中国家特别有用？

(2) How much ITS experience is transferable from the major industrialized countries to these countries?

主要工业发达国家有多少经验可以移植到这些国家？

(3) What are the most effective and mutually beneficial means of cooperation between these countries?

这些国家间采用哪种合作方式最为有效并互惠？

(4) How could ITS applications, technologies, and systems be adapted to the special requirements of transitional and developing countries?

ITS 应用、技术和系统等如何适应转型及发展中国家的特殊需求？

(5) How can we design "sustainable ITS" at both the national and the local levels within the special constraints of these countries?

如何在这些国家的特殊约束条件下在国家和地方层面设计"可持续发展的 ITS"？

(6) What are measurable benefits (if any) of ITS applications in these countries, that can be used to convince the decision makers in these countries to deploy ITS?

这些国家中，哪些 ITS 应用带来可度量的效益（如果有的话），可以用来说服决策者实施 ITS？

(7) How could ITS applications have assured interoperability and contribute to the regional integration of the national road network of these countries?

ITS 应用如何能保证互操作性并为这些国家道路网的区域性整合做出贡献？

7.1.2 Diverse Requirements 不同的需求

Understanding what the special requirements of transitional and developing countries are, and the extent to which these special requirements affect ITS development and applications in these countries are challenging for all ITS actors. For example, the level of GNP per inhabitant has many direct and indirect consequences that cannot change in a couple of decades.

对所有 ITS 的实施者来说，理解转型及发展中国家交通运输的特殊需求是什么以及这些特殊需求对 ITS 发展和应用的影响范围都是具有挑战性的。例如，人均国民生产总值（GNP）水平会产生很多直接和间接的后果，而这些后果在 20 年内都不会发生变化。

For example, the frequency of vehicle breakdowns is significantly higher in these countries than in major industrialized countries due to the aged vehicle fleets and poor road conditions. Thus, the benefit/cost ratio of incident detection devices in tunnels and elsewhere in urban areas should in principle be much higher in transitional and developing countries.

再比如，由于转型及发展中国家的车辆老龄化并且道路状况相对较差，这些国家的车辆故障率要明显高于主要工业发达国家。因此从原理上说，在转型及发展中国家的隧道和城市其他地区安装事件检测设备的效益成本比应该会比较高。

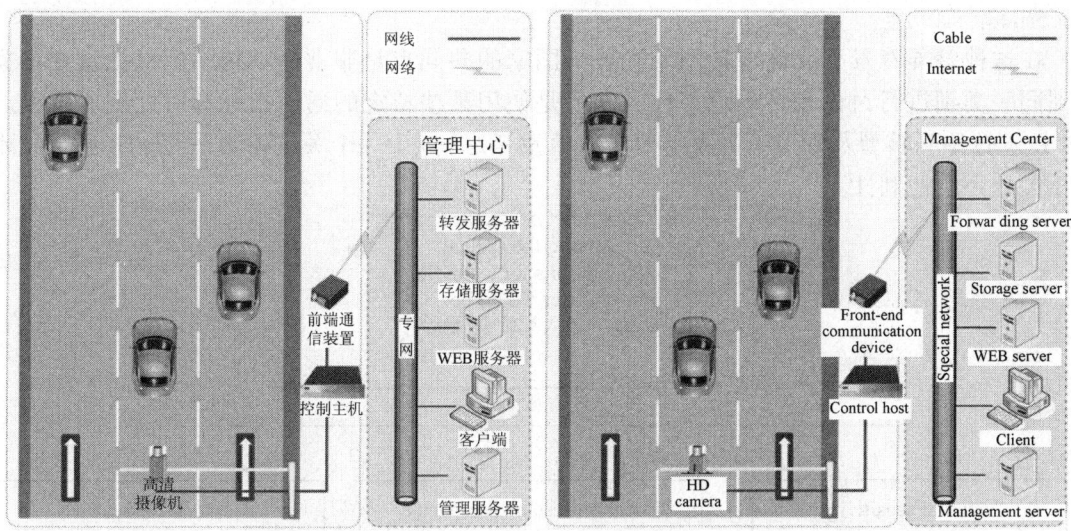

Figure 7.3　Traffic incident detection system
图 7.3　交通事件检测系统

In terms of the context for ITS deployment, there is a great diversity within and between the many transitional and developing countries in the world. The diversity lies in at least the following three dimensions:

关于 ITS 部署的背景，在许多转型及发展中国家内部以及国家之间都有很大的差异。这种差异至少体现在以下三个方面：

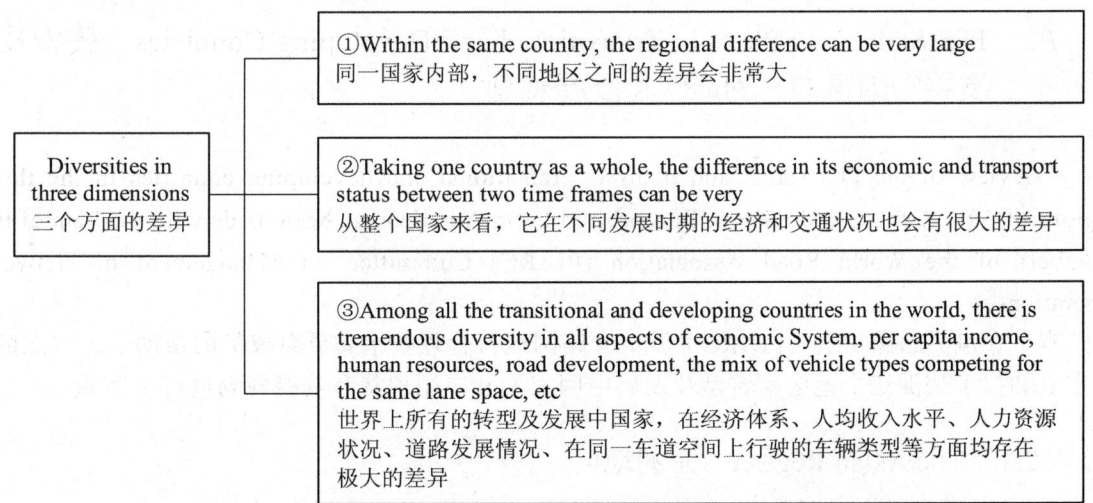

Figure 7.4　Diversities in three dimensions
图 7.4　三个方面的差异

Given these diversities, it would be difficult to identify commonalities among the transitional and developing countries and it would be hazardous to group all these countries together in the discussion. However, the use of certain common yardsticks can be helpful. ITS technology transfer involving transitional and developing countries may require careful consideration. A key consideration is the ease with which the ITS enabling technologies can be introduced in the region concerned.

在这种差异背景下，确定转型及发展中国家的共同点是非常困难的，而且把这些国家规划到同一类别进行讨论是带有危害性的，但是使用某些特定的通用指标却对此有所帮助。将 ITS 技术转移到转型及发展中国家需要予以慎重考虑，其中一个关键因素是将 ITS 可行技术引入相关地区的便利性。

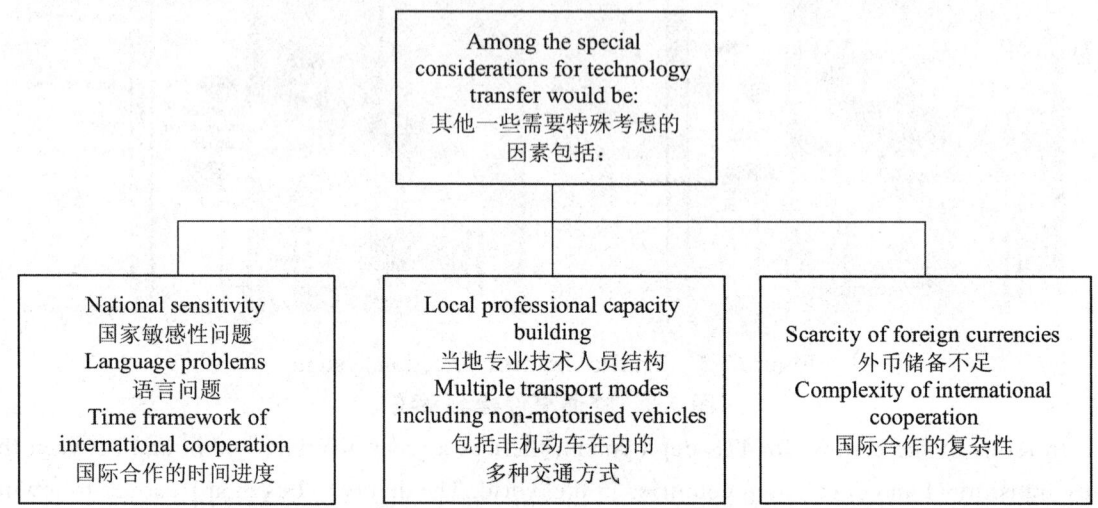

Figure 7.5　Special considerations for technology transfer

图 7.5　一些需要特殊考虑的因素

7.2　ITS Status and Plans in Transitional and Developing Countries　转型及发展中国家 ITS 的现状和发展规划

A review of the ITS status and plans of transitional and developing countries in the three regions of Asia, Central and Eastern Europe, and Latin America has been made with the help of the members of the World Road Association (PIARC) Committee on Management of Network Operations.

本节在世界道路协会（PIARC）委员会路网运行管理技术委员会成员的帮助下，对亚洲、中东欧和拉丁美洲三个地区的转型及发展中国家 ITS 应用现状和发展规划进行了回顾。

7.2.1　The Asian Region　亚洲地区

The following is a summary of ITS situations in six Asian transitional and developing countries (China, India, Indonesia, Malaysia, Philippines and Thailand).

下面是对亚洲 6 个转型及发展中国家（中国、印度、印度尼西亚、马来西亚、菲律宾和泰国）ITS 现状的一个小结。

(1) Asian Region Characteristics Relevant to ITS Applications　与 ITS 应用相关的亚洲地区特征

The six major characteristics of the Asian region that have impacts on ITS development are as follows:

亚洲地区影响 ITS 发展的 6 个主要特征如下：

(1) The primary objective is to reduce the problems of traffic safety and congestion in the large cities.
基本目标是减少大城市的交通安全和拥堵问题。

(2) There is an urgent need to cope with the large number of motorcycles and bicycles by considering such measures as installing appropriate vehicle detectors for these vehicles as well as automobiles.
迫切需要考虑采取诸如安装车辆检测器的措施来应对大量的摩托车和自行车。

(3) The common practice of involving private concessionaires through the build, operate, and transfer (BOT) approach has often led to the problem of lack of interoperability of electronic toll collection (ETC) systems.
通过建设-经营-转让（BOT）的方法获得私有特许经营权的一般实践方式通常会导致电子收费系统（ETC）缺乏互操作性。

(4) Multiple languages using non-Roman alphabets have led to the need for a two-byte format instead of the more conventional one-byte format for text handling in ITS equipment.
使用非罗马文字的多种语言导致ITS设备在文本处理中必须使用双字节文字处理方式来代替更为常规的单字节文字处理方式。

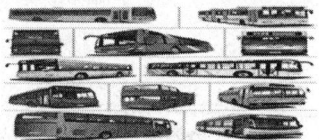
(5) Public transport facilities such as buses and trains play a very important transportation.
公共汽车和列车等公共交通设施在运输系统中扮演着非常重要的角色。

(6) ITS that have been introduced may not have been used effectively.
已经引进的ITS设备可能并没有被有效利用。

(2) Common ITS Applications and Organizational Characteristics　共同的 ITS 应用和组织特点

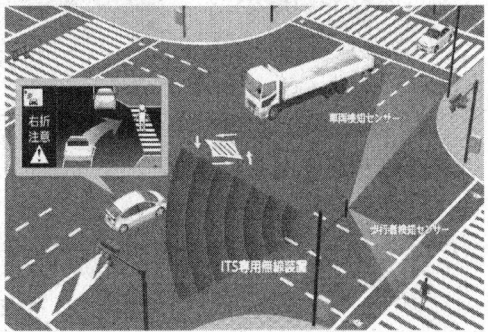

Figure 7.6　ITS Applications

图 7.6　ITS 应用

Area traffic control (ATC) has been or is being introduced in many large cities. Some of these cities have also deployed such "high-tech" devices as smart cards, GPS, and fiber optics.

区域交通控制（ATC）已经或正在被引入许多大城市。其中一些城市还部署了一些"高科技"设备，如智能卡、GPS 和光纤等。

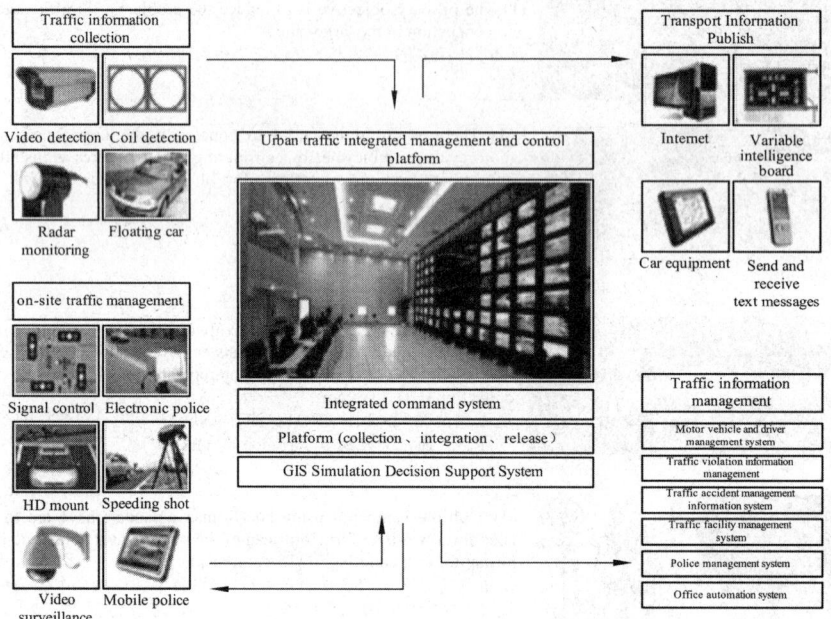

Figure 7.7　ATC system

图 7.7　区域交通控制系统

The second most common ITS application in the Asian region is the ETC system。

亚洲地区的第二个最普遍的 ITS 应用就是电子收费系统。

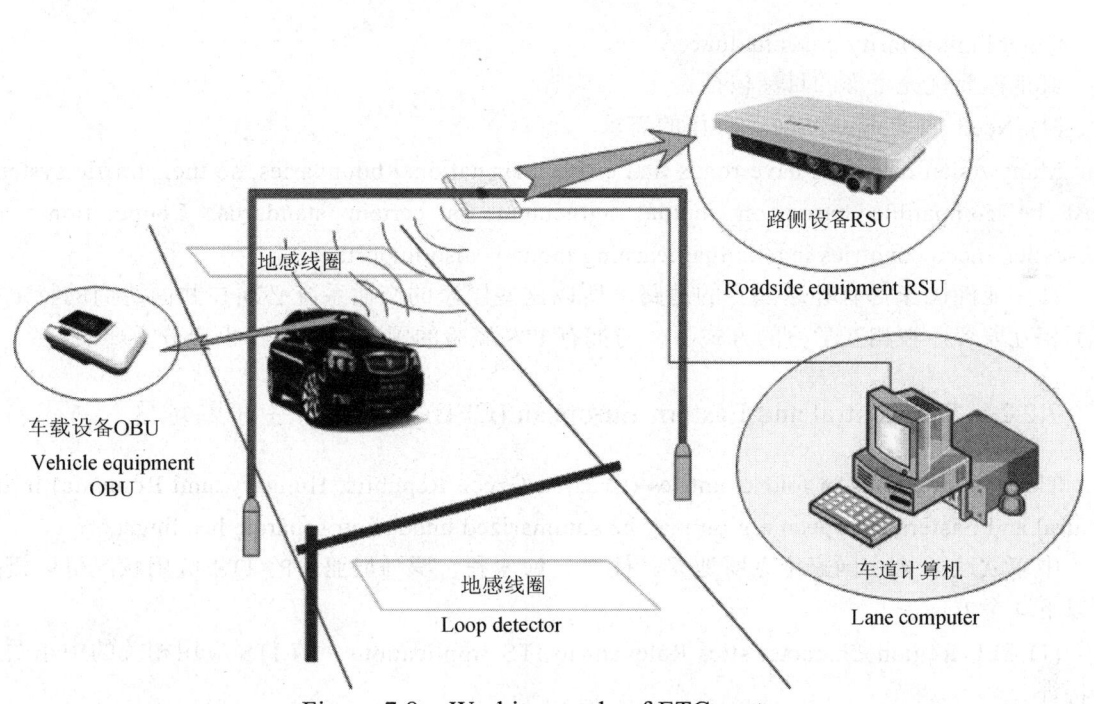

Figure 7.8　Working mode of ETC system
图 7.8　电子收费系统工作方式

(3) Urgent Requirements for the Future　未来的迫切需求

The most urgent requirements are to use ITS to maximize utilization of current roads and to incorporate ITS into future road infrastructure.

对 ITS 最迫切的需求是使用 ITS 来最大化地利用现有道路，并且把 ITS 和未来的道路基础设施结合到一起。

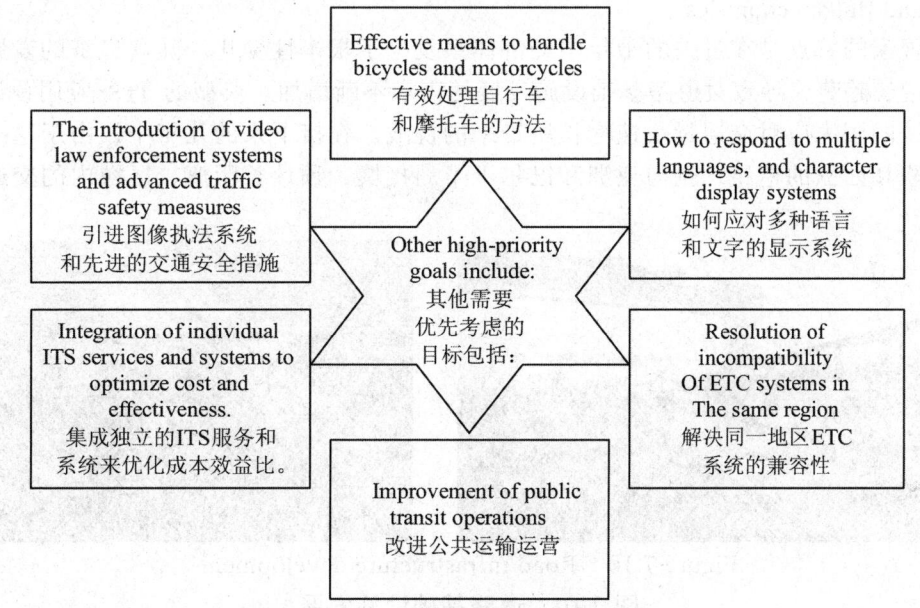

Figure 7.9　Other high-priority goals
图 7.9　其他需要优先考虑的目标

Other high-priority goals include:

其他需要优先考虑的目标包括：

(4). Need for Cooperation　合作的需求

Many Asian countries have roads that cross their national boundaries, so their traffic systems must be compatible based on mutual agreement on certain standards. Cooperation with ITS-experienced countries in a mutual learning mode is also important.

许多亚洲国家都有穿越国界的道路，所以这些国家的交通系统必须在共同协商的特定标准下相互兼容。在相互学习的方式下，与拥有 ITS 经验的国家进行合作也十分重要。

7.2.2　The Central and Eastern European (CEE) Region　中东欧地区

The ITS situations in four countries (Croatia, Czech Republic, Hungary, and Romania) in the Central and Eastern European region may be summarized under four separate headings.

中东欧地区 4 个国家（克罗地亚、捷克、匈牙利、罗马尼亚）的 ITS 应用状况可以概括为以下 4 个方面：

(1) CEE Region Characteristics Relevant to ITS Applications　与 ITS 应用相关的中东欧地区特征

The transitional are characterized by the fundamental change in their economic systems during the past decade. Economic progress has been accompanied by traffic growth, resulting in an increasing demand for road infrastructure development. Major ITS applications are expected to help the countries in this region meet the challenge of traffic growth. In the coming years, a significant increase of long-distance inter-regional traffic is expected due to the pivotal location of the region between the territories of the former Soviet Union and Western Europe, and ITS land connections with Asia and Balkan countries.

转型国家的特点是在过去的十年中经济体系发生了根本性变化。随着经济的发展，交通量呈现出增长趋势，导致对道路基础设施发展的需求不断增加。典型的 ITS 应用预计将会帮助这一地区的国家应对交通量快速增长所带来的挑战。在接下来的几年中，由于这一地区是连接前苏联和西欧的枢纽，且与亚洲和巴尔干半岛接壤，预计长距离、区域内的交通量将会显著增长。

Figure 7.10　Road infrastructure development

图 7.10　道路基础设施发展

(2) Status and Plans for ITS Activities　ITS 活动的现状和计划

ITS has been recognized in the Central and Eastern European region as a new option for the operation and management of road networks to reduce the harmful effects of traffic growth caused by motorization. Surveillance of traffic, road, and weather conditions has been recognized as a prerequisite for developing the databases for ITS-supported traffic control and management. A number of countries in the region have already begun to develop such databases. For example, Romania started a project to establish an automatic data acquisition system for the public road network by 2000.

在中东欧地区，ITS 被看作一种运营和管理道路网的新选择，它可以有效减少因机动化带来交通量增长所造成的不良影响。对交通流、道路和天气条件的监测被看作是建立支持 ITS 的交通控制与管理数据库的必备条件。这一地区的一些国家已经开始建立这样的数据库。例如，罗马尼亚在 2000 年以前已经开始进行建立公共道路网自动数据采集系统的项目。

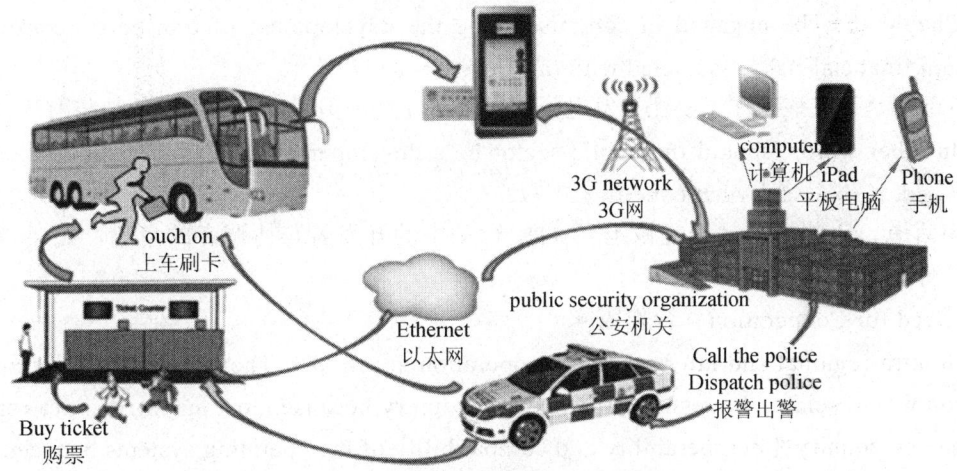

Figure 7.11　Automatic data acquisition system
图 7.11　自动数据采集系统

Academic institutions in the region have been playing active roles in ITS development in cooperation with the governmental organizations. In Croatia, the Ministry of Science and Technology has worked with the University of Zagreb since 1997 to strengthen their theoretical and experimental bases for ITS activities. Intensive efforts are being made in Croatia to develop digital map databases.

这一地区的科研单位在与政府部门合作开发 ITS 的过程中发挥了积极促进作用。在克罗地亚，科技部从 1997 年就开始与萨格勒布大学合作来加强 ITS 理论研究和实验基地建设。同时，克罗地亚正在致力于开发电子地图数据库。

(3) Transport Policy as an Urgent ITS Requirement　运输政策作为一项迫切的 ITS 需求

All Central and Eastern European countries have either joined the European Union or are under the EU accession process. Major national objectives are to sustain accelerated ITS deployment and alignment to EU standards and directives, and to benefit from technical, institutional and financial support of the European Union. Their objectives and policies for medium-term transport development tend to be derived from the *European Transport White Paper*. Given the past history and economic system in the region, there is a need to determine whether and when directive or incentive measures should be used to encourage ITS implementation.

中东欧地区的所有国家要么已经加入欧盟要么处在加入欧盟的进程中。国家层面的主要目标是保证加速的 ITS 部署并调整到欧盟的标准和方向上来，并且获得欧盟在技术、法规和财政上的支持。这些国家中期交通发展目标和政策来自于《欧洲运输白皮书》。介绍过这一地区的历史和经济体系后，需要确认是否或何时采用指导性的或激励性的措施来鼓励 ITS 的实施。

Alongside a policy on institutional capability should be some clarification of the role of public agencies in ITS activities.

关于机构职能的政策应该明确公共机构在 ITS 行动中所扮演的角色。

① Should public organizations actively participate in ITS research instead of merely supporting it?

公共组织是否应该积极参与到 ITS 的研究中，而不仅仅是支持 ITS？

② Should they be engaged in commissioning the development of transport electronics and take certain financial risks associated with this development?

公共部门是否应该专注于委托开发电子交通设备并且承担因开发而引起的某些财政风险？

③ In other words, should the public sector be a developer as well as the coordinator of ITS activities and, if so, under what conditions?

换句话说，公共机构是否应该担当 ITS 行动中的开发者与协调者的角色？如果是，那么在什么条件下才可以实现？

(4) Need for Cooperation　合作需求

Both intra-regional and inter-regional cooperation are in ITS. The full implementation of ITS application would seldom be restricted to a single country because most major road networks span more than one country. Interoperability and compatibility of the operating systems between various countries is very important. These countries encounter major problems in transport safety, security and efficiency.

ITS 涉及跨区域和区域内合作。对 ITS 应用的全面实施很少局限于单个国家，因为大多数主要路网都跨越了一个以上的国家。不同国家两两间的运营系统的互操作性和兼容性就显得十分重要。

Introduction of ITS is very slow for economic reasons. In an analysis conducted in Newly Independent States countries, ITS have been identified as a means to improving security and efficiency.

由于经济原因，ITS 的引入是非常缓慢的。对 NIS 国家进行的一项分析表明，ITS 已经被确定为一种提高道路安全和效率的方法。

7.2.3　The Latin American Region　拉丁美洲地区

Countries considered in this region include Argentina, Brazil, Chile and Mexico, which together represent a large portion in this region in terms of population, land area and current ITS applications. The summary of ITS situations in these countries may be grouped under three headings.

这一地区考虑的国家包括：阿根廷、巴西、智利和墨西哥，这些国家从人口、国土面积、ITS应用现状等方面也代表了大部分地区的特征。这些国家ITS现状可以分以下三个方面表述：

(1) Regional Characteristics Relevant to ITS Applications　与ITS应用相关的地区特征

The five major local characteristics of the Latin American region that have an impact on ITS development are as follows:

拉美地区影响ITS发展的5个主要地区特征如下：

① The economic cycles in these countries are very marked. There have been big variations in monetary exchange rates and long periods of investment shortage, following periods of large investment to catch up on service quality and productivity.

这些国家的经济周期是非常明显的。这些国家货币汇率浮动很大，并且长期性投资缺乏，接下来的一段时期需要大量投资来提高服务质量和生产力水平。

Figure 7.12　Currencies of different countries

图7.12　不同国家货币

② The highly uneven wealth distribution creates remarkable differences in the living style and transportation needs among the different social groups. The fatality rate of road accidents in this region is among the highest in the world.

财富分配的高度不均衡导致不同社会阶层的生活方式和交通需求有显著差异。这一地区交通事故的死亡率处于全世界的最高水平。

Figure 7.13　Highly uneven wealth distribution

图7.13　财富分配高度不均

③ Road authorities have let major road concessions, usually the portion with greater traffic volumes. Users are now more critical, demanding more and better roads.

道路权威机构已经在主要道路实施了特许经营，这些道路通常都承担着较大的交通量。现在的道路使用者更为挑剔，他们需要更多更好的道路。

Figure 7.14　Road with great traffic volumes
图 7.14　交通量较大的道路

④ During the strongest investment cycles, the private sector has had a greater participation than observed in other regions due to the shortage of public funds. This has in turn affected the completion of the core projects, resulting in severe recurrent congestion in urban areas for large cities.

在最强劲的投资期内，由于缺少公共资金支持，私人部门已经更多地参与了许多事情，而不是像其他地区的私人部门那样作为旁观者。这也就影响了核心工程的完工进度，导致目前一些大城市城区交通的严重拥堵。

Figure 7.15　Traffic congestion
图 7.15　交通拥堵

⑤ Public transport authorities are in the process of re-engineering their structures and functions to play a new role in the region. In some countries, such as Brazil, the previous road administrations have been replaced by public agencies and a central office focusing on intermodal transportation. Nongovernmental ITS organizations have emerged, which facilitate interactions of the public and private sectors to encourage and support ITS deployment.

这一地区的公共运输权威机构正在重新组织自身的结构和职能以扮演新的角色。在一些国家，如巴西，以前的道路管理已经由公共机构和专注于多式联运的中心办公室接手。同时，非政府的 ITS 组织开始出现，致力于推动公共和私人部门联合起来，激励并支持 ITS 部署。

(2) Common and Special ITS Applications　通用的和特殊的 ITS 应用

ETC systems are currently the most common ITS applications in Latin America. These systems have been deployed on some of the main expressways under concession in Mexico, Argentina, Brazil, and Chile. Most important cities in the region have already deployed traffic control strategies, which include:

电子收费系统是拉丁美洲地区最常见的 ITS 应用。这些系统被部署在墨西哥、阿根廷、巴西和智利实施特许经营的一些主要高速公路上。这一地区的大多数重要城市都已经部署了交通控制战略，包括：

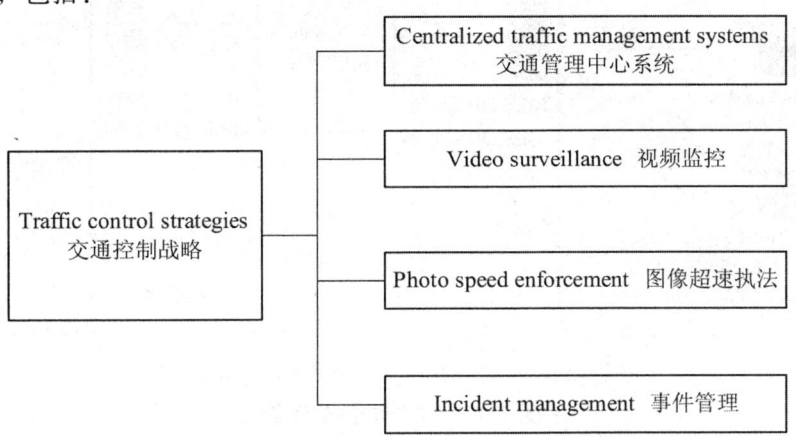

Figure 7.16　Traffic control strategies

图 7.16　交通控制战略

Commercial vehicle operations (CVO) services that are being planned or starting to be implemented include the control of overweight trucks, tracking of vehicles and hazardous cargo, and facilitation of international border crossings. An integrated data system has been partially developed by the Brazilian federal highway network to consolidate data of traffic flow, traffic safety, and GPS tracking of cargo. Advanced technologies are being used for both ticketing and operations.

一些国家正在将商用车辆运营（CVO）服务列入计划，同时正在开始实施包括超载卡车控制、车辆及危险货物跟踪等项目，而且建设了便于横穿国际边境的工程。一种数据集成系统正在通过巴西联邦公路网予以部分开发，以统一交通流、交通安全和货物的 GPS 跟踪等数据。其他一些先进的技术正在票务和运营中不断得到应用。

(3) Urgent Requirements for the Future　未来的迫切需求

① Despite efforts to achieve interoperability between ETC applications inside each city, there are still things to be done to improve users' convenience and to further increase ETC penetration. Regional ETC standardization is less pressing since most large cities are far apart in the region and each city functions independently from each other. On the other hand, it is important to integrate other ITS standards and policies at the regional level in order to give clear signals to the market.

除了努力实现每个城市内的 ETC 应用具备互操作性外，仍然有提高道路使用者便利性、进一步提高 ETC 渗透率的工作要做。区域 ETC 标准化工作并不紧迫，因为这一地区内的大多数大城市之间的距离很远，并且每个城市的功能都是相互独立的。另一方面，在地区层面集成其他 ITS 的标准和政策却非常重要，这样可以为市场指明方向。

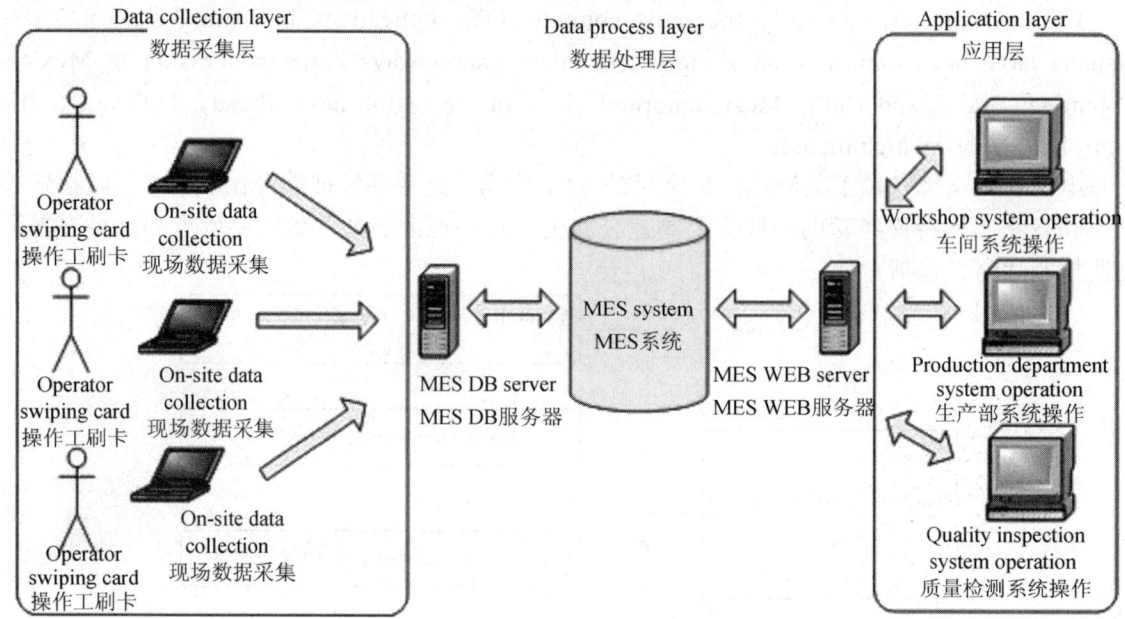

Figure 7.17　Integrated data system
图 7.17　数据集成系统

② Financial sources and private involvement need to be addressed. There are successful Public/Private Partnerships (PPP) and Build, Operate and Transfer (BOT) experiences. Local government must provide consistent and sustainable policies for financing and investing in transport projects. Overcrowded cities require deployment of ATC systems and ITS-aided enforcement of traffic laws and regulations. Multilane free flow ETC would also improve traffic flow and safety at the toll plazas as well as on the toll roads.

财政来源和私人部门的参与，需要予以强调。曾有过公私合作伙伴关系（PPP）以及建设-经营-转让（BOT）方式的成功经验。当地政府部门必须为交通运输项目提供稳定且持续的财政和投资政策支持。人口过多的城市需要部署区域交通控制系统，并且利用 ITS 辅助执行交通法律和规章。多车道自由流 ETC 也将改善收费站点及收费道路上的交通流和安全性。

③ Another priority in Latin America is further improvement of public transport services, given that large segments of the population rely on these for their mobility. Significant improvement in reliability, comfort, safety, scheduling, passenger information, and travel time reliability can be achieved only by using ITS-based techniques. Not to be ignored are the lower-grade highway networks reaching out to rural areas. The appropriate ITS applications to meet the needs of the large populations in rural areas in a cost-effective manner are yet to be defined.

另一个需要在拉美地区优先考虑的问题就是如何进一步改善公共交通服务。因为这一地区很大比例人口的出行是靠公共交通完成的。只有通过使用基于 ITS 的技术才能获得公共交通在可靠性、舒适性、安全性、调度、乘客信息服务以及出行时间上的改善。同样不能忽视的是这一地区延伸到乡村的低等级路网，这需要在成本效益方式下确定合适的 ITS 应用来满足大量居住在农村地区人口的出行问题。

7.3 Myths and Realities 误解和现实

As we can see, ITS-related issues vary considerably between transitional and developing countries. However, there are several common misunderstandings about ITS in these countries that need to be dispelled before further steps can be taken to develop ITS for their benefit. Four myths about ITS in transitional and developing countries can be identified, which may be refuted by realities, as described below.

正如我们所见，不同发展中国家的 ITS 相关问题差别很大。然而，在进一步应用 ITS 以期取得收益之前，需要澄清一些在转型及发展中国家普遍存在的对 ITS 的误解。转型及发展中国家中关于 ITS 的四个误解能被确认，且都可以用事实来驳倒，如下所述：

Myth1: "ITS technology is too sophisticated and costly and hence unsuitable for transitional and developing countries."

误解 1："ITS 技术对转型及发展中国家来说过于高深，而且成本太高，因此不适用于转型及发展中国家。"

Reality: There is already a wide range of ITS applications in these countries. Some of the ITS technologies deployed are low-cost with high payoffs, and some transitional and developing countries have applied "high-tech" devices as smart cards, GPS, and fiber optics in full-scale ITS deployments. For example:

现实情况：这些国家的 ITS 应用已经很广泛。其中的一些 ITS 技术部署是低成本、高产出的，并且一些转型及发展中国家已经在全面部署 ITS 中应用了诸如智能卡、GPS 和光纤等"高技术"设备。

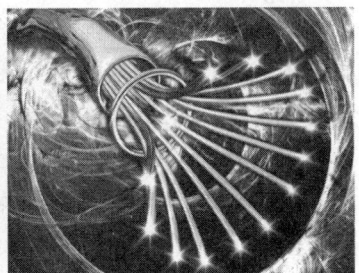

Figure 7.18 "High-tech" devices in full-scale ITS deployments
图 7.18 应用到 ITS 的"高技术"设备

ATC and ETC systems are the two most common ITS applications in these countries. For example, the World Bank ITS Toolkit reported that Kuala Lumpur installed ATC based on a SCATS signal system in 1980 and, by 2000, had 98 intersections under control by the system. Bangkok is progressing with a SCOOT system. Several transitional and developing countries around the world have already deployed ETC systems on a large scale. By and large, ITS benefits to these countries are similar to the benefits to the major industrialized countries, ranging from safety, congestion relief, to augmentation of road capacities.

区域交通控制和电子收费系统是这些国家中两个最通用的 ITS 应用。例如，世界银行 ITS 工具包报告称吉隆坡从 1980 年开始安装基于 SCATS 信号的区域交通控制系统，到 2000 年为止，共有 98 个交叉口受控于此系统。曼谷正在安装 SCOOT 系统。世界上一些转型及发展中国家已经开始大规模部署 ETC 系统。总的来说，这些国家应用 ITS 所取得的效益与主要工业发达国家相似，包括提高安全性、缓解拥堵，以及增加道路通行能力。

Myth 2: "Transitional and developing countries need no more than ITS products bought from major industrialized countries."

误解 2："转型及发展中国家只需要向主要工业发达国家购买 ITS 产品即可。"

Reality: ITS deployment is much more complex than buying and operating the necessary equipment. Effective ITS deployment requires the resolution of a host of institutional issues, including operational and financial viability for the entire system life cycle.

现实情况：ITS 部署绝不仅仅是购买和运用必需的设备那么简单，实际情况要复杂得多。有效实施 ITS 需要一系列政策上的解决方案，包括整个系统生命周期的运营和财政可行性。

Several transitional and developing countries have adapted ITS to their specific needs. For example, Brazil has developed its own "ITS Handbook" for this purpose. Hungary and other Central and Eastern European countries insist on ITS compatibility insurance with the European Union to prepare for their ITS integration with the Union. Clearly, these countries attach different priorities to various transportation objectives. "Deep adaptation to our important special requirements" is a key phrase in the current request of decision makers in many transitional and developing countries. Special attention needs to be given to ITS education and training, nurturing of ITS champions and well-informed advocates with access to high-level policy makers and to the limited financial resources in these countries.

一些转型及发展中国家已经根据它们的特殊需求来应用 ITS。例如，巴西根据这一目的编制了本国的"ITS 手册"。匈牙利和其他中东欧地区国家强调保证 ITS 与欧盟兼容，这样就为它们的 ITS 融入欧盟做好准备。很明显，这些国家的不同运输目标有不同的优先权。"深度适应我们重要而特殊的需求"是目前转型及发展中国家决策者需求中的一个关键短语。还要特别注重进行 ITS 教育和培训，培养 ITS 拥护者和能够接近这些国家的高层政策制定者和有限的财政资源博识的拥护者。

Myth 3: "ITS can be used to completely replace road infrastructure investments."

误解 3："ITS 可用以完全取代道路基础设施的投资。"

Reality: ITS can help to utilize the existing road infrastructure and reduce investment in the future infrastructure. To meet growing traffic demand and relieve congestion, ITS should be used along with additional road infrastructure investment. China and India are two of the good examples where such an approach has been seriously followed. Minimum infrastructure is absolutely necessary, and so is basic ITS (data collection and surveillance) to support more advanced ITS.

Figure 7.19　ITS education and training
图 7.19　ITS 教育和培训

现实情况：ITS 有助于充分利用现有道路基础设施，并且降低未来对基础设施的投资。但为满足不断增长的交通需求，缓解拥堵，ITS 应该与其他附加的道路基础设施投资一起使用。中国和印度是严格遵守这种方式的两个好例子。减少基础设施投资绝对有必要，基础的 ITS（数据采集和监控）也是如此，从而以支持更高级的 ITS。

Decision makers in transitional and developing countries are aware that ITS applications cannot "solve" their complex transportation problems in one swoop. They agree that ITS technologies can and should be part of the step-by-step solution. However, these evolutionary implementations must be done within a strategic framework, which would include a well-conceived ITS architecture, in order to avoid chaos and inefficiency in the future.

转型及发展中国家的决策者了解 ITS 应用不能一下子"解决"本国复杂的交通运输问题，但他们同意 ITS 技术能够也应该作为逐步实施的解决方案的一部分。然而，这些不断变化的实施方案必须在一个明确的战略框架下进行，其中包括缜密细致的 ITS 体系框架，以避免将来可能发生的混乱和低效。

Myth 4: "Our need for new ways of solving transportation problems is so urgent that we should embark upon large-scale ITS deployment without taking time for planning studies."

误解 4："我们对解决交通运输问题的新方法的需求十分迫切，所以我们应该开始大规模地部署 ITS，不用花时间进行规划研究。"

Reality: Truly sustainable ITS deployment and orderly reaping of ITS benefits require careful planning. Full-scale ITS deployment should be preceded by the establishment of a framework plan, and other preparatory steps.

现实情况：真正可持续发展的 ITS 部署和有序按部就班地获取 ITS 效益需要缜密的规划。大规模部署 ITS 之前，应该先制定框架规划、ITS 体系框架以及其他的准备性步骤。

Effectively achieving the anticipated ITS benefits and maintaining these benefits on the long term are exciting but very demanding tasks for the transportation professionals in transitional and developing countries. Take ITS training for example. Even though the elite in these countries are often very well trained, the average technicians may lead ITS projects to practical difficulties. Unless the technicians themselves are also given adequate training and appropriate incentives are provided for them to remain on the job for a sufficient period of time, the ITS equipment will not be properly maintained and operated to produce the anticipated benefits.

高效获取预期的 ITS 效益，并长期保持这种效益对转型及发展中国家的交通运输专家来说是一个令人兴奋但又费神的任务。以 ITS 培训为例，尽管这些国家中的一些高层人才通常已经接受了很好的培训，但普通技术人员可能会导致 ITS 项目的实际困难。除非这些普通技术人员自身得到了足够的培训和适当的激励以保证他们能在岗位上工作足够长的时间，ITS 设备才能保证正确维护和运转来产生预期效益。

There are other issues and serious risks in ITS deployment, both technical and institutional. Fortunately, the worldwide ITS experience is now sufficiently rich and is beginning to be shared so that the decision makers in all countries can take advantage of these lessons learned and formulate their approach to ITS deployment accordingly.

在 ITS 部署中还会遇到其他问题和严重风险，包括技术上的和政策上的。有幸的是，目前在世界范围内已经有足够丰富的 ITS 经验，并且世界各国已经开始分享这些宝贵经验，这样一来，所有国家的决策者都可以充分利用这些经验，并相应地制定他们的 ITS 部署方法。

7.4 Advice to Transitional and Developing Countries 对转型及发展中国家的建议

The advice given in this section has been extracted from a number of workshops and e-mail discussions under the aegis of the World Road Association (PIARC), and participants in these discussions included decision makers and experts from both industrialized countries on the one hand, and the transitional and developing countries on the other. The advice applies in general but may need to be adapted to specific countries or local situations. The advice is divided into three sets of issues – planning and institutional, economic and financial, and technological.

本节提出的建议取自许多由世界道路协会（PIARC）资助的研讨会和电子邮件讨论，以及这些讨论的参与者，其中既包括工业发达国家也包括转型及发展中国家的决策者和专家。此建议可以通用，但是可能需要针对特殊国家和当地形势进行相应调整。这些建议分为三个方面，即规划和制度问题、经济和财政问题以及技术问题。

7.4.1 Planning and Institutional Issues Careful Planning 规划和制度问题

(1) Careful Planning 缜密的规划

Understanding possible ITS activities and their natural sequencing is a key to good planning for ITS deployment. It is important to understand and analyze the transport problems clearly before trying to devise and prioritize ITS solutions. Some early, very-low-cost actions, both technical and nontechnical, can be very beneficial for the long term. For example, following cooperative institutional agreement and compatibility specifications, a transitional or developing country would want to invest early in the collection of reliable and timely traffic information to provide the base for effective ATMS and ATIS applications. Similarly, creating a national ITS program and organization would be a significant step forward for general consensus building and for coordinating targeted actions at the national and international levels. Many developing countries, such as Argentina, have recently created their national ITS organizations.

理解可能发生的 ITS 行动及其自然顺序是对 ITS 部署进行良好规划的关键所在。在尝试制定 ITS 解决方案并给它们排定优先级之前，透彻理解和分析运输问题十分重要。不论在技术还是非技术领域，一些早期的低投入行为从长远角度来看是非常有益的。例如，按照合作制度的协议和兼容性条款，转型或发展中国家将愿意早期投入到可靠和实时的交通信息采集方面，为高效使用 ATMS 和 ATIS 提供基础支撑。与之类似，建立一个国家 ITS 规划和组织将为达成国家和国际层面上的共识和协调目标行为而迈出重要的一步。许多发展中国家，如阿根廷，近期创建了自己的国家 ITS 组织。

Careful planning will take into account the local culture and transport profile so that ITS can be adapted and customized to meet the particular needs of each country. Cities should have some basic traffic management measures in place before ever embarking on ITS, e.g. lane marking, proper junction layouts, etc. It would help to look at neighboring countries, not only to learn from their ITS experience, if any, but also to cooperate with them in order to avoid isolated solutions. Taking an ITS study tour to major industrialized countries can help to develop future ITS visions for transitional and developing countries. Some tours have been able to pick up applicable experience from major industrialized countries, for example in the area of applying ITS for accident reduction on toll roads.

缜密的规划要考虑到当地文化和运输概况，从而来调整和定制 ITS 以应对每个国家的特定需求。实施 ITS 之前，城市应该适当拥有一些基本的交通管理措施，例如车道标线、合适的交叉口设计方案等。借鉴邻国的做法将大有裨益，不仅为学习他们的 ITS 经验，如果有的话，而且要与之合作来避免孤立的解决方案。对转型及发展中国家来说，去主要工业发达国家进行一次 ITS 技术的学习考察有助于拓展对未来 ITS 的设想。一些考察能够从主要工业发达国家中挑选出可用的经验，例如应用 ITS 减少收费公路上的交通事故。

Figure 7.20　Basic traffic management measures
图 7.20　基本的交通管理措施

ITS consist a wide range of services and products, some of which are now very well established (e.g. traffic light coordination). Even for those applications, adapting to local conditions is always necessary (e.g. to make coordinated traffic signals work in the mixed traffic of cars and non-motorized vehicles). Transport agencies in the transitional or developing country have an important responsibility to lead this adaptation, including analysis of functional specifications, interactions with consultants and instructions to suppliers.

ITS 包括大范围的服务和产品，其中有一部分现在已建设得非常完备（如，交通信号协调）。即使是这些十分成熟的应用，也有必要根据当地的状况做出调整（如，在机动车和非机动车混行道路上配置协调的交通信号)。转型或发展中国家的交通运输机构对于引导这种调整负有重要责任,包括分析功能规范、与供应商进行咨询和指导性的互动。

On a more strategic level, some transitional and developing countries have learned about the importance of the role of technological infrastructure in ITS deployment. If there is no support in national development policies, all infrastructure systems run the risk of becoming short-term economic undertakings. The development of ITS as well as road infrastructure, would then fall entirely on self-supporting solutions, and become isolated from other national information and communications infrastructure. It is important to provide near-term incentives to the private sector to be involved in ITS. However, such involvement should support longer-term policy objectives. A superior policy would be to anchor ITS development, including ITS national architecture, on the concept of National Technological Infrastructure.

从更具战略性的层次来讲,一些转型及发展中国家已经认识到技术基础设施在 ITS 部署中所扮演角色的重要性。如果没有国家发展政策支持,所有的基础设施系统将会承担短期经济担保的风险,然后,ITS 和道路基础设施的发展将会全部变成自给自足的方案,并从其他的国家信息和通信基础设施中独立出来。为私营部门提供近期激励以使其介入 ITS 十分重要,然而这种介入应该支持长期的政策目标。更高级的政策将在国家技术基础设施概念上稳固 ITS 发展,包括国家体系框架。

(2) Involvement of Stakeholders 利益相关者的参与

One of the important lessons learned from ITS deployment is that resolving institutional issues is a key to success, and addressing them takes time and commitment – thus the advice: "Do not start too late. Involve all key stakeholders early on." Transitional and developing countries can take advantage of this experience by understanding user needs as the starting point for ITS development and attacking institutional issues before it is too late. One of the very first steps in the development of a national ITS architecture is to involve all major stakeholders to understand, suggest, define, and agree on a set of prioritized ITS user services. Therefore the process of ITS architecture development can serve the purpose of assuring early involvement of stakeholders. In recent years, transitional and developing countries like Chile, the Czech Republic, and Mexico have developed national ITS architecture involving their respective stakeholders – a step sometimes supported by US Trade Development Agency with financial assistance.

从 ITS 部署中学到的重要一点就是解决制度上的问题是成功的关键所在,而且解决这些问题需要时间和决心,因此,建议是:"不要过晚着手,及早让所有重要的利益相关者参与。"为避免过晚,转型及发展中国家可以通过理解用户需求作为 ITS 发展的起点,并通过挑战制度上的问题来利用这一经验。较早地发展国家 ITS 体系框架的步骤之一是吸纳所有的主要利益相关者,来使他们理解、提出建议、定义以及同意一套优先的 ITS 用户服务。因此 ITS 体系框架发展过程能够对确保利益相关者的早期介入起作用。近几年,转型及发展中国家,像智利、捷克、斯洛伐克和墨西哥,已经发展和建立了国家 ITS 体系框架,其中包括各自的利益相关者,这一阶段有时会得到美国贸易发展机构以财政援助方式的支持。

Early involvement of ITS stakeholders can help anticipate (and resolve) both technical and institutional problems, which may be difficult to solve at a later stage. For example, large urban motorways may be very difficult to convert to tolling years after construction, for political and physical reasons: politically, because drivers used to travelling on expressways at no charge are likely to object to paying any tolls; and physically, because freeways were not designed to provide space for retrofitting toll plazas. Even in major industrialized countries, institutional issues often delay the implementation of ITS. The foresight and the pace at which multiple relevant agencies are able to develop effective cooperation (for information exchange and coordinated operations) is often the critical factor for the success of many ITS applications. On the other hand, involving stakeholders may cause tremendous delays. Procedures based upon historical and cultural conditions, with the blessing of ITS champion(s), must be creatively designed and fitted to a particular country or situation.

尽早吸纳 ITS 利益相关者能够帮助预测（和解决）技术和制度上的问题，这些问题或许在今后阶段很难予以处理。例如，大型城市快速路在建成后若干年或许很难转变成收费公路，这源于政治和物理上的原因：政治上，由于经常行驶于不收费快速路上的驾驶员很可能反对缴纳任何通行费；物理上，由于快速路在设计上并未提供空间来改进收费站。甚至在主要工业发达国家，制度问题经常拖延 ITS 的实施。一方面，能够使多种相关机构形成高效合作（为达成信息交换和协调运营的目的）的远见和步调通常是诸多 ITS 应用得以成功的关键因素；但另一方面，吸纳利益相关者可能会导致极大延误。所以伴随 ITS 拥护者的祝福，基于历史和文化条件的实施流程，ITS 必须被予以创造性地设计，并适用于特殊的国家或形势。

Another way to involve and convince stakeholders is to organize pilot projects on key ITS applications. A good example of this approach is that taken by the CONNECT project, which has been promoted by ERTICO and the Austrian authorities, with the support of the European Commission. The project involves major stakeholders in ITS cross-border applications through pilot and demonstration projects in Poland, Czech Republic, Slovakia, Slovenia and Hungary.

另一种吸纳、说服利益相关者的方法是在关键 ITS 应用上组织试点工程。一个很好的实例是 CONNECT 工程，它由欧洲智能运输系统协会（ERTICO）和奥地利当局共同推进，同时也得到欧洲委员会的支持。通过波兰、捷克、斯洛伐克、斯洛文尼亚以及匈牙利的试点和示范，这项工程吸纳了 ITS 在跨边界应用上的主要利益相关者。

(3) Staged and Proactive Planning 分阶段和预见性规划

ITS planning should include both prudent and sequential steps for deployment and forward-looking stages to reach long-term goals in a smooth and flexible manner. Appropriate progression of ITS deployment is a prudent strategy for building confidence on the part of the users as well as the implementers. All countries need to "walk before you run", especially those with limited financial resources.

ITS 规划应该既包括严谨、有序的部署步骤，又包括以平和、灵活的方式达到长期目标的高瞻远瞩的发展进程。恰当的 ITS 部署进程是一种为用户和实施者建立自信心的严谨策略。所有国家，尤其那些财政资源有限的国家，都需要"在跑前先学会走"。

While many major industrialized countries have essentially completed road infrastructures, some of the transitional and developing countries still have their major road building programs ahead of them. For these countries, transport schemes should allow for ITS technology to be inserted at a later date when it becomes affordable. For example, China's transport plan includes a highway construction program to build "five north-south and seven east-west" trunk roads, totaling 35,000 km, to expressway standard. In such countries, the policy makers must think seriously about installing ITS infrastructure (traffic detectors, etc.) and communication infrastructure (fiber optics, etc.) along with the new road infrastructure. The sequencing and timing of installing various infrastructure elements would require careful thought. For example, the infrastructure for the optical fiber network could begin with simply laying the conduits at the time of road construction. The timing for pulling the fibers through the conduits and installing increasingly sophisticated terminals will depend on the ITS demand as well as other demands for communications. The point is that simultaneous planning and installation of the three infrastructures would save future costs by avoiding expensive retrofits. This approach has been recognized and followed by the newly independent states (NIS countries – former states in the Soviet Union) as well.

虽然许多主要工业发达国家已经从本质上完成了道路基础设施建设，但是部分转型及发展中国家仍然有主要道路建设项目摆在他们面前。对于这些国家，应该在稍后的时段，在能够承担得起的时候，允许ITS技术进入交通运输发展计划。例如，中国运输规划包括建设达到高速公路等级的"五纵七横"公路干道建设项目，合计35 000 km。在这些国家，政策制定者必须要严肃考虑到随同新的道路基础设施一起安装ITS基础设施（如交通检测器等）和通信基础设施（如光纤等），同时需要对多种基础设施元件的安装顺序和时间给予充分考虑。例如，建设光纤网络基础设施可以首先在道路建设时期简单铺设管道，随后，在管道中布设光纤以及安装日益复杂的终端机的时间将取决于ITS需求以及其他通信需求。关键点在于同步规划安装三套基础设施将以避免昂贵的设施更新费的方法为未来节省资金。独联体国家（NIS国家——苏联的国家）也已经认识到这一点，并遵循了此种方法。

Figure 7.21　Traffic detector
图7.21　交通检测器

Another forward-looking step is to develop an expanding education and training program for transportation professionals and decision makers relevant to ITS. The near-term target would include awareness-level materials and courses for decision makers and the general public, as well as operational and maintenance staff for ITS projects. In the long run, ITS curricula and college-level courses need to be developed to train the next generation of transport and ITS professionals. Road users (including the pedestrians), also need to understand ITS and be educated on how to use ITS-based applications to their advantage so that they are willing to accept change. Concerns about the educational level of ITS users in transitional and developing countries affecting their ability to use ITS is unfounded – the rapid penetration of cellular phones in transitional and developing countries, even among their low-income families, shows otherwise. In many countries, enforcement is the leverage point to apply ITS technology. Many ITS applications would fail if regulations cannot be enforced on the drivers, pedestrians, toll payers, and/or transport network operators. In many cases enforcement is a political and institutional problem rather than a technological one for transitional and developing countries.

另一种有远见的步骤是为交通运输专业人员和 ITS 相关决策者开发一个拓展教育和培训计划。短期目标将包括为决策者、公众和运营维护 ITS 工程的员工提供常识水平的资料和课程。从长远角度讲，需要为下一代交通运输和 ITS 专业人员开设 ITS 课程以及专业水平的培训课程。道路使用者（包括行人）也需要了解 ITS，并接受如何使用 ITS 为自身利益服务的教育，以使其愿意认同这种转变。有人担心转型及发展中国家道路使用者的教育水平有碍他们使用 ITS，但是这些国家的手机普及程度很高，低收入人群也拥有手机，因此这一担心根本不存在基础。在许多国家，强制执行是应用 ITS 技术的杠杆作用点。如果不能针对驾驶员、行人、通行税缴纳者和/或道路路网运营管理运营商来执行相关规章制度，则会导致许多 ITS 应用以失败告终。对转型及发展中国家来说，诸多实例表明：强制执行与其说是一种技术问题，不如说是政策和制度问题。

7.4.2　Economic and Financing Issues in ITS Investment　ITS 投资中的经济和财政问题

With few exceptions, transitional and developing countries suffer from a lack of finance in general, and a lack of ITS investment in particular. The funding agencies often insist that ITS in general, and ETC in particular, be built into transport infrastructure projects, based on the rationale that ITS can contribute to transport efficiency in terms of financial and monetary savings.

鲜有例外，转型及发展中国家通常会遭受财政匮乏问题，特别是 ITS 投资短缺问题。基于 ITS 能够在货币和金融储蓄方面对运输效率起作用的基本理论，投资机构通常坚持将 ITS，尤其是 ETC，纳入到运输基础设施建设项目中。

(1) ITS Benefits　ITS 效益

Understandably, traditional methods of road building, as opposed to ITS solutions, are often preferred and regarded as more immediately beneficial. However, with more experience and better understanding of ITS, many transitional and developing countries are convinced not only by the operational benefits of ITS, such as improved traffic management resulting in reduction of heavy traffic congestion in their cities, but also by additional benefits such as increased safety and security. The latter has been experienced not only internally in terms of reduction of vehicle theft and hijacking (e.g. through GPS vehicle tracking, as the example in figure 7.19), but also between countries at their border crossings in terms of increase of efficiency and reduction of time delays.

可以理解，人们更喜欢传统道路建设方式，并认为其能够带来更直接的收益，反对 ITS 解决方案。然而随着经验的积累以及对 ITS 理解的加深，许多转型及发展中国家不仅被诸如由于改善交通管理而减少城市交通拥堵的 ITS 运营效益所说服，而且被诸如提高交通安全和公共安全的附加效益所说服。后者已经为人们所体验，不仅减少了国内车辆失窃和劫车案件（例如，通过 GPS 跟踪车辆，如图 7.19 中的例子），而且在跨越国与国之间的边界时提高了效率、减少了时间延误。

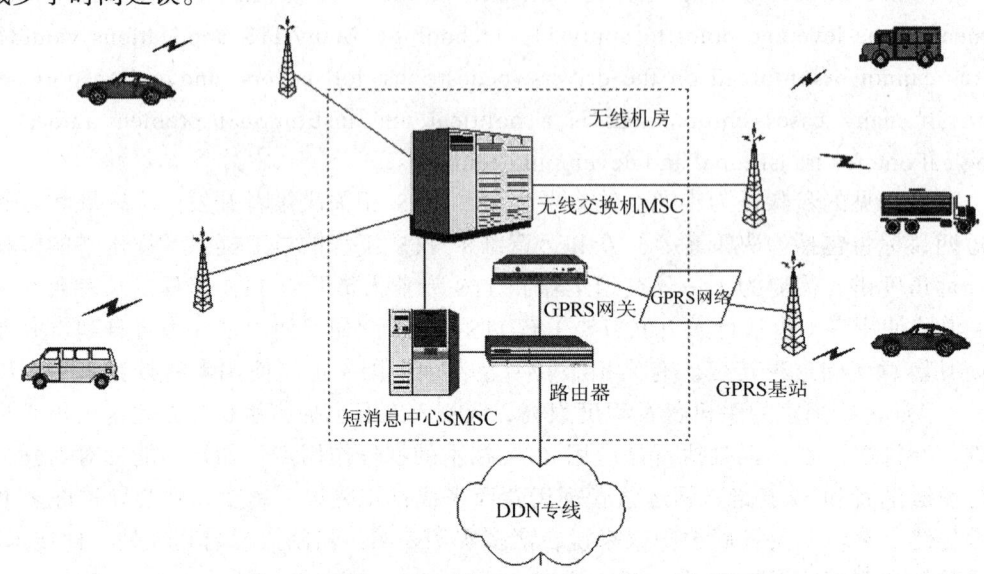

Figure 7.22　Tracking vehicles through GPS
图 7.22　通过 GPS 跟踪车辆

Cost reduction through ITS has been experienced in transitional and developing countries in both economic and social terms. For example, a reduction in transport costs, which enables countries in transition to be more economically competitive, is a benefit especially important to those countries with high concentrations of engineering equipment production, for which transport costs are a significant factor. A surprising benefit of ITS in social terms is poverty reduction and community development, resulting from improved access to transport by the poorest people who need to travel to work to earn a living. Since many examples of ITS projects in transitional and developing countries are still in their early stages the benefits are not yet known nor have been assessed. A good understanding and application of evaluation procedures will provide significant assistance to the funding process, making valid conclusions from pilot projects, and developing sustainable public/private partnerships for ITS deployment.

由 ITS 所带来的费用减少已经在转型及发展中国家的经济和社会方面均有所体现。例如，运输费用减少是一份收益，使得转型国家更具经济竞争力，这对那些工程设备生产高度密集型的国家尤为重要，运输费用对他们而言是一个重要因素。ITS 在社会方面的惊人效益是贫困减少和社区发展，究其原因是由于改善了最贫困人们的交通运输，他们需要出行去工作谋生。由于转型及发展中国家的许多 ITS 项目仍处于初级阶段，所以效益既不为人知也尚未经过评估。充分理解并应用 ITS 评估流程将为投资进程、从试点工程中得出正确结论以及发展公-私的合作伙伴关系提供重要辅助来保障 ITS 的顺利实施。

(2) ITS　成本

Operations and maintenance (O&M) costs of ITS equipment each year can average some 10 to

15% of the capital investment. Thus underscoring the importance of proper maintenance of ITS equipment, Depreciation must also be considered in life cycle costing.

ITS设备的年运营维护（O&M）成本大约平均占基本投资额的10%~15%。因此，必须强调正确维护ITS设施的重要性，同时，在全寿命周期成本中也必须要考虑折旧。

Economic and financial analyses for ITS projects in transitional and developing countries should fully take into account certain major differences between them and the major industrialized countries. For example:

转型及发展中国家ITS项目的经济和财政分析中应该充分考虑这些国家与主要工业发达国家之间的某些主要差异。例如：

① The ratio of labor to capital costs could be much lower (sometimes more than ten times lower) than that in major industrialized countries.

这些国家的劳动量和资本成本间的比率可能会低于（有时超过十倍低于）主要工业发达国家。

② The imported ITS capital equipment (both hardware and software) includes royalty charges and/or amortized R&D costs incurred by the suppliers in the industrialized countries.

进口ITS的主要设施费（涉及硬件和软件）包括版权费和工业发达国家厂商提出的分期偿还的研发成本费。

③ The competition between various sectors for equipment to be paid for in scarce foreign exchange may be very severe in some of these countries.

在部分这些国家中，由于缺少外汇，不同部门之间对于设备费的支付竞争可能会比较激烈。

Thus, certain "intermediate" ITS technologies would be more appropriate for these countries so that the equipment could use more locally available spare parts and maintenance services and allow progressive transfer of imported parts to local manufacturing (see the next section on appropriate technologies and other technological issues).

因此，这些国家较适合某些"中间"ITS技术，这使得设备能够使用更多的当地可用空闲资源和维护服务，并且可允许将进口部件进一步转换为当地生产（见下一节关于适应技术和其他技术问题）。

7.4.3　Technological Issues　技术问题

(1) Intermediate Technologies　中间技术

Since ITS embodies the application of information technology to transport problems, the possession of some basic knowledge of ITS technology, or at least the understanding of a common ITS vocabulary, would be needed to discuss technological issues effectively.

由于ITS体现了信息技术在解决运输问题方面的应用，所以掌握一些ITS技术的基础知识或者至少理解常见的ITS词汇，将为高效讨论技术问题所需。

Once the functions of ITS are understood, it is not difficult to identify how some of the basic functions could be delivered with long-proven technologies. For example, radios are a cheap and effective form of technology for disseminating real-time traffic information and can be applied immediately for this function without resorting to the advanced ITS technologies such as traffic maps on the Internet, which can be developed at a later stage.

一旦 ITS 的功能为人所理解，则不难确定一些基本功能如何能够随着久经考验的技术而传达。例如，无线电广播是一种发布实时交通信息的既便宜又高效的技术形态，并且此功能可被立刻应用而不必求助于先进的 ITS 技术，例如下一阶段开发的在互联网上的交通地图。

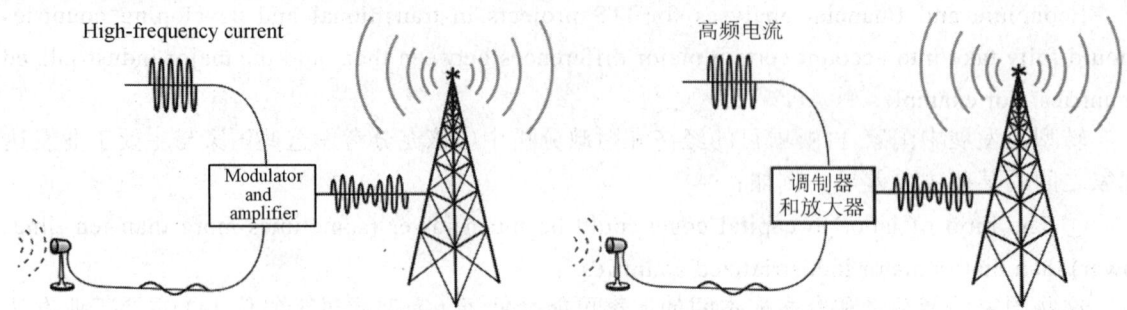

Figure 7.22 Radios technology
图 7.22 无线电广播技术

Intermediate ITS technologies for advanced public transport systems (APTS) are therefore high on the agenda. An example of intermediate ITS technologies for APTS are to provide information at the bus stops on the lapse time since the last bus has left (using simple timers reset by local beacons). This is in contrast with the high-tech approach to providing information on the arrival time of the next bus (which would require automatic vehicle location and communication networks). In this case, the value of the information provided by the intermediate technology to the bus passengers is still high but at a much lower cost and using much less sophisticated technologies.

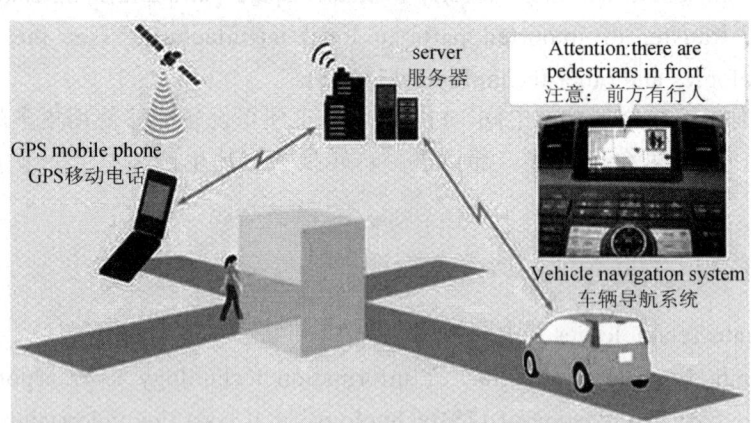

Figure 7.23 Intermediate ITS technologies
图 7.23 ITS 中间技术

ITS 中间技术应用于 APTS 的一个实例是，在公交车站提供自最后一辆公交车驶离站台算起所逝去时间的信息（使用由当地信标重新设置的简单计时器）。这与提供下一辆公交车到站时间信息的高科技方法（需要自动的车辆位置和通信网络）形成对比。在这个实例中，通过中间技术为公交车乘客提供的信息价值仍旧很高，但是所用成本和所用技术复杂程度却都非常低。

(2) Advanced Technologies　先进技术

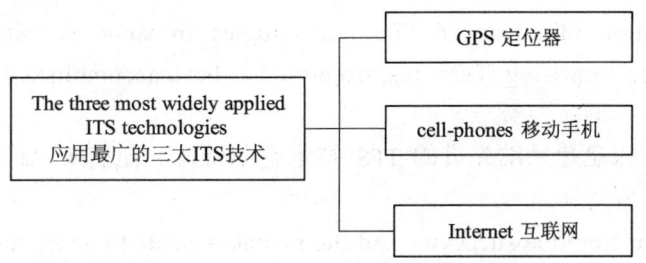

Figure 7.24　Three most widely applied ITS technologies
图 7.24　应用最广的三大 ITS 技术

Brazil has introduced technologies relating to incident management, safety and vehicle inspection. Mexico has not only cooperated with USA in applying ITS to facilitate border crossings but also applied automatic road illumination in ITS own cities, and installed in-vehicle ITS, which monitor speeds, vehicle flow, congestion and directions. The multilane free flow (MLFF) tollgates, beginning their operation in Santiago, in 2004, are among the most advanced ETC systems in the world. In Slovakia an integrated Motorway Information and Control System integrates many technologies to support road monitoring and maintenance.

巴西已经引入涉及到事件管理、交通安全和车辆监管的技术。墨西哥不仅与美国合作应用 ITS 来促进跨国界交流，而且在城市中应用道路自动照明，且安装车载元件来监控速度、流量、拥堵以及方向。多车道自由流（MLFF）收费站是世界上最先进的 ETC 系统之一，2004 年始运营于圣地亚哥。在斯洛伐克，一种综合高速公路信息控制系统集成了许多技术来支撑道路监测和维护。

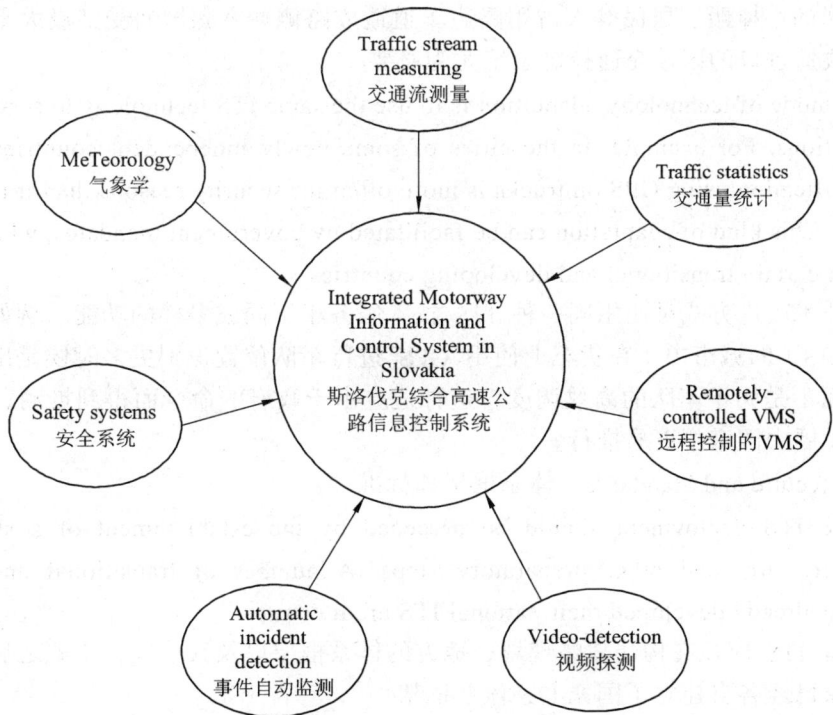

Figure 7.25　Integrated Motorway Information and Control System in Slovakia
图 7.25　斯洛伐克综合高速公路信息控制系统

The rapid adoption of advanced ITS technologies in some transitional and developing countries should not be surprising. Their leapfrogging has been accomplished with two late-comer's advantages:

转型及发展中国家迅速采纳先进的 ITS 技术毫不奇怪。他们实现跳跃式的发展，且具有两大后发优势：

① They can learn from the successes and the mistakes made by more developed countries and can benefit from the latest systems on offer, thereby saving on R&D costs;

他们能够从相对较发达国家的成功和失误中学习，并且能够受益于最新上市的系统，从而节约研发成本；

② By starting from scratch, they are less constrained by legacy systems.

由于白手起家，他们很少受已有系统限制。

(3) Adapted Technologies　　适宜的技术

When adopting ITS technologies and systems from other countries, transportation professionals in the transitional and developing countries should avoid the temptation of carbon copying the industrialized countries application approach because of different physical and human factors. For example, the frequently applied ATC systems can be greatly affected by roadside friction arising from occupation of the curb lanes by itinerant hawkers, dwellers, etc. Adaptation, sometimes re-engineering, of the imported ATC is therefore necessary.

当采纳其他国家的 ITS 技术和系统时，由于物质因素和人为因素差异，所以转型及发展中国家的专业人员应该免受复制工业发达国家应用方法的诱惑。例如，常见的区域交通控制系统会因巡回的小摊贩、居民等人占用路边车道造成路侧冲突骤增而受到极大影响。因此，调整或重新改造进口的区域交通控制系统尤为必要。

Another mode of technology adaptation is to use the same ITS technology to serve different or multiple functions. For example, in the cities of some newly independent countries (NIS), fleet location identification using GPS on trucks is more often for security reasons than it is for efficient fleet dispatch. This kind of adaptation can be facilitated by government mandates, which may come more easily in certain transitional and developing countries.

另一种技术改进方式是使用同一种 ITS 技术服务于不同或多样的功能。例如，在一些独联体国家（NIS）的城市中，在货车上使用 GPS 进行车队位置识别更多时候是出于公共安全因素考虑，而不是用于车队的高效调度，这种适应由于政府的命令而得到推动，此法可能在某些转型及发展中国家中更易推行。

(4) Architecture and Standards　　体系框架和标准

Full-scale ITS deployment should be preceded by the establishment of a strategic plan, regional architecture, and other preparatory steps. A number of transitional and developing countries have already developed their national ITS architectures.

全面部署 ITS 应该在构建战略规划、地方的体系框架以及其他预备步骤之后。许多转型及发展中国家已经各自建立了国家 ITS 体系框架。

A much harder question for transitional and developing countries, even after they have developed their own ITS architecture, is what to do when there are no widely accepted international standards for specific ITS technologies at the critical interfaces identified within their ITS architecture.

甚至在他们建成了自己的 ITS 体系框架之后,对转型及发展中国家来说更为困难的问题是如何处理那些已经在他们 ITS 体系框架确立的,但未被广泛接受的国际标准的关键接口上的特殊 ITS 技术。

7.4.4　Choice of Standards for EFC　EFC 标准的选择

ETC is among the first ITS applications in many transitional and developing countries in the world. The electronic transponder system using dedicated short range communications (DSRC) is the dominant ITS technology for ETC (and for electronic fee collection or EFC in general) in the past 15 years.

在世界上有很多转型及发展中国家,电子收费是最早的 ITS 应用之一。在过去 15 年中,使用专用短程通信(DSRC)技术的电子转发器系统是 ETC(电子收费通常也成为 EFC)的主要 ITS 技术。

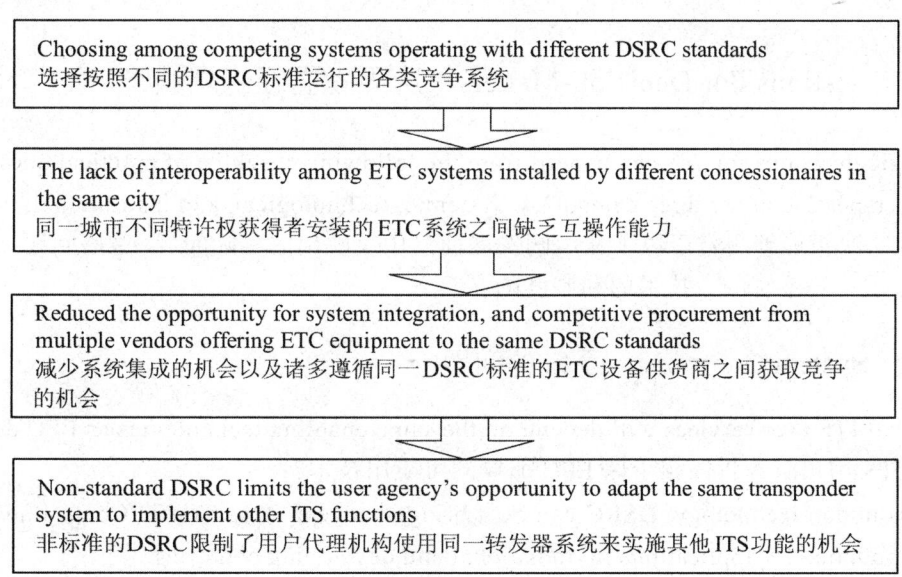

Figure 7.26　Problems faced in the EFC standards selection process
图 7.26　EFC 标准选择过程面临的问题

The choice of EFC standards may depend on the need for additional user services and vice versa. Since EFC is often a forerunner of ITS user services, a poor choice of standards might hamper the implementation of other ITS user services. Choosing EFC standards on a narrow basis without considering the broader ITS perspective could be a missed opportunity, which could turn out to be costly to correct in the long run.

选择 EFC 标准可能要根据附加用户的服务需求。由于 EFC 通常是 ITS 用户服务的先驱,所以选择标准失误将会阻碍其他 ITS 用户服务的顺利实施。不考虑广阔的 ITS 前景,就在狭义基础上选取 EFC 标准将会错失机会,且最终将因对其进行纠正而造成重大损失。

> **Dedicated Short-Range Communications (DSRC) Standards**
> **专用短程通信（DSRC）标准**
>
> In spite of a worldwide effort (through both CEN and ISO) in the past decade to develop a common DSRC standard, the EFC systems available on the international market do not comply with a single standard. The CEN standard allows both infrared and microwave for DSRC, each having its own relative advantages. In the USA, a frequency band around 5.9 GHz has been designated by the Federal Communications Commission (FCC) for DSRC applications. However, the current ETC systems in North America are continuing to operate at 915 MHz, and these systems are primarily what the transitional and developing countries can acquire from North America. Meanwhile basically new ETC systems are emerging based on GPS or licence plate readers that do not depend on DSRC at all.
>
> 过去10年中，尽管世界范围内的机构（通过CEN和ISO）致力于发展通用DSRC标准，但可用于国际市场的EFC系统并未遵循单一标准。CEN标准允许在DSRC中使用红外线和微波技术，且每种技术均具有与它自身相关的优点。在美国，联邦通信委员会（FCC）正式指定将5.9GHz左右的频段应用于DSRC。然而，北美目前的系统仍旧继续沿用915MHz频段运营，这些系统是转型及发展中国家能够从北美获得的最初系统。同时出现了基于GPS或车牌识别技术的新型ETC系统，它们根本不依赖于DSRC。

7.5 Questions For Decision-Makers 决策者面临的问题

Strategic decisions for ITS can benefit from the following checklist of practical questions from a broader perspective under three categories: systemic, technological, and institutional.

ITS 战略决策能够得益于以下从广阔发展前景中反映出的实际问题，这些问题分为下述清单所列的三类——系统的、技术的和制度的。

7.5.1 System Questions 系统的问题

(1) What ITS user services will depend on the same enabling technologies as EFC does?
什么 ITS 用户服务将依赖于像 EFC 那样的可应用技术？

As a common technology, DSRC can be a bridge between Area Traffic Control and EFC, the two most common ITS applications in transitional and developing countries.

作为一种通用技术，DSRC 能够起到连接区域交通控制和 EFC 这两种在转型及发展中国家中最重要的 ITS 应用的桥梁作用。

(2) How would the priorities of ITS user services affect the choice of EFC standards?
ITS 用户服务优先顺序对 EFC 标准选择的影响程度如何？

The relative importance of the various user services might affect the relative ITS of various DSRC standards. In case there exists a large legacy system using a particular DSRC standard for some high-priority EFC services, the tendency is to keep the same standard in order to protect the large investment on the current EFC system.

多种用户服务的相对重要性可能会影响到具有多种 DSRC 标准的相应 ITS。一旦存在一个使用特别的 DSRC 标准为高优先权的 EFC 服务的大型现有系统，则发展趋势是保留同一标准来保护对现有 EFC 系统的巨大投资。

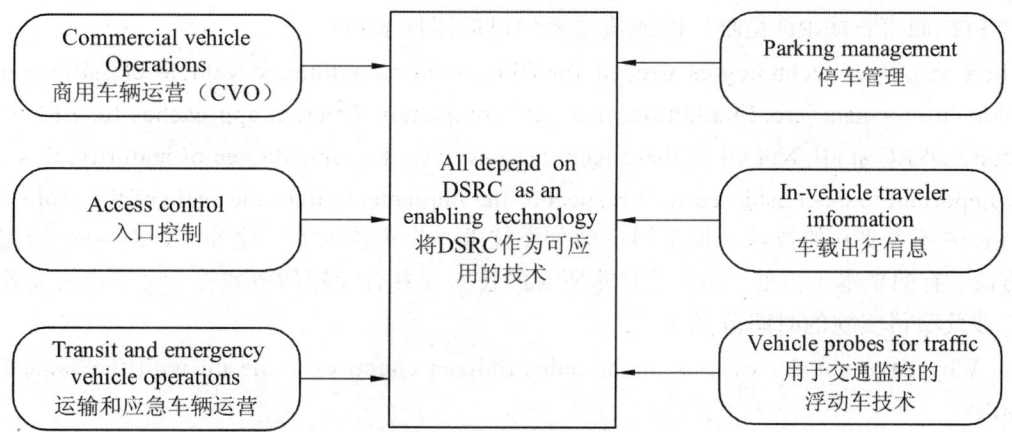

Figure 7.27 All depend on DSRC as an enabling technology

图 7.27 将 DSRC 作为可应用的技术

(3) Should I take time to develop an ITS system architecture to define how the different components should fit together?

是否该花费时间研发一套 ITS 系统体系框架来定义如何将不同组成部分进行组合？

System architecture development starts with identification of major stakeholders and their prioritization of user services. The time taken for ITS system architecture development can save much time for ITS implementation in the long run.

研发系统体系框架始于对主要的利益相关者和他们的用户服务优先权的确认。花费时间研发 ITS 系统体系框架将最终能够为实施 ITS 节省大量时间。

(4) What is the relationship between system architecture and standards?

系统体系框架和标准之间的关系是什么？

System architecture can be used to identify where standards are needed now and in the future. Standards are concrete specifications to assure that the hardware and software components from competing vendors in the system do fit.

系统框架能够用于鉴定现在和未来哪里需要标准。标准是确保系统中来自相互竞争的卖方间的硬件和软件组件相互配合的具体条目。

(5) How should an ITS framework plan consider EFC?

ITS 框架规划中应该如何考虑 EFC？

A good ITS framework plan should consider both long-term and near-term objectives and issues related to all ITS user services. The plan should provide a basis for timely and prudent sequencing of all ITS user services including EFC, which by itself should not be introduced as a fashionable thing to do.

一个好的 ITS 框架规划应该考虑到与所有 ITS 用户服务相关的长期和短期目标及问题。规划应该为适时和审慎的所有 ITS 用户服务序列提供基础支撑，其中用户服务包括 EFC，而不应像对待新型事物那样把它单独引进。

7.5.2 Technological Questions 技术的问题

(1) Is DSRC the only or the most important, enabling technology for EFC?

对 EFC 而言，DSRC 是唯一的或最重要的可应用技术吗？

There are other technologies needed for EFC, such as automatic vehicle classification, fee collection enforcement, etc. In addition, there are completely different approaches for EFC that do not require DSRC at all. Not all of these technologies have the same degree of maturity; this aspect is very important to be considered with respect to the implementation time scale of the project.

EFC 中还需要其他技术，如车辆自动分类技术、收费技术等。此外，针对 EFC 的完全不同的方法，有的根本不需要 DSRC。并非所有的技术都具有同样的成熟度，这一点需要着重考虑，它涉及项目实施的时间范围。

(2) Why have not the various major industrialized countries come up with the same DSRC standards?

为什么多个主要工业发达国家未达成同一 DSRC 标准？

Figure 7.28 Automatic vehicle charging technology
图 7.28 车辆自动收费技术

Each DSRC standard has a historical background, including industrial competition and legacy systems that reflect the priority of ITS user services and technology development in the country. It helps to understand the historical backgrounds of the various standards as this may help the country decide which standard would be the most appropriate to adopt.

每个 DSRC 标准都有其历史背景，包括工业竞争和遗留系统，这反映了本国优先用户服务和技术发展。这有助于理解多个标准的历史背景，并且有助于国家决定最适宜采纳哪个标准。

(3) What are the cost implications for different DSRC standards?

不同的 DSRC 标准中，成本的含义是什么？

In general, active tags are more expensive than backscatter (or reactive) tags. EFC devices at higher frequencies are generally more expensive than those at lower frequencies. However, the cost differential may change with time, as is the case with most electronic devices.

通常情况下，主动标签比反向散射（或被动）标签更贵。较高频的电子收费系统设备一般比低频的设备贵。但是正如大多数电子设备那样，成本的差异可能会随时间推移而变化。

(4) Why shouldn't I try to leverage on the telecommunication infrastructure instead of making heavy investment on a DSRC infrastructure?

为什么不应该试图投资到电子通信基础设施从而取代投巨资于 DSRC 设施？

The use of GPS/GSM is an example of EFC that does not require heavy investment on a DSRC infrastructure. However, the infrastructure needed for enforcement needs to be less costly than a DSRC infrastructure and this depends particularly on the network configuration, the fee policy, the type of traffic, etc. EFC systems based on GPS/GSM have advantages and disadvantages. In addition, once a DSRC infrastructure is established for EFC, it becomes an existing infrastructure that can be leveraged by other ITS applications.

在 EFC 中使用 GPS/GSM 是不需要投巨资于 DSRC 基础设施的一个例子。虽然用于强制执法的基础设施需要低于 DSRC 基础设施的投资花销，但这特别要依据网络结构、收费政策、交通类型等条件定度。基于 GPS/GSM 的 EFC 系统兼具有优点和缺点。此外，一旦为 EFC 搭建了 DSRC 基础设施，它将是一个实实在在的基础设施，并能够为其他 ITS 应用所影响。

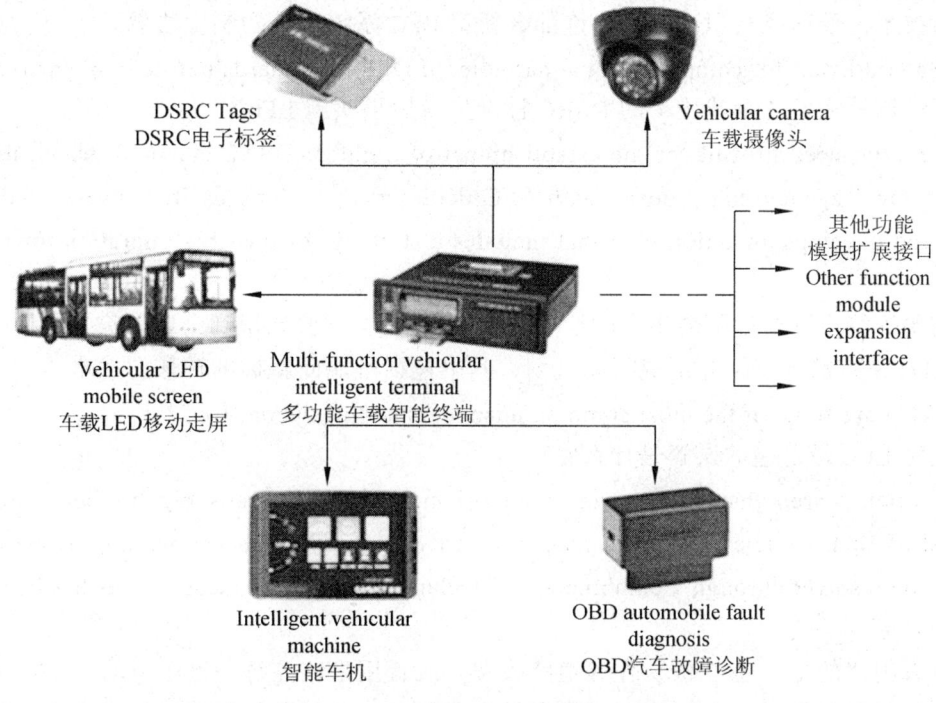

Figure 7.29　DSRC infrastructure
图 7.29　DSRC 基础设施

(5) Is interoperability among EFC systems essential and is it guaranteed if they all comply with the same standard?

EFC 系统的互操作性是否非常重要？如果它们遵照同一技术标准是否保证了互操作性？

Compliance with the same technical standard is a necessary, but not sufficient, condition for interoperability. Institutional arrangements are also necessary for achieving interoperability of EFC systems. ETC interoperability within a metropolitan area would give users much convenience as they move frequently from one part of the area to another. However, such interoperability may not be as important between metropolitan areas that are far apart.

遵照同一技术标准是实现互操作性的必要条件而非充分条件。制度上的安排也对实现

EFC 系统中的互操作性十分必要。位于大城市中 ETC 的互操作性将在用户频繁地从一处移动到另一处的时候给予他们更多便捷。但是，这种互操作性或许对彼此相距较远的两大城市之间的交通并不重要。

7.5.3　Institutional Questions　制度的问题

(1) What are the institutional pre-requisites for EFC deployment?

部署 EFC 系统，制度方面的前置要求是什么？

These vary from one country to another. Among the pre-requisites to be considered is the legislation to support EFC enforcement, interagency agreements on technical standards, and regulations for financial institutions to allow new forms of EFC deployment.

这因国家不同而各有差异。需要考虑的前置要求中包括立法来保障 EFC 强制执法，多个机构间就技术标准达成共识，以及允许部署新型 EFC 系统的金融制度法规。

(2) Should I wait for complete global harmony of DSRC standards before implementing EFC?

是否应该等完备的全球统一的 DSRC 标准出台后再实施 EFC？

There is no need to wait for the establishment of a global DSRC standard, which may never happen. A local agency can proceed with EFC deployment as long as it is aware of the global situation and develops an action plan that includes a strategy for possible migration toward a new standard.

不需要等待或许永远不会出台的全球 DSRC 标准。只要意识到全球形势，当地机构就能够推进 EFC 系统的部署，并形成行动规划，其中包括可能向新标准转移的战略。

(3) What are some of the most common misunderstandings about EFC?

一些对 EFC 最普遍的误解是什么？

It is often feared that EFC means road pricing, or EFC means big brother watching the movement of each vehicle. There are indeed security and privacy issues in EFC. However, these issues can be resolved through a combination of technical and policy measures, as has been done in many countries.

最令人担忧的是，EFC 被认作是道路收费，或者用来监控每一辆车运动。EFC 确实存在安全和隐私问题。但是，正如许多国家所做的那样，这些问题能够通过技术和政策相结合的方法予以解决。

(4) Is it important to educate the public and the politicians about EFC?

对公众和官员进行 EFC 培训是否重要？

Education is needed to avoid the above-mentioned misunderstandings. In addition, the users need to be educated about EFC operations in order to avoid confusion during the startup or transitional.

需要通过培训来避免产生上述错误。此外，需要对用户进行关于 EFC 运营的培训来避免他们在系统启动阶段或过渡阶段产生疑惑。

(5) How should I consider the possibilities of technology transfer and local manufacturing of EFC components?

应该如何考虑技术转化和在当地生产 EFC 组件的可能性？

These need to be discussed with the alternative vendors and may affect the choice among competing EFC systems of different standards.

这需要与不同的厂商讨论，并且这或许会影响到从遵循不同标准的具有竞争性的 EFC 系统中所进行的选择。

(6) Should a transitional or developing country pick a major industrialized country and follow ITS historical path and adopt ITS standards for EFC implementation?

转型及发展中国家是否应该选取一个主要工业发达国家，参照其历史发展道路并采纳它的标准进行 EFC 实施？

While there are merits in this approach, especially if the ITS user services priorities are similar between the two countries, appropriate variations from the historical path should also be considered.

虽然此法有可取之处，尤其是在这两国的 ITS 用户服务优先权相似的情况下，但是也应该考虑到要从其历史发展道路上作适当的变化。

(7) Where can I get neutral and objective advice and opinions about the pros and cons of competing standards?

能从哪里获取关于竞争性标准间的利弊的中立且客观的意见和建议？

Consultants with appropriate experience and international organizations like the World Road Association (PIARC) are potential sources of objective advice and opinions. Transitional and developing country representatives should look to the annual ITS World Congresses and IBTTA meetings to learn about the latest EFC and ITS developments and make their own independent judgments.

具有适当经验的顾问和诸如世界道路协会（PIARC）这样的国际组织都是提供客观意见和建议的潜在资源。转型及发展中国家代表应该关注每年的 ITS 世界大会和 IBTTA 会议来学习最新的 EFC 和 ITS 发展，得出自己的个人判断。

7.6 Advice to Major Industrialized Countries 对主要工业发达国家的建议

This brief section is to offer some advice to the representatives of major industrialized countries for consideration when they approach transitional and developing countries for cooperation in ITS activities.

这一节的目的是为主要工业发达国家的代表提一些建议，关于当他们与转型及发展中国家合作 ITS 事务时该如何考虑。

(1) Decision-makers in transitional and developing countries who are beginning to consider investment in ITS look for advice from experts of the major industrialized countries based on lessons learned in the policy and institutional area. In depth analysis of local situations and ITS needs, made together with local consultants and demonstrated by a pilot project, is often a necessary step for long-term cooperation.

开始考虑为 ITS 投资的转型及发展中国家的决策者会向主要工业发达国家的政策和制度

领域的专家们寻求建议。对本地形势和 ITS 需求进行深入分析，咨询当地顾问，而且通过试点工程予以证明通常是进行长期合作的必要步骤。

(2) The objective of sustainable long-term relationships requires that they have mutual respect for each other's long-term interests. The structure of the supplier consortium could well include a local partner. The supplier from the industrialized country can bring mature solutions, technologies and equipment. The local partner can provide ITS expertise in the understanding of local needs and culture, and can conduct part of the activities at lower costs.

实现建立长期可持续关系的目标需要互相尊敬对方的长期利益。供货商联盟的结构能够很好地吸纳当地的合伙股东。工业发达国家的供应商可以拿出成熟的方法、技术和设备。而当地合伙股东则提供他们在理解当地需要和文化方面的特长，并在低成本下实施部分事务。

(3) Technology adaptation is a two-way street. Not only professionals in transitional and developing countries, but those in industrialized countries, should also try to adapt ITS technologies to better suit the needs and conditions of the transitional and developing countries. Vendors from major industrialized countries can be more competitive in transitional and developing countries if they bring products designed to be robust and if they provide good after-sale services.

技术适应是双向的。不论是转型和发展中国家的专业人员，还是工业发达国家的专业人员都应该努力改善 ITS 技术，以更好地迎合转型和发展中国家的需求和形势。如果主要工业发达国家的供货商带来健康设计的产品，并且提供良好的售后服务，则他们在转型和发展中国家中能够拥有更强的竞争力。

(4) The higher rate of human errors in transport system operations in transitional and developing countries also creates opportunities for ITS technology transfer from major industrialized countries. Electronic means for finding many lost freight cars on the railways and automated block signal control in railways to avoid human errors.

在转型及发展中国家的运输系统运行中，高比例的人为错误也为从主要工业发达国家中转移 ITS 技术提供了机遇。运用电子方法在铁路上找到许多丢失的货车，运用自动闭塞信号控制来避免人为失误。

(5) The increasing trend of privatization of transport system operations in transitional and developing countries represents another set of opportunities for ITS technology transfer from major industrialized countries. Countries and transport sectors undergoing policy and institutional changes are particularly susceptible to new concepts like ITS.

转型及发展中国家的运输系统运营越来越有私有化的倾向，这表明了另一类从主要工业发达国家中转移 ITS 技术的机遇。经历政策和制度变化的国家和运输部门尤其易受如 ITS 这样的新兴事物影响。

(6) "Twinning" arrangements between public agencies and road infrastructure operators from the transitional and developing countries and their counterparts in the industrial world could provide a long-term partnership and create an "enabling environment" for mutual learning between them.

将转型及发展中国家以及工业发达国家的公众机构和道路基础设施运营商进行同等安排，能够提供长期的合作关系，并为国与国之间的相互学习创造"可能的环境"。

7.7 Conclusions 结论

Many transitional and developing countries have begun to invest extensively in ITS. In addition to the advice given in Chapter 6 applicable to all ITS programs and projects, it is hoped that those from the transitional and developing countries will find the additional advice given in this chapter useful, and relevant to their circumstances.

许多转型及发展中国家已经开始大规模投资于ITS。除了第六章所提及的应用于所有ITS项目和工程的建议之外，希望那些来自转型及发展中国家的人们能发现这章所述的其他有用且与自身环境相关的其他建议。

One of the very first steps in the development of a national ITS architecture is to involve all major stakeholders to understand, suggest, define, and agree on a set of prioritized ITS user services. Therefore the process of ITS architecture development can serve the purpose of assuring early involvement of stakeholders. For example, large urban motorways may be very difficult to convert to tolling years after construction, for political and physical reasons: Politically, because drivers used to traveling on expressways at no charge are likely to object to paying any tolls; physically, because freeways were not designed to provide space for retrofitting toll plazas. Even in major industrialized countries, institutional issues often delay the implementation of ITS. The foresight and the pace at which multiple relevant agencies are able to develop effective cooperation is often the critical factor for the success of many ITS applications. On the other hand, involving stakeholders may cause tremendous delays.

较早地发展国家ITS体系框架的步骤之一是吸纳所有的主要利益相关者，来使他们理解、提出建议、定义以及同意一套优先的ITS用户服务。因此ITS体系框架发展过程能够对确保利益相关者的早期介入起作用。例如，大型城市快速路在建成后若干年或许很难变成收费公路，这源于政治和物理上的原因：政治上，由于经常行驶于不收费快速路上的驾驶员很可能反对缴纳任何通行费；物理上，由于快速路在设计上并未提供空间来改进收费站。甚至在主要工业发达国家，制度问题经常拖延ITS的实施。一方面，能够使多种相关机构形成高效合作的远见和步调通常是诸多ITS应用得以成功的关键因素；但另一方面，吸纳利益相关者可能会导致极大延误。

A good example of this approach is that taken by the CONNECT project, which has been promoted by ERTICO and the Austrian authorities, with the support of the European Commission. The project involves major stakeholders in ITS cross-border applications through pilot and demonstration projects in Poland, Czech Republic, Slovakia, Slovenia and Hungary.

一个很好的实例是CONNECT工程，它由欧洲智能运输系统协会（ERTICO）和奥地利当局共同推进，同时也得到欧洲委员会的支持。通过波兰、捷克、斯洛伐克、斯洛文尼亚以及匈牙利的试点和示范，这项工程吸纳了ITS在跨边界应用上的主要利益相关者。

Chapter 8　What about ITS in the Long-Term
第八章　ITS 的发展趋势

This chapter looks to the future, at a number of directions that ITS might take in the next 10 to 20 years. It provides guidance on the benefits of "visioning": a forward planning tool which can be useful beyond the normal 5 to 10 year planning cycles, particularly for understanding uncertain circumstances which differ considerably from today.

本章从 ITS 未来 10 到 20 年内可能发展的几个方向展望未来，就是在"设想"的效益基础上提供引导，这种前向的规划工具也许在通常 5 到 10 年规划周期以外还可用，特别对理解与现在差异很大的不确定现象很有帮助。

8.1　Future Scenarios　未来的情景

Problems such as traffic congestion, global warming and environmental sustainability are forcing us to review our long-term plans for transport. Our aim must be to develop and improve the safety, security and effectiveness of the transportation systems where we can.

诸如交通拥挤、全球变暖以及环境可持续发展等问题迫使我们必须审视我们的长期交通规划。我们现在的目的必须是尽我们所能，开发和改进运输系统的安全、安保和有效性。

Figure 8.1　Global warming
图 8.1　全球变暖

8.1.1 Future Transport Strategies 未来交通战略

(1) Advanced Transportation Management 先进的运输管理

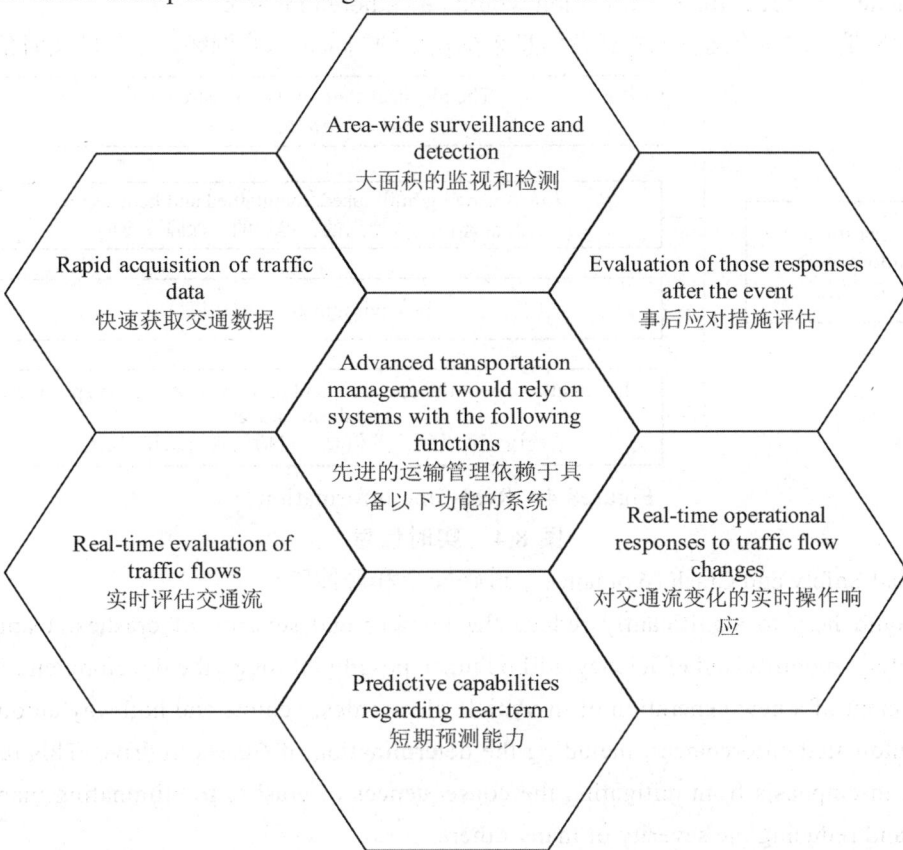

Figure 8.2 Effect of advanced transportation management
图 8.2 先进运输管理的作用

Figure 8.3 Better detection and operational tools
图 8.3 更好的监测和运营工具

(2) An Integrated Network of Transportation Information　运输信息的集成网络

This vision is of an integrated national network of operating information systems for all transport modes. The real-time information would be gathered include:

这一设想是针对所有运输方式运营信息系统建立的国家级综合网络，采集的实时信息包括：

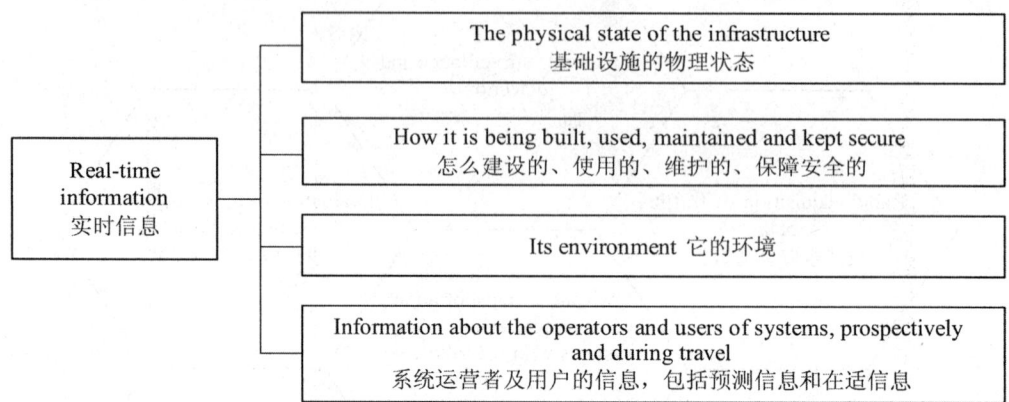

Figure 8.4　Real-time information

图 8.4　实时信息

(3) Road Safety and Crash Avoidance　道路安全和碰撞防护

ITS could help to significantly reduce the number and severity of crashes. Unprecedented levels of safety, mobility and efficiency will be made possible through the development, integration and deployment of a new generation of in-vehicle electronics, vehicle and highway automation and selective automated enforcement, including the determination of fitness to drive. This represents a major shift in emphasis from mitigating the consequences of crashes to eliminating many of them altogether and reducing the severity of many others.

ITS 有可能帮助显著减少碰撞次数和减轻碰撞的严重性。通过开发、集成和实施新一代车载电子装置、车路自动化以及可选择的自动化执法，包括对驾驶适应性的确定，使得空前的安全性、机动性及有效性成为可能。这意味着工作重点的重大转变，从减轻碰撞的后果到消灭一些可能的碰撞以及降低另外一些碰撞的严重程度。

Figure 8.5　Haval H6 safety test

图 8.5　哈佛 H6 安全试验

(4) Automatic Crash and Incident Detection, Notification and Response　碰撞和事件自动检测、发布和响应

Getting emergency response teams as quickly as possible to the scene of a crash or other injury-producing incident is critical to saving lives and reducing other adverse consequences of crashes. To achieve this, public safety providers must receive timely notice of the incident, be efficiently routed to the scene and to the hospital and be aware of and able to convey the nature and degree of the injuries. Information is also needed to minimize system disruption and to return traffic conditions to normal.

应急响应队伍尽早到达碰撞地点或其他有伤害的事件地点，对挽救生命及减少负面后果有重要意义。为达到这个目的，公众安全提供者必须及时得到事件的通知，必须尽快到达出事地点及医院，必须意识到并能够传达伤害的性质和程度，还需要最小化系统中断并恢复到正常交通状态的信息。

Figure 8.6　Traffic incident detection system
图 8.6　交通事件检测系统

8.1.2　ITS Visions and Visioning　ITS 设想和憧憬

Visioning is the process by which stakeholders, an organization or a community, envisions the future it wants and plans on how to achieve it. Once an organization has envisioned where it wants to go, it can begin to work consciously toward that goal.

憧憬是这样一个过程，即利益相关方、组织或团体可以设想未来，并且规划怎样实现。一旦这个组织框定了他们的发展目标，就能够开始有意识地朝这个目标去努力。

By articulating where it wants to go, an organization can consciously and purposefully begin to create the future it desires rather than simply reacting to prevailing trends and external forces of change.

通过清晰描述想达到的目标,一个组织就能够有意识并有目的地开始创造想要的未来,而不是仅仅被动地响应流行趋势及外界变化。

Visioning can occur at many scales, from individual, to community, regional, national, or even global. Most visioning projects for transport planning occur on a community-wide basis. Priorities and performance standards can be part of visioning. Priorities are set to distinguish essential goals. Performance standards allow an evaluation of progress toward goals over time.

憧憬有很多层面,从个人到社区、地区、国家甚至全球。大多数交通规划的憧憬项目都以社区为基础,优先级和性能标准是憧憬的一部分内容。设置优先级是为了突显主要目标,性能标准用于朝目标发展过程中对进度的评估。

Figure 8.7　Effect of visioning
图 8.7　憧憬的作用

The "US National ITS Program Plan: A Ten-Year Vision" illustrates how to approach long-term thinking about ITS. The development of the intelligent transport systems of today required a long-term commitment 20 years ago, to a transport vision of the future.

"美国国家 ITS 项目规划:十年设想"描述了怎样去实现 ITS 的长远目标。今天开发的 ITS 系统需要 20 年前对交通未来发展前景长远的承诺。

Organizations with responsibility for providing, maintaining and operating road and highway infrastructure need to know the scale, nature and magnitude of the problems they will face in the future, so they can develop strategies in response and target resources appropriately.

负责提供、维护、运营道路和高速公路基础设施的机构需要知道他们未来面临问题的规模、性质和数量级,以便他们可以恰当地制定响应策略和配备目标资源。

Figure 8.8   In-car screens: front and back seats
图 8.8   车内显示屏和车座后背显示屏

What is a Vision? 设想是什么？

A vision is something you want to happen: 设想是希望发生的事情：
- Sweden's "Vision Zero"; 瑞典的"Vision Zero"；
- US National ITS Architecture; 美国的国家ITS框架；
- Japan's Smart way concept; 日本的Smart way概念；

It has to be attainable. 这些必须是可达到的。

The uncertainty of the future means that no single vision can claim to be accurate. Realizing a vision may require a process of working backwards in order to decide how to go forward, a process known as "Back-casting".

未来的不确定性意味着任何一个设想都不是精确的。实现设想需要后向工作的过程以便确定怎样向前推进，这个过程称作"Back-casting"。

8.2   Forward-thinking ITS Programs and Projects   前瞻性的ITS系统计划和方案

8.2.1   The European Union "eSafety" Initiative   欧盟"eSafety"行动

"Saving lives in transport is not an option; it is now a social and political imperative and no wonder when some 40,000 people a year die on Europe's roads, the equivalent of a large commercial airplane crash per working day! Would we accept that?" Max Mosley, Chairman of ERTICO (ITS Europe) at that time, explained the importance of this target.

ERTICO（ITS Europe）主席 Max Mosley 当时这样解释该目标的重要性："在交通中挽救生命是必须的，现在它是社会和政治的职责，因为欧洲每年有 4 万人死于道路交通，相当于每个工作日都有一架大型商业飞机坠毁！难道我们能接受这个事实吗？"

The 40,000 fatalities he was referring to result from no less than 1,300,000 road accidents each year in the 15 countries in the EU as at 2001. Not only is this a huge cost in human terms but also in financial terms, with road accidents estimated to cost €160 billion annually (US$200 bn). By 2010, the aim is to halve this figure to 20,000 and then, in the next 10 year period to 2020, to move towards a "zero fatalities" scenario.

他所说的每年 4 万的道路死伤数字来源于 2001 年欧盟 15 个国家每年不少于 1 300 000 件的道路交通事故，这不仅是人力的巨大消耗，也是财力的巨大浪费。据评估，道路交通事故每年消耗 1 600 亿欧元（2 000 亿美元）。到 2010 年的目标是把这个数字减半到 20 000，并且在接下来的 10 年到 2020 年，达到零死亡。

Figure 8.9　Driver assistance system

图 8.9　辅助驾驶系统

(1) Safety enhancing technologies　安全增强技术

Many new vehicles are already equipped with some safety enhancing technologies. In addition, many vehicle manufacturers and after-market suppliers offer real-time traffic information and route guidance systems. In the period to 2010, efforts will be concentrated on improvements in vehicle safety and making everyone, from vehicle drivers to garages selling cars, more aware of key safety features such as these.

很多新车已经安装了安全增强技术。另外，很多汽车制造商和配件提供商提供实时交通信息和路径引导系统。从现在起至 2010 年之间，工作的重点主要是改善车辆安全以及使从汽车驾驶员到加油站工作人员的每个人都更加认识这些安全系统的主要特征。

Figure 8.10　Blind spot detection (BSDS radar)

图 8.10　盲点检测器（BSCS 雷达）

Other examples of existing and planned safety enhancing technologies being promoted by the eSafety initiative include:

eSafety 规划中用于增强安全的其他例子包括：

• Adaptive cruise control 自巡航控制
• Anti-collision systems 防碰撞系统
• Anti-lock brake system 防抱死制动系统
• In-vehicle emergency call 车载紧急呼救
• Collision mitigation/pre-crash systems 碰撞减轻/碰撞预防系统
• Drowsiness detection systems 睡意检测系统
• Electronic stability programs 电子稳定装置
• Enhanced floating car data 增强的浮动车数据
• Intersection support 交叉口支持
• Lane-keeping systems 车道保持系统
• Real-time traffic and travel information 实时交通和出行信息
• Speed alert systems 速度预警系统
• Vision enhancement 视野拓展

(2) Joint public-private working 公-私联合工作

Key stakeholders have been working for many years to develop and implement these safety-related technologies. However, it has become obvious that only coordination of these efforts can help to ensure attainment of the ambitious road safety targets for casualty reduction. Consequently, in 2002, a joint industry-public sector initiative – the eSafety Working Group – was established, with the objective of cutting the number of accidents by using ITS. The focus was advanced ITS technologies which would address the involvement and interaction between the driver, the vehicle and the road environment in order to improve road users' chances of avoiding and surviving accidents. The Working Group proposed 2 recommendations which give guidelines to accelerate the research, development, deployment and use of Intelligent Integrated Safety Systems.

关键的利益相关方多年来一直致力于开发和实施与安全有关的技术。然而很明显，只有把这些工作都协调起来才有助于确保实现减少道路交通事故的宏伟目标。因此，2002年一个工业和公共部门的联合组织——eSafety 工作组成立了，其目标是通过 ITS 减少交通事故。工作重点是可用于增强驾驶员、车辆和道路环境之间互相关联及互相作用的先进 ITS 技术，以便提高道路使用者避免交通事故或在事故中生还的几率。工作组给出两个建议，对促进、开发及推广应用智能的综合安全系统有指导意义。

(3) The eSafety Forum eSafety 论坛

In early 2003, an eSafety Forum was set up as a platform to promote and monitor the implementation of the recommendations made by the Working Group.

2003年初，eSafety 论坛作为促进和监督以上工作组建议的平台而成立了。

The eSafety Forum is divided into Working Groups that address the key issues or technologies targeted by the recommendations. Themes include:

Figure 8.11 Forum involves all the road safety stakeholders
图 8.11 该论坛涉及所有道路安全相关方

eSafety 论坛分成不同的工作组,每个工作组分别关注建议中提到的关键问题或技术。主要包括:

① Accident Causation Data: This group is working towards setting up a European wide database of accident causation. Comprehensive data is available in some countries and automotive manufacturers and insurance companies also have substantial data sets. In the first phase, the Working Group is formulating a methodology and framework which will allow more effective use of the existing data. In the second phase, the Group will analyze in more depth the user needs on accident causation data with a view to being able to evaluate the effectiveness of possible counter-measures and to make recommendations for further actions needed for effective, homogenous accident causation collection and analysis.

事故致因的数据:该工作组致力于建立欧洲范围内道路事故致因数据库。一些国家可能得到综合数据,并且汽车制造商和保险公司也有一些真实数据。第一阶段,工作组制定方法和框架,从而更有效地利用现有数据。第二阶段,工作组将深入分析基于事故致因数据的用户需求,目的是能够评估可采取对策的有效性,以及能够为将来进一步收集和分析同类事故致因数据提供有效的建议。

② Emergency call (eCall): This group is working on an integrated strategy for Pan-European emergency services. Where a vehicle is involved in an accident, an eCall will be initiated automatically and accurate vehicle location and additional safety related information will be passed to the Public Services Answering Point, thus reducing emergency response times.

紧急电话(eCall):该工作组致力于全欧洲范围紧急服务的综合策略研究。在车辆发生事故的地方 eCall 就自动启动,并且车辆的精确位置以及与安全有关的相关信息也被传输到公共服务应答点,因此缩短了应急响应时间。

③ Human-Machine Interaction (HMI): With increasingly more complex in-vehicle systems, HMI is a major concern. In 2000, the EC published a *Recommendation on Safe and Efficient In vehicle Information and Communications Systems*. This group is assessing the situation in the light of technical progress in collaboration with the industry and Member States and will propose further measures on HMI if necessary.

人机交互（HMI）：随着车载系统的日益复杂，HMI 引起人们的关注。在 2000 年，欧盟发布了《安全有效车载信息和通信系统的建议》。本工作组联合工业界及成员国根据技术进步来评估状态，并且在需要时给出 HMI 的进一步建议。

Figure 8.12　Emergency call
图 8.12　紧急电话

Figure 8.13　Autopilot and human-machine interaction
图 8.13　自动驾驶与人机交互

④ International Co-operation: The objectives of this group are to strengthen the synergies and avoid duplication with similar work taking place in other regions, e.g. North America and Japan. International co-operation is expected to cover in particular HMI issues, certification and testing methodology and procedures, harmonization and standardization, legal issues, impact and socio-economic benefit analysis and benchmarking/best practice.

国际合作：本工作组的目的是强调合作和避免相似工作在不同地区比如北美和日本的重复发生。预期的国际合作内容涵盖 HMI 问题，证明、实验方法论和方案，协调和标准，法律问题，影响和社会经济效益分析以及基准制定/最好的范例。

⑤ Research and Development: EU-funded research programs have already contributed towards the development and implementation of many leading edge Intelligent Vehicle Safety

Systems but further research is still needed in a number of technologies. The focus of this working group is to determine the priorities for further research based on analysis of accident causes and the impact of potential countermeasures.

研究和开发：欧盟资助的研究项目已经致力于很多前沿智能车辆安全系统的研究和实施，但是很多技术还需要进一步的研究。该工作组的重点是基于事故原因分析及可能的应对措施效果分析而确定进一步研究的优先领域。

Figure 8.14　Future driverless bus
图 8.14　未来无人驾驶巴士

⑥ Real-time Traffic and Travel Information (RTTI): In 2001, the Commission published a recommendation on the deployment of TTI services in Europe. This group provides further analysis and recommendations for accelerating the take-up of the recommended measures for accessing public sector data, enabling the establishment of public-private partnerships and the provision of reliable, high quality RTTI services in Europe.

实时交通和出行信息（RTTI）：2001年，委员会发布了在欧洲推广应用TTI服务的建议。该工作组就加速落实获取公众部门数据的建议、建立公私合作关系的建议以及在欧洲提供可靠、高质量RTTI服务的建议，提供更进一步的分析和建议。

Figure 8.15　Real-time traffic and travel information
图 8.15　实时交通和出行信息

⑦ Road Maps: The market introduction of Intelligent Vehicle Safety Systems involves policy, technological, societal, business, legal and consumer aspects. From the public sector point of view, it has to be possible to estimate the market introduction timetable and to use this information to plan for investments and to determine what other measures are required to enable take-up. This working group promotes the development of industry road maps and based on them, develops corresponding public sector road maps, which predict product development and deployment and indicate the investments required for improvements in road networks and the information infrastructure.

道路地图：智能车辆安全系统的市场导入涉及政策、技术、社会、商业、法律和顾客等方面。从公共部门观点来看，估计市场导入时间表及使用该信息去规划投资并确定还需要采取什么措施。该工作组不仅开发行业道路地图，并基于这些地图开发相应的公共部门道路地图。这些工作可以预测产品的开发和推广，并且指出完善道路网络和基础设施信息所需的投资。

⑧ Safety Plenary Sessions: The main tasks of these sessions are to discuss the topics covered in the Working Group reports and to try to reach consensus views on recommendations for implementing the proposed actions.

安全全体会议：这些会议的主要目的是讨论该工作组报告中的主题，并且极力就实施推荐活动的建议达成一致意见。

⑨ eScope: The eSafety Observatory project directly supports the eSafety initiative and has established an eSafety "observatory" which monitors and stimulates progress in the eSafety activities and will become an easily accessible and up-to-date resource for information on the priority eSafety topics.

eScope：eSafety 监测项目直接支持 eSafety 计划，并且已经建立了 eSafety 监测台，用来监视和仿真 eSafety 活动进展，并且变成对 eSafety 优先主题更容易获取和更新的信息资源。

(4) The eSafety vision: cooperative systems　eSafety 设想：合作系统

Research has shown that more safety benefits are possible with co-operative systems, where the in-vehicle systems interact with one another and with the benefit of information about the road ahead. Therefore the proposition that has emerged from eSafety is that road vehicles eventually will need to communicate and share data with each other in real time. The underlying objective is to deliver better quality of information, support and protection for all road users. In response, eSafety experts from the public and private sectors have provided a vision for cooperative systems: "Road operators, infrastructure, vehicles, their drivers and other road users will cooperate to deliver the most efficient, safe, secure and comfortable journeys. The vehicle-vehicle and vehicle-infrastructure co-operative systems will contribute to these objectives beyond the improvements achievable with stand-alone systems."

研究表明通过车载系统的相互配合以及与前方道路信息的配合，可以达到更好的安全效果。因此，eSafety 建议道路上的车辆最终需要相互通信并且实时共享数据。其目标是为所有的道路使用者提供更高质量的信息、支持和保护服务。相应地，来自公共和私营部门的 eSafety 专家已经对相互合作的系统有了一个设想："道路运营者、基础设施、车辆、驾驶员以及其他的道路使用者将联合打造最有效、安全、保安及舒适的旅程。车-车及车-路合作系统除改善现有独立系统的功能外,还将对以上这些目的做出贡献。"

Figure 8.16　In-vehicle systems
图 8.16　车载系统

8.2.2　Sweden's"Vision Zero"瑞典的"零死亡"

Sweden's "Vision Zero" long-term road safety goal was a forerunner to the European eSafety initiative and illustrates very well the value of a commitment to long-term planning for ITS. It can never be acceptable that people are killed or seriously injured when moving within the road transport system. It centers on an explicit goal, and develops into a highly pragmatic and scientifically-based strategy. According to "Vision Zero", this responsibility is shared by all those who have an effect on, or participate in road traffic:

瑞典的"零死亡"长期道路安全目标是欧洲 eSafety 计划的先驱,并且很好地描述了 ITS 长期规划任务的价值。人们在瑞典的道路交通系统中移动时死亡或严重伤绝对不可接受。其重点在清楚的目的,并且演变成一个高度程序化和科学化的策略。根据"零死亡",责任由所有对道路交通有影响或参与道路交通的人共同承担:

In 1997, the *Road Traffic Safety Bill* founded on "Vision Zero" was passed by a large majority in the Swedish Parliament. Sweden is already among those countries with the lowest number of traffic fatalities in relation to its population. However, this is not enough, and Swedish road safety work is based on a refusal to accept human deaths or lifelong suffering as a result of road traffic.

1997 年,根据"零死亡"而起草的《道路交通安全法案》由瑞典议会大多数人投票通过。根据瑞典的人口基数,这个国家已经步入最低道路交通事故伤亡数字的国家行列。然而,这还不够,瑞典道路安全工作基于这样一种认识:拒绝接受人类因为道路交通而死亡或者终生忍受道路交通伤害。

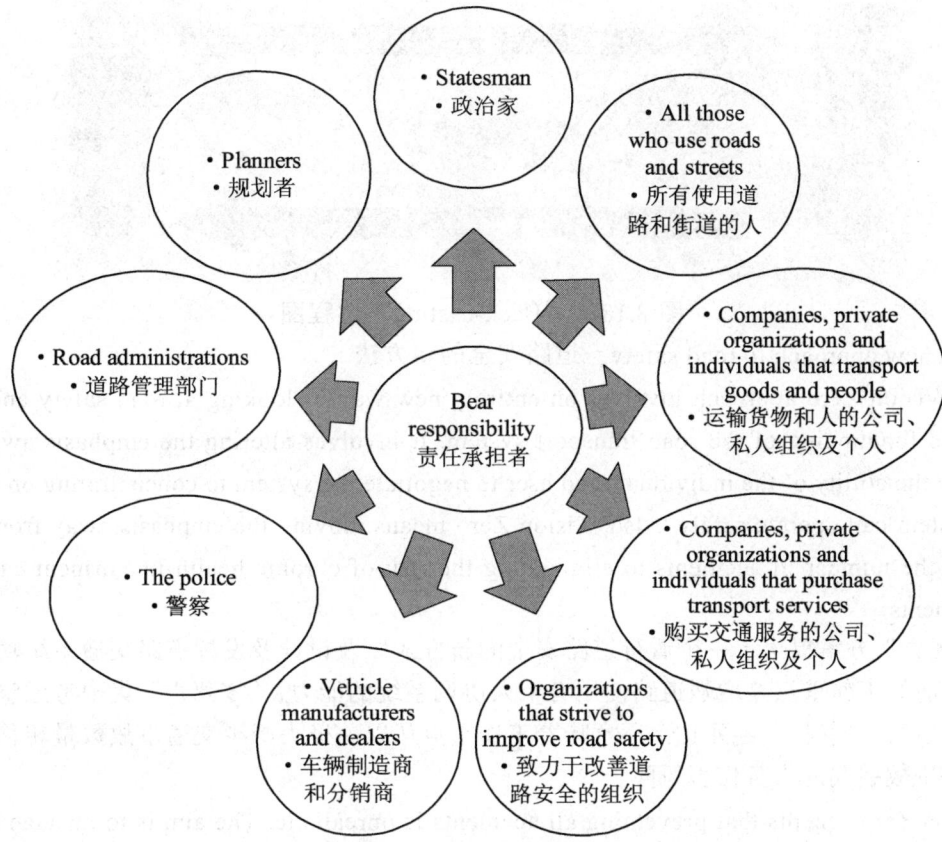

Figure 8.17 Traffic accident responsibility
图 8.17 交通事故责任

Through a process of "back-casting", as shown in Figure 8.18, specific intermediate goals or stepping stones have been identified in the migration process of reaching the long-term goal of no deaths or serious injuries on the roads which is implicit in the vision.

通过图 8.18 所示的"back-casting"过程,在向最终目标道路交通无死亡或无严重伤害迈进过程中,几个具体的中间分目标或分步骤已经明确。

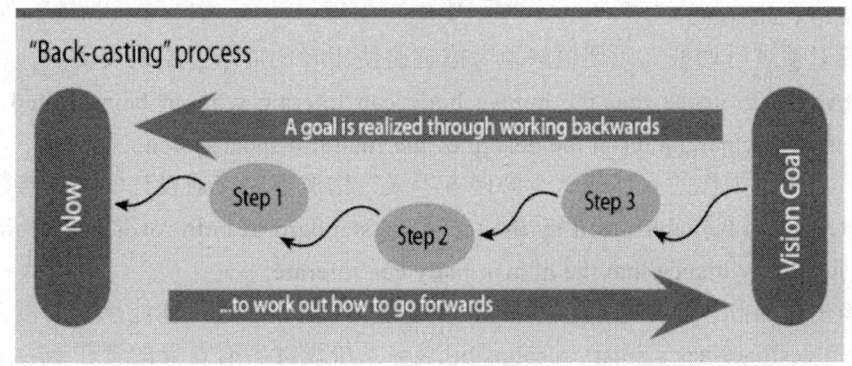

Figure 8.18 Diagram of the "Back-casting" process

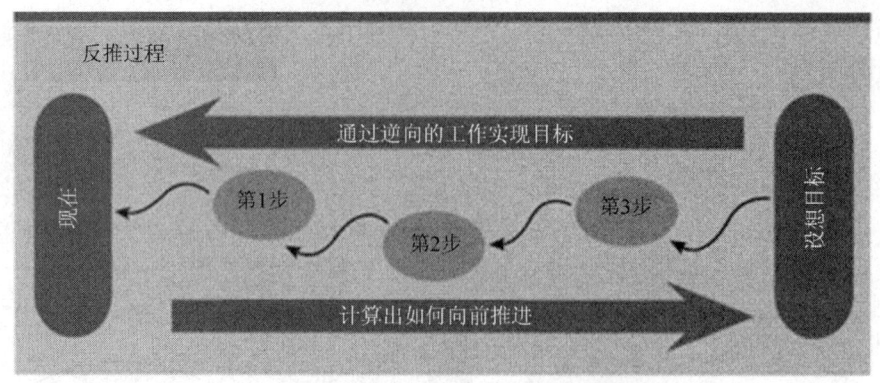

图 8.18 "Back-casting" 过程图

(1) A new approach to road safety　道路安全的新方法

The Vision Zero approach involves an entirely new way of looking at road safety and of the design and functioning of the road transport system. It involves altering the emphasis away from enhancing the ability of the individual road user to negotiate the system to concentrating on how the whole system can operate safely. Also, Vision Zero means moving the emphasis away from trying to reduce the number of accidents to eliminating the risk of chronic health impairment caused by road accidents.

"零死亡"方案提出了一个看待道路安全的新方式以及设计及发挥道路交通系统功能的新方法。以前的工作重点是增强道路使用者个人协调系统的能力，"零死亡"集中考虑整个系统怎样安全运行。同时，"零死亡"还意味着工作重点从以前极力减少交通事故数量转移到彻底清除道路事故引起的人身伤害风险。

Vision Zero accepts that preventing all accidents is unrealistic. The aim is to manage them so they do not cause serious health impairments. The long term objective is to achieve a road transport system which allows for human error but without it leading to serious injury. The strategic principles of Vision Zero are:

"零死亡"承认杜绝所有的交通事故是不现实的，其目的是对交通事故进行管理以便不对人身健康造成严重伤害。其长期的目标是营造一个道路交通系统，即使有人为错误发生也不至于对人身造成严重伤害。零死亡的战略原则如下：

① The traffic system has to adapt to take better account of the needs, mistakes and vulnerabilities of road users.

交通系统必须进行调整，以便更好地考虑道路使用者的需求、错误及弱点。

② The level of violence that the human body can tolerate without being killed or seriously injured forms the basic parameter in the design of the road transport system.

不致死亡或严重损伤的人体能承受的侵害等级，构成道路交通设计的基本参数。

③ Vehicle should be determined by the technical standard of both roads and vehicle so as not to exceed the level of violence that the human body can tolerate.

车速应该由道路和车辆的两类技术标准来确定，以便不超过人体能承受的侵害等级。

(2) System designer has primary responsibility　系统设计者有首要的责任

While the concept envisages responsibility for safety split between both the designers and users of the system, the designer has the final responsibility for "fail-safe" measures:

尽管把道路安全责任分摊给系统设计者和使用者共同承担，但设计者对失效的措施负最终责任：

① System designers are responsible for the design, operation and the use of the road transport system and are thereby responsible for the level of safety within the entire system.

系统设计者负责道路交通系统的设计、运营和使用，因此负责整个系统内部的安全等级。

② Road users are responsible for following the rules for using the road transport system set by the system designers.

道路使用者负责遵循道路设计者指定的道路运输系统使用规则。

③ If the users fail to comply with these rules due to a lack of knowledge, acceptance or ability, the system designers are required to take the necessary further steps to counteract people being killed or injured.

一旦道路使用者因为缺乏知识、接受力或能力而没有遵照使用规则，则要求设计者采取进一步的必要措施以避免人们死亡或受伤害。

(3) Operational principles　运行的原理

① At political level: not allowing road traffic to produce more health risks than other means of transportation or other major technological systems.

政治层面：不允许道路运输产生比其他运输方式或其他主要技术系统更高的健康风险。

② At professional level: seeing serious health loss due to traffic accidents as an unacceptable quality problem of products and services connected with road transportation.

职业层面：把由交通事故引起的健康损害看成是与道路运输产品和服务有关的不可接受的质量问题。

③ At individual level: playing an active part in placing demands on society and manufacturers for safe road traffic.

个人层面：积极对社会和制造商提出关于安全道路交通方面的要求。

(4) Action strategy　执行战略

An action plan is necessary in order to achieve a safe road system:

为营造一个安全道路系统，执行规划非常必要：

① To prevent accidents leading to serious injury;

预防导致严重伤害的交通事故；

② To reduce the severity of injury in the event of an accident;

降低交通事故事件中伤害的严重性；

③ To ensure that the severity of injuries received is minimized through efficient rescue service, health care and rehabilitation.

确保事故伤害的严重性通过有效的营救服务、健康保健和复原达到最小。

8.2.3　Roads to the Future in the Netherlands 荷兰的未来道路

Roads to the Future provide incentives for innovation by combining long-term thinking with short-term action. It develops future scenarios and translates these into concrete proposals in the form of demonstrations and pilot projects.

"未来道路"通过长期考虑和短期行动的结合来为创新提供激励，它构想未来的场景，并以演示及示范工程的形式转换成具体的建议。

(1) The Roads to the Future Vision　未来道路设想

The vision of a better organized, more efficient infrastructure by the year 2030 with a focus on the creation of added value for the future society gives direction to the program. In the period from 2001–2020, core values are safety, sustainability, and accessibility.

设想到2030年有一个组织更好、更有效的基础设施，其重点是为未来社会带来附加值，这个设想提供了发展方向。在2001年到2020年期间，核心价值是安全、可持续发展和可达性。

Roads to the Future is not regarded as a task for government alone, rather it is based on the conviction that problems of accessibility can only be solved by close collaboration between the market, government and centers of expertise. This basic principle underlying the various "Roads to the Future" pilot projects has already been put into practice. A close and enthusiastic partnership between government and commercial consortia has already produced some interesting ideas. RtF seeks innovation and is not limited to any one discipline. RtF seeks views from diverse social backgrounds to give some critical thought in to particular themes and topics with a view to turning the results of this dialogue into concrete pilots for innovation. The theme is that there should be a pleasant environment for living, working and recreation, without nasty smells, air pollution, noise and vibrations.

"未来道路"不仅仅是政府的任务，而是基于这样的信念：可达性问题只能通过市场、政府和专业技术中心的紧密配合来解决。贯穿于"未来道路"系列示范工程的这个基本原理已经得到贯彻落实。政府和商业银行的紧密合作已经带来值得注意的思路。"未来道路"寻求革新，并且不局限于任何学科。"未来道路"寻求来自不同社会背景的观点，针对特定主题给出具体想法，把这些结果变成具体的创新性示范工程，其主题是应该有令人愉快的生活、工作和娱乐的环境，没有肮脏的气味、空气污染、噪声及振动。

(2) Working method: themes and pilots　工作方法——主题及示范

Linking long-term vision to short-term action is characteristic of RtF's working method. This is done through dialogue with external partners.

把长期设想和近期行动结合起来是"未来道路"工作方法的特点。通过与外部合作伙伴的对话来达到目的。

"Roads to the Future" is cyclical: In each cycle, the team interpreted the element of long-term thinking in its own way. The first RtF cycle started in 1996, and the third cycle in the spring of 2002. For this cycle the mission is to find appealing pilot projects, showing that the Netherlands Ministry of Transport and Public Works (Rijkswaterstaat) explores options outside its existing framework in the fields of infrastructure and mobility. The current themes are:

"未来道路"是循环的。在每个周期中，团队都以自己的方式解释长期思考的元素。第一个"未来道路"周期开始于1996年，第三周期开始于2002年春天。这轮的任务是找到有前景的示范工程，说明荷兰交通与公共事务部探索基础设施和流动性领域现有框架之外的出路。当前的主题是：

① Tailored Information: Well-informed when on the road.

订制的信息：在路上获得足够的信息。

RtF wants to initiate a dialogue about future information provision to travelers. In practice our way of travelling often becomes a matter of habit – we take the car because it's there and because we took it yesterday. Information technology already offers so much and we have access to an unprecedented amount of information but can we actually process all this information? Or should we move towards identifying highly tailored information in order to make better choices that will make travelling more efficient and pleasant for everyone? Is investing in technology the solution, or should we invest in social-psychological or sensory-physiological knowledge? What are the opportunities to actually reach road-users and others in order to provide them with optimal information?

"未来道路"想启动给出行者提供信息的讨论。实际上，我们的出行方式常常变成习惯问题——我们乘车是因为车在那儿，并且我们昨天就乘车。信息技术提供了那么多，并且我们也获得了前所未有的大量信息，但是实际上我们能够处理所有这些信息吗？或许我们应该再往前走一步，给出高定制化的信息以便更好地做出选择，使出行对每个人都更有效、更愉快？在技术上投资是解决方案吗？或者我们应该投资社会心理学或者感知心理学知识？给道路使用者和其他人提供可选信息时，他们实际得到的是什么？

② Enriched travelling time: Make travelling time, well spent.

丰富旅行时间：愉快地度过旅行时间。

RtF seeks views and ideas about travelling and the options for high-quality mobility in the future. There are many different ways of getting around, each with its own advantages and disadvantages. If travelling can also become an experience, travelling time can be made more valuable-time that can be used for other activities. Initiatives already exist in response to the idea of combining travelling time with other activities. Petrol stations sell more than petrol alone and the car has become an extension of the office. Is the traveler better off with all these developments? And where is all this eventually leading us?

"未来道路"需求关于未来出行的观点和想法以及对高质量机动性的选择。走动有很多方式，但每种都有其优缺点。如果旅行也能变成一种体验，则旅行时间就可以更有价值，可用于做其他的事情。针对把旅行时间和其他行为联系到一起的想法，已经有一些初步的尝试。加油站不仅仅是卖汽油，小轿车也已经变成办公室的延伸。出行者真的从这些演变中获益了吗？所以这些将把我们引向何方？

③ The Multifunctional Road: Roads and motorways of the future will have more functions than transport alone.

多功能道路：将来的道路和高速公路除运输外还有更多的功能。

Smarter, multifunctional and more intensive use of the space taken up by infrastructure and better co-ordination with the environment will be key concepts. Because the road is multifunctional it will have greater social benefits, not only in the technical sense but also in societal terms. RtF has already taken initiatives to tackle the nuisance caused by the road as much as possible at the source. A good example is the new silent road surface. What specific social, economic and ecological opportunities (or others) are there for residents, road managers and road users to add value to the road?

对由基础设施占据的空间进行更智能、更多功能及更密集地使用，以及更好地与环境进行协调，将成为未来工作的重点。因为道路是多功能的，所以它将有更大的社会效益，不仅在技术层面，而且在社会层面。"未来道路"已经采取行动尽可能解决由道路引起的破坏，包括对资源的破坏，新型安静路面就是一个很好的范例。对于居民、道路管理者和道路使用者来说，还有什么特定的社会经济和生态机会来增加道路的价值吗？

Figure 8.19　Roads to the Future
图 8.19　未来道路

④ Intelligent Networks: better connections, new forms of management.
智能网络：更好的联结，管理的新形式。

Most of the components of our infrastructure were developed independently of one another in the last century. As a result, the transport networks do not always interconnect seamlessly. Can we make the networks connect better through smarter management so that traffic flow becomes more controllable? And how can we bring this about? Mobility is self-perpetuating: more capacity generates new demand. More roads are not the solution but smarter use of the network is. RtF wants to initiate a dialogue on the strengths and weaknesses of our current networks. What can we learn from other network managers in the areas of water, energy and telephony? Is the management of all road networks by one party a realistic idea? Must we consider several providers? What means are there to control traffic flows?

20 世纪，基础设施的大部分元素都是独立开发建设的，结果交通网络常常不是无缝链接。我们能通过智能管理使网络更好地联结以便交通流变得可控一点吗？怎样才能实现这个目的？机动性问题总存在：更大的通行能力带动新的需求，更多的道路不是解决办法，而更智能地使用道路才是解决途径。"未来道路"想启动关于我们现有网络优势和弱点的讨论对话。我们能从水、能源和无线电话网络管理者那里学到什么经验？所有道路网络由一个团体管理是否理想？我们必须考虑几个提供商？有什么措施提供交通流？

Figure 8.20　Vehicle Tracking
图 8.20　车辆跟踪

(3) Future Transport: new transport systems　未来交通：新的交通系统

The car is not necessarily the means of transportation for the future. Its development started some hundred years ago, and since the end of the 1960s the car has been the dominant means of transportation. But will that still be the case in forty years' time? It is conceivable that other means of transportation will be developed in that period.

未来小汽车并不是必备的交通方式，小汽车的发展开始于几百年前，并从 20 世纪 60 年代末成为交通的主要方式，但是这种状况还能继续持续 40 年吗？可以设想在这段时间里还有其他的运输方式开发出来。针对这个主题，相关的示范工程有：

① Missing Link: The network infrastructure was developed in the last century. Because of these independent networks, connections are not always optimized.

缺少连接：网络基础设施是 20 世纪开发出来的，因为各个网络相互独立，所以连接常常不容乐观。

② City box: Inner-cities often suffer from traffic congestion. City box might be the answer to these problems. City box is a logistic concept for the transportation of goods and providing shops.

城市盒子：城市内常遭受交通拥挤的痛苦，城市盒子可能是该问题的解决方法，对于货物运输和商店来说"城市盒子"是一个物流概念。

③ Optimal corridor: If data from all transportation providers could be "matched" in one system, travelers could use this information to find the best possible route to their destination: the optimal corridor.

最佳走廊：如果来自所有运输供应商的数据都能在一个系统中进行匹配，出行者就能用这些信息选择出自己到达目的地的最佳路径：最佳走廊。

④ Future service areas: The road and its environment are developing. Future service areas will probably be very different from current service areas. Inhabitants, users, managers and licenses and their opinions will be considered in this pilot.

将来服务领域：道路和环境总在不断发展，将来的服务领域很可能与现在很不相同。该项目就研究考虑居民、用户、管理者、领到执照的人以及他们的选择问题。

⑤ Waste products: Polluted mud can be used for building roads, especially when using new techniques for cleaning. These new techniques are preferred over dumping. Roads can become "self-cleansing" roads.

垃圾产业：污泥可用于建造道路，特别是使用清洁新技术处理之后。这些新技术在垃圾处理方面很受欢迎，道路可能变成"自清洁"系统。

⑥ Traffic forecast: If traffic could be forecasted, travelers could choose their preferred options for travelling. Instead of being dependent of the current situation on the roads, early information helps travelers to make travelling more pleasant.

交通预测：如果交通可以预测，那么出行者就可以选择喜欢的方式出行。与现在依赖道路状况不同的是，早期的信息可使得出行者旅行更愉快。

⑦ In-car information: Our roads are full of information. What if all this information could be offered on an in-car system? Maximum speed, parking facilities, next service station: your in-car information system provides the information you need. Could this be reality in the future?

车载信息：我们的道路到处都充满信息。如果这些信息全部送到一个车载系统上，会是什么样子？最大速度、停车设施、下一个服务站，你的车载系统把这些信息都提供给你。这在将来能成为现实吗？

⑧ Close contact: Mobility is a commodity, long distance travelling is common. But experiencing travelling could be better. If travelling time could be enriched by using working facilities in your car, or the opportunity to get in touch with fellow travellers, travelling time will become more pleasant than it is today.

紧密接触：机动性是日常需要，长距离出行很常见，但是体验式的出行会更好。如果旅行时间通过车载设施或通过与其他旅行者接触变得丰富多彩，那么旅行时光将比现在更令人愉快。

⑨ Bonus driving: Most motorists are familiar with fines and penalties for speeding or other offences, but why couldn't this be just the other way around? Why not a bonus for good behavior? Which bonus could be linked to what behavior?

奖励驾驶：大多数驾驶员对超速或其他违规行为的罚款或惩罚很熟悉，但是为什么不可以用其他形式来处理这些问题？为什么不可以对良好驾驶行为进行奖励？什么样的奖励应该可以与什么样的驾驶行为相对应？

Figure 8.21　Future Vehicles
图 8.21　未来车辆

(4) From RtF vision to reality　从"未来道路"设想到现实

Roads to the Future has yielded a number of useful innovations since 1996. But what happens to the innovative ideas after they have been realized in a pilot project? For this purpose, RtF appointed a "Propagation Manager" in the main team with the primary objective of giving shape to the path from innovation to implementation. A promising pilot will eventually be handed over to the market, passed on within the Ministry of Transport, Public Works and Water Management, or developed further by RtF itself.

自 1996 年起,"未来道路"已经带来很多有用的创新,但是当这些创新想法在示范工程中实现之后发生了什么呢?针对这个问题,"未来道路"指派一个"推进经理",主要目的是为创新到实施铺平道路。有发展前景的示范工程最终都被推向市场,交给荷兰交通、公共事务与水管理部,或者"未来道路"再开发。

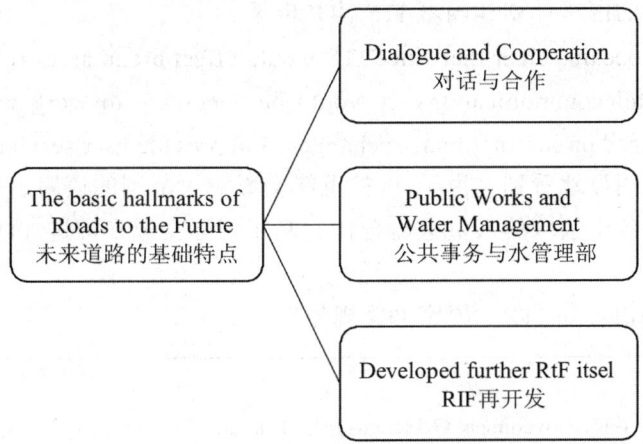

Figure 8.22　The basic hallmarks of Roads to the Future

图 8.22　未来道路的基础特点

Naturally, the pilots yield important results themselves. But the RtF participants also gain valuable experiences with regard to processes. In the innovation program they learn to think in "unconventional" ways and acquire skills which are useful at Rijkswaterstaat.

很自然,示范工程本身会产生重大成果,但是"未来道路"参与者们在这个过程中也获得了有价值的经验。在创新项目中,他们学会了运用传统方式思考,并且获得在荷兰交通、公共事务与水处理部工作很有用的技能。

National ITS Plan for Japan
日本国家ITS规划

Five organizations working together to achieve a common vision:
五个组织一起工作得到共同的设想:
- National Police Agency　日本警察厅
- Ministry of International Trade and Industry　通商产业省
- Ministry of Posts and Telecommunications　邮政省
- Ministry of Construction　建设省
- Ministry of Land, Infrastructure and Transport　国土交通省

8.2.4　Car navigation systems in Japan　日本的车载导航系统

Japan has had an all-embracing vision for Intelligent Transport Systems since the early 1970s. The public sector has taken the lead in large national programs to implement nationwide ITS services. Two national ITS systems, VICS (Vehicle Information and Communication System) and ETC are now widely served. The fast progress seen in Japan is based on the historical accumulation of physical and data infrastructures. The fast evolution is also due to an ambitious national master plan and the national system architecture for ITS.

从 20 世纪 70 年代早期开始，日本就有了全方位的 ITS 远景规划，公共部门在全国范围内实施 ITS 服务的大型工程中占主导地位，两大国家级的 ITS 系统 VICS（车辆信息与通信系统）和 ETC 都已经得到广泛使用。日本的快速发展，基于基础设施自然条件和数据的长期积累，也源于雄心勃勃的国家计划和国家 ITS 体系框架。

In the process, it became clear that since ITS would affect broad areas of road, traffic, vehicles and information and telecommunications, it would be necessary to work with people in various fields, promote ITS based on international exchanges, and provide user services to meet their needs.

在发展过程中很明显地看到，由于 ITS 可能会影响大范围的道路、交通、车辆和信息与无线通信，因此需要各个领域的人员进行合作、基于国际交流来推进 ITS 以及提供用户服务来满足用户需求。

(1) National planning for ITS　国家 ITS 规划

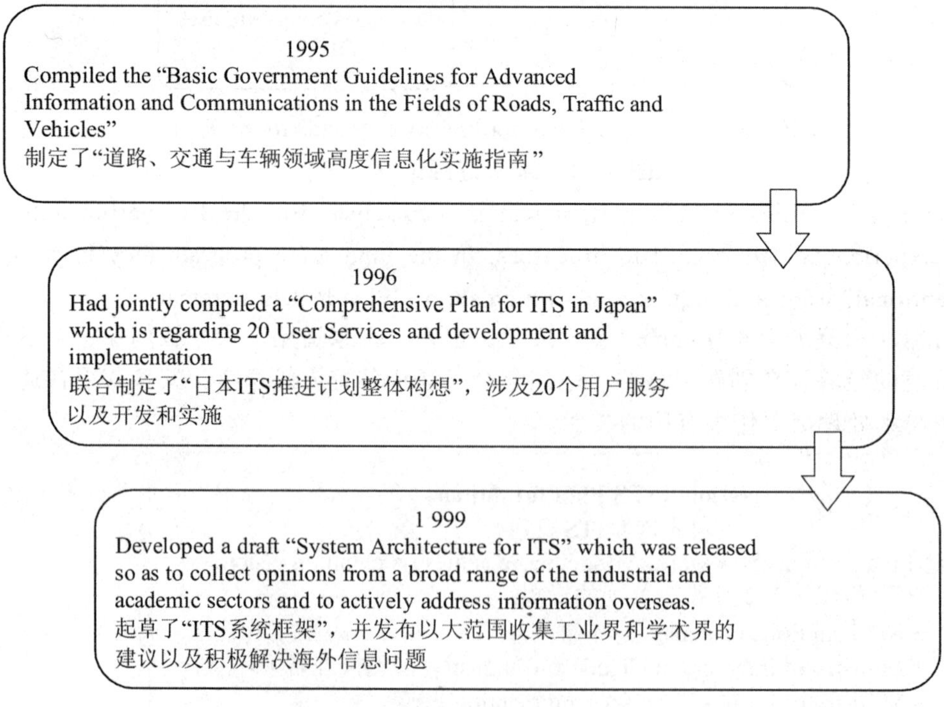

```
┌─────────────────────────────────────────────────┐
│                      1995                        │
│ Compiled the "Basic Government Guidelines for   │
│ Advanced Information and Communications in the  │
│ Fields of Roads, Traffic and Vehicles"          │
│ 制定了"道路、交通与车辆领域高度信息化实施指南"   │
└─────────────────────────────────────────────────┘
                         ↓
┌─────────────────────────────────────────────────┐
│                      1996                        │
│ Had jointly compiled a "Comprehensive Plan for  │
│ ITS in Japan" which is regarding 20 User        │
│ Services and development and implementation     │
│ 联合制定了"日本ITS推进计划整体构想"，涉及20个   │
│ 用户服务以及开发和实施                          │
└─────────────────────────────────────────────────┘
                         ↓
┌─────────────────────────────────────────────────┐
│                      1999                        │
│ Developed a draft "System Architecture for ITS" │
│ which was released so as to collect opinions    │
│ from a broad range of the industrial and        │
│ academic sectors and to actively address        │
│ information overseas.                           │
│ 起草了"ITS系统框架"，并发布以大范围收集工业界  │
│ 和学术界的建议以及积极解决海外信息问题          │
└─────────────────────────────────────────────────┘
```

Figure 8.23　National planning for ITS

图 8.23　国家 ITS 规划

(2) Enabling factors: the existence of a digital map database　　成功因素：数字地图数据库的存在

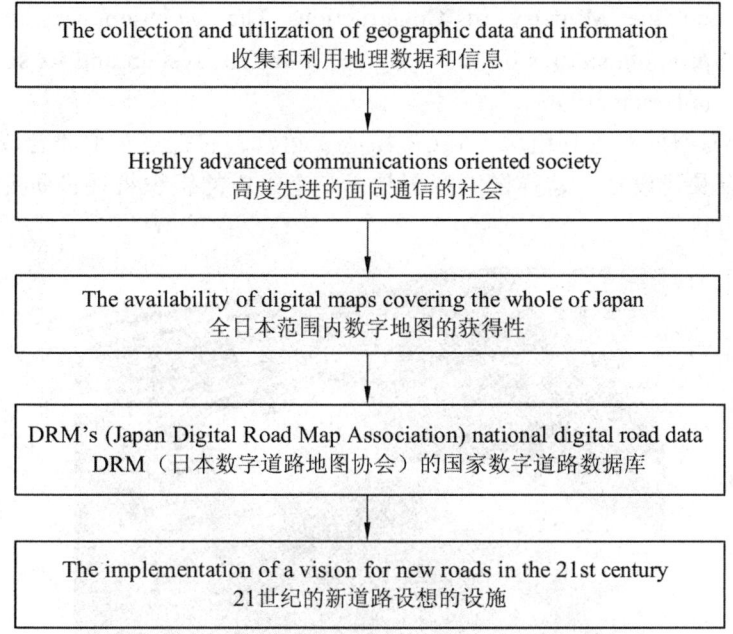

Figure 8.24　The flow chart of a digital map database
图 8.24　获得道路数据库的流程图

① VICS (Vehicle Information and Communication Systems) deployment　　VICS 车辆信息与通信系统的部署

"Advancement in navigation systems" was one of the areas of development envisioned in the National ITS Plan and VICS was one of the first developments.

"导航系统的先进化"是国家 ITS 规划中预定开发的领域之一，VICS 是首先要开发的内容之一。

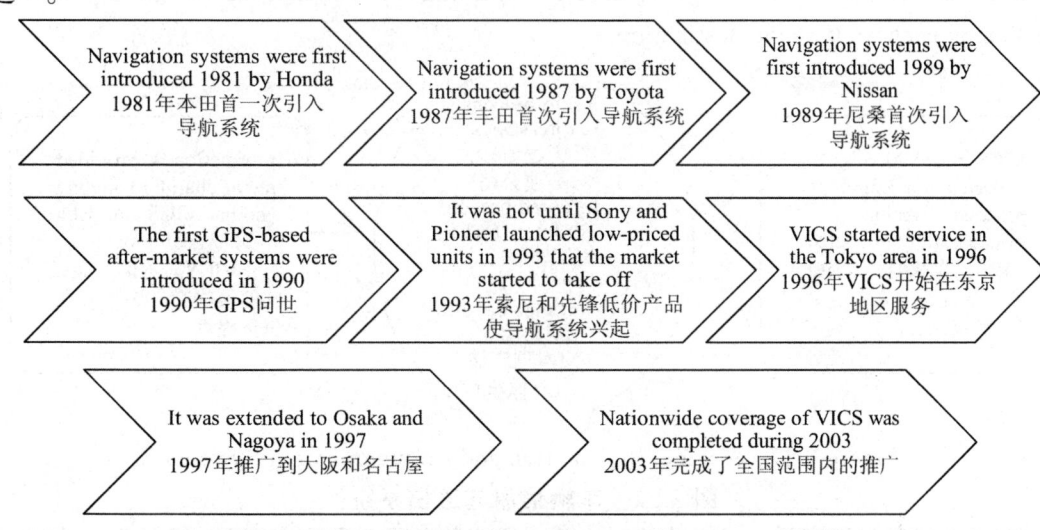

Figure 8.25　Development history of Japanese VICS
图 8.25　日本 VICS 发展历程

VICS is operated by a dedicated nonprofit organization (VICS Center) which brings together three ministries in one organization: the National Police Agency, the Ministry of Posts and Communications, and the Ministry of Construction. The intention was that an integrated organization would promote studies on the design of a unified system and its smooth operation in the actual stage of implementation.

VICS 由一个专门的非盈利组织（VICS 中心）运营，它把三个部联合成一个组织：日本警察厅、邮政省以及建设省。这样做的意图是：一个集成的组织将促进研究设计统一的系统以及实施阶段的顺利。

Figure 8.26　Vehicle information
图 8.26　车载信息

When a car navigation system is equipped with the VICS function, the driver can obtain road and traffic information in real time. If the car navigation system is a model that determines routes to the driver's destination, it can automatically recalculate the expected time of arrival based on traffic congestion, or figure out a detour to avoid the traffic congestion. While driving, the driver sees information on a display inside the vehicle, including information about driving time and congestion on each route to the destination.

Figure 8.27　Vehicle Information and Communication Systems
图 8.27　车辆信息与通信系统

当车辆导航系统配备了 VICS 功能时，驾驶员能够获得道路和交通的实时信息。如果说导航系统能为驾驶员确定通往目的地的路径，则它能自动基于交通拥挤程度重新计算达到目的地的预期旅行时间，或规划出绕开交通拥挤的替代路径。驾驶过程中，驾驶员可以看到车载显示屏上显示的交通信息，包括到达目的地每个路径的驾驶时间和拥挤程度。

(3) An iterative process 迭代过程

Since 1996, the Japanese have been working towards the goals identified in their "Comprehensive Plan for ITS in Japan". All nine areas in the master plan are assumed to enter into the deployment stage from the 21st century. Nationwide, projects such as VICS and ETC are working well, but the next stage of Japan's vision for ITS will involve integrating many of these standalone systems into a more comprehensive system. Future challenges are primarily integration and standardization.

自 1996 年开始，日本一直致力于努力实现"日本 ITS 推进计划整体构想"制定的目标，其中假定主计划中的 9 个领域在 21 世纪都进入推广应用阶段。全国范围内，诸如 VICS 和 ETC 的工程都运转良好，但是日本 ITS 设想的下一阶段将把很多这些孤立的系统集成一个更复杂的系统。未来的挑战主要是集成和标准化。

A good example of this integration is "Smartway" which is being developed by the Ministry of Land Infrastructure and Transport. "Smartway" is an infrastructure based intelligent transport system which will integrate Electronic Toll Collection (ETC), Advanced Cruise Assist Highways Systems (AHS) and the Vehicle Information and Communication System (VICS). "Smartway" is a conceptual highway which will enable a wide range of information to be exchanged among users. It is based on advanced communication technologies comprising roadside sensors and detectors, optical fibre networks and vehicle based sensors.

一个很好的集成例子是"Smartway"，它由国土交通省开发研制。"Smartway"是一个基于 ITS 的基础设施，集成电子收费（ETC）、先进的巡航辅助公路系统（AHS）以及车辆信息和通信系统（VICS）。"Smartway"是一个概念性的公路，它使用户之间大范围的信息交换成为可能，它包括由路侧传感器和检测器、光纤网络以及基于车辆的传感器组成的先进通信技术。

8.2.5 Co-operative vehicle-highway system in USA 美国的车路合作系统

The history of the development of the Automated Highway System (AHS) in the US provides a good example of how a project with a powerful vision has managed to continue its momentum, despite many changes in direction and setbacks along its path.

美国自动公路系统（AHS）的开发历史是个很好的范例，说明了一个具有强有力设想的工程如何保持其发展势头，尽管在前进道路上有很多方向改变和挫折。

(1) AHS during the 1980s and 90s 20 世纪 80 年代到 90 年代的 AHS

For many years the vision of an Automated Highway System (AHS) has been popular in the United States. The modern revival of interest began in 1986, leading to the development of Automated Highway Systems. Using State transport research funds, this partnership made significant progress in developing technologies and strategies for deploying automated vehicles and the associated supporting infrastructure. This research stimulated interest from USDOT and resulted in inclusion of a provision for AHS testing and demonstration in the federal *Intermodal Surface Transportation Efficiency Act of 1991*. Subsequently, the US DOT sponsored an ambitious program carried out by the National Automated Highway System Consortium (NAHSC) whose mission was to develop a prototype automated highway system for the United States and to demonstrate AHS technology by 1997.

多年以来，自动公路系统（AHS）的设想在美国很受欢迎。但1986年，自动公路的梦想才又复苏过来，引导了自动公路系统的研发。运用州运输研究基金，该合作在自动车辆的开发技术和推广策略方面以及相关支撑基础设施方面取得重要进展。该研究激发了美国运输部的兴趣，并促成了1991年联邦综合地面运输效率法案规定AHS测试和示范的内容。随后，美国运输部资助了一个宏伟的研究计划，由国家自动公路系统联盟（NAHSC）执行。该研究计划的主要任务是为美国研发自动公路系统的实验模型并在1997年展示AHS技术。

(2) Co-ordinated Vehicle Highway Systems (CVHS) today 今天的车路协调系统（CVHS）

Despite the cancellation of the NAHSC program, there is still substantial national and international interest in CVHS. After exploratory meetings during 1998–1999 with potential partners, Caltrans and the University of California PATH program devised an initiative called the Phoenix Project whose mission is to continue CVHS research, development and deployment with public, private and academic partners in the US and abroad. They maintain a vision of "accepted, institutionalized and mainstreamed national and international Automated Highway Systems, actively contributing to congestion relief". Activities related to "providing vision" include creating a vivid picture of the future of AHS, defining goals as the programs evolve worldwide, and defining deployment strategies, primarily to sustain interest in the concept and enhance credibility.

尽管取消了NAHSC项目，国内和国际上仍然有人对CVHS研究感兴趣。1988~1999年期间，通过与未来合作伙伴进行几轮探索性会议后，加州运输部和加州大学PATH项目设计了Phoenix工程计划，其任务是和国内外的公立、私立及学术机构合作继续研究、开发和推广CVHS。他们坚持一个"可接受的、制度化的、主流化的国家和国际自动公路系统，积极致力于减轻交通拥挤"的设想。与提供设想有关的活动包括为未来的AHS设计一个清晰蓝图，当该程序在全世界范围内发展时，定义目标、定义推广应用策略，主要维持人们对该概念的兴趣以及增强可信性。

Figure 8.28　Luminous road
图 8.28　发光道路

(3) Changing directions　改变方向

During the 1990s terms such as "dedicated lanes" and "platooning" were associated with the idea of building specialized infrastructure for automated highway systems. But the prospect of vehicle platoons, however eye-catching, seemed unlikely to become a reality. Instead, the focus of first generation vehicle-highway automation has switched to automated vehicles operating on existing roads with no extensive infrastructure modifications required. These vehicles may cluster in "designated lanes" or benefit from being on auto-pilot, with traffic flow benefits achieved through vehicle co-operative systems as well as vehicle-infrastructure interaction.

在 20 世纪 90 年代，诸如"专用车道""车队"等术语都和为自动公路系统建设专用基础设施的想法联系在一起，然而不管车队的期望多么吸引人的眼球，似乎都不可能变成现实。不同的是第一代车路自动化的重点已经转化为在现有的道路上实现车辆的自动操作而不需要对现有基础设施进行大范围修改。这些车辆可以集中在"指定车道"或者从自动驾驶中获益，通过车辆系统之间的合作以及车与基础设施之间的交互作用而实现交通流的收益。

Figure 8.29　Bus lane
图 8.29　公交专用道

(4) Potential prospects and problems　潜在的期望和问题

Fully automated vehicle operation offers the advantages of safe travel, more efficient traffic flows, and convenience to the driver. This capability has been prototyped and demonstrated extensively during the nineties, thereby establishing technical feasibility. Current research focuses on refining system approaches. For the nearer term, Low Speed Automation (LSA) is expected to be very popular as a convenience item. LSA systems would be engaged in slow-speed congested traffic conditions, so that the driver can relax instead of controlling the vehicle under these tedious conditions. When the congestion clears and speeds increase, the driver would resume control.

车辆全自动化运营提供了安全旅行、更有效的交通流以及方便驾驶员等优点，这些好处已经在 20 世纪 90 年代的模型中充分地展示出来，因此技术是可行的。现在的研究重点是精炼系统方案，近期则是期望低速自动化（LSA）作为便利的项目受到欢迎。LSA 系统将用于低速拥挤的交通状况，以便驾驶员在这些乏味的状况中不再控制车速而是开始放松，当拥挤状况消失开始加速，驾驶员又恢复控制。

This system brings with it potential problems:
这样的系统带来一些潜在问题：

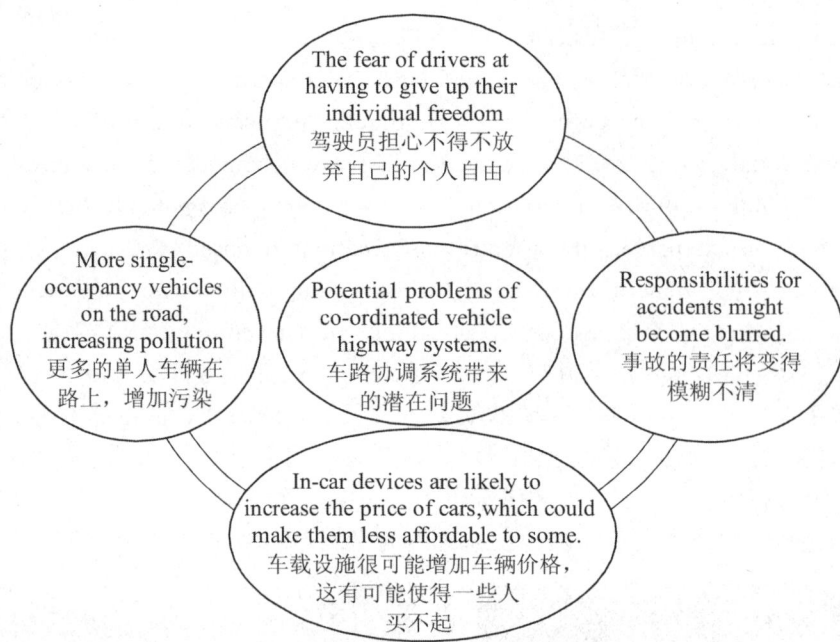

Figure8.30　Potential problems of co-ordinated vehicle highway systems

图 8.30　车路协调系统带来的潜在问题

(5) Realizing the AHS vision　实现 AHS 设想

The US vision for an automated highway system has remained clear and consistent for many years and this has advanced the development of automated highway systems. Although the original concept has dispersed itself into numerous programs and technologies world-wide and adapted to the needs of individual regions, the momentum for change has continued and automation is expected to thrive early in the 21st century in all aspects of private vehicle, commercial, transit and specialized vehicle operations.

Figure 8.31　Smart freeway

图 8.31　智能高速公路

美国 AHS 的设想已经非常清晰和持续很多年了，并且已促使了 AHS 的研究开发。虽然最初的概念已分散到世界范围内几个不同的项目和技术中,并且被调整以满足不同地区的要求,但是变化的势头还在继续,而且期望自动化在21世纪的私人车辆、营运车辆、公交车辆以及特种车辆的所有业务中得到繁荣发展。

8.2.6 South African Vision for transport　南非的交通设想

South Africa is a good example of a transitional country which has adopted a visionary approach to the planning of ITS. The visioning process began in 1994, through a series of Green and White Papers, and extensive consultation with stakeholders at each step in the process.

南非是一个转型国家的好例子,它采用憧憬的方式规划ITS。通过一系列绿皮书和白皮书,憧憬的过程开始于1994年,并且在开发的每个阶段都与相关方面进行广泛的协商。

(1) Moving South Africa　前进中的南非

The Moving South Africa project was designed to produce a program for strategic action that extends the short to medium-term policy formulation documented in the Transport White Paper into a long-term strategic formulation exemplifying the trade-offs and choices necessary to realize the vision.

"前进中的南非"项目被设计成制定战略行动的项目,该战略行动可把交通白皮书中描述的短中期政策拓展成长期战略政策,并说明实现设想所需要的折中和选择。

Customers described a system that did not meet their evolving requirements and that reflected old priorities and objectives.

顾客描述了一个不能满足他们需求并且体现陈旧优先级和目标的系统。

① Urban passengers described a system oriented towards commuting in from segregated townships, racially separated bus systems and unregulated taxis.

城区的旅客描述的系统是分离的城镇间的通勤服务、分人种的公共汽车系统和无节制的出租汽车。

② Freight customers saw biases towards import substitution and against export competitiveness of value-added products, a failing rail service, an inefficient port system and, uniquely, world class bulk freight systems.

货运客户看见了对进口替代的偏好和对增值产品出口竞争的反对、失败的铁路服务、效率低的港口系统和独特的世界级大货运系统。

③ A review of the providers showed clearly that the system as a whole has been systematically under investing in capital replacement with most modes near the outer limits of the useful lives of their assets.

对提供商的调查清晰地表明,这些系统作为一个整体已经在资本置换下被系统地购买,大多数模式已经接近其资产的使用寿命。

This highlights the key operational concern framed by the customer and provider research: the ongoing sustainability of the sector as a whole. The immediate objective of the strategy is to avert this crisis by creating a program of strategic action that prevents its evolution into a fully blown crisis in the next few years. The key question is how to manage through the constraints of human and financial capital and timing, in order to create sustainability in the reconfigured system.

这里强调了由客户和提供商研究确定的主要业务内容：作为一个整体的行业的可持续发展性。该战略的直接目的是通过制定一个战略行动的项目来避免这个危机，该战略行动可以预防此危机在今后的几年里演变成全面暴发的危机。主要问题是怎么通过限制人、资金和时间来管理，以在重构系统中保持可持续性。

> **South African Vision for Transport 南非的交通设想**
>
> The following is an extract from a speech by Minister Dullah Omar at an ITS Awareness Symposium, June 2000: "We have, in the transport field, formulated an ambitious vision for South Africa for the year 2020. The transport vision, as formulated in the action agenda of the Moving South Africa initiative, is that by 2020, transport in South Africa will meet the needs of freight and passenger customers for accessible, affordable, safe, frequent, high quality, reliable, efficient and seamless transport operations and infrastructure. It will do so in a constantly upgrading, innovative, flexible and economically and environmentally sustainable manner."
>
> 以下内容节选自Dullah Omar部长在2000年6月ITS研讨会上的讲话："在交通领域，我们已经为2020年制订了雄心勃勃的南非交通设想。正如在'前进中的南非'计划行动进度表中规定的，交通设想是到2020年，南非交通将满足货运和客运顾客对可达性、付得起、安全、频繁使用、高质量、可靠性、有效性以及无缝联结的交通业务和基础设施的要求。它将以持续更新、创新、灵活、经济、环保、可持续发展等方式进行。"

Roads were seen as a high quality low marginal cost transport option, supporting increasing car dependence. At the same time, destructive competition between transport modes on the roads, and between road and rail, further undermines the efficacy of the public transport system. Rural roads were seen as woefully inadequate, and provision for special needs customers as very weak.

道路被认为是高质量、低边际消耗的运输选择并且支持增加小汽车的依赖性。同时，道路上运输模式之间的破坏性竞争以及道路和铁路之间的破坏性竞争进一步破坏了公共运输系统的效率。郊区道路被认为严重不足，满足顾客特殊需求的功能更弱。

(2) The Role of Transport 交通的角色

Transport should be viewed as an enabling industry, with the Department of Transport acting as a provider department within government, framing the strategy around delivery against customer goals. Transport is a critical input to other industries, and the goals of the sector should be to meet the national and social (non-transport) objectives of the nation.

应该将交通应该看作是一个授权行业，交通部在政府内扮演供应商部门的角色，围绕客户目的确定策略。运输对其他行业是关键的输入，部门的目的应该是满足国家和社会的（非交通）目标。

(3) Customer Research and the Strategic Challenges 客户研究和战略挑战

The Moving South Africa (MSA) team evaluated the performance of the transport system against national and customer objectives and identified the critical gaps, or strategic challenges to be confronted. These challenges clustered into two categories: those outside the transport system requiring prior choices to be made by others outside the transport sector, and those within the system requiring choice and action from the South Africa National DOT, or provincial or local transport authorities, or providers or stakeholders.

"前进中的南非"项目组评估了运输系统针对国家和客户目标的性能，找出了关键的差距或面临的战略挑战。这些挑战分成两类：交通系统以外的挑战要求由交通部门以外的部门来做优先选择，交通系统内部的挑战要求南非国家交通部或省、地方交通部门，或提供商或者利益相关方来做选择或采取行动。

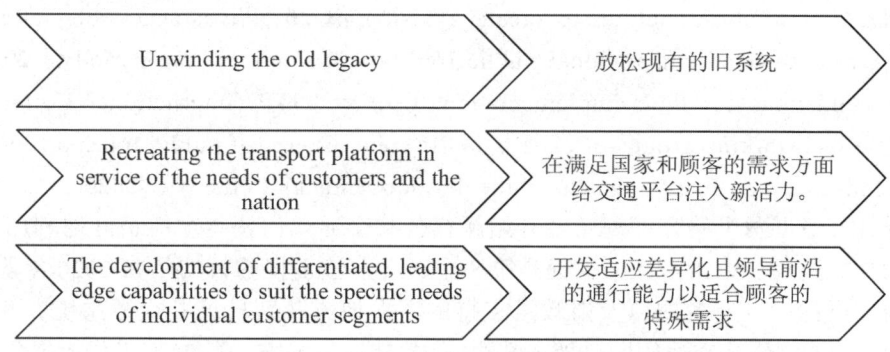

Figure 8.32　Strategic action
图 8.32　战略行动

The challenges from customers:
来自顾客的挑战：

① Building the long-term financial sustainability；建立长期财务可持续性；

② Balancing the risk alignment and affordability；平衡风险序列和可供应性；

③ Enabling the system to create human capacity for new roles；使系统能够产生新角色的人力资源；

④ Dealing with the lack of sustainability in the system. 解决系统可持续性的欠缺。

(4) Strategy Recommendations　战略建议

The guiding premise of the strategy is customer satisfaction. The strategy disseminates a detailed vision for transport, a set of ideas that integrates the needs of transport customers and policy makers, while ensuring that the system can deliver on these needs in a sustainable fashion into the future. This integrated vision is critical to guide implementation in the decentralized delivery environment in South Africa, yielding a system which is aligned around its core choices. The choices break into three tiers:

战略的指导前提是顾客满意。战略为交通传播了一个详细的设想，该设想是一系列的想法，集中了交通顾客和决策者的需求，同时确保系统以可持续的方式把这些需求延续到未来。该集成设想对在南非分散的环境中指导实施至关重要，形成一个围绕核心选择排列的系统。这些选择可分成以下三个层次：

① The breadth and reach, or density of the system
宽度和范围或者系统的密度

② The desired scale of the system and the optimal role of modes
系统的理想规模以及模式的最佳角色

③ Enhancing the platform for transport providers
运输提供商强化平台

8.2.7　A Vision for Public Transport in Europe　欧洲公共交通的设想

Two recent research initiatives from the European Commission have set out to understand how public transport can best adapt to exploit the benefits and challenges of ITS. The VOYAGER project is the first of these, set up to create a vision of attractive, accessible, effective, and financeable European local and regional public transport systems for the period to 2020, and to make recommendations for their implementation. Led by UITP (International Union of Public Transport), various working groups of experts in different aspects of public transport looked at the long-term trends and their likely impacts on the developments up to the year 2020.

欧盟委员会最近两个研究计划已经开始解释公共交通如何调整才能最好地利用 ITS 的收益及应付 ITS 的挑战。VOYAGER 工程是第一个，设立该工程的目的是在 2020 年前创建一个有吸引力的、可达的、有效的以及财政可支持的欧洲地方及区域公共交通系统，并为其实施提供建议。由 UITP（公共交通国际联盟）领导，公共交通不同方面的专家工作组展望直到 2020 年的长期发展趋势及其对开发的可能影响。

(1) The VOYAGER vision　VOYAGER 设想

Future lifestyles are likely to place a growing emphasis on personal choice, and so public transport operators will come under increasing pressure to develop collective services that are personalized or individualized in some way. Demographic trends point to greater numbers of elderly people and increased levels of immigration within Europe.

将来的生活方式越来越强调个人的选择，因此公共交通运营者面临越来越大的压力，要开发在一定程度上个性化或个人化的组合式服务。人口趋势向老龄化发展，并且在欧洲内移民加剧。

VOYAGER also argues that ITS can be used for a better understanding of travel patterns, so enabling the public transport sector to deliver better-tailored services by analyzing its market more accurately.

VOYAGER 也认为 ITS 可用于更好地理解出行模式，所以使公共交通部门能够通过更准确地分析市场来承担更好的定制化服务。

① One avenue for individualization is the greater use of personal mobile information terminals.

个性化的形成是更大量地使用个人移动信息终端。

② The development of more user-friendly designs for ITS applications is a must.

为 ITS 应用系统开发用户更友好的设计是必须的。

③ Lifestyle preferences will involve an increased expectation of safety and security.

生活方式的喜好将伴随安全和安保期望的增加。

(2) Impact of GALILEO　GALILEO 的影响

The development of a solid ITS infrastructure that will support the evolution of public transport services is going to be a challenge. However, the forthcoming European GALILEO satellite radio navigation system could potentially have a very profound effect. GALILEO is expected to enable continued development of locational services currently provided by GPS but with greater availability, a generally higher degree of precision and better continuity of service provision for some (particularly urban) applications. Location-based services which are available at present are expected to be enhanced and made more accurate and more available by GALILEO's 30 satellites in optimized orbits.

开发支持公共交通服务的稳固 ITS 基础设施将是个挑战。然而,即将来临的欧洲 GALILEO 卫星无线导航系统可能具有深远的影响。期望 GALILEO 能够完成现在由 GPS 提供的定位服务,但是服务范围更广,对一些应用(特别是城区应用)提供精度更高更连续的服务。现有的基于位置的服务,期望通过在优化轨道的 30 个 GALILEO 卫星,能够得到加强,并且服务更精确,应用范围更广。

The VOYAGER ITS group argues that a clear definition of the business model between content owners and service providers has to be developed. Alongside this, there needs to be the development and maintenance of databases necessary for realizing these services. VOYAGER is clear that value-added services such as traveller location based services or highly reliable positioning systems for airline management, should be paid services, but the business model to be shared between content owners and final service providers is not yet well structured for transport. Another challenge will be the transition from GPS to GALILEO; where it is not yet clear what level of investment is needed to make the change or to combine the two systems. Transport operators and industry providers both need to be convinced that the use of GALILEO makes commercial sense in order to make the transition. In this respect, a possible obstacle is that there may be a significant period needed for the service development phase before reaching credibility.

VOYAGER ITS 组认为货主和服务提供商之间的业务模型必须清晰定义,同时需要开发和维护实现这些服务必需的数据库。VOYAGER 很清楚诸如基于出行者位置的服务或者为航空管理部门提供的高可靠性定位系统等增值服务,应该是有偿的,但是货主和最终服务提供商之间共享的业务模型还不适应于交通。另一个挑战是从 GPS 到 GALILEO 的转换,在这里还不清楚需要什么级别的投资来实现这个转变或者把两个系统联系起来。为实现过渡,交通运营者和行业提供商都需要被说服使用 GALILEO 能带来商机。在这方面,可能的障碍是在达到可信赖之前,需要一个重要的阶段来开发服务。

Adoption of these value-added services might be held back by an underdeveloped ITS culture amongst public transport stakeholders. Heavy emphasis on the quantity aspects of public transport (i.e. number of journeys provided) may eclipse important quality aspects, bringing with it a risk of limited funds for innovation and ITS. The ITS industry and those aligned with its objectives therefore need to champion the importance of ITS in the future development of quality public transport services.

这些增值服务的采用可能会被公共交通利益相关方落后的 ITS 观念遏制,对公共交通数量的强调将冲淡质量的重要性,也将带来革新和 ITS 资金不足的风险。因此,ITS 行业及其盟友需要支持 ITS 在将来开发高质量公共交通服务方面的重要性。

(3) The ROSETTA vision ROSETTA 设想

The second of the EC initiatives was the ROSETTA project. This was a support measure for the EU Information Society Technologies (IST) research program which drew together the results and findings of a number of IST projects in order to support their effective application in Europe.

欧洲委员会第二个计划是 ROSETTA 工程，这是对欧盟信息社会技术（IST）研究项目的支持措施，它把一系列 IST 项目的研究结果和发现组合在一起便于其在欧洲的有效推广应用。

① ROSETTA identified some key points, one them being a wider understanding of the potential role for ITS in the public transport industry.

ROSETTA 确定了一些要点，其中之一是广泛地理解 ITS 在公共交通行业中的潜在作用。

② ROSETTA also foresaw the role of ITS in enabling public transport to operate in a more flexible, demand-responsive way.

ROSETTA 也预测了 ITS 能够使公共交通以更灵活、响应需求的方式运营。

(4) A new form of Public Transport 公共交通的新方式

Both VOYAGER and ROSETTA envisage a situation where public transport could quickly become more responsive to the needs of the customer, both in terms of operation and in terms of information. Alongside this, transit vehicles may increasingly have ITS capabilities engineered into them at the design and construction stage, rather than having to be retro-fitted. In this "accelerated" scenario, increasing suburbanization and diffusion of travel patterns mean that much public transport would increasingly move towards having demand-responsive characteristics. ITS would then enable public transport to adapt its service network to this new environment, but a major challenge would be to present the increasingly flexible service in a way that users could understand. ITS will permit solutions to this challenge but these may take time to develop. If this view of the future is accepted, regulatory regimes would have to change to allow buses and taxis to provide complementary seamless travel, while still enabling both these sectors to achieve profit levels that allow continued investment.

VOYAGER 和 ROSETTA 都假设了一种状态，就是公共交通能够很快地依据业务和信息更好地响应客户的需求。同时公交车辆在设计和生产阶段就可能有日益增多的 ITS 性能，而不是事后不得不安装。在这个"加速"的场合，日益郊区化和出行模式的分散化意味着很多公共交通有日益明显的需求响应特点。那么 ITS 将使公共交通能够调整自己的服务网络以适应新环境，然而主要的挑战是以用户能够理解的方式展现这日益灵活化的服务。ITS 允许针对这些挑战的解决方案，但是，需要时间来开发。如果接受了将来的这些观念，那么管理领域将不得不改变，允许公交车和出租车提供补充性的无缝联结出行，同时仍然使这两个部门能获得持续投资的收益水平。

8.3 Delivering the Future of ITS 描述 ITS 的未来

To achieve a future vision of ITS requires a commitment by numerous stakeholders to initiatives to lay the ground and pave the way for the predicted advances. There is growing realization that the truly difficult issues in ITS are not technical, but social, institutional and political. Considerable challenges lie ahead, but these represent opportunities too.

为实现 ITS 设想，需要很多的参与者共同履行责任。为预期的发展奠定基础并铺平道路。

实现 ITS 是个逐渐的过程，其实 ITS 的真正的困难不是技术问题，而是社会、制度和政治问题。虽然前面有相当的挑战，但同时也是机遇。

The demands of both the external and internal environment for transport operations are generating changes in the culture of both service providers and users.

运输业务内外环境的需求正在改变着服务提供商，这些改变暗示了观念上的深刻变化：

① From an engineering-dominated environment to multidisciplinary staffing;

从以工程学为主的环境到多学科交叉配置；

② From fragmented jurisdictions to high levels of cooperation;

从支离破碎的条块分割到高层次的合作；

③ From focus on speed and capacity to a focus on reliability and information;

从重点为速度和通行能力到重点为可靠性和信息；

④ From independent vehicles and infrastructure to a new level of coupling;

从独立的车辆和基础设施到新级别的耦合；

⑤ From a modal focus to a multimodal approach;

从一个模式重点到多模式方案；

⑥ From arms-length public and private sectors to new forms of cooperation;

从保持距离的公私部门到新形式的合作；

⑦ From reactive to proactive support of public safety operators.

公共安全业务员从应对性支持到主动性支持。

(1) Public Sector Roles, Relationships and Funding 公共部门的角色、关系和资金

The widespread use of ITS depends on mainstreaming ITS into the basic funding/planning process and seeking appropriate funding mechanisms. Over the next decade, increased funding for ITS programs needs to be available to plan and deploy new systems, to support operations of those systems and to hire and train the skilled personnel to manage the systems. Governments at all levels will provide much of this funding through traditional resources. However, innovative finance techniques including direct funding and user incentives, as well as private sector initiatives will play an important role.

ITS 的广泛应用依赖于将 ITS 回归至基本的资金/规划业务流程的主流中，并且寻找适当的资金运作机制。下一个十年，针对 ITS 项目所增加的资金需要设计和配置新的系统，支持这些系统的业务，并雇佣和培训熟练的员工管理这些系统。各级政府将通过传统的渠道来提供大部分资金，然而，革新的财务技术，包含直接投资、用户激励以及私有部门的创新，将发挥重要的作用。

(2) Initiatives to Achieve Extensive ITS Products and Services 获取广泛 ITS 产品和服务的倡议

Governments need to help accelerate deployment by:

政府需要通过以下手段帮助加速推广应用：

① Encouraging and endorsing the sale of appropriate products and services;

鼓励和批准适当的产品和服务的销售；

② Providing access to data and services;

提供数据和服务的接口；

③ Providing market incentives to users;

给用户提供市场刺激；

④ Removing barriers that impede private sector participation.

消除阻止私营部门加入的障碍。

(3) Human Factors　人为因素

The sheer volume of information can create potential problems: overload, distraction and confusion. This applies to both users of the transportation system and to the people who operate the system. Human factors are not just about avoiding information overload; it also means delivering information in the most effective, most timely way and designing controls and displays — both in vehicles and at the control centers — which are intuitive, consistent and easy to use correctly. Understanding human factors is a fundamental key to the effective delivery of the benefits of ITS.

猛增的信息量也会带来一些潜在的问题：过载、分散注意力以及混乱。这种情况对运输系统的用户以及系统操作人员来说都一样。人为因素不仅仅考虑怎样避免信息过载，而且也考虑怎样以最有效快捷的方式传输信息以及在车载和控制中心进行显示，以便这些信息能够被直觉地、一致地且容易地正确使用。理解人为因素对于有效实现 ITS 的效用非常重要。

8.4　Conclusions　结论

Increasing congestion is a major problem worldwide. Concerns about safety, security and our environment and its sustainability, have become important global issues. The "predict-provide" method of road-building is no longer seen as the answer to tackling the problems of traffic congestion and environmental degradation. Intelligent Transport Systems will make a growing contribution to the provision of transport services in future.

日益拥挤的交通是世界范围内的重大问题。对安全、安保、我们的环境以及可持续发展的关注已经变为重要的全球问题。道路建设"预测-提供"的方法不再被认为是解决交通拥挤和环境恶化问题的答案。未来，ITS 将在提供运输服务方面发挥越来越重要的作用。

In time, the ITS methods described in this book will become mainstream for road network operations in many regions. There are no guarantees of success, but it is hoped this book will help to point ITS practitioners in the right direction.

届时，本书描述的 ITS 方法将在很多地区成为道路网络运营的主流。虽不能保证成功，但希望本书将有助于把 ITS 从业人员指向正确的方向。

附录 1　运输评价方法在 ITS 中的应用

后续几页表格概括了在交通运输评价领域的一些主要技术，读者可借此对本主题进行深入研究。该表只做粗略指导，而更本质的交通运输建模知识，参见 Hensher 和 Button 的专著。加拿大的维多利亚运输政策研究院提供了一个在线的用于运输项目成本效益分析的指南，它提供了这个领域中研究的详细信息以及把这些信息应用于规划和政策分析的内容，包括效益评价的章节。

运输评价方法在 ITS 中的应用

评价	它用来做什么	如何做	我何时该用它	我从哪买它	它的局限性是什么
对将要和已经实施阶段都适合的方法					
"内心的感觉"/常识	ITS 因为很明显，所以常常被简单地使用	有大量可靠的证据表明那是一类特定的值得花钱的投资项目，那么直觉就是做，而不是去做深入的研究。多准则分析可对直觉形成检验，或者帮助对决策者解释这种"常识"	如果道路交叉口拥挤，不用进行大量的交通模型训练来确定交通信号是否改善交通流，而且成本是可预测的，同样也适用于公共交通实时信息服务	找到那些被证实值得投资的系统的可靠信息。信息源包括 IBEC 网和美国运输部 ITS 成本效益在线数据库	很昂贵的系统常常需要评价，即使仅仅是"关键因素分析"。新的 ITS 项目应该评价，因为没有证据显示投资的价值。在不同环境中有不同效果的 ITS 也应该单独评价。以下网站对多准则分析进行了解释：http://www.imf.org/external/np/mdm.gwu.edu/Forman/DBO.pdf
定性分析方法	提高标准，并提供规划和评价 ITS 时的基准	重点在群体、用户组、市民组以及质量周期，参加由独立机构协调的结构化讨论	信息源：投资规划、冲突评价以及考虑所有相关观点的暗示	运输咨询和市场研究公司	必须采取措施，确保包括来自所有适当的相关参与者的提问，并且确保重点群体和小组的成员能够在平等的基础上发挥作用。这些技术可补充定性调查，但不应用于取代定性分析
出行调查	提供如下统计信息：道路使用者的旅行目的以及出行方式	可用一系列方法：交通计数，问卷调查，自动牌照调查，旅行日记等	作为交通模型的输入数据，以及作为规划 ITS 服务和检验变化的出行数据源	运输咨询和市场研究公司	平庸的调查设计、薄弱的现场技术以及低相应率都影响统计的准确性和调查的可靠性，导致产生错误的调查结果。质量控制和调查方法的一致性在研究的前后都特别重要

续表

评价	它用来做什么	如何做	我何时该用它	我从哪买它	它的局限性是什么
对将要和已经实施阶段都适合的方法					
交通建模	显示ITS系统对交通的影响	交通模型估计交通网络中的交通流、延误和超时揭示如果没有进行投资，将发生什么，以及如果投资了，将发生什么	如下场合：目标是改变交通流、交通量和速度等，有关ITS的公布数据不足以制定"常识性"投资决策	机构内的建模者或运输顾问	交通模型基于假设，其关于未来交通成长的假设常常受到挑战，模型中的其他假设也一样。另外模型中也用到一些关于人们如何反应、什么在激励他们等假设。该项科学还在继续发展，因此交通模型也应当不断更新和经常评估
一般成本建模	大多数交通运输成本效益分析的基础，它揭示人们对ITS的响应是什么	非常基础，考虑现在的出行"成本"以及采用新的ITS的"成本"，并且在对成本变化的基础上预测行为变化	用于对ITS响应假设的不利范围，在这些场合，ITS应用几乎都是基于"常识"但需要一些计算。它也是任何在用交通模型的关键所在	机构内的经济学家或运输顾问。关于一般的成本模型及其在交通运输领域的应用，见Button 1982年的文章和网站www.Bolton.ac.uk/Campus/builtenv/modecho.html	一般的成本是个相当简单的概念，它相对地受它所描述的内容的限制。一般成本模型只考虑货币化的成本，但不适用于ITS涉及的一些政策。的确，ITS能够支持的几个政策选择，将增加而不是减少一般的出行成本。ITS的目的常常是改变旅行时间的变化性而不是总体旅行时间，或增加其他市政设施
效用模型	效用模型极力简化人们对变化所得的描述，它们与一般成本模型相似，但其设计却更好地反映用户信息	利用统计分析来测度不同人群从改变中得到的"效用"或"好处"	当用户行为对ITS努力实现的结果重要时，例如ITS努力鼓励人们改变出行方式，放弃自驾车，改用公共交通工具	专业运输顾问，大学统计学或经济学机构，不是业余爱好者的工作	好的效用模型是非常强大的工具。McFadden获得诺贝尔奖所做的工作仅仅是运用这种方法建立的政策和商业模型的冰山一角。模型的形式非常简单，但也可变得复杂。由于许多效用模型采用意向数据推理价值，因此也曾经引起对其"真实性"的怀疑，但是这些模型也可以使用历史数据（参考文献3，4，5）
判别分析	建立对一种变化可能响应的一种简单方法。如上面描述的模型一样，它试图估计当变化发生时不同的人群将做什么	找到各组之间最本质的不同，许多模型运用假设去对人群进行分类，然后分析不同类型人群的反应。判别分析研究这些数据，看哪些人群将根据响应被替代	当需要行为模型、有数据但又不想花太多钱用来训练时有用。它也可用于实用模型数据分类的初步筛选	机构内的运输和统计顾问。是个简单的工具，它比其他方法需要更少的计算，并依赖更少的假设条件	判别分析的美妙之处在于它涵盖经济成本（一般成本模型中的内容），而且它能够用于分析行为变化和对社会及环境的影响。其缺点是不精确。该方法不明白人们的行为为什么是这样，它仅仅估计人们的行为举止会怎么样。是Quarmby第一次描述判别分析对于更严密的交通模型产生类似结果（参考文献6）

续表

评价	它用来做什么	如何做	我何时该用它	我从哪买它	它的局限性是什么
对将要和已经实施阶段都适合的方法					
成本效益分析	比较实现相同效果的各种选择的成本	为不同投资背景列出输出或结果	如下场合：ITS产生的收益有时候没有金钱价值或者很难用金钱来描述，比如挽救的生命数量，减轻了受伤者的伤势严重度等。成本效益分析也是评价ITS系统的框架，ITS系统大多数都是"常识"性并需要结构化的判定，也适用于不需要进行建模的小型ITS系统	成本效益分析是内部工具箱的一部分。首选是效用经济学的咨询顾问、运输咨询顾问或环境界咨询顾问	通常使用相似的带假设的交通建模输入，这些假设是关于设有相应措施的结果。当工程目的明确并且ITS性能评估没有争议时，该方法是个优秀的方法。亚洲开发银行用一系列经济学分析指导方针对成本效益分析提供了指导（参考文献7）
实施前评估					
"后推法"	交通评价往往依赖预测，预测是基于问题的评价方法，而"后推法"是着眼于我们想要结果的评价方法	"后推法"问我们在未来十年或二十年中要从路网运营管理中得到什么，以及为得到那种结果我们现在必须做什么	当ITS是演绎一种设想或实现一种机遇而不是解决问题的时候。Nijkampetal建议ITS作为避免"技术推动"的一种手段，在"技术推动"情景中，安装ITS仅仅因为它是一种新技术	后推法工作组可以由社会科学家或交通或环境顾问领导。OECD描述了这个步骤，在机构内部执行不错	"后推法"的优点在于能够用清晰的规划构建未来设想并提供前进的动力；不利之处在于它不能在计划阶段提供足够的信息判断某个特定的投资是否有助于达到目标或物有所值
生活资产品质	生活资产品质是一种非货币化的系统化评价方法	对环境和规划决策开发却很容易延伸到交通运输领域。这种方法起源于这样一种观点：环境、经济和社会提供了一系列的好处，并且改变应该保护和提高这些好处	以下场合：ITS将给我们带来更多的好处，但对一般的成本模型使用的因素有负面影响。举例来说，ITS用于重新分配路面空间的场合	环境顾问可能用这种方法，它可在内部完成	一个缓慢的过程，需要广泛的协商以及可能反复修改，而且也不能产生清晰的成本收益分析，但可以依据它做出合理的决定。关于如何以及何时进行生活资产品质的评估，详见 www.qualityoflifecapital.org.uk

续表

评价	它用来做什么	如何做	我何时该用它	我从哪买它	它的局限性是什么
实施后评估					
消费者满意度调查	测量用户是否觉察到给他们带来好处的影响	在 ITS 采取措施的前后，测量人们对其的感受	当 ITS 方案旨在改善用户舒适度或社区的宜人设施时	市场研究公司；社会研究公司；大多数运输顾问	很多调查采用"Likert 等级法"来询问是否事情是这样，例如，"非常坏—有点坏—同样—有点好—非常好"。这样调查的价值很有限，Likert 自己也提醒说，等级是针对态度而不是完整的措施。这种调查的倾向是得出一些不切实际的乐观评价。 设计能产生有效结果的客户真正满意度调查问卷并不容易（参考文献 10）
依条件而定评价/固定的选择/关联分析	测量行为怎样对 ITS 作出响应。固定的选择的益处在于不用过去的行为做指导。其他交通模型是"展示的选择"，使用过去对改变的响应来获得将来改变的价值	一个产品或服务不同组成部分的实用性严格评估建立在平衡基础上，这种平衡由一个高度组织化的面谈问答来完成	如下场合 ITS 初为人知，或者 ITS 支持的运输政策新近出现。关于模型的形式、洞察在哪里可以用到这些模型以及如何最好地设计它的信息，请浏览网站：www.spss.com/spssbi/conjoint/，以及 Ampt, Swanson and Nelson and Towriss and Carson	运输顾问和一些市场研究公司	风险是回答者不在纸上写出他们实际的选择。回答者也许没看到成堆使用的新 ITS 系统。研究人员没描述新产品的缺陷，只描述优点。一些回答者也许不能预测他们将来能做什么——在信息和通信技术领域，一些发展已经引导人们居住地远离工作地点，那么在调查中他们将预测什么呢？令人害怕的是关联分析将获得错误的答案，而且答案（它产生的数据和值）的实质与错误是如此吻合以致导致了错误的投资决定（参考文献 11，12，13）
ITS 内部评价/ITS 影响评估	测量交通/时间等的改变	ITS 送出或返回数据。这些数据能够显示目标结果随着时间的变化。以前数据基准线需要与实施以后得到的内部数据进行比较	在技术可行的每个案例使用	把测量结果纳入 ITS	ITS 本身通常只能测量一些定量的结果，而一些诸如用户信心等的目标虽然可以被含蓄地表达，但是不能被测量；ITS 通常也无法测量对公共交通的支持，例外的应用是票务或收费系统

参考文献和注释

[1] Hensher D A and E J Button (eds). "Handbook of Transport Modelling". Pergamon, 2000.

[2] http://www.vtpi.org/tca/.

[3] McFadden D. "Disaggregate behavioural travel demands RUM side: a 30-year retrospective". Dept of Economics, University of California, Berkeley, 2000.

[4] Ben-Akiva M and S R Lerman, "Discrete Choice Analysis: Theory and Application to Travel Demand". MIT Press, Cambridge , 1997.

[5] Fischhoff B, B Goitein and Z Shapira. "The Experienced Utility of Expected Utility Approaches". In feather N T (ed) "Expectations & Actions:Expectary-Value Models in Psychology", Hillsdale, New Jersey,1982.

[6] Quarmby D A. "Choice of Travel Mode for the Journey to Work: Some Findings". Journal of Transport Economics & Policy, Vol 1. 1967. For the form of the model, see www2.chass.ncsu.edu/garson/pa765/discrim.htm.

[7] Asian Development Bank, www.adb etc.

[8] Nijkamp P, G Pepping and D Bannister. "Telematics and Transport Behavior". 1996.

[9] OECD. "Project on Environmentally Sustainable Transport". Working Group on National Environmental Policy, Working Group on Transport, 2002.

[10] Likert R. "A Technique for the Measurement of Attitudes". Archives of Psychology, Vol 22, No 140. 1932.

[11] Ampt E ,J Swanson and A D Pearman. "Stated Preference: too much Deference". In Ortuzar J de D(ed)"Stated Preference Modelling Techniques". PTRC, 1999.

[12] Nelson P S and J G Towriss. "The Monetary Valuation of the Environmental Impacts of Road Transport: A Stated Preference Approach". European Transport Conference, PTRC, 1999.

[13] Carson R T. "Contingent Valuation: A Users Guide". Dept of Economics,University of California 1999.

附录 2 ITS 单元成本

本附录中的成本来自于美国运输部 ITS 成本效益数据库,时间截止到 2004 年 3 月。他们在美国范围内,给出了资金成本的数量级和实施不同 ITS 组成涉及到的运营和维护成本。由于在城市和乡村建设的地点不同、地形、工作方便性以及许多其他因素如通信成本、系统整合成本、软件开发成本、物资和人力成本、获得技能、税务规则等的不同,地方的成本可能与这些数字差异较大。

虽然已尽力确保表中给出的数字是可靠的,但建议读者在为他们自己的 ITS 项目概算之前,应确保这里给出的信息适用于他们的当地情况。运营和维护成本很难归属于某一特定的 ITS 系统,应该认真对待。软件的成本数据是基于现有商业产品的,并没有覆盖成套系统和开发成本。如果需要更详细和更新的信息(包括设备生命周期的估算)请参见美国运输部网站。

ITS 单元成本

子系统/单元成本元素	资金成本 千元(美金) 低	资金成本 千元(美金) 高	运营维护成本 千元(美金) 低	运营维护成本 千元(美金) 高	备注
路侧通信 RS-TC					
管道设计与安装——走廊或一部分	50	65	0.02	0.02	每英里成本,包括一个建设工程的钻孔、挖坑、管道(3 或 4 英寸;8~10 cm)。成本可能是建设工程的一部分,也可能是空中安装的一部分
双绞线安装	12	12	0.02	0.02	每英里成本
光缆安装	20	50	0.02	0.02	每英里成本,包括一个建设工程的钻孔、挖坑、管道(3 或 4 英寸;8~16 cm)。成本可能是建设工程的一部分,也可能是空中安装的一部分
900 兆赫无线扩频	9	9	0.15	0.4	每次接通成本
微波通信	10	20	0.5	1	每次接通成本,成本由塔/天线安装决定
电话箱	4	5.9	0.7	0.7	资金成本包括电话箱和安装。运营维护成本是每单元(每年)用于服务维护合同和年蜂窝通信网服务费
路侧检测(RS-D)					
通道感应线圈监视	3	8	0.5	0.8	两组(4 个线圈),不包括安装
交叉口感应线圈监视	9	16	1	1.6	四方向,两个车道/路径
通道机器视觉传感器	21.7	29	0.2	0.4	一个传感器两个出行方向,不包括安装
交叉口机器视觉传感器	20	25.7	0.2	0.2	四方向交叉口,一个路径一个摄像机,不包括安装

续表

子系统/单元成本元素	资金成本 千元（美金）		运营维护成本 千元（美金）		备注
	低	高	低	高	
通道无源声波传感器	3.7	8	0.2	0.4	一个传感器覆盖 5 个车道。低成本基本传感器，安装套件，接线盒，和终端橱柜卡。高成本包括基本传感器带有天线、太阳能充电器、电池和电池组、无线基站、可以处理多达 8 个传感器
交叉口无源声波传感器	5	15	0.2	0.4	四个传感器，四个方向交叉口
通道遥感交通微波传感器	3.3	6	0.1	0.1	一个传感器两个旅行方向，不包括安装
交叉口遥感交通微波传感器	18	18	0.1	0.1	4 个传感器、4 叉交口。包括安装在现有基础设施
主动式红外传感器	6	14			传感器探测两个方向移动，能确定车速、分类、行车位置
被动式红外传感器	0.7	1.2			传感器覆盖一个车道，能确定车辆数量、流量、类别
闭路电视摄像机	7.5	17	1.5	2.4	能摇摄、倾斜、变焦（PT2）的彩色摄像机
闭路电视摄像机塔	2	12			低成本是 35 英尺（9.3 m）的塔，高成本的是 90 英尺（27.5 m）的塔。包括基础、铝杆、管、劳力
行人检测——使用微波	0.6	0.6			
环境监测站[（速度或气象站）全景摄像机环境监测站是更大道路气象信息系统的基础组成部分（见交通控制中心子系统下的道路气象信息系统）]	10	50	1.9	4.1	路径和地表温度传感器，雨量传感器（类型和概率），风量监测器（强度和方向），大气温湿度传感器，可见度传感器，远程处理单元。每 5 年更新费用为 64 000，操作管理部分包括调校，设备维修，损坏设备更换
安装	75	136	60	60	35 毫米胶片摄像机每年操作管理费用，注意：经销商的合约权限大多包括维护、进行系统的内勤功能
摄像机机降系统	5	8			通常系统包括 50 英尺（15.2 m）的钢柱。机械操作的机降系统可以使用所有类型的柱子（如，钢、混凝土、铝、玻璃纤维），实际上任何能增加的高度和任何智能交通系统柱上设备（如监视摄像机、雷达检测器），包括安装成本
路侧控制（RS-C）					
连接信号系统局域网	40	70	0.4	0.8	连接信号系统的局域网
对信号控制的信号控制器升级	2.5	10	0.2	0.5	每个交叉口

续表

子系统/单元成本元素	资金成本 千元（美金）		运营维护成本 千元（美金）		备注
	低	高	低	高	
信号控制器	11	17.5	0.2	0.9	包括每个交叉口交通信号控制器和橱柜的安装
交通信号	95	115	2.4	3	为一个信号（四个交叉口）、管道、控制器、检测的安装。低成本对应的感应线圈检测；高成本对应的是非侵入性的检测
匝道控制	30	50	1.5	3.5	每个地点。包括控制、电源等
车道控制软件	25	50	2.5	5	现场的硬件和软件，软件为现成的技术，单元价格不能反映产品开发成本
车道控制闸门	100	150	2	3	每个地点
定时车道信号	6	8	0.6	0.8	每次
道路信息（RS-I）					
路侧信息标志	56	84	2.5	3.8	为 HOV 和 HOT 登陆固定的信息
可变情报板	54	129	2.4	6	较小的低成本的可变情报板（VMS）一般安装在公路主干道上。高速公路上一般安装全屏、显示3行文字的、巨大的、高成本的 LED 型可变情报板（VMS）。这里成本包括安装，包括800 m 连接中心的数据传输线
可变情报塔架	25	125			悬臂结构的成本低，门架结构的成本较高，它可以跨越3~4个车道，塔架的维修要求尽量少
可变情报门架					悬臂结构的成本低，龙门架结构成本较高，它能够跨越3~4个车道，门架要求尽量少的维护
公路无线广播	16	32	0.6	1	10 瓦特 HAR，包括处理器、天线、发射机、电池备份、橱柜、货架安装、照明、座椅、连接器、电缆、许可费。超级 HAR 成本增加 9~10k 美元（大天线用于增强信号）
公路无线广播标志	5	5	0.3	0.3	带有闪光指示灯、控制器、可变信息的能力的 HAR 标志
路侧移动信标	5	8	0.5	0.8	双项地点（每个地点）
可变速度显示标志	3.7	5			低端为可变限速显示系统。高端包括速度静态标志、速度探测器（雷达）和显示系统
收费站（TP）					
电子收费读写器	2	5	0.2	0.5	读写器（每车道）
高速摄像机	5	10	0.5	1	成本包括1个摄像机和两个车道

续表

子系统/单元成本元素	资金成本 千元（美金）		运营维护成本 千元（美金）		备注
	低	高	低	高	
电子收费软件	5	10			包括 COTS 软件和数据库
电子收费结构	10	15			主要结构
遥感定位（RM）					
闭路电视摄像机	2	1.5	0.1	0.3	
摄像机与现有系统的整合	2	2.5			每站
信息亭	9.55	50	1	5	包括用于室内和室外的硬件、圈地、安装、调制解调器服务器和地图软件
信息亭与现有系统的整合	2.2	27.4			软件费用为 COTS（低）和开发成本（高）
为交互式信息亭的升级	5	8	0.5	0.8	交互信息显示接口（升级现有接口）
为交互式信息亭软件的升级	10	12			软件为 COTS
公共交通状态信息标志	4	8			安装在公共交通终端的 LED 显示屏，用于提供车辆到达信息。成本有质量、尺寸和控制器能力决定
智能卡售货机	37	40	1.85	2	用智能卡的售票机
智能卡售货机的软件和整合	3	5			软件为 COTS
紧急事件响应中心（ER）					
大区域基础设施、通信	4000	4000	600	600	用于人口>750 000。基于购买的建筑。包括基础设施内的通信设备如设备架、复用器、调制解调器等
小区域基础设施、通信	2800	2800	400	420	用于人口<250 000。基于购买的建筑。包括基础设施内的通信设备如设备架、复用器、调制解调器等
紧急事件响应硬件	15	30	0.3	0.6	设施，如设备架、复用器、调制解调器等，包括 3 个工作站
紧急事件响应软件	70	150	0.5	3.5	包括紧急时间响应计划数据库、车辆跟踪软件、实时交通协调
紧急事件响应劳动力			50	165	两人。所有工资费用包括基本工资、加班费、效益等
紧急事件管理通信软件	5	10	2.5	5	在 4 个地点间的共享数据库。千元/地点
E-911 和 Mayday 升级	105	180	1.7	2.5	数据通信转换软件，E911 接口软件、处理器和 3 个工作站
紧急车辆车载（EV）					
通信接口	0.3	2	0.02	0.02	紧急车辆通信。千元/车
信息服务提供商（ISP）					
大区域交通基础设施、通信	4000	4000	400	600	用于人口>750 000。基于购买的建筑。包括基础设施内的通信设备如设备架、复用器、调制解调器等

续表

子系统/单元成本元素	资金成本 千元（美金）		运营维护成本 千元（美金）		备注
	低	高	低	高	
小区域交通基础设施、通信	2800	2800	400	420	用于人口<250 000。基于购买的建筑。包括基础设施内的通信设备如设备架、复用器、调制解调器等
信息服务提供商硬件	40.5	49.5	0.8	1	包括2个服务器和5个工作站
系统整合	90	110			与其他系统整合
信息服务提供商软件	275	550	13.8	27.5	包括数据库软件（COTS）和交通分析软件
地图数据库软件	15	30			软件为COTS
信息服务商提供劳动力			175	250	
调频副载波租金			120	240	每年的工资，加班费，管理费，利润等（美国价格）
交互信息的硬件升级	18.9	23.1	0.4	0.5	包括一个服务器和两个工作站
交互信息的软件升级	250	500	12.5	25	路径规划软件（包括开发成本）
为交互信息增加的劳动力			100	150	两班倒，每个职员5万到7.5万，工资成本包括全部基础工资，加班，管理费用，利润等
路径导航软件升级	250	500	12.5	25	路径选择软件，COTS
地图数据库路径导航升级	100	200			地图数据库软件升级
紧急路径规划硬件升级	13.5	16.5	0.3	0.4	包括一个服务器
紧急路径规划软件升级	50	100	2.5	5	路径选择软件，COTS
动态合乘硬件升级	5.4	6.6	0.1	0.2	包括两个工作站
动态合乘软件升级	100	200	5	10	软件包括一些开发费用
动态合乘增加的劳动力			100	150	两班倒每个职员5万到7.5万，工资成本包括全部基础工资、加班、管理费用、利润等（美国价格）
浮动车信息采集软件升级	250	500	12.5	25	软件包括COTS和一些开发费用
交通管理中心（TM）					
大区域的基础及一般性设施	4000	4000	400	600	人口>750 000，基于购买建筑，包括设施内部通信设备，如设备架、多路（复用）器、调制解调器等
小区域的基础及一般性设施	2800	2800	400	420	人口<25 0000，基于购买建筑，包括设施内部通信设备，如设备架、多路（复用）器、调制解调器等
信号控制的硬件	15	30			包括3个工作站
信号控制集成及软件	180	220			软件和集成，安装，一年维护，软件为COTS

续表

子系统/单元成本元素	资金成本 千元（美金）		运营维护成本 千元（美金）		备注
	低	高	低	高	
信号控制劳动力			486	594	成本包括操作劳动力（2个人50%工作时间，共10万），交通工程（1个人50%工作时间，共10万），升级时间计划（所有10个系统，每系统每月2千），信号维护技工（2个人，7.5万），工资成本包括全部基础工资，加班，管理费用，利润等（美国价格）
交通监测集成软硬件	135	165	6.8	8.3	处理器和软件
交通监测集成	225	275	11.3	13.8	与其他系统的集成
快速路控制硬件	15	30	1	1	包括3个工作站
快速路控制集成及软件	180	220			软件和集成，安装，一年维护，软件为现货技术性供应，单元成本不反映开发费用
快速路控制劳动力			225	275	操作劳动力（2个人50%工作时间，共10万），维护技工（2个人，7.5万），工资成本全部计算在内，包括基础工资，加班，管理费用，利润等（美国价格）
车道控制硬件	5.4	6.6	0.3	0.4	包括1个工作站和19个监视器
车道控制集成及软件	225	275	11.3	13.8	控制器软件开发、集成、升级。软件已为本地安装而调整，另外，软件为COTS
车道控制劳动力			90	110	两个操作员各50%，10万
COTS区域控制软件、集成	330	440			软件和集成，安装，一年维护，软件为COTS，与TMC集成
实时交通自适应信号控制系统	120	150	20	20	基于运行于中心计算机的商业应用包，高成本未包括用户界面软件包和事故管理
区域控制劳动力			180	220	操作员劳动力（2个人50%工作时间，共10万）交通工程（1个人50%工作时间，共10万），维护合约，工资成本全部计算在内包括基础工资，加班，管理费用，利润等（美国价格）
事故检测视频监视器墙	40.5	49	2.0	2.5	包括5个19英寸视频监视器，和3×3=9个监视器墙
事故检测硬件	81.7	119	4.0	6.0	包括4个服务器，5个工作站，2个激光打印机
事故检测集成	90	110	4.5	5.5	与其他系统集成
事故检测软件	90	110	4.5	5.5	软件为COTS，包括开发成本
事故检测劳动力			630	770	操作员劳动力（4个人，共10万，1个经理，15万），2个维护技工7.5万（美国价格）

续表

子系统/单元成本元素	资金成本 千元（美金）		运营维护成本 千元（美金）		备注
	低	高	低	高	
事故响应视频监视	2.7	3.3	0.14	0.17	包括1个19英寸监视器
事故响应硬件	2.7	3.3	0.14	0.17	包括1个工作站
事故响应集成	180	220			与其他系统集成
故响应软件	13.5	16.5	0.68	0.83	软件为COTS
事故响应劳动力			90	110	事故管理协调员1个，10万（美国价格）
自动化事故调查系统	15	15			包括工作站，三角架，单极天线，自动集成，辅助绘图软件
交通事故疏散硬件	5	10	0.25	0.5	包括一个工作站
交通事故疏散软件	18	22	0.9	1.1	软件为COTS
交通事故疏散集成	90	110	4.5	5.5	与其他系统集成
交通事故疏散劳动力			90	110	操作员劳动力1个，10万。工资成本全部计算在内包括基础工资，加班，管理费用，利润等（美国价格）
动态电子付费软件	22.5	27.5	1.13	1.38	包括软件安装和一年维护，软件为COTS
动态电子付费集成	90	110	4.5	5.5	与其他系统集成
浮动车信息收集硬件	5	10	0.5	1	包括1个工作站
浮动车信息收集软件	18	22	1.8	2.2	包括软件安装和一年维护，软件为COTS
浮动车信息收集集成	135	165	13.5	16.5	其他系统集成
浮动车信息收集劳动力			45	55	操作员劳动力1个（每天工作4小时，一年10万）。工资成本全部计算在内包括基础工资，加班，管理费用，利润等（美国价格）
铁路道口监控软件	18	22	1.8	2.2	包括软件安装和一年维护，软件为COTS
铁路道口监控集成	90	110			与其他系统集成
铁路道口监控劳动力			45	55	操作员劳动力1个（50%，一年10万）。工资成本全部计算在内包括基础工资，加班，管理费用，利润等（美国价格）
道路气象信息系统(RWIS)	25	25	0.4	2.5	道路气象信息系统包括环境监测站、CPU、带有RWIS软件的工作站，通信设备。所有RWIS的组成部分都包含在交通管理中心里，除了环境监测站的成本。（见上面的路侧检测）每5年更换CPU，成本为4千，运营管理成本包括通信和可选的天气预报和气象服务

续表

子系统/单元成本元素	资金成本 千元（美金）		运营维护成本 千元（美金）		备注
	低	高	低	高	
公共交通管理中心（TR）					
大区域的基础及一般性设施	4000	4000	400	600	人口>750 000，基于购买建筑，包括设施内部通信设备，如设备架、多路（复用）器、调制解调器等
小区域的基础及一般性设施	2800	2800	400	420	人口<250 000，基于购买建筑，包括设施内部通信设备，如设备架、多路（复用）器、调制解调器等
公共交通中心软硬件、集成	830	1750	6	12	包括3个用来追踪车辆和排班的工作站，数据库和信息储存，时刻表，调校软件，实时出行信息软件和集成，软件为COTS
公共交通中心附属建筑空间			6	9	智能交通系统技术所需的附属空间，每平方英尺12~18元，500平方英尺（46.5 m^2）
公共交通中心劳动力			50	250	三个职员劳动力，7.5万，工资成本全部计算在内包括基础工资，加班，管理费用，利润等（美国价格）
自动排班升级和集成	245	540	0.4	0.8	处理器、软件升级，安装和一年维护，软件为COTS，与其他系统如电子付费的集成是支出主要部分
电子付费远期升级	40	60	0.8	1.2	软件为COTS，自动乘客技术处理软件附加成本为2.5万。具体是几十万成本由系统决定
车辆定位界面	10	15			车辆定位界面
车辆定位设备	275	275	16.5	16.5	
安保系统视频监视	15	20	0.75	1	每位置5个
安保系统硬件和集成	305	590	1.1	1.9	包括服务器3工作站，主要成本是与其他系统集成
安保系统劳动力			202	247	3个职员劳动力，每个7.5万，工资成本全部计算在内包括基础工资，加班，管理费用，利润等（美国价格）
收费管理（TA）					
收费管理软硬件	50	95	5	9.5	个人电脑，2个工作站，打印机，调制解调器，数据库协调软件，软件为COTS
运营车辆检查站（CC）					
检查站结构	50	75			路侧结构——主线/W车道指示信号
信号板	10	15	1	1.5	路侧信号板
信号指示器	5	10	0.3	0.5	信号指示器系统
路侧信标	5	8	0.5	0.8	用于电子滚屏的路侧信标（未包括在路侧子系统中）信标修理和替换

续表

子系统/单元成本元素	资金成本 千元（美金）		运营维护成本 千元（美金）		备注
	低	高	低	高	
路侧信标的线路	10	20			从信标到路侧的专用线路通讯（1英里向上流）（1.6 km）
检测站软件，集成	180	215	0.1	0.1	工作站，软件和集成
安全及适当性电子记录（SAF-ER)数据信箱	7.5	9.2			带打印机及无线网调制解调器的便携式计算式，该调制解调器可在现场或检测站下载、记录及上传托运者的安全数据库记录
检测系统	50	75	2.5	3.8	营运车辆通讯设施（基于无线的单元）及接口
安全检测的软件更新	40	80	0.8	1.6	安全数据库添加，结果写进车辆标签处理器，软件是COTS
手持安全设施	3	5	0.3	0.5	用于营运车辆检测，该设备或者测量数据本身，或者从车上读数据，每个地方有3个
用于引用和事故记录的软件更新	20	40	1	2	该软件用于把引用和事故信息添加到营运车辆
动态称重设施	14	21	1.4	2.1	包括WIM固定载荷单元和到路侧设施的界面，软件是COTS
动态称重设施的线路	1	2	0.1	0.2	线路通讯（本地线）
信号指示器	5	10	0.3	0.5	信号指示器系统
路侧信标	5	8	0.5	0.8	用于电子滚屏的路侧信标(未包括在路侧子系统中)信标修理和替换
路侧信标的线路	10	20			从信标到路侧的专用线路通讯（1英里向上流）（1.6 km）
检测站软件，集成	180	215	0.1	0.1	工作站，软件和集成
安全及适当性电子记录（SAF-ER)数据信箱	7.5	9.2			带打印机及无线网调制解调器的便携式计算式，该调制解调器可在现场或检测站下载、记录及上传托运者的安全数据库记录
检测系统	50	75	2.5	3.8	营运车辆通讯设施（基于无线的单元）及接口
安全检测的软件更新	40	80	0.8	1.6	安全数据库添加，结果写进车辆标签处理器，软件是COTS
手持安全设施	3	5	0.3	0.5	用于营运车辆检测，该设备或者测量数据本身，或者从车上读数据，每个地方有3个
用于引用和事故记录的软件更新	20	40	1	2	该软件用于把引用和事故信息添加到营运车辆
动态称重设施	14	21	1.4	2.1	包括WIM固定载荷单元和到路侧设施的界面，软件是COTS
动态称重设施的线路	1	2	0.1	0.2	线路通讯（本地线）

参考文献

[1] Highway Industry Development Organization. ITS Handbook[M]. UC Berkeley Transportation Library, 1998.
[2] Bob McQueen, Judy McQueen. Intelligent Transportation Systems Architectures[M]. Boston: Artech House, 1999.
[3] John C. Miles. ITS Handbook[M]. Boston: Artech House, 2004.
[4] Ayman Smadi, Kate Miner. Intelligent Transportation Systems (ITS) Statewide Plan[R]. Bismarck: North Dakota Department of Transportation, 2004.
[5] Joseph M. Sussman. Perspectives on Intelligent Transportation Systems[R]. Massachusetts: Massachusetts Institute of Technology, 2004.
[6] 张国伍. 智能交通系统工程导论[M]. 北京：电子工业出版社，2003.
[7] 陆化普，李瑞敏，朱茵. 智能交通系统概论[M]. 北京：中国铁道出版社，2004.
[8] 杨兆升. 智能运输系统概论[M]. 北京：人民交通出版社，2005.
[9] John C. Miles，陈干，王笑京. 智能运输系统手册[M]. 北京：人民交通出版社，2007.
[10] 王众托. 系统工程[M]. 北京：北京大学出版社，2010.
[11] 曲大义，陈秀锋，魏金丽. 智能交通技术及其应用[M]. 北京：机械工业出版社，2012.